# Macroeconomic Instability and Coordination

ECONOMISTS OF THE TWENTIETH CENTURY

**General Editors:** David Colander, *Christian A. Johnson Distinguished Professor of Economics, Middlebury College, Vermont, USA*, and Mark Blaug, *Professor Emeritus, University of London, UK, Professor Emeritus, University of Buckingham, UK, and Visiting Professor, University of Amsterdam, The Netherlands*

This innovative series comprises specially invited collections of articles and papers by economists whose work has made an important contribution to economics in the late twentieth century.

The proliferation of new journals and the ever-increasing number of new articles make it difficult for even the most assiduous economist to keep track of all the important recent advances. By focusing on those economists whose work is generally recognized to be at the forefront of the discipline, the series will be an essential reference point for the different specializations included.

A list of published and future titles in this series is printed at the end of this volume.

# Macroeconomic Instability and Coordination

Selected Essays of Axel Leijonhufvud

Axel Leijonhufvud

*Professor of Economics, University of California, Los Angeles, USA and Professor of Monetary Economics, University of Trento, Italy*

ECONOMISTS OF THE TWENTIETH CENTURY

**Edward Elgar**
Cheltenham, UK • Northampton, MA, USA

Published by
Edward Elgar Publishing Limited
Glensanda House
Montpellier Parade
Cheltenham
Glos GL50 1UA
UK

Edward Elgar Publishing, Inc.
136 West Street
Suite 202
Northampton
Massachusetts 01060
USA

A catalogue record for this book
is available from the British Library

**Library of Congress Cataloguing in Publication Data**

Leijonhufvud, Axel.
    Macroeconomic instability and coordination : selected essays of Axel
Leijonhufvud/Axel Leijonhufvud.
    — (Economists of the twentieth century series)
    Includes bibliographical references and index.
    1. Macroeconomics.   2. Economic policy.   3. Financial crises.   I. Title.
II. Economists of the twentieth century.

HB172.5.L45 2000
339—dc21
                                                                    00–034121
ISBN 1 85278 967 0

Typeset by Manton Typesetters, Louth, Lincolnshire, UK.
Printed and bound in Great Britain by Biddles Ltd, *www.biddles.co.uk*

# Contents

# Acknowledgments

I wish to express my appreciation to the respective editors and/or publishers for their permission to reprint the following articles:

'What Would Keynes Have Thought of Rational Expectations?', in G.D.N. Worswick and J.S. Trevithick, eds, *Keynes and the Modern World*, Cambridge: Cambridge University Press, 1983.

'Did Keynes Mean Anything? Rejoinder to Yeager', *Cato Journal*, Spring/ Summer 1988, reprinted here as 'Keynes's Contribution to Theory'.

'Keynesian Economics: Past Confusions, Future Prospects', in A. Vercelli and N. Dimitri, eds, *Macroeconomics: A Survey of Research Strategies*, Oxford: Oxford University Press, 1992.

'Keynesianism, Monetarism, and Rational Expectations: Some Reflections and Conjectures', in Roman Frydman and Edmund S. Phelps, eds, *Individual Forecasting and Aggregate Outcomes: 'Rational Expectations' Examined*, New York: Cambridge University Press, 1983.

'What Was the Matter with IS-LM?', in Jean-Paul Fitoussi, ed., *Modern Macroeconomic Theory*, Oxford: Blackwell, 1983.

'Hicks on Time and Money', *Oxford Economic Papers*, November 1984, supplement. (Simultaneously published as D.A. Collard, D.R. Helm, M.F.G. Scott and A.K. Sen, eds, *Economic Theory and Hicksian Themes*, Oxford: Oxford University Press, 1984.)

'Monetary Policy and the Business Cycle under "Loose" Convertibility', in Anthony Courakis and Charles Goodhart, eds, *The Monetary Economics of John Hicks*, supplement to *Greek Economic Review*, Vol. 12, 1990.

'Theories of Stagflation', *Revue de L'Association Francaise de Finance*, December 1980.

'Inflation and Economic Performance', in Barry N. Siegel, ed., *Money in Crisis: The Federal Reserve, the Economy, and Monetary Reform*, San Francisco: Pacific Institute, 1984.

'Constitutional Constraints on the Monetary Powers of Government', in Richard B. McKenzie, ed., *Constitutional Economics: Containing the Economic Powers of Government*, Lexington Books, Mass.: D.C. Heath Co., 1984.

'Rules with Some Discretion: Comment on Barro', in C.D. Campbell and W.R. Dougan, eds, *Alternative Monetary Regimes*, Baltimore, MD: Johns Hopkins University Press, 1986.

'High Inflations and Contemporary Monetary Theory', *Economic Notes*, Vol. 21, 1992.

'Notes on the Theory of Markets', *Intermountain Economic Review*, October 1970.

'Capitalism and the Factory System', in Richard Langlois, ed., *Economics as a Process: Essays in the New Institutional Economics*, Cambridge: Cambridge University Press, 1986.

'Information Costs and the Division of Labour', *International Social Science Journal* (special issue on *Economic Growth Policies: Theory and Reality*), May 1989.

'Problems of Socialist Transformation: Kazakhstan 1991', in Lazlo Somogyi, ed, *The Political Economy of the Transition Process in Eastern Europe*, Hants: Edward Elgar, 1993.

'The Nature of the Depression in the Former Soviet Union', *New Left Review*, No. 199, May–June 1993.

'Ideology and Analysis in Macroeconomics', in Peter Koslowski, ed., *Economics and Philosophy*, Tübingen: J.C.B. Mohr, 1985.

'Time in Theory and History – Or Why I Am not a Historian', *Agricultural History*, Winter 1986.

My thanks also go to the very helpful and efficient staff of Edward Elgar and particularly Alison Edwards.

# Preface

Like cells, organisms or ecologies, economies are complex adaptive systems. What such systems have in common is the capacity for self-regulation of the activity levels of their various components. These capacities are never unbounded. Beyond certain limits, they will break down. More generally, their effectiveness will depend both on internal structural characteristics of the system in question and on the magnitude of external shocks to which they are exposed.

What are the limits to an economy's capacity to coordinate the activities of its members? How does the behavior of the system change under extreme conditions? In what ways does its performance depend upon the institutions that govern the market process? In what circumstances might the coordinating capabilities of the economy be improved by institutional design or by deliberate intervention in markets? These exemplify the coordination questions which have been my main interest as an economist. I regard them as the central ones in macroeconomics. With one exception, all of the essays in this volume deal with them. This could be said also of my book *Information and Coordination* (1981a), but Parts III–V of the present collection are a good deal more 'institutionalist' than that earlier one.

The essays in Part I attempt to put the development of macroeconomics from Keynes to Lucas in historical perspective. The misunderstandings of Keynes's *General Theory*, which I worked on thirty years ago, remain important even today because of the sequence of later muddles that they originated and that eventually led to the virtual disappearance of the coordination problem from macroeconomic discussion. My paper from the Keynes centennial conference in Cambridge (Chapter 1) outlines the story as I see it. Two short sketches in this paper get their own chapters later: the 'Swedish Flag' story is told at greater length in Chapter 2 and the section on monetary regimes is elaborated in Chapter 6. As an appendix to Chapter 1, I have included a short piece from 1988 pointing out that evidence from Keynes's *Collected Writings*, which had appeared subsequent to my 1968 book, proved my interpretation of the *General Theory* to have been correct, contrary to the assessments of Yeager, Grossman, Coddington and others.

Chapter 2 was written for the introductory session to a summer school on 'Alternative Approaches to Macroeconomics'. This was the first of four such schools hosted by the University of Siena at the Certosa di Pontignano for which E.S. Phelps and I were responsible for the programs. Ned Phelps has some responsibility also for Chapter 3 (although, let it be said, not for its content). It was written some years previously for a conference on rational expectations arranged by him and Roman Frydman. My concerns about the New Classical economics at that time were two, namely that it left no room for the effective demand failures that I saw as the theoretical legacy of Keynes, and that the emblematic model of anticipated inflation reflected a theory of inflations that was seriously misleading with regard to their economic costs and social consequences. The 'blueback scheme' with which I sought to dramatize the deficiencies of that model is sketched in this chapter, to recur repeatedly in Part II.

The friendship of John and Ursula Hicks has been one of the privileges of my life. No other author's work was as helpful to me in graduate school as that of John Hicks. Although his late works did not find the audience of his most famous contributions, I have found that they also reward close reading. Three of the chapters in this volume are essentially 'Hicksian'. My attempt to size up *IS–LM* (Chapter 4) dates from a session arranged by Jean-Paul Fitoussi where Sir John was the other speaker on the same subject! Used in static textbook fashion, I maintained, *IS–LM* had sown confusion in the Keynes and the classics discussion, in the liquidity preference versus loanable funds controversy, and finally in the Monetarist debate. If the underlying theory is understood as one of an adaptive system, where agents modify their behavior in the light of current market outcomes, it is possible to make sense of *IS–LM* and to handle it without danger to life or limb. In the wake of the rational expectations revolution, however, such adaptive theorizing was rather out of fashion.

What I most admired about John Hicks was his ability to ponder a difficult question for decades on end without ever fooling himself that it could be resolved or disposed of by some facile assumption or other. Chapter 5, which was written for a *Festschrift* to his 80th birthday, traces one such struggle through fifty years, namely his persistent attempts to find a treatment of time that would accommodate both history and equilibrium.

Hicks insisted that 'monetary theory belongs to monetary history'. The paper dedicated to Hicks from an Oxford conference devoted to his monetary economics (Chapter 6) tries to follow his lead in fleshing out the distinction between monetary regimes relying on convertibility and on quantity control, respectively. The interpretation of the cyclical patterns of money, prices and output hinges on whether variations in the money supply are to be interpreted as endogenous changes in inside money (as in a convertible regime) or as primarily exogenous changes in outside money (as will be the case when quantity control is driven by fiscal exigencies).

During most of the period that the papers in this collection were written, my main preoccupation was to try better to understand the disorganizing effects of inflation. Back in the 1970s, professional opinion quite generally trivialized these effects. The welfare costs from the inflation tax were often portrayed as of a lower order of magnitude than those of unemployment. It did not seem to me that economists knew what they were talking about. But my first attempt to articulate a contrary view (Leijonhufvud 1977, written in 1974), although it made a number of valid points, was not very satisfactory and no one paid much attention to it. Chapters 7 through 11 return to the fray.

'Theories of Stagflation' (Chapter 7) came about as an attempt to convince a classroom of French students that the simultaneous occurrence of inflation and unemployment did not prove the bankruptcy of all the macroeconomics that had gone before.

The 'blueback' currency reform idea was one I had used for years in class as a pedagogical device to make students think twice (at least) about what might be wrong with the anticipated inflation model. My standard punchline had been: 'if real world inflations were like those assumed in the model, we could cure them overnight. Since we cannot get rid of inflation that easily, there must be something wrong with the model.' Chapters 8 and 9 use the idea in this way. I doubt that it ever occurred to me that bluebacking might be found useful in any actual policy context. But, thanks to the initiative of Daniel Heymann, it came to be used in Argentina in the 1985 Austral Plan – and it worked. Overnight, disinflation was achieved without significant redistributive effects. Variants of bluebacking were then tried in Brazil and Peru the following year. But disinflation does not by itself bring stabilization. In none of these cases were the fiscal reforms required to stabilize at low inflation achieved, so all three of these 'heterodox' plans eventually failed. So the popularity of bluebacking was fleeting. While it lasted, however, Heymann and I became concerned that it might be used in the wrong circumstances, since the quite restrictive conditions under which it would work were not well understood. The paper that we wrote to spell these conditions out appears here for the first time in print as Chapter 10. Chapter 11 also stems from my collaboration with Daniel Heymann. It is in the nature of an interim report on the work we did for our 1995 book, *High Inflation*.

For more than two decades, I argued the dangers of inflation at virtually every opportunity. Today, I find myself somewhat mysteriously in the minority again – on the other side of the issue. Now, low or even zero inflation targets are suddenly supposed to be the be-all and end-all of monetary policy. This is rather baffling, since the theory of the costs and consequences of inflation that is still taught remains on the whole as it was in the early 1970s. Exclusive attention to inflation targets will mean neglect of credit policy. At a

time when one credit crash after another is heard around the world, I doubt
that this can remain the state of the art for very long.

Several of the papers in this volume (for example, Chapters 4, 7 and 18)
had their beginnings in the classroom. The simple example in Chapter 12 of
how a collectively adaptive market process may be modeled is one such
which goes back more than thirty years. When I did my work on the 'Economics of Keynes', I thought of his system as composed of markets like this.
For some twenty years, starting in 1971, I taught a course in European
economic history for undergraduates as my annual respite from a money and
macro diet. A much appreciated stay at the Institute for Advanced Study
under the aegis of Albert Hirschmann allowed me to tie some of these
lectures together in what is here Chapter 13, a piece continued in the chapter
following. I do not understand the hold that the neoclassical constant returns
production function has over the profession, unless it be that it is handy to
manipulate. But it gives us no clue as to why economic growth brings increasing differentiation of productive functions, or why so high a proportion
of international trade goes in cross-shipments of products of similar factor
intensities, or why capital hires labor and controls production rather then vice
versa, or why the 'factory-system' brought unionization and a new type of
industrial conflict, or why, with the factories, unemployment becomes a novel
social problem, quite different from the 'vagrancy' of the past. The production theory tradition that runs from Adam Smith to Allyn Young (via, among
others, Karl Marx!) brings understanding of these and a host of other interesting issues.

One of these issues is the 'nature of the depression in the former Soviet
Union', as I argue in Chapter 17. By a twist of fate, I came to do some work
on market 'reform' during what was to be the last year of the USSR. That
story is told in Chapter 16. For a UCLA economist to lecture the Central
Committee of the Communist Party (of Kazakhstan) on supply and demand
was a unique experience. But thinking of the Gosplan economy as a 'factory
system' writ large made me skeptical of 'big bang' reforms which seemed not
to pay sufficient attention to the myriad complementarities that imparted such
rigidity to the inherited system and made it, therefore, so vulnerable to all
sorts of supply interruptions. These reservations, as I found out, did not fit the
line of American foreign policy journals at the time.

I am grateful to my wife, Earlene Craver, for many discussions of the
issues in this part, where her insights as a contemporary historian became
especially valuable to me. Her constructive criticism also helped make the
arguments of Chapters 8 and 9 clearer.

All of these essays were written during the many years that I served on the
UCLA faculty. Putting them together has given me many occasions to remember with gratitude how much I learned from my colleagues, and especially

from Armen Alchian, Robert Clower, Harold Demsetz, Jack Hirshleifer, Ben Klein, John McCall, Joseph Ostroy and Finis Welch. In more recent years, Daniel Heymann, Kumaraswamy Velupillai, Dan Friedman and Peter Howitt have been the friends that have influenced me most.

Joannes Mongardini at UCLA was tremendously helpful to me in putting these essays together and obtaining all the permissions. So, somewhat later, were Alberto Baldlessari and Maurizio Binelli, at the University of Trento, in completing the bibliography.

# PART I

# Keynesianism, Monetarism and Rational Expectations

# 1. What would Keynes have thought of rational expectations?

The Keynes centenary celebrations would be more festive if the Keynesian tradition were in intellectual good health and vigor for the occasion. Unfortunately, it is not. Unsuccessful policies and confused debates have left Keynesian economics in disarray.

In recent years, the intellectual excitement in macroeconomic theory has centered around the development of the rational expectations approach. Many economists have concluded that rational expectations spells the end of Keynesian economics – and many more seem to fear that this is so, even while they dispute it. What has caused the most commotion, however, is not so much rational expectations *per se* but rather the so-called New Classical economics. *Rational expectations* is but one of the characteristic components of New Classical economics. The other two are *Monetarism* and *market clearing*.

It does not seem particularly fruitful to speculate on how Keynes might have reacted to theoretical developments taking place thirty years or so after his death.[1] Economists who still regard themselves as 'Keynesians' (in some sense) will, however, have to define their positions *vis-à-vis* these new developments. What should we learn from this recent work? What criticisms of Keynesian economics have to be accepted? What lessons of Keynesian economics must not be abandoned? How can they most persuasively be reasserted?

The relevance of Keynes's contributions to current concerns is best reaffirmed by providing good, clear answers to these questions. Many retorts to the New Classical economics have been impatient outbursts, tinged with moral indignation. They have gotten us precisely nowhere. Quite generally, Keynesian economics has adapted badly to opposition. As a consequence, it is losing the battles for the best young talent in economics. In the United States, this has been true for a decade or more. To the younger generation of economists, Keynesian economics – all of it, not just Keynes himself – belongs to the history of economic thought.[2]

## MONETARISM IN THREE LESSONS

How did Keynesian economics end up in such a sorry state? Although some of us have not conceded defeat, it is obviously a widely held view that Keynesianism was vanquished by Monetarism. James Tobin has distinguished two Monetarist creeds: Mark I and Mark II.[3] It is useful, I think, to distinguish two stages in the development of his Mark I Monetarism and correspondingly to recognize three stages of the long controversy.

In the first stage, through the mid-1960s,[4] the discussion concerned the Monetarist causal interpretation of money–income correlations. The stability of the demand function for a well-specified stock of 'money' and the predominance of supply over money demand in the determination of that money stock were the core tenets of this stage I Monetarism. In claiming that monetary policy would be an effective regulator of nominal income, this Monetarism differed markedly from Keynesian views of that time. In almost every respect the policy doctrine advanced by Friedman and Brunner was diametrically opposed to that of the Radcliffe Report.

In the second stage of the controversy, many Keynesians embraced the Phillips curve and the Monetarists challenged its stability. Arguments based on the anticipation of inflation became central to the debate for the first time. Although not logically entailed by labor market anticipation of inflation, the natural rate of unemployment hypothesis was made a Monetarist doctrine. This natural rate doctrine sharpened the crowding-out arguments against fiscal stabilization policies. The Monetarists found use for the anticipated inflation model (AIM) also in accounting for Gibson's paradox, that is, the (pro-cyclical) pattern of nominal interest rates. Friedman's presidential address (1968) authoritatively summarized this stage II Monetarism.

In the third stage, Lucas (1972) succeeded in providing a model, carefully built on rational expectations foundations, within which Friedman's (1968) conjectures about the short-run and long-run Phillips curves hold true. A breakthrough in the systematic modeling of informational assumptions, this immensely influential paper married the rational expectations approach to stage II Monetarism from the outset. Sargent (1973) generalized the policy-ineffectiveness proposition, which was then further developed by Sargent and Wallace (1976) and Barro (1976). 'New Classical economics' gained currency as the label for this stage III Monetarism.

The reason for distinguishing between stages I and II is that the former is capable of a 'weak' and a 'strong' interpretation of the money–income correlation. In the strong version, exogenous changes in a purely supply-determined money stock interact with a stable money demand function to 'cause' the observed movements in money income. The 'weak' version allows a reciprocal influence from real income movements via real money demand to the money stock. The weak version nonetheless implies that control of the money stock will yield control of money income. Recall the oft-quoted summing up in Friedman and Schwartz's *Monetary History*:[5]

> Mutual interaction, but with money rather clearly the senior partner in longer-run movements and in major cyclical movements, and more nearly an equal partner with money income and prices in shorter-run and milder movements — this is the generalization suggested by our evidence.

Sufficiently diluted, stage I Monetarism can be made weak enough, obviously, to be stomached by almost all Keynesians, most of whom use a stable money demand function in any case. Stage II Monetarism, however, pretty much excludes this weaker interpretation. In the absence of monetary shocks, employment stays at the natural rate level. The permanent income corresponding to the natural rate of unemployment determines the demand for real balances which is, therefore, a constant in the absence of monetary shocks. This leaves us with 'money causes income', *without* the reciprocal influence. It is this strong version, consequently, that is carried over into stage III New Classical theory.

Where, then, did Keynesianism founder? At stage II, obviously, on the Phillips curve or, more generally, on the failure to incorporate inflation rate expectations in the Keynesian model. When American inflation picked up steam, the misbehavior of the Phillips curve and the inflation premium in nominal interest rates became obvious for all to see. Monetarists, who had predicted these things by reasoning from the neoclassical anticipated inflation model, made enormous headway within the economics profession and without. Keynesians, who had continued to argue the usefulness of the Phillips curve and to disparage the empirical relevance of the anticipated inflation model, lost face and lost influence.

It was a debacle. A bad enough debacle that the profession proclaimed the long controversy a Monetarist victory and, by and large, turned its interest elsewhere. This collective reaction left a number of things muddled.

First, the Phillips curve and Gibson's paradox were both late-comers among the issues of the Monetarist controversy. When the verdict was rendered on the basis of the obvious significance of inflationary expectations, the original (stage I) issues were not thereby settled. Rather, they were forgotten, or at least tabled for a number of years. I would agree with Tobin that 'the question whether money causes income or income money or both is still undecided'.[6]

Second, the stable Phillips curve had not been an integral part of earlier Keynesian theory. It was added on to that theory in the 1960s, not without opposition from some Keynesians.[7] It is not obvious, therefore, that the destruction of this excrescence by unfolding events should be regarded as tantamount to the demolition of the central structure.

Third, although the natural rate hypothesis is pedagogically effective as the polar opposite to the stable Phillips trade-off hypothesis, it is not the case that empirical rejection of the latter establishes the former. Suppose that fully anticipated, purely nominal shocks have no employment effects. Other things (such as changes in the 'marginal efficiency of capital') might still have such effects. The ability to anticipate inflation (or 'absence of money illusion'), then, does not by itself imply some sort of strong stability of the economic system around full employment, be it 'natural' or not.

## THE OUT-OF-FOCUS KEYNES

What do the three stages of Monetarism have to do with Keynes? How do we bring Keynes into some sort of relation with developments decades after his death?

In all the debates over Keynesian economics in the last twenty years or so, there is one Keynes that has remained curiously out of focus: Keynes, the monetary reformer. This is true also in my own writings. After more than fifteen muddled years of inflation, preoccupied as we are with intractable problems of monetary stabilization, it seems natural to give some thought to the Keynes who gave so many years of his life, from Versailles to Bretton Woods, to the cause of a stable and workable international financial order.

The Phillips curve debacle coincided in time with the elimination of the last vestiges of the Bretton Woods system. The heritage of Keynes, the theorist, came to grief when the legacy of Keynes, the monetary reformer, had been squandered. Is this just a curious coincidence? Or should we make more of it?

Keynesian theory failed to incorporate inflation expectations. Before the Great American inflation, the theory was widely accepted as an adequate guide to reality. Once inflation picked up momentum and became both high and volatile, the Keynesian neglect of nominal expectations became fatal. But the international monetary order that Keynes had striven for should have had responsible international central bank policy by the reserve currency countries and everyone else disciplined by fixed exchange rates. In such a regime, rational agents should not have volatile nominal expectations, and a theory in which they do not is appropriate to the regime.

This is a rational expectations argument. The concept of 'monetary regime' figures prominently in the more recent rational expectations literature. It links expectations and institutions. It may be defined as follows: a monetary regime is a system of expectations that governs the behavior of the public and that is sustained by the consistent behavior of the policy-making authorities. Since the responses of an economy to shocks or policy actions depend on the public's expectations, we need, in effect, a different short-run macrotheory for each different regime.

The regime approach is a highly useful one – certainly, one of the most useful developments to come out of the rational expectations movement so far. I suggest we use it on Keynes and ask what regimes (if any) his theory would fit and also what his opinions were of various regimes. First, we need to consider his treatment of expectations.

## EXPECTATIONS

It used to be one of the proud boasts of Keynesian economics that it incorporated expectations in a significant way. Sir John Hicks in his first review of *General Theory* gave pride of place among the book's contributions to its treatment of expectations:[8]

> If we assume given, not only the tastes and resources ordinarily assumed given in static theory, but also peoples' anticipations of the future, it is possible to regard demands and supplies as determined by these tastes, resources and anticipations, and prices as determined by demands and supplies. Once the missing element – anticipations – is added, equilibrium analysis can be used, not only in the remote stationary conditions to which many economists have found themselves driven back, but even in the real world, even in the real world in 'disequilibrium'.
>
> This is the general method of [*General Theory*]; it may be reckoned the first of Mr Keynes's discoveries.

The claim Hicks made for Keynes was that, by bringing in expectations in the right way, he had succeeded in significantly extending the scope of equilibrium analysis. This is precisely the claim now being made for Lucas, Sargent and colleagues although for rather different reasons. Keynes extended the use of the Marshallian equilibrium method by treating long-term investment expectations as exogenous determinants of his short-run income equilibrium. Lucas extended the use of neo-Walrasian equilibrium analysis by making short-run nominal expectations strictly endogenous again, while shifting to a stochastic equilibrium concept that allows realizations to diverge from expected values.

By the early 1930s, business cycle theorists had come to realize that use of the equilibrium toolbox could be strictly justified only for stationary and perfect foresight processes.[9] This pretty much excluded business cycles – and there was no other toolbox. Keynes's new method successfully *evaded* this dilemma. Lucas's new method attempts to *solve* it.

That, however, is not the whole story. Keynes's innovation concerned the long-term expectations of real magnitudes, while New Classical economics theory has dealt mainly with the short-term expectations of nominal magnitudes. Keynes, on the whole, ignored nominal expectations, and the rational expectations pioneers have only recently begun to turn their attention to long-term investment expectations.

Keynes's own treatment of short-term expectations should give pause to anyone tempted to attack New Classical economics on the grounds that it assumes too much foresight on the part of agents:[10]

> [I]t will often be safe to omit express reference to short-term expectation in view of the fact that in practice ... there is a large overlap between the effects on employment of the realized sale-proceeds of recent output and those of the sale-proceeds expected from current input.

The omission of 'express reference' is achieved, of course, by simply equating expected and realized real income, a procedure subsequently embedded in the Keynesian cross, in *IS–LM*, and thus in the entire Keynesian literature. This is 'perfect foresight' such as the rational expectations people have not allowed themselves to indulge in! Keynes, I think, would have appreciated the considerable weakening of this assumption achieved through the use of a stochastic equilibrium concept.

Long-term expectations are another story. In the early stages of the rational expectations debate, *the* issue was the Phillips curve, and the focus, therefore, was entirely on expectations over the most immediate future only. The ability of agents to infer more or less correctly the immediate price-level consequences of current monetary policies was emphasized to the neglect of their inability to infer much of anything about the future nominal values that will emerge from longer sequences of discretionary policy actions.[11] As a consequence, this early rational expectations literature provides very little in the way of theoretical foundation for the opposition to inflationary policies (and discretionary policies in general) that also characterizes it.[12] This temporary neglect does not mean that the rational expectations approach implies negligible social costs of inflation. Nor does it mean that it somehow precludes sensible study of this problem on which Keynes held such strong views.[13] On the contrary, progress beyond the point reached in the *Tract* requires, I think, careful specification of the 'inflationary regime' in question – requires, in other words, a rational expectations approach.

Nonetheless, long-term expectations pose the question of how far the endogenization of expectations can be taken. Elsewhere, I have used a distinction between 'well-behaved' and 'ill-behaved' expectations (see Leijonhufvud 1983d, reprinted as Chapter 3 below). Well-behaved expectations bear a stable relationship to the observable state variables of a macroeconomic model and can therefore be treated as fully endogenous. Expectations are 'ill-behaved' if not explainable by the model. If, in addition, they are unobservable (or unmeasurable), ill-behaved expectations will spell trouble for our ability to forecast.

In these terms, Keynes's short-term expectations were (excessively) well-behaved, but his long-term expectations ill-behaved in that they shifted for reasons not incorporated in the model. The rational expectations approach to this problem will, of course, be to strive for a behavior description in which long-term investment expectations are completely endogenized.[14] Keynes would presumably have raised philosophical objections to so foolhardy an attempt to harness the 'dark forces of time and ignorance' with the actuarial calculus.

From the standpoint of rational expectations methodology, a refusal to attempt to endogenize all expectations is perhaps nothing but obscurantism. The Keynesian trick of explaining income movements by invoking exogenous (and perhaps also unobservable) 'shifts in the marginal efficiency of capital' appears as nothing more than putting a verbal label on our quantitative ignorance. Clearly, we are better off the more success this ambitious rational expectations program has. Meanwhile, a label for one's ignorance is a very useful thing – if it helps remind one that one *is* ignorant.

## PRICES AND QUANTITIES

During the course of the Monetarist controversy, it was often said that the two sides differed in their explanations of changes in nominal income but 'were in the same boat' when it came to explaining the breakdown of nominal income changes into their price and quantity components. But surely the two approaches do not belong in the same boat? Throughout the entire history of modern macroeconomics, I feel, there has been something profoundly unsatisfactory, something thoroughly befuddled, about our handling of the relationships between nominal and real magnitudes.

I have no precise diagnosis for what the problem has been. I do have a hunch about it, namely that the trouble may stem from a failure to keep straight the differences between monetary (or nominal) and real business cycle hypotheses.

Any business cycle 'story' would have, as two of its elements, first, a shock or disturbance, and second, the failure of some endogenous variable or variables to adjust appropriately to the shock. The disturbances could be nominal or real (or, of course, mixed) and so could the adjustment failures. Thus, we obtain the 'Swedish flag' classification of Figure 1.1, where the mixed cases are slighted for the purposes of the present discussion.

A '(purely) nominal disturbance' is one that requires a scaling up or down of all nominal values for the re-equilibration of the system. Thus, nominal

Propagation

| | Nominal | Mixed | Real (intertemporal) |
|---|---|---|---|
| Nominal | *N/N* | | *N/R* |
| Mixed | | | |
| Real (intertemporal) | *R/N* | | *R/R* |

Impulse

*Figure 1.1   Adjustment 'failures'*

shocks are neutral by definition. A 'real shock' is one that requires some reallocation of resources and, correspondingly, changes in real relative prices. Keynes's shifting 'marginal efficiency of capital' (MEC) is the case we will deal with here (oil shocks and other new-fangled inventions will be ignored). MEC shocks change perceived intertemporal opportunities and require, therefore, adjustments in intertemporal prices, that is, in the structure of real rates of interest.

In a nominal/nominal (*N/N*) theory, the disturbance requires a rescaling of nominal values. A truly exogenous change in a purely supply-determined money stock might approximate such a case. If money wages (for instance) were to be inflexible – for whatever reason – the maladjustment would show up in changes in employment. Friedman's (1968) explanation of deviations from the natural rate of unemployment exemplifies this brand of theory.

In the diagonally opposed real/real (*R/R*) case, the MEC shift requires a reallocation of resources between production for present and for future consumption. (To the extent that intertemporal substitution elasticities in labor-supply versus leisure choices are of significant magnitude, it may also call for a change in the present 'natural' level of employment.) If the intertemporal price structure proves inflexible, saving and investment cannot be appropriately coordinated and the maladjustment, again, shows up in changes in employment. Keynes's (1936) *General Theory* is, of course, of this variety.

If we could have had a Monetarist controversy of this clear-cut *N/N* versus *R/R* variety, modern macroeconomics would be more easily understandable than is now the case. That a failure of nominal values to adjust to a nominal disturbance will mean trouble is not a very complex idea. That a failure of relative prices to adjust to a real disturbance likewise spells trouble is not that much harder to grasp.

The actual discussion has seldom been that straightforward. First, the most widely accepted version of Keynesian economics combines shifts in MEC with rigidity of money wage rates. This *R/N* story is not at all as transparent as our first two examples. If we start with a real disturbance requiring changes in the allocation of resources and in relative prices, but not in the level of nominal values, why should rigid money wages give us trouble? At best a crucial link is missing from this story. At worst it is confused.

One of the consequences of 'Keynesian' economists shifting their ground in this way was a rather confused altercation with the Monetarists over unemployment theory. In this discussion, the Monetarists – who are obliged to invoke some nominal adjustment failure to explain how the real cycle results from nominal shocks – were steadfast in denying any rigidity of wages, while the Keynesians, who should have no particular use for the assumption, eventually made it the touchstone of Keynesian doctrine.[15] Probably, nothing could have done more to make wage rigidity seem an essential Keynesian tenet than the objections to it of Karl Brunner and Milton Friedman.

At the same time, of course, Friedman assumed temporary 'stickiness' of wages to explain how nominal shocks would cause temporary deviations of unemployment from its 'natural rate'. In constructing an equilibrium model with the properties conjectured by Friedman, Lucas transformed the temporary maladjustment into an intertemporal one. The canonical version of New Classical economics, therefore, has nominal disturbances causing misperceptions of the real rate of return, which give rise, in turn, to intertemporal substitution adjustments in employment.[16]

Thus the New Classicists have, in effect, shifted the Monetarist position from an *N/N* one to an *N/R* one. This moves the muddled conflict over unemployment theory onto the *R/N* to *N/R* off-diagonal, which frankly does not help much. It leaves us with Keynesians blaming sticky money wages confronting Monetarists blaming real return misperceptions.

The slow quadrille continues. It may be that most American Keynesians see little difference between the *R/N* and *N/N* positions. From *IS–LM*, one learns that both monetary and real shocks can produce changes in nominal income; it appears, then, that the point one must insist on is that changes in nominal income produce changes in real output and employment only if money wages or prices are sticky. Quite a few former Keynesians, moreover, have come to agree that it takes monetary impulses to produce aggregative movements. These people actually occupy the original Monetarist position (at $N/N$) but still regard themselves as quite non-Monetarist in their insistence on the inflexibility of wages; they do so with some reason, since the leading younger Monetarists have vacated these premises in favor of a position (at $N/R$) allowing a principled insistence on market-clearing wages.

Meanwhile – are you following me? – doubts have arisen in the rational expectations camp concerning the Monetarist causation hypothesis. Indeed, Sims has moved already from a reconsideration (1980) to rejection (1983) of the monetary business cycle explanation. Here I must ask you to stand by for further developments. It is, as yet, too early to tell whether Sims will lead the New Classical economists to occupy the original Keynes position (at $R/R$), while the old Keynesians make themselves at home in Friedman's quarters (at $N/N$).

This will remind you, I am sure, of that great Cambridge contemporary of Keynes, Sir Dennis Robertson (1954):

> [H]ighbrow opinion is like a hunted hare; if you stand in the same place, or nearly the same place, it can be relied upon to come round to you in a circle.

Whether Robertson was here expressing a rational expectation or merely voicing the autoregressive prejudice of his five lagged decades in the profession, I will not presume to judge. If, in this clockwise dance, highbrow opinion were to come back to 'nearly the same place' as Keynes, it may still not be perceived as a vindication, for by now the term 'Keynesian' is little more than a label for the hindmost.

The long controversy between Keynesians and Monetarists is thus a very complicated story. That acknowledged, I will proceed 'as if' the basic conflict, all along, had been between a Keynesian real disturbance/real maladjustment theory and a Monetarist nominal disturbance/nominal maladjustment theory.

## MONETARY REGIMES

There are two basic but contrasting conceptions of how control of nominal values can be achieved, which we may call the *quantity principle* and the *convertibility principle*, respectively. Monetary regimes may be distinguished *inter alia* according to how closely they approximate a system of pure quantity control or one of pure convertibility control.[17]

The quantity principle seeks control of the price level through control of some monetary aggregate usually referred to loosely as the 'quantity of money'. The logically tidiest version of such a system will be on a pure fiat standard. It requires central banking. The private sector must be prevented from creating perfect substitutes for the government-controlled 'money', since otherwise control of the latter might not achieve control of the general price level. Hence the system usually has government monopoly of the note issue and more or less far-reaching governmental control of the banking system. Basically, the government decides on the quantity of money and the private sector sets the price level.

An extreme version of this regime would arise if the government, in changing the quantity of money, did so only by means of currency reforms that change the nominal value of outstanding contracts and of the real balances held by the public. (The 1958 French replacement of old with new francs is an example.) In this unrealistic case, the 'nominal scalar' case, the government could directly manipulate the nominal scale of all real magnitudes.

The convertibility principle, in contrast, requires the government to set the legal price of some commodity (such as gold), allows banks to produce 'money' redeemable into the commodity, and lets the private non-bank sector decide the quantity of paper money and bank deposits it desires to hold. Suppose, just for a moment, that the government could set the legal nominal price of a basket of commodities, and that redeemability of money into baskets could be made operable. Such a 'basket case' monetary regime would be the diametric opposite to the 'nominal scalar': the government sets the price level and the private sector determines the quantity of money.

We may thus consider a spectrum of institutional possibilities, with the commodity standard regimes toward the convertibility control extreme at one end and the fiat regimes toward the quantity control end. Early banking history shows us systems relying altogether on convertibility for monetary control. The present system retains no shred of convertibility, but relies altogether on governmental quantity control. In between, we could array, in rough historical sequence, the managed gold standard, the gold exchange standard, and the Bretton Woods system in its various stages of ascendancy and decline. The historical process has not been a smooth and gradual transition from commodity to fiat standards, of course. War-time lapses into inconvertible paper were repeatedly followed by the re-establishment of regimes in which convertibility had a more or less significant role to play. With some backing and filling, the secular process has nonetheless been away from convertibility and toward quantity control of fiat money.

Most of the historical experience relevant to the present discussion is not well represented by either of my two extreme cases. Nonetheless it is instructive to note what kind of monetary theories and monetary policy doctrines would fit these extremes. We should also ask what relationship might be established between the previous classification of business cycle theories and the present one of monetary regimes.

Obviously, the quantity control fiat standard is made for Monetarist theory. In Friedman's theory (particularly stage II), the central bank sets the quantity of money and the private sector adjusts first nominal income but ultimately only the price level. The monetary authorities can control nominal magnitudes but, in equilibrium, real ones are beyond their grasp. Attempts to control what cannot be controlled produce undesirable results. Pursuit of a low interest target, for instance, would eventually produce explosive inflation. Monetary policy should be directed at monetary targets, and the latter should not be adjusted with an eye to variables, such as employment, that are ultimately beyond nominal control. And so on.

The (unrealistic) case of 'basket convertibility' would be a convenient one for Radcliffe monetary policy doctrine. The price level is set and the public rationally expects its future to be regulated by convertibility. The non-bank public's trading of real IOUs for real deposits with the banking system determines the monetary aggregates. To the extent that the central bank can affect the terms of this exchange, that is, mainly the real rate of interest, it will have some small degree of influence on real investment, output and the real money stock, but control of the nominal scale of real magnitudes in the economy is essentially beyond its powers. Monetary policy operates within narrow limits to affect real credit conditions and liquidity. The use of interest targets does not carry any imminent danger of nominal instability in this setting where both the price level and price expectations are kept in check by convertibility.

Now, of course, not even the late 19th century gold standard resembled this 'basket convertibility' regime at all closely. It had an anchor for nominal values in the sense that price level fluctuations were constrained to those of the relative value of gold in terms of other commodities. Mean reverting price-level expectations helped stabilize prices. Even so, a variable supply of new gold, small and price-inelastic non-monetary demand and vanishing non-bank monetary demand meant that the bounds that gold convertibility put on the price level could be uncomfortably wide. The wider these bounds, the more room the system gave for the 'credit cycle', as Keynes called it.[18] Management of the standard, for reasons beyond merely protecting the solvency of the banking system against 'drains', became increasingly desirable.

The last attempt, in the 1920s, to control nominal values through gold convertibility ended in total disaster. Convertibility for the public disappeared and was never seen again. One by one, the features of the commodity standard were removed, making central bank control increasingly important. With redeemability gone, the public could no longer protect itself against inflationary policies. Until 1971, small open economies were still disciplined to some degree by fixed exchange rates but retained a significant ability to sterilize reserve flows, particularly in periods when capital flows were restricted.[19]

The international system of multiple fiat regimes, snakes, tunnels, dirty floats and flexible exchange rates is far removed from the old gold standard world. But although the peoples of the Western world have had to become accustomed to the instability of nominal values, and even though the correct anticipation of nominal changes is of the utmost importance in such a setting, the present system of multilateral monetary mismanagement does not closely approximate my 'nominal scalar' extreme.

So, our historical experience lies well inside these extremes. But the never-ceasing theoretical debate juxtaposes two traditions of monetary analysis, each of which interprets that experience as if it 'essentially' belonged close to one of the extremes. Very often, moreover, the battle between Monetarism and the 'new view' over the interpretation of some regime midway between the extremes is carried out in terms that suggest that the two theories are regarded as mutually exclusive, so that one must be true and the other false.[20] My own unprincipled belief is that both theories are about half true and that we can be dangerously misled if we base policy wholly on one to the total exclusion of the other.

## REGIMES AND CYCLES

Turning now to business cycle theories, it is clear that those postulating purely nominal shocks are relevant only at the fiat extreme, whereas at the convertibility extreme only real shock hypotheses are admissible. The (strong) Monetarist causal chain from exogenous money shock via nominal inflexibility to real output and employment is familiar. The Keynesian chain from changes in real intertemporal prospects via real interest rate maladjustments to real income and endogenous movements in inside money, even if familiar, is out of fashion. We may sketch both an equilibrium and a disequilibrium version of it.

In the equilibrium version, we start with a rise (exogenous in relation to the model specified) in the future real income perceived as derivable from present factor employment in some sizeable sector of the economy. All agents are equally informed about this change in the situation and all evaluate it in the same way. The entire system responds as would Robinson Crusoe, therefore. Suppose, for the sake of argument, a high degree of intertemporal elasticity of labor/leisure substitution, so that we obtain a significant supply response to this change in the future return to present labor. This will allow a temporary equilibrium employment expansion in one sector without equal contraction elsewhere. Hence, the natural rate of unemployment is not a constant but depends on the marginal efficiency of capital. The expansion of output is financed by an expansion of bank and non-bank trade credit. As income increases, more real money balances are demanded, so that the additional saving matching the increased investment ends up being partly intermediated by the banking system. Investment, real interest rates and employment all rise, and the expansion of the banking system (and of non-bank credit) allows this to happen without downward pressure on money prices.

Note that this sketch follows the rational expectations equilibrium ground rules, although it is non-Monetarist. The money stock varies with income for purely endogenous reasons. Employment co-varies with money income for reasons that have nothing to do with nominal misperceptions or other maladjustments of wages or prices.

The disequilibrium version is the Wicksell–Keynes story. Here it is *not* the case that all agents get the same information. Individual firms see improvements in the future return to present activity, but no one has an overview of what is happening to the economy-wide marginal efficiency of investment. Since, historically, the average real rate of return has not been a volatile variable, speculation stabilizes the real rate of interest and firms adjust their rates of investment to it. When the real interest rate fails to find its 'natural' level, household saving and business investment are not properly coordinated. In the upswing, (over)-expansion of credit allows investment to exceed planned saving, putting upward pressure on money prices and wages. In recession, the contraction of credit will similarly put downward pressure on prices. The cycle, therefore, would leave a Phillips-curve pattern of observations, even in this system where nominal values are anchored by convertibility.

Suppose this is a serviceable description of the kind of cycle that occurs toward the end of our spectrum, where convertibility more or less guarantees against the occurrence of purely nominal shocks. What then happens to the cyclical behavior of the economy as the historical trend away from convertibility control takes it toward pure quantity control? What does *not* happen is that the Keynesian $R/R$ cycle fades out to be replaced by a Monetarist $N/N$ cycle. Two things might happen. Either the quantity control is handled in such a way that shocks requiring adjustments in the nominal scale of real magnitude do not occur; or it is mismanaged, in which case an $N/N$ cycle is superimposed on the $R/R$ one.

Recent history presents us with about two decades of one and two of the other. What seems most interesting about the Bretton Woods regime in retrospect is that a system of expectations basically appropriate to an economy with convertible money was sustained by quantity control and with the central convertibility mechanism removed. A system of price-level expectations consistent with the convertibility principle means that people expect prices to revert to the longer-term trend if and when they go above or below the trend. For such expectations to be maintained when the economy is not in fact on a standard where non-discretionary, objective factors determine the trend, the central bank must, in effect, 'mimic' such a standard. It does so by imposing monetary restraint above the trend and applying monetary stimulus below it. The government must also maintain the faith that this pattern of behavior will be continued indefinitely. An (at least implicit) monetary constitution will be of help in this regard. For small open economies, a habit of defending a fixed exchange rate may be the way to accomplish this task – if, that is, the reserve currency country behaves responsibly. This can be a big 'if'. In any case, public confidence in the indefinite maintenance of this pattern of monetary control will require budgetary policies consistent with this objective.[21]

In the United States, monetary stability was maintained in this way until the mid-1960s. With the private sector firmly expecting a quite low and not very variable rate of inflation, the Federal Reserve System could affect the availability and price of 'real' credit to some extent. Monetary policy could play a limited, but constructive, role in attempts to stabilize employment. But the continuance of the regime required continued restraint on the part of the authorities.

The one-time Keynesian (or Radcliffe) doctrine of the 'ineffectiveness' of monetary policy would seem to have served, however inadvertently, as a myth protecting the Bretton Woods regime. Like the belief in the stickiness of nominal wages, it is a doctrine fitting a true convertible standard – where the monetary authorities cannot play around with the nominal scalar, rational agents will not expect that adjustments in the nominal scale of contracts will be needed. When the Friedmanite doctrine that the quantity of money is an effective regulator of nominal income gradually gained acceptance, however, it was inevitable that advocates of discretionary policy would put it to use. To economists who explained unemployment by the stickiness of money wages, this Monetarist doctrine suggested that the stock of money might serve as an effective regulator of employment. If so, it was almost a moral imperative that it be used. But vigorous manipulation of the supply of outside nominal money will destroy the system of expectations that makes nominal values relatively inflexible. The Phillips curve will then start to misbehave.

## INVOLUNTARY UNEMPLOYMENT

At the outset I noted that the New Classical economics was made up of rational expectations, Monetarism and market clearing. It remains to comment on the last of the three.[22]

The equilibrium approach has caused more uproar among Keynesians than any other aspect of the work of Lucas, Sargent et al. The reason is that the market-clearing assumption is taken to be inconsistent with 'involuntary unemployment', a concept that most Keynesians feel obliged to defend to the bitter end of their creed. Much ink has been spilt and a considerable volume of hot air expended, therefore, in criticizing or satirizing the rational expectations approach on this score. From the rational expectations side, scorn is heaped on the arbitrary fix-price constraints of 'disequilibrium' theory, while the concept of excess demand is declared inoperational and the notion of 'involuntary' behavior spurned as inexplicable in utility-maximizing terms.

In my opinion, however, the issue has hardly been joined, so that not much can be sensibly said about the debate as it relates to Keynes. One reason for this is that few if any people on either side care much about what Keynes might have meant by 'involuntary unemployment', and that most proceed to use the term as if whatever associations happen to come to mind are good enough at least for polemical purposes.[23] The term, without a doubt, is one of the most unfortunate new coinages in the history of economics. This does not mean that the problem to which the term refers is therefore nonsensical. Keynes was concerned with a systemic problem that could be defined neither in terms of individual decision situations nor in terms of interactions between buyers and sellers in a single market. His 'involuntary' unemployment is the result of *effective demand failures*.[24]

Two distinct effective demand failures are involved in Keynes's persistent involuntary unemployment state. One is the intertemporal ($R/R$) one discussed above, which arises because[25]

> a decision not to have dinner to-day ... does not necessitate a decision to have dinner or to buy a pair of boots a week hence or a year hence or to consume any specified thing at any specified date.

Hence, it does not pay to organize all the markets for specified things at all specified dates. In their absence, it is possible to have an effective excess supply of present goods to which there corresponds a notional excess demand for future goods which is nowhere registered in a market. The other failure, predicated on the prior occurrence of the first, occurs between the spot markets for labor and consumption goods, because unemployed people without money cannot bid for consumption goods so that an effective excess supply of labor may have as its Walras' Law counterpart an ineffective excess demand for goods.

Now, this kind of situation does not have fix-price rationing as a prerequisite. Suppose atomistic markets where, every day, sellers of commodities and buyers of labor post prices and wages, and buyers of commodities and sellers of labor have to decide on their demand-price and reservation-wage schedules.[26] These prices are set using the best information available. Suppose further that agents find a way to carry out all transactions compatible with these prior valuation decisions. 'Markets clear'. If, however, the system has been perturbed in some way such that not all agents are equally informed about the developing situation, these information asymmetries will make realized transactions deviate from their 'equilibrium' volume (if by 'equilibrium' we mean the transactions that would be consistent with plans based on some universally shared view of what the true situation is). So the 'market clears' at a 'disequilibrium' volume.

In the first round of a Keynesian recession, demand-price schedules for capital goods shift down, because expectations about their future rental values have deteriorated and the rate of interest at which expected rentals are discounted has not declined commensurably. The derived demand for labor in those industries consequently declines, but suppliers of labor, who have little reason to believe that realizable real wages have declined throughout the entire system, keep their reservation wages up. So the market clears at reduced employment with not much change in the observed wage level.

Now, this first round outcome may be described in various ways. To say, as I once did to my frequent regret, that '[I]n the Keynesian macrosystem the Marshallian ranking of price- and quantity-adjustment speeds is reversed'[27] is too mechanical to be helpful. It reads as an open invitation to fix-price rationing modeling of the sort that pays little attention to the determination of prices. In my 1968 story, prices were not 'rigid', but held up temporarily (in atomistic markets) because of speculation based on 'inelastic expectations'. This story does not give both sides of the labor market the same information sets. But it does not otherwise differ significantly from the way in which later rational expectations models deal with variations in employment.[28]

In the New Classical models, however, tomorrow is another day (drawn from a distribution of pretty nice days). Tomorrow you try it again, starting from scratch. Today's decline in employment has no persistent consequences. (A reason for persistence, in fact, has to be invented.)

In Clower's version of the Keynesian story, the temporary curtailment in employment means that tomorrow's consumption demand is constrained by today's realized income. The derived demand for labor in the consumption goods industries is now also affected. By a familiar route, multiplier repercussions bring the system into a state where the inability of the unemployed to back their notional consumption demands with cash is a major reason for the persistence of unemployment. The unemployment that persists in the system *for this reason* Keynes called 'involuntary'.[29,30]

Now, I agree that the theory of effective demand failures raises more questions than it answers and also that it has made no progress (as far as I know) for several years. But the nature of the problem that it poses should be clear. Individuals interact on the basis of incomplete information. The consequence is a price vector reflecting the incompleteness of information and a pattern of realized transactions which leaves some agents disappointed. Will this set in motion a learning process that leads to a coordinated solution? If price adjustments were governed by notional excess demands, then neo-Walrasian stability theorems will tell us under which conditions the answer is yes. Effective demand theory argues, I think persuasively, that there is no reason to suppose that, whatever the trial-and-error process that capitalist economies rely on, the successive trials will in fact be governed by these notional errors. Consequently, *tâtonnement* stability theorems are suspect.

To my knowledge, the New Classical literature contains nothing of any relevance one way or another to these issues. When 'excess demand' is simply dismissed as an inoperational concept, inquiries into its 'notional' or 'effective' nature are somewhat discouraged. The oft-paraphrased point that 'rational agents will act to exhaust perceived gains from trade' may serve very well as a pedagogical note of caution *vis-à-vis* certain fix-price construc-tions, but as a contribution to our understanding of the stability of general equilibrium, it ranks somewhere below the Law of Jean-Baptiste Say.

This debate, to repeat, has not been joined.

## THE 1920s AND THE 1980s

To many people, my assigned subject is worth discussing mostly in so far as it leads up to a stand for or against Mrs Thatcher or President Reagan. It should be developed in adversary terms: Keynes versus rational expectations; aggregate demand management in a world of sticky wages versus policy ineffectiveness in a world of neutral money; re-inflation versus continued disinflation. My own belief, in contrast, is that this way of seeing the issues gets neither Keynes nor the rational expectations people right. I do not believe it gets the alternatives currently before us right, either.

There was one period, in the early 1920s, when Keynes had to deal with a monetary regime resembling our own, which is to say, a system of flexible exchange rates, unbalanced budgets and unanchored fiat currencies. His main reaction to it, evidently, was that it urgently demanded monetary reform. The *Tract* was not a book about how best to muddle along from year to year within the existing system. It argued for a change of regime.

The 1920s have recently drawn the renewed interest of balance-of-pay-ments theorists and monetary economists. In a recent paper on the problem of 'Stopping Moderate Inflations', Sargent (1981) compares the methods of Poincaré and Thatcher. He criticizes Mrs Thatcher for carrying through with disinflation without reforming the policy regime, and attributes the 1926 Poincaré 'miracle' to a systematic fiscal and monetary regime change.

The diagnosis of the French situation and the precise recipe for the miracle had been given by Keynes more than two years before Poincaré reluctantly acted on these lines. Keynes's diagnosis, item by item, was then exactly the one that Sargent has now rediscovered.[31] For example:

> What ... will determine the value of the franc? First, the quantity, present and prospective of the francs in circulation ... (T)he quantity of the currency, depends mainly on the loan and budgetary policies of the French Treasury ... What course should the French Treasury now take in face of the dangers surrounding them? It is soon said. First, the government must so strengthen its fiscal position that its power to control the volume of the currency is beyond doubt.

Obviously, Keynes had an adequate working knowledge of that 'unpleasant Monetarist arithmetic'![32] A more detailed reading of Keynes and Sargent only makes the agreement between the two even more remarkable.

The *Tract on Monetary Reform* is a very Monetarist book. Many latter-day Keynesians like to think that Keynes successfully kicked this habit soon afterward and went on to write the *Treatise*, which he in turn discarded as the *General Theory* began to take shape in his mind. But it is also possible to see this progression less as a series of radical changes in Keynes's fundamental theoretical beliefs than as reorientations of his theoretical efforts to meet changing problems.

This characteristic of Keynes's work – that he adapted his theory to changing problems – has often been remarked upon. Practical political economists approve; pure theorists disapprove. Rational expectations economists might recognize in this adaptability of Keynes's something more than an engaging or irritating character quirk. Rational expectations theory tells us that the short-run effects of particular disturbances or policy actions will depend upon the expectations of the public and, therefore, on the regime that the public believes to be in effect. We need a different applied macrotheory for each monetary regime. The lesson is that we all must, like Keynes, adapt our theories to a changing world.

The *Tract* denounced 'instability of the standard of value' in strong, colorful terms. We do not find Keynes retracting these opinions later. Instead, throughout the rest of his life, he strove for an international economic order that would anchor nominal values and provide 'fixed' exchange rates while leaving scope for discretionary domestic policies and, in particular, giving Britain time to adjust.[33] His work in theory, subsequent to the *Tract*, assumed a regime in which the nominal scale of real magnitudes was not being manipulated. The influence of nominal expectations on behavior was correspondingly neglected. His theory did assume, of course, that one would have to face a business cycle even in the absence of nominal shocks. Absence of obstacles to money wage adjustment does not suffice to guarantee rapid convergence on the natural rate of unemployment in this theory, since intertemporal coordination failures ('saving exceeding investment') are not corrected by changes in nominal values.[34] The strong version of Monetarism, therefore, cannot hold in this theory.

## CONCLUSIONS

Keynesian economics used to be the mainstream. Now, the younger generation of macrotheorists and econometricians regard it as just a backwater, look to Monetarism for navigable channels, and find their real white water thrills in the technically demanding rapids of rational expectations. This ageing Keynesian thinks the main channel is still where it used to be. But obviously it has silted up, is full of accumulated debris, and must be thoroughly dredged and cleared before one can hope that it will see much traffic again.

Mainly, I suggest, the Keynesian tradition has had trouble in keeping the analysis straight on nominal versus real shocks and adjustments. This happened to surface in the squabble over the Phillips curve. But the trouble goes deeper and begins earlier. When I was a student, over twenty years ago, two of the tenets (for example) that were taught to us as 'Keynesian' were (1) that nominal wages were rigid, and (2) that monetary policy could not bring about sizeable changes in nominal income. Both propositions are basically true if we can take a framework of monetary stability as part of the (unstated) *ceteris paribus* conditions. Both are false as matters of general theory. As it happens, you will be alright as long as you firmly believe both of them. Unlearning (2) while still holding on to (1) led to confusion and produced the Phillips curve debacle.

One does not revive Keynesian economics by insisting that nominal wages are sticky or by denying that governmental money creation causes inflation. The doctrine that unemployment is produced by the interaction of nominal income changes (without distinction as to their cause) with sticky wages keeps pointing us in the wrong direction, namely toward using nominal instruments to try to bring about real change.

Keynesians should learn from Monetarism (if need be) that manipulation of the nominal money stock has strong effects on nominal income in discretionary fiat money regimes. From rational expectations they should learn that nominal expectations (of price-setting agents in particular) are endogenous in regimes where the nominal scale is subject to manipulation; also that stabilization policy is better thought of in terms of the design of policy regimes with desirable overall, long-run properties rather than in terms of one short-horizon policy choice at a time. But there are also fashionable things they should refuse to learn. We do not have sufficient reason to accept the strong version of Monetarism; we have reason to reject the natural rate of unemployment doctrine;[35] and we have no reason to pay much attention to rational expectations denials of effective demand failures and the possibility of involuntary unemployment.

We should seek a return to a monetary order that should as far as possible minimize nominal shocks. They do us no good but cause us much harm.[36] A return to monetary stability – *if* we can find a way – requires us to forswear policies that are built on the hope of exploiting temporary money-illusions, or the incomplete indexing of contracts, or other information imperfections. This includes forswearing fiscal deficits financed by borrowing today but by money creation tomorrow.

In a world where the nominal scale were firmly anchored, business fluctuations would presumably still take place (and they would probably leave behind a record of observations looking much like a stable Phillips curve). It is conceivable that these would be socially optimal in some sense or other, but we have no substantive reasons to give much weight to this possibility. The amplitude of these real cycles and the incidence of their social cost can be modified by policy regimes designed to have real effects on real variables: unemployment insurance, functional finance, built-in stabilizers. The lessons of Hansenian Keynesianism would come back into their own.

As in the 1920s, so in the 1980s: the times call for monetary reform. That will be easier said than done. Simple money growth rules, assuming their operational feasibility, are probably too tight as constraints on systems where not only does '(nominal) money cause (nominal) income' but '(real) income also causes (real) money'.[37] We should have no longings for the 'barbarous relic'. And there can be no returning to Bretton Woods. From Keynes, the monetary reformer, we get a useful suggestion on where to start: 'First, the government must so strengthen its position that its power to control the volume of the currency is beyond doubt' (1971a, p. xxi). However, he provides hardly any help beyond that point. As is proper for an economist, I am thus led to a dismal conclusion – namely, that we have to start thinking for ourselves.

## APPENDIX 1.1    KEYNES'S CONTRIBUTION TO THEORY

Professor Yeager may be justified in his complaint that I have defended my interpretation of Keynes of twenty years ago merely by 'emphatic reassertion'. I have tried consistently to refrain from rearguing my case, when I have had nothing much to add to it, in response to the various commentaries and criticisms that have been raised against it. Repetition of that sort has seldom proved productive. At some point, one must simply leave it to readers to make their own judgments without boring them with one's insistence on having been right. When Yeager alluded to the matter in his recent paper (Yeager 1986), I wished merely to signal that I do not concede to his critique (or, very much, to Grossman's). But this time, there was also something to add, namely the previously unknown evidence from Keynes's *Collected Writings XXIX* (Keynes 1979), which has appeared in the interim. Yeager's 'Reply' (1988) makes clear, however, that mere reassertion plus that reference will not do. I owe him an explanation of how it fits in.

I do not want to argue that Keynes 'was right all along'. So that is not the issue. What is at issue is the theme of my 1968 book, (Leijonhufvud 1968c) which maintained that the *General Theory* contained a novel and important theoretical idea, that this idea was central to Keynes's conception, and that this idea was not developed, or even preserved, in the later development of Keynesian economics. This 'promise which the Keynesian tradition has not fulfilled' (p. 386) inheres in the idea of 'effective demand failures'.

In his 1973 'Keynesian Diversion' article, Professor Yeager declared that, according to his reading of Keynes, while much in the *General Theory* strikingly resembles 'the supposedly vulgar Keynesianism of the income-expenditure theory', Keynes 'falls short of articulating anything resembling … the Clower–Leijonhufvud story', (Yeager 1973, pp. 156–7). Similarly, Professor Grossman's 1972 review article, 'Was Keynes a "Keynesian"?', concludes that 'the most plausible answer' to the question of its title 'is that Keynes did not have in mind anything resembling Clower's interpretation of the consumption function … and that he had no vision of the sort attributed to him by Leijonhufvud'. Yeager now quotes Alan Coddington (in his 1976 article) as finding our interpretation to be the result of 'reading not so much between the lines as off the edge of the page.'[38] This line is so witty, it is rather a pity that it misses the whole book!

At the time I was writing, the established interpretation of Keynes was that he had explained unemployment by postulating rigid wages. (Today, this is also the re-established interpretation – one sees this old canard repeated almost wherever Keynesian economics still rates a mention.) The rigid wages hypothesis was not a novel idea in Keynes's day. That the explanation of why labor fails to sell must start from the presumption that wages are too high and won't come down is a notion that is in all probability older than is economics as a discipline. The idea that Keynes sought to differentiate himself from the 'classics' and start a 'revolution' by reasserting this old platitude is not necessarily the 'most plausible' reading of the *General Theory* – particularly since it is definitely to be found only 'off the edge of the page'.

In 1968, I tried to show that there was a theoretically far more interesting, alternative reading of the *General Theory*, and therefore – and this was really the point – that there had existed in 1936 an 'alternative future' for Keynesian economics to the one realized. I did confess (rather too readily and too often, I now think) that this alternative reading was 'speculative' rather than literal on some points. But I also maintained that it made more sense. In particular, it allowed a coherent interpretation of how Keynes did differentiate himself from the 'classics', where no such coherent interpretation was previously available.

Mass unemployment is a symptom of coordination failure. 'Wrong' prices that won't budge is one possible explanation of such failures. Another possibility, the one that Clower and I explored, is that freely competitive, flexible prices might fail to move in such a manner as to generate the price signals required to coordinate activities. The 'market forces' governing the adjustment of prices (and of rates of output, employment and consumption) will not always drive prices toward the equilibrium configuration where the desired transactions of all parties are consistent. Although there are no obstacles to price movements, the price system may thus fail to communicate all the information required to enable agents to exhaust potential gains from trade.[39]

In an imaginary economy, so organized that the offer of any particular good would constitute an 'effective' demand for any other good desired by the supplier, such effective demand failures would not occur. They occur in systems where money appears on one side of all transactions and thus is the only good traded in all markets. For an individual agent in a money economy, the sale of labor and purchase of wage goods, for instance, must then be separated by the acquisition and disposal of money; whether the agent's desire to acquire wage goods is communicated as an effective demand thus becomes conditional on the realization of the sale of labor. To capture the theoretical possibility of this kind of coordination problem, therefore, it is vital to think in terms of a model in which money is the means of exchange. 'Barter' models will not do.

Today, the New Classical economics has made it utterly commonplace to discuss macroeconomic problems from this information perspective. (This is so even though the New Classicals have waved the magic wand of rational expectations over most of the things that Clower and I thought of as information problems – and have thus made them vanish from discussion.) In the mid-1960s, no one wrote about Keynesian unemployment or other macroeconomic issues in those terms. So the contention that Keynes had already thought in such sophisticated 'modern' terms thirty years earlier was received with the suspicion to which Yeager, Grossman and Coddington gave expression.

I came to consider the question whether all this 'was in Keynes' quite late in my own work. (Chapter 2:3 of my 1968 book was not part of my dissertation.) At that stage, I would not have been averse to claim the originality that Yeager in 1973 sought to accord me! But in revising my manuscript for publication I had to form a judgment on the question. A careful re-reading of the *General Theory*, Chapter 2, 'The Postulates of the Classical Economics', was more convincing than anticipated. From the standpoint of the theory of effective demand failures, the chapter made perfect sense. Moreover, all of Keynes's objections to classical theory were part and parcel of the same argument.

It was clear what Keynes's definition of 'involuntary unemployment' meant and why he had phrased it in such a seemingly awkward, contrived way. It was clear why he harped on Professor Pigou treating the wage bargain as if it were a barter bargain when he (Pigou) knew it was a money bargain. It was clear what were Keynes's objections to Say's Law (unemployed labor is not an effective demand for wage goods, and current saving does not constitute effective demand for future consumption). And finally, it was clear why he claimed that the three 'classical' assumptions, which he argued must be discarded, 'all amount to the same thing in the sense that they all stand and fall together, any one of them logically involving the other two' (Keynes, p. 12).

As far as I am aware, there is to this day no alternative interpretation of Keynes's Chapter 2 in the literature that makes *coherent* sense of it. Almost all authors simply ignore Keynes's elaborate definition of involuntary unemployment and substitute their own opinion of what the words might usefully (or, in the case of Lucas, uselessly)[40] mean: most of them end up thus labelling some concept of unemployment that Keynes went to the pains of explicitly listing as 'voluntary'. Some have read his discussion of why Pigou is unjustified in treating wage negotiations as dealing with exchanges of labor for wage goods as showing that he assumed the labor supply decision (but not the consumption decision) to be affected by money illusion. And the most common interpretation of his attacks on it has been that he was attacking Say's Law in the sense (or nonsense)[41] *later* invented by Oskar Lange. This makes Keynes's critique of 'classical' theory, I noted (p. 101), into a 'motley assortment of outlandish propositions'. Hence,

> One must conclude, I believe, that Keynes' theory, although obscurely expressed and doubtlessly not all that clear even in his own mind, was still in substance that to which Clower has recently given a precise statement. (p. 102)

This is the conclusion to which Yeager, Grossman and Coddington take exception. (None of them, however, has tried his own hand at making sense of Chapter 2.)

Still, I had to admit, an argument that rests on coherence of interpretation does not compel assent. If Grossman, Yeager and others did not accept it, I could not very well force them to do so. My interpretation did involve a fair amount of reading between the lines. Some scholars will object to anything but a literal reading, but I see nothing illegitimate about it – it is, literally, the only 'inter-legent' thing to do. But why, if this was his message in substance, did not Keynes spell it out more clearly?

Some things he did not need to go into. In trying to understand the relationship between Keynesian macroeconomies and the neo-Walrasian general equilibrium theory of the early 1960s, Clower and I came to delve into such matters as the absence of the Walrasian auctioneer, 'false trading' and the appearance of realized sales proceeds in the (consumption) demand function. There is no reason why someone, coming to the problem from a Marshallian background in the 1930s, should have trod this tortuous path. Alfred Marshall's demand function, for instance, was constrained by realized income to begin with.[42] So there are a number of elements of the 1960s discussion that one should not expect to find parallelled in the *General Theory*.

Nonetheless, before the *Collected Writings* had appeared, the evidence that Keynes had a clear conception of effective demand failures was to a large extent indirect. Keynes could so easily have made the matter indubitable by some simple illustrative example – but had not done so. I put my classroom examples into print to help make the point. The posited context was a state in which, at today's (fix-)prices, the supply of labor exceeds employment and the supply of wage goods is exceeded by demand – if in the latter we include what the employed would have bought had they found jobs. Why should we not predict tomorrow's wage to be set lower *and tomorrow's wage-good prices higher*, and tomorrow's quantities to be moving smoothly in the directions required to eliminate the 'rationing' due to the initial pricing mistakes?

> Clearly, because in that [Keynesian] system *all exchanges involve money on one side of the transaction*. The workers looking for jobs ask for money, not for commodities. Their notional demand for commodities *is not communicated* to producers ... The individual steel-producer cannot pay a newly hired worker by handing over to him his physical product (nor will the worker try to feed his family on a ton-and-a-half of cold-rolled sheet a week) ... In an economy of self-employed artisans our problem simply cannot appear. If it does appear in a posited system, say, of big farmers 'higgling and haggling' with prospective farm-hands over the room and board and other direct material benefits that are to constitute the real wage, it will be most smoothly solved in a thoroughly Walrasian manner. (Leijonhufvud 1968, pp. 89–91)

I could not find anything that plain in Keynes,[43] and that left a nagging doubt. I have told the rest of the story before, but without putting it fully into context (as I have here tried to do). To repeat (1983, p. 198n):

> When Volumes XIII and XIV of the *Collected Writings* appeared, I skimmed them solely to see whether my interpolations had been too imaginative. Somewhat to my consternation, I could not find anything that seemed relevant to the problem one way or another! In the Fall of 1974, I visited Cambridge ... and took the opportunity of a dinner at King's to ask my host, Lord Kahn, and also Lord Kaldor and Professor Robinson whether the Circus had not discussed Chapter 2 of the *General Theory* and why no background material had come to light. They did not recall any such discussions – which left me somewhat mystified.
>
> Some time ago, Mr. C.W.S. Torr brought to my attention that the 'Tilton laundry hamper' had contained the answer. Much of Vol. XXIX is devoted to some discarded introductions to the *General Theory* in which 'the contrast between a Co-operative and an Entrepreneur Economy' is treated as fundamental.
>
> Keynes's 'Co-operative Economy', as it turned out was one in which labor is bartered for goods, so that the supply of labor is always an effective demand for goods. In his 'Entrepreneur Economy' the Clowerian rule applies: labor buys money and money buys goods but labor does not buy goods. In the entrepreneur economy, therefore, effective demand failures are possible and so, consequently, is involuntary unemployment.

That, I think, should settle the matter (see Keynes 1979, pp. 63–102).

My own reaction to reading Keynes's volume XXIX was that of at last coming on a piece of the puzzle that I had long conjectured should have existed! The contrasts drawn between the 'Cooperative Economy' (in some places also called the 'Real-Wage Economy') and the 'Entrepreneurial Economy' involved precisely the simple, straightforward, unmistakeable conceptual experiments that had been missing. Hence my statement in commenting on Yeager: 'it so happens that on these particular points we now do know precisely what [Keynes] meant' (1986, p. 415).

Yeager does not think so. His 'Reply' asks:

> [W]hat significance attaches to what Keynes said or supposedly said or supposedly meant in rough drafts that he *discarded*? The fact that he wrote certain ideas down, considered them, and then *discarded* them would suggest that they were not what he meant.

Ignoring what did not get into print, Yeager's conclusion suggests, would 'serve the integrity of the history of economic thought and also the very substance of money/macro theory'. Indeed!

Yeager ends on a rhetorical note: 'is it not time at last to give up the delusion that Keynes really had this theory right all along?'. There are two, somewhat related, delusions that I most definitely would not want to propagate. One is that all the novel theoretical ideas in the *General Theory* were correct and valuable. Keynes's liquidity preference hypothesis of interest rate determination, for instance, I consider to be 'theoretically unsound, empirically false, and practically dangerous'.[44] I also part from Keynes on the scope of the effective demand failure possibilities discussed above.[45] The other delusion is that, in trying to understand the development of our subject, we should assume that Keynes (or anyone else) had powers of logical closure, that is, presuppose that he understood fully all the logical implications of a theoretical structure, whether his own or one or those, such as *IS–LM*, that were proposed by others as interpretations of his thought. But I also regard it as a delusion that Keynes had nothing worthwhile to contribute.

Yeager is simply unwilling to consider Keynes's understanding of 'monetary disequilibrium' as on a par with that of Harry Gunnison Brown, Herbert J. Davenport or Clark Warburton. Yet, it is hard to find anything in the picture Yeager gives of their theories beyond the quantity theory with 'frictions', albeit intelligently elaborated. Keynes, too, has written intelligently within this genre. His *Tract on Monetary Reform* belongs to it. By the *General Theory*, his theory has become more complicated: a generalized excess demand for money may result not just from a contraction of the money supply, but also from an increase in the amount demanded induced by real shocks; in the case of a real intertemporal (saving–investment) disequilibrium, a new relative price vector has to be found for equilibrium to be restored, so just a balanced deflation will not do; even in the absence of significant 'frictions', the adjustment process may fail to home in on the equilibrium price vector because of effective excess demand failures.

Keynes did not get all this 'right all along'. But he was venturing (as we now have every reason to know) into exceedingly difficult territory. The questions that he tackled were not of the sort that would better have been ignored. Monetarism highlights some basic truths that should not be lost from sight – as, admittedly, they tended to be at times during the high tide of Keynesianism. But we also have to be concerned about real shocks, about the intertemporal coordination problem and about effective demand failures. A macroeconomic theory that grapples seriously with these problems is not just a useless diversion.

## NOTES

1.  In the past, I have sometimes been accused of claiming knowledge of 'what Keynes really meant'. The present title was assigned to me by Royal (Economic Society) decree. In trying to write a paper to fit it, I have had occasional bouts of the unworthy suspicion that it was meant to goad me into some sort of spiritualist seance before witnesses. I would like to declare from the outset, therefore, that I have not been in touch with Maynard about this!

2.  A recent Lucas and Sargent paper (1979) is entitled 'After Keynesian Macroeconomics'. It deals, however, to a very large extent with econometric issues outside the scope of my discussion.

3.  See Tobin (1981). For the material in this section, see also Laidler (1981, 1983).

4.  Friedman's (1956) 'Restatement', through the years in which Friedman and Schwartz's (1963a) *Monetary History* and related works by Cagan, Brunner and Meltzer were absorbed by the profession.

5.  Friedman and Schwartz (1963a), p. 695.

6.  Tobin (1981), p. 41.

7.  See especially Phelps (1968). I may also refer to my own comment on Phelp's paper.

8.  Sir John Hicks (1936), reprinted as '"The General Theory" a First Impression', in Hicks (1982) p. 86.

9.  See Hicks (1933), reprinted as 'Equilibrium and the Cycle' in 1982. Compare also Lucas (1980), reprinted in Lucas (1981), especially section 5.

10. See Keynes (1936), pp. 501. My colleague Robert Clower reads this passage simply as assuming static expectations. Even on that reading, however, the solution states of Keynes's model will be perfect foresight equilibria.

11. See Leijonhufvud (1984a, 1983d – Chapters 8 and 3 respectively in this volume).

12. That the New Classical economics does not provide sufficient reasons for its strong aversion to inflationary policies is a complaint often voiced by critics. See, for example, Tobin, *op. cit.*, or Hahn (1983), pp. 101ff.

13. Keynes (1971b), 'Preface'. It is true, of course, that Keynes's thought changed and developed from the *Tract* on. It is also true, however, that the world of the *Tract* resembles our current regime of fiduciary standards and flexible exchange rates more than does the world of the *Treatise* or that of the *General Theory*. One must insist, moreover, that we do not have evidence from Keynes's later years that would indicate a change of mind on his part with regard to the consequences of inflation.

14. Early in his career, Lucas was best known for his work on investment. He returns to it, in the context of a complete macromodel and from a rational expectations perspective, in Lucas (1975). For the growing interest of the rational expectations group in explaining the cyclical behavior of investment, see the 'Introduction' to Lucas (1981). For recent work, see, for example, Kydland and Prescott (1982).

15. See, for example, Okun (1981), Gordon (1981) or Solow (1980).

16. See Lucas (1975) and Barro (1980).

17. I have discussed the material in this and the following sections more extensively in Leijonhufvud (1982, 1984b – the latter reprinted as Chapter 9 below).

18. Keynes (1971b).

19. For an assessment of the scope for independent monetary policies, see Darby, Lothian et al. (1981).

20. For the strong anti-Monetarist position, see Kaldor (1982).

21. See the 'Unpleasant Arithmetic' of Sargent and Wallace (1981), and Keynes's advice to Poincaré quoted p. 21 below.

22. The following remarks will deal only with 'involuntary unemployment', which is the aspect of the matter that has the most to do with Keynes. For a broader discussion of the equilibrium methodology of the New Classicists, see the last section of Leijonhufvud (1983d) and also Leijonhufvud (1983a).

23. Lucas (1978), for example, concludes his discussion of the concept as follows: 'In summary, it does not appear possible, even in principle, to classify individual unemployed people as either voluntarily or involuntarily unemployed depending upon the characteristics of the decision problems they face.' Lucas may have had in mind, perhaps, Barro and Grossman (1971), Benassy (1975) or Malinvaud (1977), but his comment is simply irrelevant to Keynes's concept.

24. One should recall that the Keynesian categories of 'frictional' and 'voluntary' unemployment covered vast territories, and especially a number of possibilities that latter-day Keynesians often like to bring into their quarrel with the rational expectations equilibrium theorists. The *General Theory* (1936, p. 6) briskly lumps into the *voluntary* category, for

instance, 'unemployment due to the refusal or inability of a unit of labour, as a result of legislation or social practices or of combination for collective bargaining or of slow response to change or of mere human obstinacy, to accept a reward corresponding to the value of the product attributable to its marginal productivity'. Note especially that the *inability* is 'voluntary'!

25. See *General Theory*, p. 210.
26. This is basically the conception from which I began in Leijonhufvud (l968c). It will not serve for long before a more structured picture of how trade is organized in the system becomes required (cf. Clower 1975).
27. Leijonhufvud (1968c), p. 52.
28. An important class of rational expectations models, exemplified by Barro (1976), has what amounts to Hicksian 'inelastic expectations' as a central feature. Most of the 'action' in realized transactions comes from a term in the supply and demand functions which measures the difference between current and expected future price. When the expected future price fails to reflect a disturbance appropriately, the result is speculative intertemporal substitution effects that affect the price and volume of transactions in the spot markets. Asymmetries of information between the two sides of the market are against the rules of the game that apply to this class of models, however. They occur only in the market where the central bank conducts open market operations.
29. See Clower (1965, 1967), Leijonhufvud (1968c, Ch. 3) and, for second thoughts on how prevalent such effective demand failures may be, Leijonhufvud (1973).
30. For further discussion see Appendix.
31. See the March 1924 'Preface to the French Edition' in Keynes (1971a, p. xvii). See also the 1926 and l928 commentaries reprinted as 'The French Franc' in Keynes (1972).
32. See Sargent and Wallace (1981).
33. See Tumlir (1983). I am grateful to Tumlir for insisting in conversation that I should go back and read Keynes on the French franc.
34. See 'The Wicksell Connection' in Leijonhufvud (1981a), especially sections 9 and 10.
35. See 'The Wicksell Connection' in Leijonhufvud (1981a).
36. See Leijonhufvud (1984a).
37. For a monetary rule allowing scope for discretion, see the discussion in Leijonhufvud (1984b).
38. Coddington (1976, p. 1268). This was said about Clower, but it was undoubtedly intended that I should feel guilt by association since the concession of having 'read between the lines' was mine.
39. The occurrence of 'false trading' at prices of the moment is a link in the chain of argument. But the theoretical emphasis is altogether on whether adjustments of prices have the system heading toward full employment or not. The orientation, therefore, is very different from that of the literature on fix-price general equilibrium rationing models developed by Barro and Grossman, Siven, and the French school of Benassy and Malinvaud.
40. Lucas (1978) argues the uselessness of the concept of 'involuntary unemployment'. I have discussed the matter in Leijonhufvud (1983d – Chapter 3 below).
41. For a detailed discussion of Lange's concept and of the damage it has done to textbook Keynesianism, see Clower and Leijonhufvud (1973).
42. Grossman's conclusion was, in part, '[most plausibly] ... Keynes did not have in mind anything resembling Clower's interpretation of the consumption function ... Keynes surely did not appreciate the essential sense in which it was inconsistent with the classical theory of markets' (Grossman, 1972). It is not easy to appraise it briefly. It is almost certainly true that Keynes had given little or no thought to the various logical inconsistencies that would arise if his consumption function was somehow plunked down in the midst of a Walrasian general equilibrium model. But he certainly knew (and said so) that his theory is inconsistent with Say's Law of markets and, of course, that his consumption function was crucial to the thoroughly anti-classical deviation-amplifying multiplier.

Grossman correctly pointed out that my characterization of Keynesian short-run dynamics as 'a reversal of Marshall's ranking of price and quantity adjustment speeds' could not be true in general, or Keynes would not have his labor demand function coincide with the marginal productivity of the labor schedule. I stand corrected on this point. But it does not follow from it that Keynes did not have a theory of effective demand failure.

43. For the *other* effective demand failure (the intertemporal one), Keynes did come up with a homely, to-the-point illustration:

An act of individual saving means – so to speak – a decision not to have dinner today. But it *does not* necessitate a decision to have dinner or buy a pair of boots a week hence or to consume any specified thing at any specified date (Keynes 1936, p. 210).

44. Leijonhufvud (1981b, p. 195).
45. See Leijonhufvud (1973).

# 2.  Keynesian economics: past confusions, future prospects

The complaint has become widespread in recent years that macroeconomics is in a confused state. Theory and practice have lost virtually all connection. The approaches generating all the theoretical excitement offer almost no guidance on stabilization policy. Policy practice proceeds on the basis of theories in which we no longer have much confidence. Keynesian and Monetarist beliefs continue to contend with New Classical ideas, with no clear-cut resolution in sight.

One way to find an intelligible pattern in this confusing contention among alternative approaches is to take them in historical sequence and consider, again, the grounds on which some substantial segment of the profession decided to transfer its allegiance from one camp to another. This is the tack taken here. The sketch to follow cannot be comprehensive. It is selective, which means, of course, that it is in some degree subjective.

## THE SWEDISH FLAG

Consider first the following 'Swedish flag' taxonomy. It classifies business cycle theories according to the hypotheses they make about the *impulses* that initiate fluctuations and about the *propagation* mechanisms that turn the impulses into persistent movements in output and employment.

A nominal impulse ($N$) is a disturbance to the system such that the re-equilibration of the economy requires (only) a change in nominal scale, that is, an adjustment of the money price level, leaving real magnitudes unaffected. Purely nominal impulses are neutral, in other words. A helicopter drop of fiat money in a Patinkin model free of distribution effects is an example. A real impulse ($R$), on the other hand, requires some reallocation of resources between industries or occupations and therefore also some corresponding change in relative prices. If it is a 'pure' case of a real disturbance, it will not require a general deflation or inflation in order to restore equilibrium (see Figure 1.1). For the immediate purposes of the flag, we deal throughout with a particular subcategory of real impulses, namely the intertemporal ones.

Close real world approximations to the pure cases may be relatively rare, so the flag is drawn to recognize 'mixed' categories both on the impulse and the propagation side. Our historical review of macroeconomic debates will not compel us to discuss them, however.

## *R/R* (KEYNES) AND *N/N* (FRIEDMAN)

How propagation comes in is best explained by going directly to the relevant cases. Start at *R/R* in the lower right-hand corner of Figure 1.1 with 'the economics of Keynes'. Various events may cause firms to change their views about the profitability of investment, that is, of employing present productive resources for the purpose of augmenting future output. If this shift of the 'marginal efficiency of capital', as Keynes called it, were in a pessimistic direction, for example, they would plan to reduce investment, thereby creating an excess supply of present resources and, implicitly, an excess demand for future goods. This disequilibrium Keynes liked to describe in terms of quantities as 'saving exceeds investment', while Wicksell preferred to describe it in terms of prices as 'the market rate exceeds the natural rate'. The appropriate system response should be that real rates of interest fall (so as to raise the price of future goods in terms of present goods). The Keynesian propagation hypothesis is that speculation prevents the real rates of interest from falling sufficiently to equate saving and investment at full employment. With the failure of the relevant relative price to coordinate intertemporal activities, the excess supply of present resources is removed by a decline in output and employment

In the upper left-hand corner, at *N/N*, we find the Monetarism of Milton Friedman or of Brunner and Meltzer, that is, Monetarism before New Classical economics. The typical disturbance is an exogenous change in the fiat money supply; the failure of the money wage to adjust immediately propagates the shock to real magnitudes so that real income and employment (and not only nominal prices) co-vary with the money stock. Note carefully that the stickiness of money wages is *essential* to this theory. Without it, the history of the US money stock is not to be transformed into a history of US business fluctuations.

## THE MONETARIST DEBATE THAT NEVER HAPPENED

A Monetarist controversy between the *N/N* and *R/R* positions would have been relatively straightforward. The theoretical cores of the two are easily grasped. The *N/N* theory asserts that the typical disturbance is nominal and that the problem with the system is that nominal prices do not adjust promptly. The *R/R* hypothesis asserts that real disturbances require changes in intertemporal prices but that the capitalist system has peculiar difficulty in producing this particular adjustment when it is needed. In each case, there is a straightforward correspondence between what the impulse requires and what the system won't do.

Note that the two theories are not mutually exclusive. It is perfectly reasonable (at least *a priori*) to take the eclectic view that certain episodes in our macrohistory were of the *N/N* type, others of the *R/R* type, and yet others, indeed, 'mixed'. But one can easily imagine a debate between two camps, one insisting on a 'real', the other on a 'monetary', interpretation of the historical record. That debate never took place.

## THE 'KEYNES AND THE CLASSICS' DEBATE

Before the Monetarists came on the scene, internal developments within the Keynesian camp had already shifted the Keynesian position into the bottom left (*R/N*) corner of the flag. The Keynesian economics that filled the text-books for three decades retained the hypothesis that shifts in the marginal efficiency of capital were the typical cause of changes in income but stressed money wage 'rigidity' as the cause of unemployment. It is curious that 'Keynesian' economics should have ended up in this position, since the wage rigidity explanation of unemployment was one that Keynes had done his best to dispute. Moreover, it is not at all obvious that the mix of a real disturbance hypothesis with a nominal inflexibility hypothesis results in a coherent theory.

This, however, was the outcome of the so-called 'Keynes and the classics' debate, which sought to isolate and define the fundamental difference be-tween Keynes's 'revolutionary' new theory and previously accepted 'classical' theory. At one stage (Modigliani 1944), two 'causes' of unemployment were distinguished in the discussion: (1) the traditional one of a money wage level too high in relation to the nominal scale of the economy (as determined by an exogenously set money supply), and (2) Keynes's novel one of an interest rate too high for saving not to exceed investment at full employment. But the Pigou-effect argument, it was eventually agreed, demonstrated that this sec-ond explanation also depended on nominal wage inflexibility and therefore should not be accepted as a distinct and independent case. In thus reasserting the generality of the classical unemployment explanation, this brand of Keynesianism lost sight of the difference between an unemployment state that could be cured by a money wage correction of a few percentage points (so as to bring wages into the equilibrium relationship with the nominal scale of the system) and one of similar extent that would require a horrifying, never-yet-experienced deflation (in order to produce a sizeable wealth effect on saving out of the increased real value of the outside money stock).

This shift of the Keynesian position switched the theoretical focus from the role of intertemporal relative prices in the coordination of saving and investment over time to the relationship between current aggregate money expenditure and money wages.


## THE MONETARIST CONTROVERSY

The Keynesian–Monetarist controversy started therefore with the Keynesians in this muddled *R/N* position being attacked by Monetarists from an *N/N* position. The Keynesians found the defense difficult. To cover all the issues and all the various stages of this 30-year debate is not feasible here. Consider first two examples from the later stages which, although hardly central to the controversy as a whole, serve to show how the discussion was affected by the Keynesian shift from *R/R* to *R/N*.

First, consider the Keynesian response to Friedman's so-called 'natural rate of unemployment' hypothesis. This hypothesis was not one of the original issues in the debate but was added rather late in the game. For present purposes, it may be stated as follows:

Employment has a strong tendency to converge rapidly on equilibrium employment. What ensures this result is simply the ordinary supply-and-demand mechanism operating on the price in the relevant market. Unemployment will be found to diverge from its 'natural rate' only when and in so far as the money wage rate temporarily lags behind its equilibrium value.

From the standpoint of Keynes's *R/R* theory, this is true if and only if intertemporal equilibrium is already assured – but false whenever saving does not equal investment at full employment income. Any Keynesian would have said so in the 1940s. But when, in the 1960s, Friedman added the natural rate of unemployment hypothesis to the structure of monetarist beliefs about the world, the intertemporal coordination problem was out of sight and out of mind among his Keynesian opponents. No one brought it up! It was not even mentioned.

So what retort was left to them? The answer given was, in effect, that Friedman was right: only lagging wage adjustment stands in the way of full employment – but that money wages are *more inflexible* than he or any other monetarist would like to believe! In this way, Keynesian economics became so strongly wedded to the notion of wage inflexibility that, by now, most of the profession thinks of it as *the* characteristic that distinguishes it from other brands of macroeconomics – and also as the basis for its advocacy of active stabilization policies. The irony of all this is of course palpable: money wage inflexibility is downplayed by the side that necessarily needs the hypothesis in the context of its own (*N/N*) theory; it is insistently played up by the side who has stumbled into this hypothesis only by mistake!

Second, consider the Keynesian response to Barro's (1974) so-called Ricardian equivalence theorem. This theorem asserts that the present value of future taxes has the same effect on aggregate behavior as an equivalent amount of current taxes; consequently, there is no reason to delay taxation, and the Keynesian proclivity for bond-financed deficit spending, rather than simply balanced budget spending, has no rational basis.

The natural Keynesian (*R/R*) retort to this should have been to insist that the discussion keep to the original context for these characteristic Keynesian fiscal policy recommendations. That context was, of course, one of unemployment due to intertemporal disequilibrium. With real interest rates at a level that will not allow saving–investment coordination at full employment, the result will be an excess supply of present factor services and an implicit excess demand for future goods. Spending now will reduce this excess supply; taxing later will reduce the excess demand. The temporal structure of the Keynesian policy fits the temporal maldistribution of excess demands left uncorrected by intertemporal price adjustments.

Barro's Ricardian theorem presupposes intertemporal general equilibrium. This is not a state of affairs that needs to be 'stabilized'. Nor has anyone ever suggested that activist fiscal policies should be used in such circumstances. Moreover, the only thing of much interest that can be said about the calculation of wealth at a market rate different from Wicksell's natural rate is that *everyone* will get the wrong result.

But, again, no one brought it up. Having lost track of Keynes's saving–investment problem, the critical replies to Barro accepted his intertemporal equilibrium assumption but argued that his aggregative conclusions might still be invalidated by distribution effects. Admittedly, intergenerational distribution effects are somewhat more interesting and slightly more amenable to empirical study than the run-of-the-mill distribution effects that always surround any macrotheoretical proposition with a penumbra of doubts. But Keynesian fiscal policy doctrine cannot be restored on this ramshackle foundation.

## SUCCESSIVE MONETARY REGIMES AND THE MONETARIST CONTROVERSY

Although conflicting beliefs about the economy's capacity for 'automatic' self-equilibrating adjustment bedevilled the debate from beginning to end and made progress even towards some 'agreement to disagree' difficult, the explicit issues at the core of the controversy concerned the role of money in the determination of income (nominal *and* real) and the effectiveness of monetary policy. The debate on these issues did not take place in the safe isolation of some ivory tower. Instead, the course it took was strongly influenced from the start by external events and, in particular, by the monetary regime changes of the last fifty years.

The experience of the 1930s formed the economic world view of early American Keynesianism in more ways than one. With regard to money, the formative memories were of a banking system that, in the wake of the Great Crash and deflation, found few of its potential borrowers creditworthy and seemed to have an almost insatiable new taste for excess reserves. Monetarism, as it first emerged, was primarily a challenge to the doctrine of monetary policy ineffectiveness that Keynesians had distilled from this experience and had carried over into a postwar world that was very different.

The younger men who were about to assume leading roles in Keynesian economics after the war – Tobin, Modigliani et al. – were not wedded to this ineffectiveness notion, however. Their differences with Friedman ran deeper. Basically, these Keynesians thought of changes in the money stock as changes in bank *credit* that had their effects on investment, output and employment via changes in real interest rates. In contrast, the Monetarists thought of changes in the money stock as changes in the 'nominal scalar' of the real economy. The actual rescaling dictated by a particular nominal impulse would, however, come about with 'long and variable lags'; in the meantime, nominal impulses had real effects. These two competing perceptions of 'what money does' fit – to the extent that they do fit – quite different monetary regimes.

Consider two basic, inherited ideas of how a society may achieve predictability and stability of the nominal price level. We may refer to them as 'convertibility control' and 'quantity control', respectively. The macroeconomic theory appropriate to a regime relying for its nominal stability on convertibility differs in important respects from the one appropriate to a regime relying on government control of the stock of money.

The main points are the following. Under commodity convertibility, the government fixes the nominal price of gold (for example) and leaves it to the banks and their customers to determine the corresponding equilibrium stocks of money and other liquid assets. Under quantity control, the monetary authorities fix the quantity of money and allow the markets to determine the corresponding equilibrium level of nominal prices. From the standpoint of the government, the first is a 'price-fixing, quantity-taking' and the second a 'quantity-fixing, price-taking' strategy.

The constraints that convertibility imposes on the behavior of the monetary authorities prevent them from bringing about sizeable changes in the equilib-

rium price level. In general, therefore, monetary policy cannot be very 'effective' if by that we mean causing large changes in nominal income. The
commitment to redeem money in gold (or foreign currency) on demand
means forgoing the option of controlling the money stock. Roughly speaking,
the money stock is determined by demand rather than by supply. In a system
where the money stock adjusts to the price level rather than the other way
around, however, the central bank can worry about the price and availability
of credit and their effects on real activity in the economy. If convertibility
were generally to be seen to guarantee the price level, the public would have
'inelastic expectations'; that is, whenever the price level departs a bit from
the longer-term trend set by the supply and demand for gold, people expect it
to return to trend. The inelasticity of price expectations reduces the amplitude
of fluctuations in money prices and money wages (even when these are
perfectly 'flexible'). With such expectations, changes in the central bank
discount rate change a real price and changes in bank reserves change the real
volume of credit supplied. The monetary authorities have some limited leverage over output and employment in such a system, therefore.

Clearly, much of this has a distinctly Keynesian ring to it. But the match
between the two theories is not perfect. The standard Keynesian model did
not have an endogenously varying but exogenously fixed money stock, just
like the Monetarist one (see, however, Tobin 1963). And Keynesians in general have not regarded the validity of their theory as in any way restricted to
convertible regimes.

Monetarist theory is best suited to the pure quantity control case. When the
economy is on a pure fiat standard, control over some nominal stock is
necessary in order to provide the system with a nominal anchor. If the
authorities try to govern real credit, and do not keep track of the money stock,
they are likely to fail at their primary task of providing nominal stability.
Interest rate targeting of monetary policy, which is a natural tactic when
convertibility takes care of the price level, threatens total loss of control over
the price level under these conditions. Monetary policy is obviously 'effective' under quantity control in the sense that it can bring about large changes
in money income (by changing the money stock and letting the price level
adjust). What is not so clear is whether it can have a reliable, predictable
effect on real activity.

Now, Keynesian economics evolved in the heyday of the Bretton Woods
system (of which Keynes, not so coincidentally, had been one of the principal
architects). Until the late 1960s, this meant that it had evolved within a
monetary regime that avoided exposing the economy to sizeable nominal
shocks – one that behaved in most respects like the convertibility model.
Keynesian theory came to embody, therefore, the ingrained analytical habits
of interpreting money stock changes in effect as changes in the real volume

of credit, and of treating monetary policy as operating chiefly through its effect on real rates of interest. As the Bretton Woods system crumbled and was swept away, these were no longer the most appropriate mental habits. On the whole, Keynesians adapted only slowly and reluctantly to the inflationary environment of the 1970s. The Monetarist analytical habit of interpreting money stock changes, not as endogenous responses to real income movements, but as nominal shocks requiring, albeit with long and variable lags, a corresponding adjustment in the nominal scale of the economy, now came into its own. Monetarists were more ready than Keynesians for a world in which nominal scale varied almost altogether independently of real variables. Keynesians tended to dwell on stagflation as a puzzling phenomenon and to hang on too long to the belief in predictable and exploitable Phillips trade-offs. This Keynesian unpreparedness to deal with an inflationary world thus handed the monetarists a series of easy victories at this stage of the debate.

## NEW CLASSICAL ECONOMICS

The New Classical movement began with Lucas's attempt to construct a microtheoretically founded model of Friedman's theory. In that theory, movements in employment could be generated by assuming either that the labor market did not clear or else that it did clear but on the basis of asymmetric expectations between the two sides of the market. For methodological reasons, Lucas did not want to make either assumption. Instead, he first produced a monetarist version of Phelps's 'islands' model. This model still belongs at $N/N$ in the flag taxonomy, but Lucas soon shifted to an $N/R$ model in which nominal impulses led to changes in the intertemporal prices perceived by transactors, who would respond by reallocating their supply of labor and their consumption of leisure between the present and the future.

For several years following its appearance, Lucas's intertemporal equilibrium business cycle model was at the 'leading edge' in macroeconomic debates. Thus the late 1970s offered the odd spectacle of a sort of Keynesian–Monetarist controversy on the 'wrong' diagonal. By now, a few years later, it seems unclear whether much of substance was learned from this clash of the two combinations of mismatched hypotheses – the supposedly 'Keynesian' $R/N$ theory and the Lucasian $N/R$ theory.

This $N/R$ theory did not become a lasting position for the New Classicals, however. Its Minnesota wing led a withdrawal from the nominal impulse hypothesis. Sims (1983) showed that the empirical support for it was much weaker than previously thought, while work by Wallace (1981), Sargent (for example, 1987) and others subverted its quantity theory foundations. These attacks from a new quarter on Monetarism in all its versions opened the way for Kydland and Prescott's 'real' business cycle theory, in which exogenous changes in anticipated productivity govern the variations in employment. This is an equilibrium model in the New Classical sense, so the fluctuations in activity that it exhibits are optimal. Propagation here becomes a matter of explaining, not departures from equilibrium, but persistence of (relatively) high or low activity states. The hypotheses favored among the real business cycle theorists use the durability of capital or its gestation period ('time to build') to spread out the effects of productivity shocks through time.

The Kydland–Prescott theory is also intertemporal. In equilibrium models where information is not dispersed, we deal in effect with a representative agent (or social planner), so the basic story can be put in time-honored Robinson Crusoe form. We may imagine that Crusoe's island has seasonal weather and that there are certain planting seasons when the future return to present effort is particularly high. Robinson's dynamic program will then tell him to behave like farmers through the ages, that is, to work long hours in the planting season and to take his leisure at times when his productivity is lower. (For the Lucas' $N/R$ theory, in contrast, we would have to imagine that the powers that be rain fiat money on him from time to time and that, whenever this happens, Robinson will draw the unwarranted conclusion that planting season has arrived.)

In Kydland and Prescott's model, employment is high, in effect, when the 'marginal efficiency of capital' is high. So we are back at $R/R$. But something has gone askew in this slow (fifty-year) dance around the flag. Consider the position now: to many erstwhile Keynesians, resistance to the New Classical economics has centered on their market-clearing assumption. Resistance, in other words, is based on wage stickiness once more. At the same time, the inflationary world of the 1970s has taught them to regard changes in the money supply as the principal cause of changes in nominal income. These new Keynesians, therefore, have arrived more or less at Friedman's old position at $N/N$ (almost as soon as it had been vacated by the New Classicals). But they use it as a base for asserting the need for active stabilization policy. Meanwhile, the New Classicals have arrived at $R/R$, once a Keynesian position, from which they argue that no stabilization policy is needed because observed fluctuations in activity are to be interpreted as optimal.

## KEYNESIAN THEORY AND THE NEW EQUILIBRIUM APPROACH

The real business cycle (RBC) version of the New Classical economics would seem to be the leading research program in macroeconomics today (cf. also Hansen 1985). At present, therefore, an appraisal of the prospects of

Keynesian economics requires redefining that tradition in relation to this contemporary vanguard in economic theory. I choose not to consider the 'Keynesian economics' (at $R/N$) but to restrict myself to 'the economics of Keynes'. The two theories to be juxtaposed, therefore, are both at $R/R$.

For nearly three decades, Keynesians (of whatever description) have had to struggle with the task of defining their differences *vis-à-vis* evolving Monetarist doctrines. This time, Monetarism – all of a sudden – is out of it. Or so it seems. Not, certainly, because it was vanquished by decades of Keynesian opposition but, instead, because it was abandoned by the younger generation that at one point was taken to be the heirs of Friedman and Brunner. The startling, dramatic thing about the New Classical school, in fact, is the speed with which, in a few years, it has moved from a monetarist $N/N$ position to one that is, if not diametrically, then at least 'diagonally', opposed at $R/R$. In terms of the history of business cycle theory, these are two very different views of the world between which we have seen unending controversy. Continuity, in this school, is not a matter of tenaciously held beliefs about the real world; it is provided, instead, by shared (and tenacious) beliefs about what is 'good economics' or good ways of doing economics.

It is not obvious that either Keynesian economics or New Classical RBC economics has absorbed the lessons that should be learned from Monetarism. But this time we may leave the Monetarist issues aside. What seems intriguing, at present, is that the vanguard has come around to $R/R$ – which is where we started with Keynes fifty years ago. No public rehabilitation for Keynesian economics results from this late-coming coincidence for, in New Classical eyes, it wasn't 'good economics'. It was never done properly, as equilibrium theory.

What was done improperly in Keynesian theory can all be encapsulated in the complaint that the Keynesians created a macroeconomics distinct from and certainly not rigorously derived from microeconomics. The New Classicals do insist on building macroeconomics from first principles – meaning essentially from postulates of 'rational' behavior. The distance from individual rationality to aggregative systemic rationality is often taken in quick stride (in part because the rational capabilities postulated for the typical agent are anything but modest). Thus the New Classical RBC models describe cycles as efficient, perfectly coordinated, dynamic responses to exogenous perturbations in productivity. (Since these responses are 'rational' from a systemic point of view, they do not require any policy intervention.) The New Classicals also obeyed this same imperative in deserting the nominal shock hypothesis, finding it in the end difficult to believe that rational agents would not remain fully informed about changes in the money stock.

Making a methodological principle of the rational behavior postulate may seem harmless or in any case unobjectionable to economists. But instructions on how to do things also tell you what things to do. So the methods deemed successful for obtaining answers in microeconomics are now determining what questions get asked in macroeconomics. And, for the first decade or so of New Classical economics, the old question, 'How good is the market system at coordinating activities?', has not been one of them.

How does this come about? At the risk of oversimplifying and thus failing to do justice to the New Classical program, let me try a loose sketch of the modeling strategy that has driven the program.

The starting point is 'rational behavior', conceived of as individual choice between perceived alternatives, and to be represented, of course, in terms of optimization subject to constraints. It is unnecessary at this point to rehearse familiar reservations about the underlying cognitive assumptions. New Classical economics, however, adds a couple of 'lemmas' to the rational behavior postulate, namely

1. that the rational agent will have learned not to make systematic mistakes but will know the structure of the economy (at least one step ahead of economists); and
2. that rational agents will not leave any gains from trade unexploited.

Broadly interpreted, the second lemma says that economists have no social function, while the first says that they are the last to learn anyway. Oh, well, a little humility will do us no harm!

Now, it was supposed that the first of these lemmas more or less does away with discrepancies between the subjectively perceived and the objectively existing reality and also, therefore, between the expectations of different agents. (Note, however, the effective challenge to this supposition by Phelps 1983b). When the pre-reconciliation of expectations can in this way be taken for granted, the second lemma will, under competitive conditions and with complete markets, transfer the rationality of the representative agent to the economic system as a whole. When gains from trade are exhausted, markets clear and are efficient. Most importantly, the law of one price will hold everywhere and will ensure that anyone using a resource takes into account its value to all other agents in the system and, therefore, that resources move without fail into their highest valued uses. The Modigliani–Miller theorem is in this broad sense an instance of the law of one price.

On the finance side of the New Classical economics, the hunt is on for other applications of Modigliani–Miller reasoning that may also have surprising or perhaps counterintuitive implications (cf. Sargent 1987). The Ricardian equivalence theorem (Barro 1974) may be regarded as belonging in this class. So does the irrelevance theorem for open market operations (Wallace 1981). Both theorems state, in effect, that the government accomplishes nothing by swapping what in the end will amount to perfect substitutes with the private sector. The proposition of the irrelevance of open market operations is one prong of a more comprehensive New Classical attack on the quantity theory. Wallace's 'legal restrictions' theory of money is another (Wallace 1983). The related Black–Fama–Hall theory is a third. It envisages a financial system in which, once legal restrictions impeding competition were removed, money would not be distinguishable from other securities, its quantity would therefore not be defineable, and debts would be settled basically in barter deals for securities (Black 1970, Fama 1980 and, for dissenting views, O'Driscoll 1986 and White 1984).

Thus, individual optimization with the two lemmas of rational expectations and exhaustion of the gains from trade produces a perfectly coordinated system, one which for most modeling purposes may be represented by one rational representative; and it is a system with no function for 'money' to perform. This should sound at least vaguely familiar. We have been here before.

From all this recent work we have learned quite a lot about how to model dynamic systems based on intertemporal optimization and so on. Perhaps we have also learned to see more clearly some of the properties of perfectly coordinated systems. But on some spiral staircase of increasing formal sophistication, we are obviously coming back again and again to the same basic issues.

The dissatisfaction over the incongruous relationship of Keynesian macro to neo-Walrasian micro was not first felt or voiced by the New Classicals. The conceptual tension between value and allocation theory and monetary and cycle theory preoccupied Frank Knight, Friedrich Hayek, Erik Lindahl, John Hicks and many others in the decade or so before the *General Theory*. From the standpoint of analytical method, the *General Theory* is itself an attempt to find an acceptable resolution. *Value and Capital* is another such attempt.

Note also that these authors did *not* see the problem of the relationship between equilibrium value theory and business cycle theory simplistically in terms of the contrast between stationary and fluctuating processes. To them, seasonal fluctuations were not part of business cycle theory precisely because they understood them to be equilibrium motions governed by (what we today call) rational expectations – and therefore not worth worrying about.

More to the point, perhaps, neither did they see this problematic relationship in terms of market-clearing versus non-market-clearing models. Lindahl and Hicks, in particular, constructed models in which all markets 'cleared' in each period. They, as well as Hayek, regarded the fulfilment of expectations (between points of time) as the troublesome aspect of the equilibrium assumption.

Those of us who came out of graduate programs in the early 1960s had been taught a micro- and a macrotheory that could not have applied to the same world at the same time. So this problem was of intense concern to many of us. Our label for it was the 'microfoundations of macroeconomics'. Quite a lot was written about it at one time (cf. Weintraub 1979).

Robert Lucas resolved this tension between micro and macro by declaring that the problem did not really exist. The appearance of a problem was due simply to the fact that macroeconomics had not been done right. The microfoundations problem would evaporate once we decided to do macrotheory in strict obedience to microtheoretical modeling principles.

That cut the Gordian knot alright. But why was this path not taken before? Let me give a personal answer: because macroeconomics (I thought) is about system coordination, and one should not adopt a method that threatens to define away the main problem. The New Classical economics has the priorities the other way around – and carrying through from individual optimizing behavior, it all but eliminates the coordination problem.

## THE COORDINATION QUESTION

The coordination question, simply stated, is this: will the market system 'automatically' coordinate economic activities? Always? Never? Sometimes very well, but sometimes pretty badly? Under what conditions, and with what institutional structures, will it do well or badly? I regard these questions as the central and basic ones in macroeconomics.

The market system does very well, with seasonal fluctuations obviously. But that is surely in large measure because of its recurrent, predictable nature which allows people to plan ahead in a coordinated fashion. Kydland and Prescott have the right modeling strategy for seasonal fluctuations. Maybe most business cycles are 'very much like' seasonal fluctuations. One should not pretend that the answer to that one is obvious. But the end of World War I, or the Great Depression, or the first oil shock, or the international debt crisis – those, surely, were not 'like' seasonal fluctuations?

The point of the coordination question is this: will the market mechanism work 'automatically' even if people are not so smart? Will it work even in cases of unprecedented, non-recurrent 'historical' developments the consequences of which are difficult (even for smart people) to foresee? Indeed, if people were no more far-sighted and calculating than Pavlovian dogs – or Battaglio's pigeons – would a system of 'free markets' coordinate their actions?

That is what we want to know about the market system. One is not much enlightened on this question by learning that an economy would work just fine if people were so smart and knowledgeable that they did not need market feedback to adjust their behavior. In rational expectations models, people do not learn about changing relative scarcities from price movements; price movements merely reflect what they have already learned more directly.

Perhaps not much is gained by ranting on about coordination in general terms. Consider, then, a specific example of a Keynesian question that is not being worked on at present. My choice is 'effective demand failures'. The effective demand failure (EDF) question concerns the 'market forces' that act on prices (and on output and consumption rates) when people have not succeeded from the outset in setting those general equilibrium prices that would have coordinated all activities.

Suppose that, in a situation of this sort, we construct the vector of 'notional' market excess demands. This is done by asking what quantities people would have liked to buy and sell at those prices and then aggregating these magnitudes. Let us suppose that we could be assured of arriving at a perfectly coordinated general equilibrium state if price adjustments were governed by these 'notional' excess demands. Then the EDF question (or one variant of it) is: do the 'effective' excess demands – that is, the actual market forces acting to force revisions of those 'incorrect' prices – always have the same sign as the notional excess demands?

The Keynesian answer is that the effective excess demands can differ in sign from the corresponding notional excess demands in cases where financial constraints are binding (Leijonhufvud 1973). This result throws doubt on traditional general equilibrium stability propositions – and therefore on simplistic beliefs about the 'automaticity' of the market system. It seems that we cannot be certain that people will always come to learn that which they did not know to begin with.

Note that there are two types of theoretical structures that will not allow us to analyse the EDF question:

1.   the fix-price general equilibrium models, commonly called 'Keynesian disequilibrium' models; and
2.   the New Classical models.

The question, 'what effective demands govern price adjustments', does not make sense either in models where prices do not adjust or in models where there are no meaningful excess demands. Thus it is an example of a question, central to Keynesian theory, that is excluded from analysis by current methodologies.

# BEYOND NEW CLASSICAL THEORY?

For those who would like to revive the coordination question, the choice would seem to be between three strategies *vis-à-vis* the currently dominating New Classical economics.

## 1. Try to Beat Them at their Own Game

This would mean to find some hole in the New Classical deductive structure that lets genuine coordination difficulties seep back in, despite rational agents, rational expectations and market clearing. The interest of the New Classicals themselves in system-states that depart from perfect coordination has centered on the possibility of the rational private sector facing a government of more doubtful caliber that is either trying to take 'unanticipated' (usually inflationary) actions or else simply exhibiting time-inconsistent behavior. Other possibilities for generating non-Pareto optimal solutions include various asymmetric information and/or externality assumptions. Here, the logical possibilities are almost endless – the problem is to come up with information asymmetries that are obviously important in explaining, not steady state aspects of system structure, but variations over time in how well the system is coordinated, or else with externalities that 'truly rational' agents cannot in the end get around.

There seem to be two fronts where an opening may be sought. One is the 'Phelps problem' (Frydman and Phelps 1983), that is, that agents must form expectations not just about parametric disturbances to the system but about each other's expectations as well. Keynes's beauty contest parable was an instance of this general problem (cf. also the reference to Haltiwanger and Waldman below).

The other is the recent literature on incomplete markets and multiple equilibria in general equilibrium models. Recent contributions have made these general equilibrium indeterminacies look much less like improbable curiosities than they did at first. With incomplete markets, the model economy is likely to have equilibria in which financial constraints are binding on subsets of agents; it may then be possible to Pareto-rank the different equilibria, showing some of them to be inefficient (see, for example, Levine 1989a, 1991). These multiple equilibria systems also open the theoretical door to exogenous shifts in the expectations of rational agents – such as that old Keynesian sunspot, the 'change in the marginal efficiency of expectations' (Farmer and Woodford 1984; Woodford 1988).

## 2.   Refuse to Play by Their Rules

In the present context, this means backing away from the 'unbounded rationality' postulate in some way. Only the experimentalists and those with a firm interest in other behavioral sciences seem willing to contemplate this at present. But note that Hart (1987), for example, is quite emphatic that the observed incompleteness of contracts cannot be rationalized in a context of unbounded rationality; progress in this area is held back by the lack of a satisfactory formalization of bounded rationality. Lucas (1986) sees no pressing need for a departure in this direction but takes a tolerant wait-and-see attitude – if someone gets a firm handle on how to model 'bounded rationality', he will take an interest in it. If we exclude Herbert Simon, the positive theoretical record of prominent critics of *homo oeconomicus* has not been encouraging. But, in my opinion, there is now reason to be encouraged by the recent work of Heiner (1983, 1986) and Leland (1988). It is worth noting also that interesting results can be obtained by assuming that only a subset of transactors fall short of unbounded rationality (Haltiwanger and Waldman 1985, 1989).

## 3.   Raise a Different Topic Altogether

If the equilibria of the New Classical models (that we have been exposed to so far) look 'too nice', perhaps it is due in part to conventional general equilibrium assumptions that have nothing to do with the knowledge and information assumptions on which most of the discussion has centered? Surely, the assumption of universally diminishing returns has been suspect all along, for instance? A number of people are already busy in this area (cf. especially Romer 1987).

# INCREASING RETURNS

So, I turn finally to a topic that has been neglected by Keynes and by Keynesians but which I think has the potential for illuminating some traditional Keynesian concerns, namely increasing returns to scale.

   The production theory that totally dominates in macroeconomics still has the Ricardian farm as the representative production unit: there are constant returns when both land and labor can be varied, smoothly diminishing returns when labor is varied with land constant. If effective demand failures can be disregarded, the unemployed Ricardian farm-worker need only adjust his asking price to his marginal product in order to induce some farmer to take him on. Finding the farm where his marginal product is the highest may take a bit of trudging around the countryside, but such search-unemployment would not constitute a social problem of great consequence. Similarly, a farmer who finds himself making losses need only cut back output to raise the productivity of his variable inputs until they earn their keep.

The macroeconomy consisting of Ricardian farms has a smoothly convex transformation surface. When events in the surrounding world economy require it to change its output mix, it suffices that some farmers move a bit of land out of corn and into wine or vice versa in the direction of the higher land rent; the adjustment can be gradual – no one needs to make a large, discontinuous move.

Suppose, instead, an economy made up of Smithian factories (Leijonhufvud 1986b – Chapter 13 below). Here, 'the division of labor depends upon the extent of the market'. Increased division of labor is productive so that the average product of inputs increases with the rate of output. A highly articulated division of labor, moreover, tends to be associated with a high degree of complementarity between inputs. Picture an economy consisting of assembly lines where a whole line comes to a halt if one machine breaks down or one worker leaves his work station.

Market clearing becomes an unclear notion in this setting. Decreasing-cost producers will be price-setters, not price-takers, and will normally always want to sell more than their current sales at the prices they have posted. It does not make sense to treat these markets 'as if' they were auction markets.

The Smithian factories form a non-linear input–output system where each firm produces under increasing returns to scale and also uses one or more intermediate products produced by other increasing returns firms. Structures of this kind can be enormously productive at high levels of activity but are, by the same token, incapable of proportional scaling down of activities. For concreteness, suppose that the typical firm has the simple production structure of two parallel assembly lines, with some work stations in common so that some machines and some operatives serve both lines. In recession, this firm shuts down one of the lines, cutting output in half, but it cannot lay off half the work force because the common work stations must still be manned. Thus, Okun's Law is a result, not of labor hoarding, but of the increasing returns technology in this system. At the reduced activity level, the firm's real unit costs are higher, but it cannot compensate itself by charging a higher (relative) price since its customer firms are all in the same position. Everyone is making losses in the recession and, while the losses may be limited, profitability cannot be restored by reducing output further.

Note that the direction of causation here goes from changes in the activity level to changes in productivity and not, as in New Classical RBC theory, from productivity to activity.

The Smithian factory worker who has been laid off cannot induce the firm to start up the idle assembly line by lowering the real wage at which he offers to work. An individual worker is not able to expand the number of production jobs by this tactic. All he might achieve is to bid the job away from someone who is still working. Implicit contracts dictating lay-offs by inverse seniority, and strong social sanctions against scabbing, are likely to evolve in this setting.

The representative firm is itself in a situation precisely analogous to that of its representative worker. It cannot induce an expansion of the entire input–output structure by cutting the supply price of its product. And a small country that is highly integrated into the international division of labor may similarly find that it is easy to inflate but, acting alone, difficult to expand real activity. These Smithian input–output systems depend on 'the extent of the market' – that is, on demand in the final goods sector – to maintain the high levels of activity required for them to show high productivity and correspondingly high real incomes. But in a highly integrated world economy, a country's final goods sector is not always under domestic control. International policy coordination looks far more important in a system of this sort than it does through Heckscher–Ohlin (Samuelson–Stolper) glasses.

In part, these economies of scale will be internal to the firm, but to a large extent they are external. The internal scale economies dictate that firms will not accumulate capital continuously, but in discrete, sizeable 'lumps'. Investment decisions are correspondingly riskier and the timing of investments trickier. The external economies mean that the profitability of one firm's investments depends upon the scale at which its suppliers and customers are operating. Economic development in such a system does not repeat past patterns, but evolves through progressive differentiation of functions and through the gradual achievement of economies of scale in more and more of these functions (Young 1928).

In a system of this sort, major changes in the allocation of resources cannot be made by continuous adjustment following some gradient procedure in the direction of the optimum. We have this problem at present.[1] The current pattern of the international division of labor has evolved in a setting of exchange rates that could not be sustained indefinitely because they required one-way capital flows of large magnitude that could not cumulate indefinitely. Thus, the world economy cannot continue to grow in the pattern set over the last fifteen years or so. The result is tremendous investment uncertainty. We do not know whether the future will be one of free or of protected markets, of monetary stability or of inflations and financial crises. How much capacity to add – and where in the world to put it – is a question that may have to be answered more by 'animal spirits' than by rational calculation in this difficult transitional period.

Again, the assumptions of the analysis just sketched certainly are not Keynesian (by any definition of the term). But perhaps that means no more than that Keynesian economics has missed an avenue that it could profitably have taken? The implications that the analysis suggests do not clash with a Keynesian view of the world – the situation of the laid-off worker, the countercyclical behavior of productivity and profits, the significance of investment uncertainty and the importance of final goods sector demand all seem to fit.

## THE PROSPECTS

Does Keynesian economics have a future? My answer is 'Yes', for two reasons. Firstly, because the coordination question is a real question that cannot be kept off the agenda indefinitely. Presumably, the current generation of theorists will pursue it with methods that are as New Classical as is at all possible. But as they come to grips with it, the substance of the work will become Keynesian, not classical (see especially Roberts 1987). Secondly because, sooner or later, we really must open up our theoretical structures so that results from the other behavioral sciences can be utilized in economics. Then the 'unbounded rationality' postulate will have to go. This, too, will have the effect of moving us away from the systemic rationality of classical economic models and readmit the 'irrational' system-states of Keynesian economics.

## NOTE

1. Written in 1987.

# 3. Keynesianism, Monetarism and rational expectations: some reflections and conjectures*

To what extent is Keynesianism discredited? Is there anything left? Did Monetarism score a total victory? Must rational expectations make New Classical economists of us all? Every teacher of macroeconomics has to wrestle with these questions – hoping against hope that some new cataclysm will not let some fantastic supply-side doctrine or whatever sweep the field before he has been able to sort through the rubble of what he once knew. I am going to sort some of my rubble. The object of the exercise is to make some guesses at how the seemingly still useable pieces might fit together.

My starting points are as follows. Keynesianism foundered on the Phillips curve or, more generally, on the failure to incorporate inflation rate expectations in the model. The inflation, which revealed this critical fault for all to see, was in considerable measure the product of 'playing the Phillips curve' policies. But the stable Phillips trade-off was not an integral part of Keynesian theory.[1] Its removal, therefore, should not be (rationally) expected to demolish the whole structure.

Monetarism made enormous headway in the economics profession and with the public when the misbehavior of the Phillips curve and the inflation premium in nominal interest rates became obvious for all to see. Few observers could continue to doubt the strong link between nominal income and money stock as the great American inflation went on and on and on. The Monetarist 'victory'[2] was impressive enough that the profession's interest turned elsewhere. But the victory was not total.[3] The Phillips curve and Gibson's paradox were both late-coming issues to the Monetarist controversy. The *original* issues were not settled, but rather more or less forgotten. Chief among these was the old bone of contention, namely the hypothesis that the money stock is exogenously determined, so that the correlation between money and nominal income can be interpreted as a causal one-way street.

In the contest between Keynesians and Monetarists over the Phillips curve and Gibson's paradox, the neoclassical anticipated inflation model (AIM) played a pivotal role. The Monetarists pushed it; most Keynesians were reluctant to grant it empirical relevance. The Monetarists were seen to have been empirically more nearly right on the issues where this model had provided their theoretical ammunition.

The AIM was again pivotal when the rational expectations group shouldered the Monetarists aside. The full logical implications of the model for the Monetarist position were not entirely welcome: if exogenous money supply changes are known to be the only aggregative shocks worth worrying about, and if exogenous money is neutral, then anticipated (recognized) money supply changes will not have any real effects. Thus rational expectations methodology applied to the Monetarist position produces New Classical economics. This development has put the monetary theory of nominal income within an (unanticipated) inch of conversion into a short-run neutrality proposition that could not explain cyclical fluctuations in real magnitudes, and hence could not give a plausible account of the monetary history of the United States from (say) 1867 to 1960.

This brief recapitulation of recent controversies suggests an agenda of four items: (1) the treatment of expectations in macromodels, (2) the anticipated inflation model, (3) the forgotten issues of the Monetarist controversy, and (4) the question of equilibrium or disequilibrium theory.


## EXPECTATIONS

Consider how the expectations business looks from the standpoint of politicians and civil servants who have to take some measure of responsibility for macroeconomic policies and their consequences.[4] The disarray among macroeconomists is apparent to them. Whose advice do they rely on?

From what they are told, the role of expectations in macroeconomics must be the crux. On the one hand, they have the 'old Keynesian' macroeconomics that once looked so solid and reliable, that had very little to say about expectations – and that now, apparently, is thoroughly discredited for its lack of attention to such ephemeral matters. On the other hand, they have the 'New Classical' economics that looks so paradoxical and speculative, that has very little to say except about expectations – and that now, obviously, gets all the attention from economists. In between, they have the already 'middle-aged Monetarism' that used rational expectations arguments to undermine the one-time Keynesian belief in a stable Phillips trade-off – but balks at the new rational expectations doctrine that fully anticipated money stock policy is totally ineffective. The 'old' advise that monetary policy alone is no way to cure inflation; the 'middle-aged' have it that only monetary policy will do, but the safe way is slow and gradual; the 'new' urge a quick, clean, indubitable end to inflationary money growth.

For policy-makers who have been around for that long, the heyday of Keynesianism must seem like the good old days. Those were the days when macromodels disgorged policy options in the form of readily understandable quantitative predictions: if you do *a*, GNP will rise by *x* dollars per annum, employment will grow by *y* per cent, and prices will go up by *z* per cent. And so on. Nowadays, economists tell policy-makers that the effects can be this or that, depending on the state of expectations. Unless one can ascertain (in some quantitative manner) what the state of expectations is or will be, therefore, it would seem that one cannot know what it is that one is doing. Unfortunately, measures of expectations do not inspire trust. Their unreliability (or unavailability) makes direct tests of all the novel propositions about the influence of expectations difficult (or impossible). So, again, whom are policy-makers to believe? And, if they cannot know what they are doing, how are they to choose from the alternative policies that different factions clamor for?

They may hope to escape from this predicament in various ways. The first hope, perhaps, is that there will be many instances where expectations will not matter after all. The second would be that, in most of the remaining cases, economists will be able to measure expectations so that their influence can be taken into account.

Vain hopes. In macroeconomics, expectations always matter. Sensible policy judgments cannot be made at all if their influence is ignored. They cannot be measured accurately for econometric purposes. Significant progress on their measurement, moreover, is unlikely.[5] For present purposes, we may as well think of them as *unobservable*.

There is a third possible avenue of escape from the expectations predicament. Expectations might be 'well-behaved' (let's call it). Expectations are well-behaved if linked in a stable manner to the system of observable variables.

In the simplest imaginable case (Figure 3.1, (A)), we would have one-to-one correspondence between the unobservable, *E*, and the contemporaneously observable, *S*, aspects of the state of the system. The unobservability of expectations then would not matter. It would not prevent us from developing reliable macromodels. (If the world generally were to conform to this simplest case, of course, the proposition that behavior is governed by expectations would be a moot point of Austrian philosophy, supported by no empirical evidence other than introspection.)

A problem first arises when each vector of observable state variables may be combined with any one of many unobservable states of expectation. With one state of expectation, a policy of demand stimulation might, for example, reduce unemployment; with another, it might produce nothing but inflation. So it matters. One may then resort to the past history of observables for the clues that will differentiate one state of expectation from another (Figure 3.1,

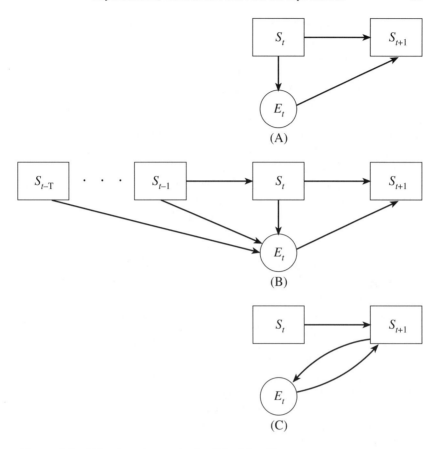

*Figure 3.1 What is going on in the 'black box'?*

(B)). The search is for a one-to-one correspondence between *sequences* of observable states and states of expectations. If that hope is fulfilled, reliable prediction is again possible.

In Keynesian theory, (long-term) investment expectations are not necessarily well-behaved, and Keynesian macromodels had, in fact, not much success in predicting investment. But for the rest, both Keynesians and Monetarists – following Koyck (1954) and Cagan (1956) – did pretty well by assuming expectations to be well-behaved in this manner. Well enough so that the 'old' macroeconomics in its time did not need to trouble us much by hedging all its predictions on the unobservable state of expectations. Its time ran out with the arrival of the great American inflation.

It is the great inflation of the last fifteen years that has destroyed faith in macroeconomics. By the same token, it is not expectations in general that have been the problem here but specifically expectations about inflation. Why should expectations about the future of the price level give us more trouble, more serious trouble, than expectations about other things?

It is tempting to jump to the conclusion that, perhaps, price-level expectations are ill-behaved, that is, not related in any stable manner to observables. Then the system can in principle not be modeled in a reliable way, and making policy is simply and unavoidably a dangerous business. But it cannot be true in general that price expectations are ill-behaved. If that were the case, we would not have had to wait until the decade of the 1970s to discover that we were in trouble.

Inflation expectations in the 1970s were not well-behaved in either of the two ways that the older macroeconomics habitually sought to rely on. Clearly, people did not form their expectations about the future of the price level just from observing the present state of the economy. Extrapolating from the immediate past, as we know by now, would have been irrational. If these linkages to the *present* and the *past* will not do, there is only one way left: assume that people's expectations match the macromodel's predictions about the *future* (Figure 3.1, (C)).

The costs of not accepting this rational expectations development are apparent.[6] If we have to give up on making expectations well-behaved, we must either start faking expectations measures or else condemn ourselves to an indefinite future of double-talk: 'The effect will be either this or that'. Of course, disassociating oneself from macroeconomics is also a way out, and one that many colleagues have found the most attractive of late.

When would this last-ditch method to make expectations behave be needed? If monetary policy were itself well-behaved, so that base money creation were some stable function of present and past observables, agents would be able to base their short-term price-level expectations on the history of those variables. So this rational expectations twist becomes important when monetary policy is ill-behaved, that is, when it is not predictable on the basis of past performance.

What limits to rational forecasting should be built into our macromodels to fit such conditions? What is it that people can and cannot know about the future of inflation? We have two clues. First, if the outside modeler must treat the state of expectations as unobservable, then inside agents will not be able to observe each other's expectations. Second, if the system poses a difficult predicament to policy-makers (who can call on all the modelers for advice), it must be worse still for agents who have to cope with the added uncertainty of not knowing what actions will be taken by policy-makers who do not know what they are doing.

Phelps's chapter in Frydman and Phelps (Phelps 1983b) begins the exploitation of the first clue. I have been trying to get some mileage out of the second (Leijonhufvud 1984a, 1984b – Chapters 8 and 9 below).

# THE ANTICIPATED INFLATION MODEL

Let us define a *monetary regime* as a system of expectations that governs the behavior of the public and that is sustained by the consistent behavior of the policy-making authorities. The reaction of the public to any particular policy action (such as a change in the growth rate of base money) will depend on the regime that is believed to be in effect. Consequently, each regime requires its own applied macrotheory; models that do reasonably well for one regime may break down badly for its successor. We can choose among the different possible monetary regimes by choosing behavior rules for the fiscal and monetary authorities.

What consistent behavior on the part of the policy-making authorities would sustain the expectations assumed in the anticipated inflation model? If the public unanimously predicts a particular constant inflation rate (to continue indefinitely), then it must be because the authorities are bound to produce it. Rational agents will not anticipate a result that no one is even trying to bring about. The model presupposes a believable precommitment by the government to create money at precisely the pace required to produce the anticipated inflation rate. The authorities operate, in effect, under a most rigid monetary discipline, having forsworn all discretionary options to 'make policy' in the future in light of the then existing conditions.

If we define a *monetary constitution* as a set of rules, binding in the short run,[7] that specify the conditions under which (base) money will be created or destroyed, then the anticipated inflation model presumes an exceedingly restrictive monetary constitution to be in effect. All meaningful constitutions must put limits on the exercise of discretionary authority. This one, however, eliminates discretion altogether.

The representation of the inflation expectations of the public by a single number, the anticipated inflation rate, seems reasonable in this instance. Individual agents who expect a higher or lower inflation rate will be taught the error of their ways in a most systematic and pedagogical manner by suffering losses in the marketplace. Individual expected inflation rates should converge, therefore, on the constitutionally dictated rate. If the regime is operated with great precision, the variance of each agent's subjective expectations should also be small. Obviously, expectations are exceedingly well-behaved under this regime.

Now, if all of this is true, it does follow that the only welfare costs of inflation are the trivial ones associated with a tax on money balances (Bailey 1956). Contrary to a widespread opinion among economists, this kind of inflation can be stopped at even smaller cost. If, initially, 'greenbacks' are depreciating in real purchasing power by $k$ per cent per year, we simply create a new 'blueback' currency and make it, by law, appreciate relative to greenbacks by $k$

per cent per year. Bluebacks grow in their legal capacity to extinguish greenback debt at this $k$ per cent rate. This currency reform does not force any redistribution of wealth. All outstanding contracts will be discharged in exactly the real terms originally anticipated by the parties. Because the inflation tax on greenbacks is $k$ per cent, and zero on bluebacks, the former will disappear from circulation. People will demand larger real balances of bluebacks than they held of greenbacks. To the extent, therefore, that the steady-state demand for money is interest-elastic, the monetary authorities must allow for the creation of a larger initial stock of bluebacks than the stock of greenbacks that is being retired, so as to avoid the emergence of deflationary pressure on the blue price level. If this aspect of the transition is only handled right, there should be not the slightest blip in the unemployment rate. We end up, painlessly, with a zero inflation rate in the blueback currency.

The anticipated inflation model implies that the social problem that we have agonized over for fifteen years could be gone by Monday. That implication is false. So the model, for all its pedagogical virtues, makes bad theory. This conclusion is of some consequence because of the model's pivotal role in the macrotheoretical controversies of the 1970s.

For want of a better name, I have called the present American monetary regime the random walk monetary standard (RWMS). This is a somewhat halting metaphor, not a technical description, but it will have to do.

Under the RWMS, the authorities decide one period at a time whether to accelerate, keep constant or decelerate the rate of money stock growth. Only current economic conditions and immediate political pressures enter into the decision. Future money growth rates are left to the future; they will be chosen at the last minute on the basis of what seems most pleasant and convenient to whoever happens then to be in charge.

In contrast to a Friedman rule (for example) that is unconditional, money creation in this regime is conditional on a great but unspecified number of things, most of which cannot be predicted very far in advance. Consider the term structure of an individual agent's inflation rate expectations. How could he predict the rate of money growth in the first quarter of 1992? Suppose he already has a forecast for the last quarter of 1991. That given, he needs to predict the acceleration or deceleration chosen by the authorities in the next quarter. But he does not know what the economic conditions and the political situation will be, or what people will be in charge, or even what economic theories they will believe in. For dates this distant, therefore, he may as well regard money growth rates (and inflation rates) as picked by a random device.[8] The individual's expected price level for 1991 is a subjective forecast entertained with very little confidence. It is likely to be an *ill-behaved* expectation, that is, one not itself predictable from current and past values of the observable variables of some macromodel.

Because there is no scientific method to forecast price levels in the relatively distant future, the distribution over all agents of individual subjective expectations is likely to show very considerable dispersion. Period by period, policy will shower profits on those who most nearly behaved as if they had anticipated it and losses on those who failed so to behave. But the profits and losses produced by frequent turnarounds in monetary policy will not teach people to make better ten-year forecasts. Consequently, individual long-term forecasts will not converge. For brevity, we shall refer to this as an *incoherent* state of long-term nominal expectations.

As we consider forecasts over successively shorter terms, more and more of the determinants of monetary policy will begin to seem predictable to the transactor. Such predictions – about who will be in office, what economic theory he will favor, and what conditions he will face, five, three, two, one year hence – will vary among agents, and so will the models by which they generate price-level forecasts from such predictions. Nonetheless, the state of expectations should become more coherent and more nearly well-behaved for shorter and shorter time horizons. At the very shortest end, behavior might approximate that of the New Classical model: agents watch contemporaneous base money growth and, in so far as they believe the state of expectations to be coherent,[9] let it affect their pricing decisions but not their immediate output and employment decisions.

This does not mean that random walk (RW) monetary mismanagement has 'neutral' consequences. On the contrary, the regime will reduce productivity, discourage productivity growth and lower the rate of capital accumulation. Longer-term commitments will be the most adversely affected. RW inflation will also exacerbate social tensions and undermine popular confidence in inherited political institutions and social arrangements. But I have argued these costs and consequences of RW inflation elsewhere (Leijonhufvud 1977, 1984a).

None of the three types of theory under discussion have done much to further our understanding of the costs and consequences of the great inflation. But of the three, the Keynesian has clearly been the most grievously wrong about inflation. It was wrong about the 'ineffectiveness' of money stock policy in changing nominal income, wrong about nominal interest rates, and culpably wrong in supporting the 'playing the Phillips curve' policies that led to our present lamentable regime. In each respect, Monetarism was the better guide in an era of developing monetary instability. As the economy learned to adapt, finally, to the incessant discretionary manipulation of a fiat money totally without anchor, the lags in responses of prices and nominal short-term rates shortened. In this respect, the rational expectations version of the Monetarist model came to look better. At the same time, however, the state of longer-term nominal expectations became increasingly incoherent and ill-behaved, with the result that neither agents nor modelers can rationally expect to do very well at predicting the relationships between money, prices and real activities.

It is not possible to have a macroeconomic science that can predict well in all possible worlds. If expectations are unobservable (or unmeasurable) and ill-behaved, macroeconomics will predict badly, policy-makers will not be able to pre-calculate the effects of what they are doing, and agents will not have well-founded ideas of what policies to expect or of each other's expectations. It is possible, however, to change the world to fit (more nearly) what macroeconomics can do – and, incidentally, make its inhabitants better off in the process.

This is accomplished, of course, by putting constitutional constraints on monetary policy. Some social institutions exist because they rationally solve problems of conjectural interdependence that cannot simply be left to the rational expectations of individual agents. The right-hand driving rule saves a lot of speculation on average opinion every morning before you hit the freeway. It also saves those who did not get it right. A monetary standard is another example. It provides a target on which individual expectations can converge. As the state of expectations coheres around the time path implied by the standard, individual agents can plan on the basis of the justified supposition that average expectation is not far off from their own. Economic activities will be more efficiently coordinated as a consequence.[10]

Suppose, then, that we had a presently unanticipated return to monetary stability – as much stability, for instance, as the Bretton Woods regime at one time supplied. How would we rate the various macrotheories in such a setting? The judgments of their relative merits given earlier make the 1970s (as experienced in the United States) the exclusive test of a macrotheory's worth. To do so is very much in tenor with the literature of recent years. But the issues on which Monetarism vanquished Keynesianism, only to be outflanked by the New Classical economics, are rather defused by the supposition of a return to stable money. Would our assessment of Keynesian theory be more favorable if we were to see it in the context of a framework for monetary stability such as might have been constructed by J.M. Keynes (to pick a largely irrelevant name not altogether at random)?

At this point, I am at the end of my reflections. Here start the conjectures.

## THE FORGOTTEN ISSUES OF THE MONETARIST CONTROVERSY

Keynesian theory failed to incorporate inflation expectations. In a world of high and volatile inflation this is a fatal flaw. But for a long time, before the great American inflation got under way, a majority of economists found the theory an adequate guide to reality. Events did not reveal the flaw. But how could this be so if the disturbances causing business fluctuations were predominantly of a nominal nature? Can the Monetarist hypothesis be the general explanation of fluctuations in a world where the Phillips curve maintains the appearance of stability?

When we come to reconsider the macrotheory of constitutional monetary regimes, the 'real' theory of business fluctuations will, I conjecture, make a comeback. The hypothesis of Keynes and most pre-Keynesian business cycle theorists that medium and long-term real expectations tend to misbehave will regain, I think, a measure of qualified acceptance. Two subsidiary conjectures are: (1) the interpretation of correlations between M2 and income for such regimes will shift back to a renewed emphasis on the endogeneity of inside money and, correspondingly, (2) Gibson's paradox will once more be seen as a pro-cyclical pattern of real interest rates reflecting underlying movements in profit expectations. These are the matters on which I think the 'old' Keynesians were more nearly right than they are currently given credit for.

The great inflation has held the truths of Monetarism before our eyes for some fifteen years without a break. But several developments in economics during this same period have actually weakened the case for a 'middle-aged' Monetarist interpretation of nominal income fluctuations in stable monetary regimes. One has been the rationally expectant youth movement's stress on deficient information about changes in outside money as the (implausible) source of business fluctuations in Monetarist theory. Another has been the Monetarist balance-of-payments model for small open economies, with its demonstration of the endogeneity of money stocks for at least $n-1$ countries in a fixed-exchange-rate world. A third, perhaps, has been the apparent difficulties that some central banks have had in hitting their money stock targets with any consistency.[11]

Some motivation for these conjectures needs to be sketched in conclusion. We should consider a monetary constitution that has much smaller long-term price-level uncertainty than the present RW regime but comparable short-term uncertainty. For concreteness, think of a managed gold exchange standard where, over the longer term, the price level is determined by the requirement to maintain fixed exchange rates, but where, in the short run, the central bank can expand or contract by letting its reserves vary. Another possibility is a money stock rule with a band within which the central bank is allowed discretion.[12]

In this constitutional (MC) system, agents will know the longer-term, 'permanent' trend (or level) of prices.[13] They will have inelastic expectations about this permanent price level. The Fisher premium in long-term nominal interest rates, if any, should be constant. Knowing the price trend, MC agents will be able to distinguish periods of 'high' and periods of 'low' prices. When such periods occur, they will expect reversion to the constitutional mean. Now, suppose for the sake of argument that this system exhibits 'cyclical' alternations of 'high' and 'low' prices and that real activity levels fluctuate correspondingly.[14] How do we explain it? Well, it depends. We are back with the half-forgotten issues of the original Monetarist controversy, before inflation expectations became the center of it.

The Monetarist and the Keynesian hypotheses regarding the cause of business fluctuations need not, of course, be mutually exclusive. It is useful, however, to proceed, to begin with, *as if* they were.

Take first the Monetarist hypothesis that the fluctuations in nominal GNP are caused by changes in the exogenous money stock. For simplicity, suppose we have a central bank that sets up a sine wave in base money around the path that will maintain the constitutional price trend over the longer run. This is a purely nominal, systematic disturbance to the economy. It is difficult to see why the system should not learn to find the rational expectations equilibrium path: in each period, nominal prices should be proportional to the base, and the short-term nominal interest rate should reflect the anticipated price change until next period. The short-term rate should trace out its own sine wave around a constant long-term nominal interest rate. But then output and employment should not react to this monetary 'policy', and so the real cycle is left unexplained.

The nominal disturbance may, of course, be less predictable than in the sine wave example. But agents do not need to predict it accurately, if they can be quite confident that movements in the nominal base are exogenously caused. As pointed out by Eden (1979), they could simply index-link all contracts to the base so as to obtain 'real' transactions prices from which nominal disturbances have been purged.

The class of hypotheses that combines exogenous monetary impulses with the inability of agents to disentangle real from nominal disturbances to explain the cycle seems to be implausible, therefore. In this Monetarist world with a constitution, short-term nominal expectations can be kept on track simply by watching the money supply, and long-term nominal expectations are kept well-behaved by the constitution.

Second, then, consider a 'real' cycle hypothesis. In order to have a clean-cut opposite extreme to the purely Monetarist theory, suppose that the monetary base obeys a Friedman constitution (but that we still have business fluctuations, although perhaps of 'moderate' amplitude). All agents know, therefore, that no disturbances emanate from the central bank. But investment expectations are not necessarily well-behaved. Forward markets for the goods that will be produced with the capital goods to be bought today are missing. (Tired old refrain?) It is possible, therefore, for agents individually to invest on the basis of expectations that are inconsistent with aggregate ongoing investment.

To keep the story close to those in the recent equilibrium cycle literature, where agents usually are pure price-takers in all markets, we may re-do the 'shifting marginal efficiency of capital' story into one in which producers mistake the future relative price of their products.[15] In the boom, the majority of producers think that the price of their product is going to go up relative to the general price level,[16] so that, by producing today for sale tomorrow, they can earn a return (intramarginally) higher than the real rate of interest. In recession, most producers make the opposite error.

The perception of higher profits in prospect may be caused, initially, by innovations in certain industries, by government spending or by political events abroad, and so forth. (Because the process never duplicates itself exactly at the individual 'island' level, transactors will not learn never to be fooled again.) The producers who first start betting on improved real profits for themselves will bid for more inputs. The expansion of the industries first affected improves business conditions in general. Prices edge up as real supply inelasticities begin to make themselves felt. The increase in the volume of transactions is financed, we may imagine, primarily through an all-round expansion of trade credit. Bank credit could be a critical component of this credit expansion but is not necessarily of predominant quantitative importance. In any case, the money supply expands endogenously.

The upswing will peak, for several reasons. Real interest rates will creep up as the banking system runs out of excess reserves. As the stock of non-bank trade credit outstanding grows in relation to sales, the rate of credit growth tapers off. Rising money prices will make the present employment of 'marginal' factors seem increasingly costly in relation to prospects of future revenues (at constitutional prices). But, mainly, producers discover that not everyone's real terms of trade can improve relative to everyone else's. As this starts to dawn on more and more people, prices that are high in relation to the constitutional mean will tempt inventory liquidation. When this gets underway, sales revenues will be used to reduce accounts payable rather than to maintain production. The volume of credit outstanding contracts, and the inside money stock falls as the recession develops.

This, of course, is simply an attempt to paraphrase the kind of story told innumerable times in the Keynesian and pre-Keynesian business cycle literature.

Repeated episodes of this sort, in the MC setting, might generate observations such that an impressively stable Phillips curve could be fitted to them. For the sake of argument we might suppose that alternating periods of high prices/low unemployment and low prices/high unemployment produce a Phillips scatter with all points virtually on a line.[17] If so, that curve still does not hold out the promise of a permanent policy trade-off. It is not exploitable because the points on the locus are not stationary equilibria; instead, these historical observations record states in which the expectations held are bound to be revised in the light of outcomes. An attempt to exploit the apparent stable trade-off will, if pursued far enough, destroy the monetary constitution without gaining its object of permanently lowering unemployment. Once the MC system is swept away, the stable Phillips curve disappears. But we have been through that, I think.

In a trade cycle of this kind, discretionary fiscal and monetary policy could possibly have a useful role in trying to reduce its amplitude and to prompt the upswing. If this is correct, my further conjecture is that such policy will be maximally effective when fully anticipated. Note, however, that we are presupposing continued adherence to a monetary constitution that regulates the monetary base and, therefore, the price level over the medium and longer run. Monetary policy in such a setting is reduced to short-term credit policy, and one expects it, naturally, to use interest rate targets. Its 'effectiveness' is likely to be limited.

For simplicity, we have dealt with the Monetarist and the 'real' (or Keynesian) hypotheses as if they were mutually exclusive. In a purely Monetarist case, where real aggregative disturbances are known not to occur, rational agents need only watch the appropriate monetary aggregate and price their wares proportionally to stay out of trouble. In a purely Keynesian case, where exogenous monetary shocks are ruled out, monetary aggregates move with more general movements in real credit; credit, moreover, expands and contracts with real output. Pricing proportionally to bank credit will not do; the safe strategy is to revise prices in response to market excess demand.

The two types of disturbances are not, of course, mutually exclusive but may be present at the same time. When, in addition, they interact, transactors will have a difficult time sorting nominal from real shocks. Suppose, for example, that the central bank is in the habit of supplying an 'elastic currency', that is, that it participates in the all-round expansions and contractions of credit so that the base will move pro-cyclically also in Keynesian processes. This, I believe, creates an information problem for the private sector that may give a more plausible reason for short-run non-neutrality of money than does the 'islands' story. When the base is seen to expand, is it an extension of 'real credit' by the central bank (that will reduce real rates of interest)? Or is it a nominal scaling up of all values in the system, so that one's prices should be marked up proportionally? Uncertainty on this score could produce stickiness of nominal prices in the face of monetary expansion.

The relationship between money and credit in the business cycle, however, is a large and difficult topic that cannot be pursued further here.

# EQUILIBRIUM OR DISEQUILIBRIUM THEORY?

One last question. Suppose the conjecture is right that the Keynesian 'real' disturbance hypothesis is due to be readmitted on at least a coequal basis with the Monetarist 'nominal' shock hypothesis. Would this have any implications for current squabbles concerning the merits of equilibrium versus disequilibrium approaches to business cycle theory? I do not pretend to have a firm answer to this question. But it ought not to be evaded altogether.

Monetarist theorists have, on the whole, rested content with the equilibrium method. In the older, Friedman version, monetary disturbances may cause temporary deviations from the natural rate of unemployment. In the newer, Lucas version, changes in unemployment are interpreted as movements between temporary equilibria. In either one, the coordination of economic activities is taken on faith. In Keynesian economics, it is problematic.[18] The problem, moreover, is essential to the Keynesian view of business fluctuations – an integral, not an optional, part of the inquiry.

The most heated discussion of the issue has centered on the 'clearing' of labor markets. The New Classicists have made the (telling) point that fix-price assumptions imply that agents allow perceived gains from trade to go unexploited; if, in contrast, one assumes all perceived gains to be exhausted, the implication is that the labor market 'clears'. At this point, the discussion easily gets derailed into unproductive arguments about the 'voluntary' or 'involuntary' nature of unemployment. That thicket had better be avoided on this occasion.

'Speculative' pricing, based on temporarily given information sets, seems to me preferable to more or less arbitrary fix-price constraints as the theoretical rationale for short-run wage 'stickiness'. So far, so good. But the matter does not end at this point. Price flexibility in this qualified sense does not by itself guarantee that the time path of the economy will be a sequence of temporary Walrasian equilibria. A Keynesian theorist would proceed to consider how the trades actually realized at the speculatively set prices during this period might affect the feasible set of trades for next period. In the standard example, reservation wages are set too high, so that labor's realized income is reduced with further consequences for consumption, and so forth.

What eliminates such income-constrained state sequences from the New Classical theory is not just the assumption that fix-price constraints are absent. The assumption that all agents have the same information sets is just as crucial. If all agents in a market receive the same news and evaluate it using the same theory, they will all agree on what change in price is indicated. The volume of transactions will not be affected by disagreements among transactors. Taking the old Keynesian example again, if the news causes revisions in the demand price and supply price of labor of equal magnitude, neither side will be surprised by, or disappointed in, the volume of transactions realized.

It is not easy to come up with a context in which the assumption of universally shared information sets seems more reasonable than in the Monetarist case of purely nominal shocks. Even so, it eliminates the Friedmanian temporary deviations from the natural rate of unemployment. These departures from equilibrium come about because firms learn of changes in the inflation rate before workers do, so that there is a transitory information asymmetry between the two sides of the market. Once workers catch on, the information asymmetry vanishes, and employment returns to the natural rate. The New Classical assumption does not allow the asymmetry to develop.

The labor market focus of the debate over the new equilibrium business cycle theory has been unfortunate. Preoccupation with the stickiness of money wages comes naturally to Monetarists: if you believe that all aggregative shocks are purely nominal, the failure of nominal prices to adjust appropriately must be the key to the explanation of unemployment. Keynesians do not believe that exogenous nominal shocks are the only disturbances, or even the typical disturbances, to worry about. Traditionally, they have been concerned about the intertemporal coordination of saving and investment decisions. In the latest round of the solemn, farcical muddle that is modern macroeconomics, we have been treated to a spectacular bout in unemployment theory featuring, in one corner, New Classicists blaming the failure of nominal interest rates to adjust to changes in money and, in the other, old Keynesians blaming the rigidity of nominal wages in the face of changes in real intertemporal opportunities.

The Keynesian case for a disequilibrium approach is best considered in an intertemporal context. The real rate of return on investment is not just some given constant. We have to presuppose that political events and technological developments, for instance, can change the real returns in prospect for broad sectors of the economy. A change in the returns perceived to be in prospect, in the unfashionable terminology of Keynes, causes a change in the marginal efficiency of capital (MEC). Such changes are real shocks – 'real' in the sense that system adjustments to them require changes in the allocation of resources and in the relative price vector, and not just some scaling up or down of nominal values. We now have (at least) the following possibilities.

A.  There is nothing in all this for macroeconomists to talk about. Real disturbances cause reallocations of resources between sectors but no movements in macroeconomic aggregates – unless monetary shocks are also involved. In the latter case, the macroeconomic effects are all attributable to those shocks.

B.  A real equilibrium business cycle: utilization of both labor force and manufacturing capacity fluctuates but does so optimally in response to correctly perceived changes in the real rate of return. The labor market is continuously in equilibrium. People choose to work more when the real rate on savings is high, *ceteris paribus* – intertemporal substitution *à la* Lucas. In this case, we assume that everybody has the same information and the same theory. They act, therefore, on the basis of mutually consistent beliefs,[19] and these beliefs are correct. The rate of capital accumulation fluctuates, but saving equals investment (*ex ante*) throughout.

C.  A real business cycle that is a sequence of temporary equilibria. Mutually consistent beliefs again, but we allow for the possibility that what everyone believes will still be wrong. Again, saving equals investment in every period. When expectations are found to have been inaccurate, both savers and investors revise their expectations to the same extent and at the same time ('between innings').

D.  A Wicksell–Keynes disequilibrium cycle wherein the market real rate of interest fails to coordinate saving and investment decisions appropriately. In cyclical expansions, investment tends to exceed saving (market rate below natural rate); in contractions, these inequalities are reversed. There are any number of variations on this theme.[20] All have in common the assumption that the expectations of entrepreneurs, taken collectively, are inconsistent with those held in the financial markets.

Of these four possibilities, (A) is the only one that is fully consistent with the New Classical economics. New Classical theory is made up, however, from Monetarist theory and rational expectations method. (B) and (C) are non-Monetarist, but are clearly compatible with the rational expectations equilibrium approach to modeling. (B) is probably the most appropriate benchmark for discussion of 'real' cycle theory.[21] A formal version of (C) would be a real counterpart to Lucas's Monetarist equilibrium cycle model (Lucas 1975). The problem comes down to the various versions of (D).

Whether (D) can be modeled using a rational expectations equilibrium approach depends on how stringently the latter is defined. Phelps's 'islands' parable, formalized by Lucas in a study that has been central to the entire rational expectations development, should be adaptable to the representation of such Keynesian processes (Phelps 1968; Lucas 1972). Each producer is his own island in regard to his expectations of future profit from present investment. There are no archipelago-wide (futures) markets to ensure the consistency of these expectations with the plans of consumers and with aggregate ongoing investment. If the MEC on the home island falls below what the producer thinks is obtainable elsewhere, he will cut back on investment and pile up his retained earnings in liquid form, and so forth. From there the Keynesian story develops as usual (Leijonhufvud 1981b, pp. 197–9).

If, however, by 'equilibrium approach' we mean modeling the economy as if it behaved like an Arrow–Debreu contingency market general equilibrium system,[22] it is clear that Keynesian processes must fall outside its purview. An Arrow–Debreu economy works like 'clockwork' going through the Markovian motions of a system in which all allocation decisions were made and reconciled at the beginning of time. Agents may have trouble predicting states of 'nature',[23] but they have no trouble with each other. Coordination of activities, given the state of nature, is not a problem. All agents have the same information on the probability distributions for future states of nature. There is no room, in this framework, for the inconsistencies of belief or expectation that are essential in Keynesian theory.

It is, perhaps, necessary in conclusion to insist that the incompatibility of the rational expectations equilibrium method with the Keynesian hypothesis is totally irrelevant to the scientific appraisal of the latter. It merely indicates the limitations that the unanimity-of-beliefs postulate builds into the method.[24]

## NOTES

*   I have profited from discussions with Carlos Daniel Heymann and from comments on earlier drafts by Earlene Craver-Leijonhufvud.
1.  I know, of course, that to some people Keynesianism means little else than Phillips curve stability, but l ask indulgence in using my own definition of the term.
2.  'Victory' and 'defeat' are terms that seem to belong on the sports pages rather than to the history of science. Here, however, no epistemological meaning is intended but only sociology of knowledge connotations. To 'win' means to attract the best new young talent. In this sense, the Monetarism of Friedman and Brunner 'won' over American Keynesianism, only to 'lose' soon afterward to the New Classical economics of Lucas and Sargent.
3.  Rejection of the stable Phillips curve does not suffice to establish the natural rate of unemployment hypothesis (Leijonhufvud 1981a, pp. 182–7).
4.  From here on, I borrow heavily from my response to Joint Economic Committee (1981) questions on the role of expectations in economics.
5.  This is not to say that expectations cannot be made the subject of very worthwhile research. See, in particular, Jonung (1981). We may be able to obtain fitted data on short-term inflation expectations. What we theoretically require, however, is the entire 'term structure' of inflation rate expectations relevant to multi-period decisions to be made currently. For some purposes, moreover, some measure of the dispersion over agents (period by period into the future) of these expectations is also needed. It is this task that seems to me hopeless.
6.  The novelty of this solution is sometimes exaggerated; this is how Keynes dealt with short-term (sales and real income) expectations in his *General Theory*.
7.  Consider, for example, a constitutional law that can be changed or amended only by majority votes in two consecutive sessions of the legislative body, the two sessions to be separated by a general election. The US Constitution is too difficult to amend, I would think, for the purpose discussed here.
8.  He cannot be confident, however, that drawings from this urn will be made at fixed intervals. Moreover, the distribution in the urn is presumably not stationary.

9.  That is, insofar as they believe that others generate their inflation expectations as they themselves do.
10. Compare the discussion of 'coordination games' by Schotter (1981). See also Sowell (1980).
11. For some reason, however, early converts to money stock targets do not seem to have as much difficulty as these last central banks in professing abandonment of interest rate targets.
12. I have in mind a rule specifying a constitutional *level* of the money supply for each date after the constitution goes into effect and a band width of $\pm x\%$ around this target. A growth rate rule with a band defined as the constitutional rate $\pm z\%$ is a different possibility.
13. And, if this trend is only implied rather than stated in the constitution, they could use some autoregressive scheme to learn it.
14. It is tempting to go on to say that prices must be 'sticky' because they move with less amplitude than nominal income and that this 'explains' the real income movements. But the implied suggestion that prices (and/or wages) 'should' move proportionally to nominal income is misleading when the shock is not a purely nominal one. Nor does it help much to substitute speculation on the basis of 'inelastic price expectations' for involuntary constraints on price sellers – as in Leijonhufvud (1968c, Chapter 2). Note that while rational agents in the MC system should have inelastic expectations about the price level over the longer run, it is not obvious that the monetary stability contributed by the constitution sketched earlier would instil inelastic price expectations over the short run.
15. This suggestion is due to C.D. Heymann.
16. Some subset may be optimistic instead that they are going to cut their real costs.
17. A series of counterclockwise loops is more likely, actually.
18. In cruder versions of Keynesianism, admittedly, coordination of activities is not problematic either – just impossible. An article of a more pessimistic faith.
19. No great matter of principle hinges on it, but I happen to prefer this terminology (that is, consistent or inconsistent beliefs). See Leijonhufvud (1981b).
20. The collection of variations discussed in 'The Wicksell Connection' (Leijonhufvud 1981b) is not by any means complete, but should suffice to try the patience of all but dedicated antiquarians with the general idea. Note also that the broad-brush taxonomy painted in the text will be judged incomplete by (E) Cambridge Keynesians who do not believe the interest rate can equilibrate saving and investment, (F) old-time Keynesians who do not think the equilibrium exists, and (G) post-Keynesians who do not think the equilibrium can be defined. We have already passed over (H) the modern muddled Keynesians who think Keynesian theory has nothing to do with saving and investment but has sticky wages as its analytical fulcrum. There are more kinds of Keynesians than one can shake a stick at! Believe me – I've tried.
21. My 'Wicksell Connection' uses (A) as the benchmark. It would have been more relevant to current debates if 1 had used (B).
22. This is the position taken by Lucas (1980) more recently.
23. Monetarist cycle theory can be cast in this frame, it would appear, only by classifying central bankers as 'ravages of nature' rather than as open market 'traders'.
24. The argument that the agents will act so as to exhaust apparent gains from trade, which the New Classicists have used against fix-price modelers, is simply irrelevant in the intertemporal context chosen here as the appropriate one for discussing the Keynesian case. With incomplete intertemporal markets, the interactions required to generate information about, and exploit, these potential gains from trade do not take place.

# 4.   What was the matter with *IS–LM*?

At a conference on 'Recent Developments in Macroeconomics', elementary *IS–LM* might be a somewhat unexpected topic. *IS–LM*, after all, has been around for a while. It ruled research for 30 years or more, and, in the teaching of macroeconomics, a better mouse-trap has still to be invented. For the last fifteen years or so, however, it has been out of favor even with many economists who do not quite know what to put in its place. And in the last decade, theoretical research in macroeconomics has moved away from this frame of reference.

Why are we bent on abandoning *IS–LM*? This would seem to be a question to which we ought to have a clear answer. An answer is needed for the appraisal of 'recent developments'. Do fix-price temporary general equilibrium models solve (or successfully avoid) the problems we had with *IS–LM*? Do rational expectations models?

Well – what were those problems?

## I

Different people are apt to have different answers to that question. Every teacher of macroeconomics has his own list of 'troubles' with *IS–LM*. But almost all of those one hears frequently mentioned are surely remediable deficiencies. Taking inventory of the most popular complaints does not seem a promising tack, therefore.

My title does not ask what is *wrong* with *IS–LM*. We are not looking for some simple error or omission. Omissions would have been remedied long ago. Fatal error is inconsistent with the long dominance of the framework. Yet somehow, *IS–LM* does not do what a good model is supposed to do; it is not dependable in producing the right answers to questions in the hands of students (for example), who may not yet understand all that much about economics but do know their algebra. It is a good vehicle for demonstrating certain relationships, which is why we continue to use it. But some questions are more easily understood or analysed without it than with it. In the end, it is probably not a short-cut to understanding macroeconomics, for knowing when to use it and when not to rely on it seems to be more difficult than the subject matter itself. Even the best economists can go wrong with *IS–LM* on occasion.

In my opinion, *IS–LM* has served us ill in three long-lasting controversies.

1.  In the *Keynes and the classics* controversy, *IS–LM* produced, in the end, widespread agreement on the wrong answer, namely that Keynes was merely doing orthodox economics with rigid wages (cf., for example, Leijonhufvud 1969, Lecture 1).[1]
2.  *IS–LM* was used to deny that the issues of the *loanable funds versus liquidity preference* controversy were of serious consequence to general macrotheory.[2] This was a mistake.
3.  In the course of the *Monetarist* controversy, *IS–LM* has proved a less than helpful framework for producing agreement between the two sides on what the empirically important issues are.[3]

I will try not to bore the reader with a rehash of my views on controversy (1). Some observations on the second point will be made. But this paper will deal mainly with the Monetarist controversy, as seen through *IS–LM* glasses darkly.


# II

There are, speaking somewhat simplistically, two broad approaches to macro-economics today. In one, which I have elsewhere called the 'spanner in the works' approach, coordination failures are explained as the consequence of rigidities in the economic system which prevent it from adjusting appropri-ately to parametric disturbances. For the individual agents of the system, the obstacle to appropriate adjustment may be coercion or past commitment to a (possibly implicit) contract or to a particular structure of physical capital. When this approach is being followed, it is usually not an important issue whether agents do or do not correctly perceive the potential gains from trade that they are in any case prevented from exploiting. Since this is so, the standard conceptual apparatus of static equilibrium theory – which assumes that agents have full information about their opportunities – may as well be utilized. Economists of this persuasion are consequently less likely to ques-tion the adequacy of standard neo-Walrasian theory as a microfoundation for macroeconomics, and also less likely to see any reason why *IS–LM* should not serve perfectly well, at least for the proper care and feeding of under-graduates.

In the other approach, which we may cheerfully call the 'mud in the eye' approach, coordination failures are explained as the consequence of the failure of agents correctly and completely to perceive the opportunities present in the system. Thus 'stickiness' of certain prices, for example, is interpreted as being due not to constraints on price-setters, but instead to their ignorance of changes in relevant market conditions. Economists who try to follow this approach find that they make lots of trouble for themselves, for all the nuts and bolts and tricks of standard models are apt to be fashioned on the assumption that agents do know market conditions. So this group has problems with static price theory and is also likely to have problems with *IS–LM*.

Perhaps it would be better to talk of 'emphases' rather than 'approaches', for the two are obviously not mutually exclusive. In pursuing, for instance, the incomplete information approach as far as it will go, one need not be committed to the belief that the world is free of institutional or other rigidities of significant consequence.

Here, however, the question of the title will be discussed altogether from the incomplete information perspective.

# III

It is sometimes complained that *IS–LM* is 'too static'. As we will see later, however, one might with at least equal justice voice the complaint that 'it is not as static as it seems'. *IS–LM*, as it is most frequently utilized, is neither static nor dynamic. It is a 'short-run period model' – the accepted term for a static model with which one tries to do dynamic analysis. We had better clarify its status in relation to the two concept pairs, 'static–dynamic' and 'long run–short run'.

The most widely accepted definition of dynamics in economics is the one due to Sir John Hicks: when the *quantities* that appear in our model must be *dated*, we are doing dynamics. For present purposes at least, I would like to amend the Hicksian definition to read: when we must *date* the *decisions* taken by various agents, we are doing dynamics. In statics, then, we need not date decisions – *because it does not matter in what sequence they are made.*

The temporal order of decisions is of analytical significance if and only if transactors have to act on incomplete information. In models where agents are assumed to have complete information, all choices are made at the same time. The multi-period general equilibrium model is the best example. It is 'dynamic' by Hicks's definition, since an infinite number of future periods adds as many dimensions to its commodity space. It is 'static' by the present definition, since the opportunities and preferences defined over this space pose just one choice for each agent and since the simultaneous market reconciliation of the choices of all agents is provided for. Everything is decided simultaneously at the origin of time in this construction.

The well-known 'cobweb' model illustrates the opposite case. Here, consumers and producers are assumed to take turns making decisions. On odd-numbered dates, consumers get to set a demand price on the output that has been produced. On even-numbered dates, producers must choose their outputs for the next period. The system oscillates because, at the time when producers have to commit themselves, they do not have, nor are they able to anticipate, the information most pertinent to the output decision: namely the price that it will fetch. If we provide the producers with sufficient additional information – for example by putting a futures market into the model, or by assuming rational expectations that will substitute for such a market – they will find the market equilibrium directly.[4] The dynamic behavior of the system becomes of no interest. The exact sequence of events no longer matters. The static supply and demand cross tells us everything we want to know.

One further illustration will help to suggest approximately where one might draw the line between 'complete' (or 'full') and 'incomplete' information. Arrow and Debreu generalized the metastatic neo-Walrasian model to deal with a probabilistically uncertain future. In their famous contingency market model, it is also true that all choices are made at the origin of time. I would like to subsume uncertain knowledge of this kind, therefore, under 'complete' information. But can this be justified?

In the Arrow–Debreu model, agents plan for all possible futures. No matter what the future brings, they have anticipated it perfectly and have concluded the contracts that are optimal to this contingency. All they learn, therefore, as the future moves into the present, is what particular Markovian railroad track the world is fated to run on. In a more fundamental sense, they have nothing to learn. They do not learn, for example, what it is like to grow old; that is, they do not 'discover' anything about themselves (and their preferences) that they had not already anticipated. In particular, they do not learn anything about the economic system that they did not already know. Their understanding does not change.[5]

Processes of this type are equilibria in the sense suggested by Hahn, in that further experience with market interaction will not teach agents anything that significantly alters their beliefs.[6] We may note also that the rational expectations approach, which assumes that agents fully understand the world that they inhabit, has produced a class of equilibrium models of the business cycle. Lucas explicitly interprets business cycles as the period by period revelation of a particular Arrow–Debreu contingent-claim time path (cf. Lucas 1980). And preceding both Hahn and Lucas, we have Hicks (1965, pp. 92–3; also cited in Hicks 1983b): 'Equilibrium over time requires … [that] there can be no revision of expectations at the junction between one "short" period and its successor'.

The older theories of business cycles were generally not equilibrium theories by these criteria. It is for the representation of these 'dynamic' or 'disequilibrium' theories that *IS–LM* has been so much utilized. In trying to understand these theories from the incomplete information standpoint, it may then be a good idea to examine the sequence of interactions that lead up to *IS–LM* solution states.

## IV

In the 'long run' of price theory, all adjustments have taken place. In the 'short run', some adjustments 'have not had time' to be completed. Originally, in Marshall, the distinctive characteristic of the short run was that stocks need not be stationary but that net investment or disinvestment may be going on. Except for the adjustment of stocks, all activities were 'equilibrated' in the Marshallian short run. More recently, new short-run notions have begun to proliferate in the literature to fit all sorts of incomplete adjustment cases.

For macroeconomics, Marshall's long run does not seem to be the most useful full-adjustment benchmark. Since, most of the time, we are dealing with growing economies, the stationarity condition is inappropriate. An economy travelling on an equilibrium growth path is 'fully adjusted' as far as the coordination of economic activities is concerned. If we are to be able to define what 'goes wrong' with the adjustment of the system, we need a clear conception of what 'full adjustment' would entail. So what should this benchmark be like?

The suggestion here, of course, is that it should be complete or full information. This term should not evoke notions of perfect foresight or costless information; rather, it should convey the sense of a situation in which agents are not going to learn anything new or surprising from continued market interaction.[7] In a full information state, agents have learned all that can be (profitably) learned about their environment and about each other's behavior. In economies that are not hampered by rigidities, adjustments will then be complete; people are not going to change their behavior. Full information states are equilibria in this sense. By the same token, incomplete information states are, of course, 'disequilibria', in the sense that, when people proceed to interact in markets on the basis of the information they possess, some of them will discover that they are acting on incorrect (and unprofitable) premises.

It would be a mistake, I feel, to press the badly used and badly worn Marshallian 'long–run'/'short–run' terms into the further service of covering also the 'full information state'/'incomplete information state' concepts.[8] Marshall had in mind the actual creation and installation, or depreciation and wearing out, of physical capital as the adjustments needed to bring about a stationary state. These are processes that necessarily take a long time – 'real', calendar time. We are concerned not with stationarity, but with the coordination of activities. The degree to which coordination is achieved depends upon the state of knowledge, and convergence to full coordination on the speed of learning. Learning can be sometimes fast and sometimes slow.

To illustrate the point, consider the complaint voiced with some frequency by Keynesians in the course of the Monetarist controversy: 'The trouble with Friedman is that he takes propositions that we all agree are true in the long run and uses them as if they were true in the short run.' What does it mean? What we all agree to be true in the long run is that money is neutral. In the long run, therefore, nominal income is proportional to the money stock. Friedman has a Monetarist theory of nominal income in the short run. Keynesians object to it because they do not think money stock policy is as effective and reliable as this would imply.[9]

Friedman might presumably say the same thing about Lucas (or Sargent, Wallace and Barro): 'The trouble with Lucas is that he takes propositions that I agree are true in the long run', and so on. What would this mean? In Friedman's theory, the long-run Phillips curve is vertical, so that monetary policy has only price-level effects in the long run. In Lucas's theory, anticipated monetary policy is neutral right away. Friedman would object, because he does not believe anticipated monetary policy to be without consequence for real variables in the short run.

When Sam played it again (fans of Casablanca will remember), his words were:

> … the fundamental things apply
> As time goes by.

The trouble here is that the 'fundamental things' might apply without much time at all going by.[10] It depends upon how much people understand and what information they receive. In the two cases just mentioned, Friedman's transactors are assumed to know more than Keynesians think is reasonable, and to know less than Lucas thinks it reasonable to assume for his transactors.

This last statement could stand some more explanation. But here we are not interested in the transmission of monetary impulses for its own sake, but only in order to find out what is the matter with *IS–LM*. There are a number of things to be done before we can return to the transmission question and look at it from the *IS–LM* angle.

## V

Full information macroeconomics (FIM) would be a useful branch of the subject. We may not be terribly fascinated with a kind of macroeconomics in which little, if anything, ever goes wrong. But FIM would be useful as a benchmark construction. Its main purpose would be to define the adjustments that must take place if the system is to adapt fully following some disturbance, such as a shift of the investment function or a change in the money supply. A knowledge of this is helpful in trying to define exactly what is the trouble assumed to occur in various macrotheories in which much, if not everything, always goes wrong.

Use of FIM constructions, on the other hand, does not commit us to the belief that the system will always or normally adapt smoothly and rapidly no matter what the disturbance; nor does it force us to preclude the very rapid convergence of the economy on full information equilibrium in certain cases. We do not want invariably to associate the notion of an FIM state with either the short run or the long.

For present purposes, we want an FIM model that will match the structure of a simple *IS–LM* model. For present purposes, also, it is not necessary (fortunately) to derive and justify the properties of the FIM model in any detail. It will be alright to 'suppose' a system with certain FIM properties, and then look at it through its *IS–LM* version. Our FIM model should, of course, have a reasonable family resemblance to Hicks's classical model. So, we suppose the following:

$$X = f(N, \underline{K}) \qquad (4.1)$$

$$N^d = f_N^{-1}(w/p) \qquad (4.2)$$

$$N^S = g(w/p) \qquad (4.3)$$

$$N^d = N^S \qquad (4.4)$$

The notation is too familiar to need explanation. The first four equations state that labor supply and derived demand for labor in a competitive, one-commodity system determine output, employment and the real wage rate in FIM states.

$$I = I(r) \qquad (4.5)$$

$$S = \underline{X} - C(\underline{X}, r) \qquad (4.6)$$

$$S = I \qquad (4.7)$$

Saving and investment determine the rate of capital accumulation and the real interest rate.

$$M^d = \underline{k}p\underline{X} \tag{4.8}$$

$$M^S = \underline{M} \tag{4.9}$$

$$M^S = M^d \tag{4.10}$$

Money supply and money demand determine the price level. For certain purposes, we will substitute a more common liquidity preference function,

$$M^d = p \times L(X,r) \tag{4.8'}$$

for the constant velocity function (4.8). For the time being, however, we are supposing that, in comparisons between FIM states, velocity will be found to be unrelated to the real rate of interest.

In this paper, we will discuss only two macroeconomic questions: (1) 'What are the effects of a change in the money supply?' and (2) What are the effects of a decline in the marginal efficiency of capital (MEC). For brevity, we will refer to the two parametric shifts as the 'monetary shock' and the 'real shock'.

The comparative statics of the above FIM model are so simple as to be obvious. The relevant results might be summarized as follows.

1. *Monetary shocks have no real effects.* Only the price level is affected; note in particular that the real interest rate is not. Conceivably, it may be a long, long run before we get neutrality, but FIM comparative statics should skip by all intervening incomplete information states in silence.
2. *Real shocks have no monetary consequences.* A decline in the MEC is interpreted here as a worsening of the terms on which a society can trade present goods for future goods – the terms being judged according to the best information available to that society. (For simplicity, think of a decline in the rate of embodied technological progress.) The rational adaptation entails a lower rate of capital accumulation, a transfer of resources to consumption goods industries and a lower real rate of interest. It does not entail unemployment, of course, or (in this FIM model) a decline in the price level.[11]

# VI

The macroeconomics we actually teach, of course, bears no clear relationship to full information macroeconomics. Instead of the static properties of some FIM model, the beginning student may be given one or the other of two crosses to bear. The first one uses a Keynesian savings–investment cross to determine (real) income. Call it 'model A'. The second employs a given money stock and a 'Cambridge $k$' money demand to determine (nominal) income.[12] Call it 'model T'.

$$pS = p[X - C(X)] \qquad (A4.1)$$

$$pI = p\underline{I} \qquad (A4.2)$$

$$pS = pI \qquad (A4.3)$$

$$M^d = \underline{k}pX \qquad (T4.1)$$

$$M^S = \underline{M} \qquad (T4.2)$$

$$M^d = M^S \qquad (T4.3)$$

Why do we start students off this way? Are these gadgets supposed to be easier to understand than an FIM model? Whether the student is fed A or T as his first introduction to macroeconomics, he has had a switch pulled on him before he even gets started. In our FIM model, in opposition to model A, savings and investment have nothing to do with the level of income, whether real or nominal; in opposition to model T, money supply and demand determine the price level and not real income or the product of the two. Full information macroeconomics may have little direct bearing on problems of unemployment and short-run stabilization policy; but why does 'relevant' macroeconomics start off by replacing FIM (4.5)–(4.7) with model A, or else by replacing FIM (4.8)–(4.l0) with model T?

As suggested in the previous section, it is not really a very good answer to say that FIM is long run and model A (say) short run. That leaves the student on his own to try to figure out why savings and investment determine income in the short run but the rate of interest in the long run.[13]

Since A and T both differ from FIM, our answer should be that certain information failures (or rigidities) are taken for granted – so much so, in fact, that they are built into elementary models as if they were inescapable features of the real world. The Monetarist controversy started off, in effect, with a confrontation between models A and T. To understand the theoretical issues in that controversy, then, it would seem desirable, as a first step, to explain how A and T, respectively, depart from a full information (all things flexible) model. This would tell us what the information problems (rigidities) are that are presumed to be ever-present – or ignored as implausible – by each side.

Model T is the simplest. In the rigidities (R) version, to the extent that prices (wages) are sticky, a change in the money stock will affect real output, $X$, and not just prices, $p$. In the incomplete information (IIM) version, anticipated changes in money affect prices, but unanticipated ones affect real income as well.

For model A, the R version would state: to the extent that intertemporal prices (that is, the interest rate) do not adjust to a change in perceived intertemporal production opportunities (that is, MEC), changes in investment will lead to changes in aggregate money income. The corresponding IIM argument would run: whereas changes in the realizable rate of profit that are generally recognized will affect only the interest rate and the growth path, unrecognized such changes will affect money income. Except that model A is more extreme than that – it asserts (R) that the interest rate never responds or (IIM) that the market never knows what is going on, so that the rational FIM adjustment (which leaves income unchanged) can be excluded as a possibility from the model.[14] Model T is more reasonable in that, specified as a theory of nominal income, it leaves the extent to which the FIM response is approximated an open question.

Two long-established stylized facts lend plausibility to A and T, respectively, as candidates for the first thing the student should learn in macroeconomics. For model A, we have the fact (SF1) that investment and GNP are positively correlated over business cycles, with investment showing a larger amplitude than other components of income. For model T, of course, we have (SF2) the positive correlation between the money stock and nominal income. The Monetarist controversy started out as a statistical contest over the dependability of these stylizations. Although no economist alive will confess to belief in either model A or model T, the issues for round one of the controversy are produced by putting the two on a collision course: the relative stability of the consumption-income and the money-income relations; the appropriate empirical components to be included in 'autonomous expenditures' or in the money supply, respectively; the 'autonomy' of investment and the 'exogeneity' of the money stock; the effectiveness of fiscal and monetary policy actions and the predictability of their consequences.

Econometric contention over these issues did nothing to bring out the information failures implicit in the debate.

## VII

From A to T, our student graduates to *IS–LM*. By linking A and T by the real rate of interest, $r$, we obtain the simplest version – a model of nominal income:

$$pS = p[X - C(X,r)] \qquad \text{(AT4.1)}$$

$$pI = pI(r) \qquad \text{(AT4.2)}$$

$$pS = pI \qquad \text{(AT4.3)}$$

$$M^d = p \times L(X,r) \qquad \text{(AT4.4)}$$

$$M^S = \underline{M} \qquad \text{(AT4.5)}$$

$$M^d = M^S \qquad \text{(AT4.6)}$$

On this loftier plane, new riddles appear. In the comparative statics of our FIM model, real and monetary phenomena were independent of one another. In *IS–LM*, as usually taught, real disturbances have monetary consequences and vice versa – unless extreme assumptions are made about the elasticities of *IS* and *LM*. Is it plausible that this two-way interdependence also stems from information failures of some sort?

Round two of the Monetarist debate necessarily had to lead on to consideration of these interdependencies as well. An A-theorist who relies on (SF1) to argue that changes in autonomous expenditures cause income movements must also explain away (SF2) as showing endogenous movements in the money stock.[15] A T-theorist similarly has to explain away (SF1). *IS–LM* gives us a handle of sorts on the interaction of real and monetary phenomena, so it became, rather naturally, the framework for debating these interaction issues.

The *IS–LM* model is used, in this type of context, as if one were doing comparative statics with a genuinely static model. Real disturbances (or fiscal policy actions) are represented as shifting *IS*, while *LM* stays put; monetary disturbances (that is, policy) as shifting *LM*, while *IS* stays put. The issues of round one were gone over again in this framework, and crowding out and Gibson's paradox added.[16] *IS–LM* curve-shifting will suggest that the values of the elasticities of the two curves are crucial to the issues of the Monetarist debate. Many of the participants accepted this suggestion. The discussion tended to presume, moreover, that these elasticities are stable properties of the system, that the results of time-series regressions give information on these steady-state elasticities, and that qualitative results from *a priori* static choice theory have a bearing on the issues in sufficing by themselves to exclude extreme values.

There are two extreme possibilities. The 'fiscalist' extreme would postulate a vertical *IS* and/or a horizontal *LM*; the Monetarist extreme, a horizontal *IS* and/or a vertical *LM*. Putting it this way tends to suggest that, surely, all moderate men of sound judgment will take a position somewhere in the middle. The trouble is that this moderate position (like the fiscalist extreme) implies that real impulses always must affect income and that monetary impulses always must change the economy's rate of growth. It implies that the rational FIM adjustments can never happen. And the Monetarist extreme will imply that real impulses never change income and that monetary impulses never disturb the growth path. In either case, 'sometimes' is the (econometrically troublesome) possibility that is being excluded by construction. This steady-state version of *IS–LM* is a model that will not allow representation of an economy that adapts more or less well to shocks depending upon the state of information.

Note that, if it were to be the case that these short-run interactions of real and monetary phenomena were due to incomplete information on the part of agents, then the steady-state elasticities view would be seen to be misleading. What the response to a particular impulse will be then depends upon the state of information and not just on steady-state behavioral parameters. What counts is the extent to which the nature and extent of the shock is recognized or unrecognized, anticipated or unanticipated, perceived as permanent or as transitory. The same impulse need not produce the same response every time it is repeated.

In order to re-examine the interaction of real and monetary phenomena in the *IS–LM* model, start back with A and T, with the propositions that are fundamental to each. Money income, in model A, will decline *if and only if* intended saving exceeds intended investment (so that we have an excess supply (ES) of commodities). In model T, money income will decline *if and only if* the prevailing state is one of excess demand (ED) for money. So far the two are consistent. But we have two contrasting hypotheses about causation. In A, a decline in investment produces the ES of commodities. In T, a reduction in the money supply produces the ED for money. If we scrutinize the A story through the suspicious eyes of a T-believer and then let an A-believer have his turn with the T story, we obtain two questions about 'transmission':

1. Why should real disturbances be expected to cause an excess demand for money and thus a change in the nominal income level (and, if money prices and/or wages are inflexible, a change in activity levels)?[17]
2. Why should monetary disturbances be expected to cause savings and investment intentions to diverge (and thus to change nominal income, and so on)?[18]

Let us begin with the second of these questions.

# VIII

The effects of an increase in the money supply are usually demonstrated by shifting *LM* rightwards. With *IS* assumed to stay put ('in the short run'), money income rises and the interest rate declines. What kind of transmission mechanism does this suppose?

*Table 4.1*

|  | *L* | *X* | *B* | *M* |
|---|---|---|---|---|
| 1. FIGE$_1$: $M^s$ increased | 0 | 0 | 0 | 0 |
| 2. Impact effects: *r* declines | 0 | 0 | ED | ES |
| 3. Inflationary pressure: *pX* rises | 0 | ED | 0 | ES |
| 4. Nominal income 'equilibrium' | ? | 0 | 0 | 0 |

In order to discuss the sequence of events, we supplement our simple *IS–LM* model with an excess demand table (Table 4.1).[19] We count four goods: labor (*L*), commodities (*X*), securities (*B*) and money (*M*). The *IS–LM* story of the once-over money injection should begin with the following course of events.

1. We assume the initial state to be a full information general equilibrium (FIGE) – all excess demands (EDs) are zero and the demands and supplies from which these EDs are computed are generated by full information individual conceptual experiments and aggregation over transactors.
2. We assume a disturbance that creates excess reserves in the banking system. The banks expand, creating an ES of money and an ED for securities. The ED that implicitly corresponds to the explicitly specified ES of money is found to be 100 per cent in the bond market, rather than distributed over all non-money markets, because the banking system is assumed to demand nothing but securities. Note, however, that we know that the ED distribution at impact of the disturbance must be as specified in the table for another reason as well. Whenever *IS* is assumed not to be shifted by the disturbance, the impact effect must be zero in the commodities markets. Holding *IS* constant when *LM* is shifted, consequently, is a *strong* assumption.
3. Next, interest rates decline in response to the excess demand for bonds and until this ED becomes zero; demand prices for assets rise relative to their current rental values and relative to their initial supply prices; planned investment thus exceeds savings, so that the state of the economy at this stage is one of money ES and commodity ED.

4. Looking at the third row of Table 4.1, both A- and T-believers will agree on what must happen next: money income will rise.

That finishes phase one of the *IS–LM* tale. It takes us from the initial FIGE at $(\hat{Y}_0, \hat{r})$ in Figure 4.1 to the *IS–LM* 'short run' at $(\underline{Y}, \underline{r})$. But this cannot be a full STOP. There has to be a further GO at $(\underline{Y}, \underline{r})$, because in the comparison of initial and terminal equilibria money must be seen to be neutral. This requires that we end up in some FIGE$_2$ with the same relative prices as in FIGE$_1$ – for example, at $(\hat{Y}_1, \hat{r})$ in Figure 4.1.

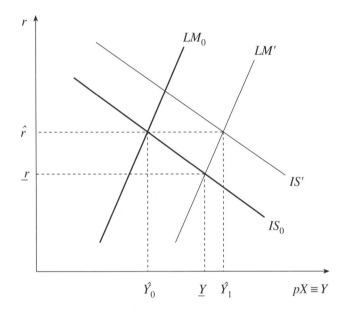

*Figure 4.1*

Phase 2 of the story might run as follows:

4. (continued) When nominal income rises, some part of this is an increase in $p$ but some part of it initially takes the form of an increase in real output, $X$, and employment. For concreteness, we may suppose that these departures from 'natural' full-information activity levels are due to a temporary information asymmetry between employers and employed. Suppose that firms learn the truth about the new price level before workers do. Observing the demand prices for their output going up in relation to money wages, firms find that they can hire labor at a reduced real wage. Workers whose perceptions of the inflation are lagging believe

they are being hired at somewhat improved real wage rates. Consequently, the two sides of the market will agree (at some money wage
between $w_o$ and $w_1$) to a volume of employment exceeding the FIGE one.
5.   As prices (and nominal rentals) increase, aggregate demand in money
terms will come proportionally to exceed the level indicated by $IS_0$ at
whatever the interest rate happens to be. So IS shifts rightwards.[20]
6.   In this process, workers discover that real wages are not what they
supposed them to be. The initial overshooting of output and employment
is corrected, so that, with $X$ declining back to $\hat{X}$, prices increase further.
The process ends up with a new FIM state, with the monetary impulse
having affected only nominal magnitudes.[21] In terms of the *IS–LM* diagram, both schedules are shown to have shifted to precisely the same
extent.

   Once the sequence is spelled out in this way, it is obvious that the analysis
definitely does assume incomplete information. It is these ignorance assumptions, moreover, rather than the steady-state interest elasticities of money
demand or investment, that count in explaining the position of the system at
stages intermediate between FIGEs. It also becomes apparent that *IS–LM* can
be a cumbersome, inappropriate framework for representing theories that
make non-standard assumptions about the knowledge of transactors and,
consequently, about the time-phasing of events.
   In the above sequence, incomplete information is implied at two points. In
phase I we have it at stage (3), where the real interest rate, and therefore the
relative prices of assets and their services, changes away from its FIM values.
Then, in phase two incomplete information is assumed at stage (4), where
activity levels and not just nominal values rise. If we replace the first one by a
full information assumption, the result is an approximation to Friedman's
theory of nominal income, where the first information imperfection is minimized but the second is admitted. In an *IS–LM* representation of the resulting
theory, the effects of a once-over money injection are shown by *simultaneously* shifting both *IS* and *LM* outward to the same extent. The phase one
sequence is short-circuited. If we replace also the second IIM assumption by
a full information one, we obtain the rational expectations theory of the fully
anticipated once-over money injection. No relative prices and no activity
levels are affected; only nominal values change. Phase two also is short-
circuited. The system jumps directly from $FIGE_1$ to a full STOP at $FIGE_2$,
without passing any *IS–LM* GO en route. 'Long-run propositions become
true in the short run'.
   Some twenty to thirty years ago, Keynesian doubts about the effectiveness of monetary policy were commonly couched in *IS–LM* terms: *IS* was
interest-inelastic and *LM* very elastic, so that shifts in *LM* (*IS* staying put)

could be seen not to have much effect on nominal income. There have been really two Monetarist counterarguments to this 'fiscalist' position, and it would probably have been helpful if the two had been more clearly distinguished than has been the case. *Monetarist counterargument no. 1* takes the sequencing of Table 4.1 for granted, and therefore concedes the appropriateness of posing the issue in terms of the *IS–LM* elasticities. Thus, in the early days of the controversy, the Monetarists were concerned to show or argue that each link in this particular transmission mechanism was more robust than Keynesians believed. In particular they argued, first, that no 'liquidity trap' was ever absolute; monetary policy was never quite a case of 'pushing on a string', but the central bank could always bring about the situation in row (2) of the table. Second, they argued that Keynesians tended to underestimate the interest elasticity of aggregate expenditures, in large part because of too narrow an interpretation of 'the interest rate'. In Keynesian theory, the term tended to signify 'borrowing cost'; in a world where elasticities of substitution between various asset types are high, the more appropriate interpretation of the phrase 'a fall in the interest rate' is that of 'a rise in the demand prices of durables relative to their rental values'. Going from row (2) to row (3) of Table 4.1, therefore, we should find a strong increase in the effective demand for output. This is because relative prices change everywhere in the economy. Monetary policy, in this account of the transmission mechanism,[22] is effective because of the pervasive non-neutrality of its 'short-run' effects.

*Monetarist counterargument no. 2* denies the above sequence and has the economy going directly from row (1) to row (3), omitting (or downplaying very much) row (2).[23] How is that story to be told? Assume a large subset of transactors who have accurate information on the supply of high-powered money and who understand that an increase in the money supply eventually must raise prices. As soon as the intentions of the central bank to expand base money become known, these agents will increase their demand for commodities at the old prices and the full information interest rate. At the same time, the increased supply of credit by the banking system is offset by the increased demand on the part of those who anticipate a rise in prices. The rate of interest does not move, and never plays any role in the transmission of the monetary impulse. We get to row (3) without it.[24] In the analysis where the standard sequence is followed, the lowering of the rate of interest (at row (2)) serves, we may conclude, to cajole *those agents who do not know what is going on* into nonetheless increasing their spending. When agents do know, there is no 'transmission problem' and the whole notion of a 'transmission mechanism' becomes somewhat meaningless.

This illustrates a more general proposition that the rational expectations literature is making exceedingly familiar: namely that fully informed agents

have no need for a price mechanism to inform them about what is happening.
Prices merely reflect what they already know.

## IX

The other question concerning the interaction of real and monetary phenomena asked why a change in the marginal efficiency of capital (MEC) should
produce a change in money income and perhaps also in employment. We take
the case of a decline in MEC and we construe this to mean, in FIM terms, that
the economy faces the problem of traversing to a new full-information general equilibrium on a lower growth path with a lower real rate of interest. In
*IS–LM*, of course, the analysis is usually begun by shifting *IS* left, keeping
*LM* in place. Again, this procedure imposes a particular sequence of events;
this sequencing implicitly rests on certain incomplete information assumptions, and hence is no more immutable than these assumptions are.

*Table 4.2*

|  | | $L$ | $X$ | $B$ | $M$ |
|---|---|---|---|---|---|
| 1. | FIGE$_1$: MEC declines | 0 | 0 | 0 | 0 |
| 2. | Impact effects: $r$ declines | 0 | ES | ED | 0 |
| 3. | Deflationary pressure: $pX$ declines | 0 | ES | 0 | ED |
| 4. | Nominal income 'equilibrium' | ? | 0 | 0 | 0 |

Once more, we may use an excess demand table (Table 4.2) to examine
phase one of the sequence.

1.  We start with the initial full-information general equilibrium.
2.  Perceived returns to investment decline. Firms decrease their demands
    for capital goods and their net issue of securities. The impact effects
    show that *IS* has shifted with *LM* constant (since ED for money is zero).
3.  Next – in the loanable funds sequence of events[25] – the interest rate
    declines in response to the excess demand for bonds and finds the level at
    which this ED is zero; with a lower rate of interest, the amount of money
    demanded at the initial level of money income will increase.
4.  Row (3), therefore, will show an ES of commodities and an ED for
    money. T-theorists and A-theorists will agree that the spending of money
    on commodities must decline until the excess demand for money in
    terms of commodities is zero.[26]

5.  If money wages fail to fall in proportion to this decline in nominal aggregate demand, there will be unemployment in the state portrayed in row (4).

That would be phase one of the usual *IS–LM* tale. It takes us from the initial FIGE$_1$ at $(\hat{X}_1, \hat{r}_0)$ in Figure 4.2 to the *IS–LM* unemployment state at $(\underline{X}, \underline{r})$.[27] Note that a significant interest elasticity of money demand is crucial to the story. Unless an excess demand for money emerges, at row (3), there will be no deflationary pressure on the level of money income and, consequently, no unemployment (whether or not money wages are sticky).

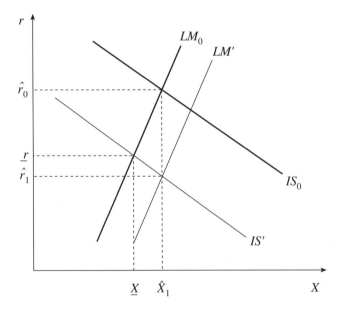

*Figure 4.2*

So liquidity preference in this general sense that money demand is interest-elastic is a *sine qua non* to any Keynesian theory of employment fluctuations.[28] The reader may recall that Modigliani (1944) came to a different conclusion in his influential assessment of Keynesian theory. Liquidity preference, Modigliani argued, was not an essential part of Keynes's story. Instead, 'the low level of investment and employment are both the effect of the same cause, namely a basic maladjustment between the quantity of money and the wage rate' (Modigliani 1944, pp. 224–5).[29] This conclusion fits Monetarist theory, where unemployment arises either from a reduction of the money stock or from money wages rising faster than the money stock. But as a

characterization of a Keynesian theory where unemployment arises in response to an unfavorable shift of MEC, Modigliani's conclusion is simply
incorrect. It is the result of an investigation of the pure statics of the *IS–LM*
model. If the *comparative statics* of *IS–LM* imposes a certain sequencing of
events, the *pure statics*, naturally, ignores sequence – and causation – altogether. Consequently, it misidentifies 'what goes wrong' – what rational
adaptation to changing circumstances agents fail to see – in the Keynesian
theory.

There are two ways (not necessarily mutually exclusive) in which the
crucial excess demand for money can be made to develop at the critical
juncture of row (3) of the story.

The first relies on the speculative demand for money. We assume a money
demand function, $M^d=f(pX, r-r^*)$, which does not significantly depend upon
the absolute level of the interest rate, $r$, but only on the difference between $r$
and the perceived 'normal' rate, $r^*$. If, then, we suppose an adverse change in
the MEC taking place, while speculators fail to realize that a lower rate of
return will be normal from now on, the system will fail to make the traverse
smoothly. An excess demand for money will develop, as in Table 4.2, and
income and presumably employment will decline.[30] If, on the other hand, the
decline in MEC is correctly perceived and seen to be permanent, $r^*$ will be
re-evaluated accordingly, and the downward adjustment of the growth rate
and of the real rate of return will proceed without creating deflationary
pressure on the income level – as in our FIM model. In this version of the
model, whether or not the real shock has monetary consequences is seen to
depend on the state of information.

The second way to generate the Table 4.2 story is the more common one.
We assume (4.8′), $M^d/p=L(X,r)$, to be the steady-state money demand function and rely on the interest elasticity of a Baumol–Tobin transactions
demand to produce an excess demand for money as the interest rate declines. In this instance, the real shock will always produce a change in the
price level, also in comparisons between FIM states. By the same token, the
*IS–LM* solution at $(\underline{X}, \underline{r})$ of Figure 4.2 is seen to be a temporary position of
the system. There should be a phase 2 to the sequence. In response to the
unemployment of stage (5), money wages and prices fall, thereby increasing the real value of the money stock until excess demand for money is
zero. In Figure 4.2, this is shown as *LM* shifting right until the new equilibrium, $\text{FIGE}_2$, is reached at $(\hat{X}_1\hat{r}_1)$.[31]

In this second story of an *IS* shift, we are supposing that people can know
the real rate of return in the system, so that there are no differences of opinion
giving rise to a speculative demand for money. Agents all perceive the decline
in MEC correctly; it is only that (when fully informed) they demand larger
real balances when the return on alternative assets has fallen. But this adjust-

ment down the steady-state demand for money function for a known decrease in the rate of profit should produce an entirely predictable decline in velocity. And, in turn, if everyone knows the extent of the required deflation, why should reservation wages and prices be sticky? If they are not, then unemployment need not develop in the move from the initial to the terminal FIGE. The system would not pass through the point $(\underline{X}, \underline{r})$ in the course of its adaptation to the decline in MEC.

Once more, we conclude that, with a bit more information at their disposal, agents would short-circuit the particular sequence assumed in the usual *IS–LM* exercise. In that case, *IS* and *LM* have to be shown as shifting simultaneously.

# X

The liquidity preference (LP) hypothesis of the interest rate mechanism maintains that the interest rate is governed by the excess demand for money: $\Delta r = f(M^d - M^s)$. It gives rise to a different sequence of events following a decline of the marginal efficiency of capital. The characteristic LP sequence is shown in Table 4.3. The impact effect of the MEC shift is, as before, an ES of commodities and an ED for bonds. Since, according to the LP hypothesis, the rate of interest will fall *if and only if* we have an ES of money, there is no interest rate response. Row (2) shows an intertemporal disequilibrium – saving exceeds investment – but intertemporal prices will not change. The Keynesian system that incorporates the LP hypothesis is altogether incapable of adjusting rationally to disturbances that require a change in the rate of capital accumulation.[32] The appropriate price mechanism, it is assumed, will never work. The loanable funds hypothesis, in contrast, asserts that the interest rate is governed by the ES of securities: $\Delta r = g(B^s - B^d)$. This price mechanism will work with well-informed speculators, and will not do the job, of course, if speculators are ill-informed. The difference between the LP Keynesian and loanable funds (LF) Keynesian models is that between a system that cannot

*Table 4.3*

|  | L | X | B | M |
|---|---|---|---|---|
| 1. MEC declines | 0 | 0 | 0 | 0 |
| 2. Output falls | 0 | ES | ED | 0 |
| 3. *r* falls | (ES) | 0 | ED(?) | ES |
| 4. Nominal income 'equilibrium' | (ES) | 0 | 0 | 0 |

work properly and one that can (and presumably often does) work, but cannot be counted on to do so without fail. That difference is not a trivial theoretical issue.

The LP sequence contains another issue that is not trivial. Comparison of rows (2) and (3) shows, first, that spending (of money on commodities) declines although the excess demand for money is zero, and second, that the decline in money income proceeds to produce an excess supply of money. This contradicts every possible quantity theory of nominal income, whereas the LF Keynesian model is consistent with quantity theory reasoning.

Keynes summarized his departures from classical theory in two propositions: (1) saving and investment determine income – not the interest rate, as the classics believed; and (2) liquidity preference and the money supply determine the interest rate – and not the price level, as the classics believed. Both propositions stem directly from the LP hypothesis (which remains the core of British Cambridge Keynesianism). They can be read off, in LP sequence, from Table 4.3.

Alvin Hansen, who was extremely influential in shaping the American Keynesian tradition, decided that Keynes's summary propositions were simple analytical mistakes and therefore meaningless. Savings and investment, Hansen argued, determine neither income nor the interest rate: they give us the *IS* schedule. And money supply and demand, of course, give us the *LM* schedule. Everything has to be determined simultaneously. This is another argument that treats the model *as if* it were a purely static one. And, again, it misses the point – an important point.

# XI

The simplest version of *IS–LM* can be produced by linking models A and T by the rate of interest.[33] But model A (especially) and model T are incomplete information models. Their solutions portray market interactions that are, at least on the part of some group of transactors, based on misapprehension of the opportunities potentially present. It is to invite misunderstandings, therefore, to treat *IS–LM* solutions as if they were the static, short-run equilibria familiar from price theory.

One must pay attention to the sequencing of events in order to understand the theoretical reasons why the system is supposed not to be in full information general equilibrium, and also in order to understand the interaction of real and monetary phenomena in the system.

*IS–LM*, handled as if it were a static construction, will pay no attention to the sequence of events. This use of the apparatus produced a nonsensical conclusion to the *Keynes and the classics* debate: namely that Keynes had revolutionized economic theory by advancing the platitude that wages too high for full employment and rigid downwards imply persistent unemployment. It failed to capture essential elements of Keynes's theory: namely that the typical shock is a shift in investors' expectations and that it is the failure of intertemporal prices to respond appropriately to this change in perceived intertemporal opportunities that prevents rational adaptation to the shock. The same 'as if static' method produced the conclusion that *liquidity preference versus loanable funds* was not a meaningful issue; that it does not matter whether the system is or is not potentially capable of adjusting intertemporal prices appropriately in response to changes in intertemporal opportunities.

The popularity and staying power of the *IS–LM* apparatus, especially in classroom teaching, rests not on its static but on its comparative static uses, however. In the course of the *Monetarist* debate, this method was employed to bolster the suggestion that the steady-state interest elasticities of the two schedules were central – or even *the* central – issues in contention. If the interest elasticity of *IS* is pretty far from infinite and that of *LM* pretty far from zero, standard curve-shifting exercises suggest that real disturbances should have monetary effects and monetary disturbances have real ones – although these interdependencies do not occur in our FIM theory. When reasonable assumptions are made about the interest elasticities of excess commodity and money demand, the *IS–LM* model seemingly will not allow the interest rate to adjust appropriately 'in the short run'. Monetary disturbances are shown to have real (allocative) effects because the interest rate changes – when in FIM it should not. Real disturbances have monetary (income) consequences – because the rate of interest does not change as far as (in FIM) it should.[34]

The reason why *IS–LM* seemingly will not allow equilibration in the short run, of course, is that it is habitually assumed that the disturbances in question will shift one reduced form and leave the other one put. Whether this procedure is justified or not is a question of some importance. Supply and demand analysis, as Marshall noted, is a useful tool in so far as the forces that shift one schedule do not also tend to shift the other. The same is true in this case. *IS–LM* as a modeling strategy – that is, first concentrating on obtaining the two reduced forms and then getting the answers by manipulating them – is really predicated on the procedure being justified. If, in response to the standard disturbances, *IS* and *LM* both shift, this modeling strategy makes little sense. When both shift more or less simultaneously, preoccupation with the elasticities is on the whole a mistake.

But FIM analysis shows that both schedules should shift – ultimately. The use of *IS–LM* 'as if' it were a comparative static apparatus is thus seen to involve the lag-assumption that one shifts before the other, that there will be a well-defined 'short-run' solution halfway in the process – and that macroeconomic policy-makers have their natural being in this halfway house. This imposed sequencing or lag structure rests on assumptions of incomplete information on the part of various groups of agents.

So, is the procedure of shifting *LM*, keeping *IS* constant – or vice versa – justified? The answer is: sometimes; perhaps often; but not necessarily or always. And that, very largely, is what is the matter with *IS–LM*.

## NOTES

1.  My own disaffection with *IS–LM*, obviously, starts here.
2.  Loanable funds versus liquidity preference started out, of course, as part and parcel of the Keynes and the classics debate. Following its wrongful dismissal from among the major issues of the latter, it has lived an independent and somewhat fitful existence as a some-time preoccupation of a small number of specialists in monetary general equilibrium theory. It is convenient to treat it as a separate set of issues here.
3.  Thus Professor Tobin would maintain, for example, that the magnitude of the interest elasticity of the *LM* reduced form is a critical issue between the two camps, while Professor Friedman maintains that it is not decisive in determining whether one is a 'Monetarist' or not.
4.  Students used to be told that the cobweb model oscillates 'because production takes time'. But the time-consuming nature of physical processes is significant only in so far as it is associated with an information lag.
5.  It is a world in which economic theory need not be taught and where the only economic research needed would be of the simplest fact-finding variety. What a threatening picture to paint on the wall!
6.  This is loosely paraphrased. For the original statement, see Hahn (1973).
7.  Disappointments or surprises of a sort may still occur. But they should then be in the nature of lottery outcomes (or harvest results), where it is too late for the winner or loser to do anything about it. Also, the outcome should not change the agent's willingness to play the game or the strategies he uses in doing so.
8.  Most of all, of course, we want to avoid calling the mathematical solution to an incomplete information model a 'short-run equilibrium'.
9.  This is not the only objection to Friedman's theory that is suggested when this loosely worded complaint is aired. But it will do for our illustrative purpose here.
10. Love at first sight is one example – a case of irrational expectations. In the drearier area of rational expectations, the example would be money at first sight.
11. If we replace (4.8) with (4.8′), however, a decline in MEC will produce not only a decline in the growth rate and a decrease in the real rate of interest, but also an increase in the amount of real balances demanded and hence a decline of the price level.
12. There is some recklessness here in the use of 'determine'. But the beginning student should not be bothered by 'missing equations' when first trying to fathom the familiar diagrams.
13. Beginning macroeconomics can be made even more challenging for him by suggesting that the reason for 'switching' what savings and investment are made to determine lies, somehow, in the short-run stickiness of money wages.
14. Worse than that, Model A clearly allows us to eliminate the *p*'s everywhere. Then it asserts, in addition, that shifts in investment must change real income, implying that the imperfection admitted as a possibility in model T is inescapably present also in A.
15. For our simple AT model to serve this purpose, its fifth equation had better be changed into $M^s = M(\underline{B}, r)$, with *B* denoting the monetary base.
16. Gibson's paradox is the positive correlation of the interest rate and price level over

business cycles. Tooke's stylized fact would be a better name for it, since Tooke was the first to pose it as an empirical challenge to monetary theories of nominal income movements. In the *IS–LM* setting, movements of the *LM* locus with *IS* stable should give rise to negative correlation between the interest rate and nominal income. In this discussion of *IS–LM* we will leave this (SF3) aside.

17. Empirically, do real disturbances cause income movements? Always, sometimes, or never? The Keynesian answer is that they always do (although Cambridge Keynesians would insist, as we will see, that they do so without creating an ED for money in the process). Monetarists think 'never' is the better conjecture.

18. Empirically, do they? Always, sometimes, or never? In the various macrotheories stemming from Wicksell (which include the Austrian and Keynesian theories), it is presumed that monetary impulses do work this way. In modern Monetarism it is presumed that they will always create an ED for commodities but not by disturbing the growth path. The clearest contrast, on this score, is that between Hayek and Friedman.

19. Also known as a one-armed bandit. For four 'lemons' in a row, the machine will pay the general equilibrium jackpot.

20. If we had chosen to draw Figure 4.1 with real income, *X*, rather than nominal income, $pX \equiv Y$, on the horizontal axis, this part of the story would be told in terms of rising prices gradually reducing real balances back to their initial level. *LM'* would be shown to shift back rather than *IS* also shifting out. For present purposes, having the diagram in terms of nominal income seems pedagogically preferable. Doing the exercise in real income has the advantage of highlighting the point of the Archibald–Lipsey critique of Patinkin, namely that real balance effects result from evaluating nominal balances at disequilibrium prices. If and when we can assume that money balances are evaluated at equilibrium prices, we regain the valid classical dichotomy, that is to say, the FIM 'independence' of real phenomena from monetary ones.

21. Except in so far as the transitory period of producing at false prices has also left a legacy of disequilibrium stocks of capital (as in Hayekian overinvestment theory).

22. It is an account that I tend to associate especially with the work of Brunner and Meltzer in the 1960s. But see also Friedman and Schwartz (1963).

23. I am thinking here of the later position of Friedman, according to which the central bank has no influence over the real rate of interest, liquidity effects on the real rate are insignificant and evanescent, and the interest elasticity of money demand is irrelevant to the effectiveness of monetary policy. In my opinion, as is clear from the text, the *IS–LM* representation of this theory should show both *IS* and *LM* shifting together at the impact of a monetary disturbance. The elasticities are then irrelevant. However, Friedman has (I think) muddied the waters by suggesting that the *IS* schedule should perhaps be drawn horizontal. See, for example, Friedman (1976).

24. Passing through the Monetarist black box that is so often the object of complaints.

25. For the contrast between loanable funds and liquidity preference, see following section.

26. Note that the liquidity preference theory of interest rate determination predicts, instead, that in the state depicted in row (3) the interest rate will rise.

27. We have chosen to put real income, *X*, on the horizontal axis in this exercise.

28. But liquidity preference, in the very different sense of the hypothesis that the ED for money governs the interest rate, is better dispensed with, however; see next section.

29. See also Leijonhufvud (1969, pp. 14ff.), where 'Keynes's special case' – as Modigliani called the liquidity trap possibility – is also considered.

30. Note that, since this unemployment disequilibrium is due to the inconsistency of the beliefs of entrepreneurs (with respect to MEC) and of securities markets investors (with respect to $r^*$), it is not to be cured by persuading wage earners that the (FIM) level of wages is too high.

31. Deflation helps in this instance, because the new FIM state that the system should reach requires larger real balances. In the earlier exercise, where the excess demand for money developed for speculative reasons, the FIM money demand function was supposed to be interest-inelastic, so that the new FIM equilibrium required the same wage and price level as the old one.

32. Model A – the 'Keynesian cross' – properly portrays a system with the dynamic properties of Table 4.3.
33. And looking elsewhere for the 'missing equation(s)' that will determine the price and output components of nominal income.
34. This maladjustment of the interest rate is the theme of 'The Wicksell Connection' (Leijonhufvud 1981b).

# 5. Hicks on time and money

Modern macroeconomic theory has been shaped to an extraordinary degree by Keynes and by Hicks. My assignment was to discuss them both, but I have found it too large for a paper. I will confine my discussion of Hicks's role to two related themes: time and money.

Even within these boundaries, the following attempt at an interpretation cannot be definitive.[1] Among the several reasons for this, one is germane: I know that I shall learn more from Sir John Hicks in the future. But I cannot know exactly what I shall learn next time I sit down to read or reread him. Hence today's assessment cannot be my 'optimal' or final one. Rather than commit myself fully, I should retain a measure of 'flexibility'.[2]

In certain types of situations, it is rational to commit oneself fully or contingently. In others, where the future contingencies cannot be enumerated or their nature anticipated, one should retain flexibility. One difference between neoclassical and Keynesian theory is that the former tends to exclude, whereas the latter must include, situations of the second sort.[3] The younger Hicks is remembered for his contributions to neoclassical economics; over the years the elder Hicks has become more insistently Keynesian in this particular sense.

## TIME AND EQUILIBRIUM

'Every economist is familiar with the accomplishments of Hicks the Younger, whether he has read him or not. That brilliant young man was supremely successful – by reformulating utility theory, by simplifying monetary theory, by interpreting Keynes and the Classics, and by reviving general equilibrium theory – in constructing the moulds into which 40 years of subsequent theoretical developments were to be cast'.[4] It is helpful to try to see the young Hicks in historical context.

What went on at the London School of Economics in the early 1930s appears in retrospect almost as important as what was going on in Cambridge. At LSE, the world of Anglo-American economics was being won over from the tradition of Ricardo and Marshall to modern neoclassical economics – or, in the terms of Hicks the Elder, from 'plutology' to 'catallactics'. If Cambridge was sufficient unto its British self, Lionel Robbins's London School encouraged the study of the Austrian and Lausanne schools, of the Americans and the Swedes. ('We were such "good Europeans" in London that it was Cambridge that seemed "foreign".')[5] Robbins brought F.A. von Hayek to London and assembled a stable of superbly talented junior people: R.G.D. Allen, Marian Bowley, John Hicks and Ursula Webb-Hicks, Nicholas Kaldor, Abba Lerner, Vera Smith-Lutz, Richard Sayers and G.L.S. Shackle. Most importantly, Robbins wrote the programmatic tract that, highly controversial in its time, has long since permeated the teaching of economics to the point where its main message has become a platitude (thus depriving its author of the Nobel Prize?). His *Nature and Significance of Economic Science* (Robbins 1932) argued the 'scarcity' definition of economics, a definition that fundamentally changed both the scope and the content of Marshall's subject. Robbins made rational means–ends calculation the core of economics.

It was the younger Hicks who demonstrated how this Robbins program could be realized. The Hicks–Allen 'Reconsideration' (Hicks and Allen 1934) recast demand theory in terms of rational decision theory. Hicks's simplification of monetary theory drew money into the orbit of marginalist calculation. 'Taking step after step along a road which seemed pre-ordained as soon as one had taken the first step' in a few years time led to the 'static' parts (Chapters 1–8) of *Value and Capital* (Hicks 1939).[6] These were the parts of Hicks's early work that, together with 'Keynes and the Classics', were to have such a profound and pervasive influence on how economics was to be taught in the United States in the era when American economics was becoming strongly predominant. Perhaps it is more accurate to say that these parts of Hicks's work were selected by the generation of American economists led by Paul Samuelson who were re-erecting the structure of economic theory using constrained optimization building blocks.

Pure decision theory, formalized as optimization subject to constraints, is essentially timeless. The choice among the foreseen outcomes of alternative actions[7] is a purely logical calculus that does not involve time in any essential way. Thus was created a durable tension between neo-Walrasian microtheory and Keynesian macrotheory which, decades later, was to culminate in crisis.

This could hardly have been foreseen. As Robert Clower has remarked,[8]

[I]t was only natural for economists generally to proceed on the presumption that general equilibrium theory had no inherent limitations ... That any even moderately 'general' economic model should [be incapable of representing Keynesian processes] ... would hardly occur naturally to any but a very perverse mind. That the elaborate Neo-Walrasian model set out in Hicks' *Value and Capital* might fail [in this respect] would have seemed correspondingly incredible to any sensible person at the outset of the Neo-Walrasian Revolution.

The younger Hicks knew that time was a problem. We find him wrestling with it in almost all the parts of his early work that did *not* become part of the American neoclassical canon. It was to become even more of a preoccupation – an unfashionable preoccupation – for Hicks the Elder.

From the first, it seems, Hicks saw it as a supreme theoretical challenge, deserving the most sustained effort, to find a mode of process analysis that would retain a role for equilibrium constructions without denying (or trivializing) change. In the early going, this amounted to finding a workable way between Walras and Pareto, on the one hand, and Knight and Hayek on the other.[9] Thirty or forty years later, the opposed alternatives – Arrow–Debreu versus Shackle or Lachmann – are clearer and also further apart. In the Arrow–Debreu construction, the rational choice of each agent is defined over all dimensions of commodity–time–contingency space; the result is that all decisions are made once and for all at the origin of time. To obtain a model in which decisions are made in temporal sequence, agents must be ignorant of some of the information that is necessary in order to calculate all optimal allocations at the beginning of time. Thus Shackle poses the issue with uncompromising force: '[T]he theoretician is confronted with a stark choice. He can reject rationality or time.'[10]

The American neo-Walrasians, from Paul Samuelson to Robert Lucas, have not seen this choice as at all difficult. In general, they have simply gone whole hog for Rationality, letting Time and Change be trampled underfoot in the philosophical muck as unfit food for economic thought. If forced (somehow) to choose, it is possible that Hicks the Younger might also have opted for rational allocation theory; Hicks the Elder almost certainly would opt for economic history. In actuality, Hicks fought fifty years to maintain a conceptual middle ground.

The issue may have come into focus at LSE precisely because all of the neoclassical schools were to some extent cultivated in the circle around Robbins and Hayek. Marshall had been aware of the problem[11] and had devised a method that at least partly evaded it. Hayek had worked on the construction of an equilibrium process 'in time' and had found himself forced back onto 'perfect foresight' assumptions.[12] Robbins had drawn the conclusion that: 'The main postulate of the theory of dynamics is the fact that we are not certain regarding future scarcities'.[13]

As matters stood around 1930, the static toolbox of economic theory was strictly applicable only to stationary, perfect foresight processes. It was not at all clear that economic theory provided any foundation for the disciplined analysis of monetary questions or business cycles. Hicks's earliest work dramatized the predicament. In particular, his remarkable 1933 paper on 'Equilibrium and the Cycle'[14] drove home a point made by Knight: that in a perfect foresight equilibrium process, people would not demand cash balances. This spelt trouble for the most sophisticated cycle theory available at the time. What became of Hayek's notion of 'neutral money' as a criterion for maintaining macroeconomic equilibrium, if in equilibrium there could be no place for money, 'neutral' or otherwise?

The Swedish followers of Wicksell had run into similar quandaries, and it was from Myrdal and Lindahl that Hicks got help with the next step. [15] The next step had to be a method of describing economic processes that (a) was not confined to just 'perfect foresight' processes, and (b) still did not force the abandonment of the entire apparatus of inherited static theory. Lindahl's temporary equilibrium method[16]

> reduced the process of change to a sequence of single periods, such that, in the interior of each, change could be neglected ... Everything is just the same as with the 'static' kind of process analysis ... save for one thing: that expectations are explicitly introduced as independent variables in the determination of the single-period equilibrium.

Thus, when the *General Theory* appeared, Hicks had been working along these lines for some time. His first reaction gave pride of place to Keynes's use of a similar device: a short-run equilibrium adapting to independently specified long-term expectations.[17] But the kinship was not all that close. Keynes had applied the 'methods of expectations' to a Marshallian short period. Marshall had invented a kind of analysis ('with some slight dynamic flavouring')[18] which definitely was 'in time' but which left the line between statics and dynamics unclear. In *Value and Capital*, Hicks developed an alternative line of attack.

The attack starts with the famous definition of 'economic dynamics' as those parts of economic theory 'where every quantity must be dated'.[19] This was an important step. The Marshallians, for example, had not taken it.

By itself, the dating of goods only adds dimensions to the commodity space considered in 'timeless' statics. Studies in efficient intertemporal resource allocation following Fisher and Hicks have improved our understanding of capital, growth and interest theory immensely. But the course of this development became quite similar to what happened to British classical theory, about which Hicks observed: 'The more precise capital theory became, the more static it became; the study of equilibrium conditions only resulted in the study of stationary states.'[20] We have to substitute 'steady' for 'stationary', of course, but otherwise the conclusion holds. It is presumably for this reason that Hicks no longer favours his old static–dynamic distinction but prefers to talk of analysis that is 'out of time' or 'in time'.[21]

Dating brings in future time, but it does not necessarily help in bringing in the passage of time. If the usual (stochastically) perfect knowledge assumptions are made, the end result will be the Arrow–Debreu contingency market model in which all decisions are made at the origin of time. There is no business left to transact at later dates. Money and liquidity can be forced into such a structure only by obvious artifice.

The present-day practice at this juncture is for the theorist to retire behind a smoke screen while intoning some incantation about transactions costs. Hicks, in 1939, did a bit better. 'What must be done is to weaken the informational assumptions of the model so as to make agents postpone at least some decisions "until they know better".'[22] Hicks discussed several types of uncertainty and decided, I think correctly, that agents' uncertainty about their own intentions was the most fundamental[23]

> [I]n particular, they know that they cannot foretell at all exactly what quantities they will themselves desire to buy or sell at a future period ... and this it is, in the end, which limits the extent to which forward trading can be carried on in practice.

This argument is the bridge by which Hicks made his escape from steady-state capital theory into temporary equilibrium theory. In the temporary equilibrium theory of *Value and Capital*, time is divided into a sequence of 'weeks'. Planned demands and supplies for the week depend on current prices and expected future prices. Current prices are determined on 'Monday' and rule unchanged for the rest of the week. On 'Sunday' (we may imagine), the parameters of the equilibrium system are updated: changes in stocks are accounted for and price expectations revised. The system is then ready for another Monday morning.

In this story, all markets cleared each Monday. Hicks understood perfectly that this assumption by itself did not preclude periods of subnormal activity in the system. The defence of the assumption that he suggested is exactly the one so strenuously insisted upon by Lucas, Barro, et alia almost forty years later. In Hicksian terms, if price expectations are inelastic, a fall in current prices will induce intertemporal substitution: supplies will be shifted from this week into next.[24] Market clearing, however, was equilibrium in a 'limited sense'; in the more fundamental sense of 'equilibrium over time', Hicks emphasized, the economic system was 'usually out of equilibrium'.[25]

This temporary equilibrium method is thus clearly distinct both from Keynes's short-run equilibrium, on the one hand, and from the New Classical equilibrium method of more recent years. It avoids some of the problems of the alternatives and deserves further exploration, therefore,[26] although, of course, it has problems of its own. But, while Hicks resumed the struggle for a systematic 'in time' analysis later – and on more difficult ground even[27] – he chose to abandon the temporary equilibrium approach.

Why? The elder Hicks has given his retrospective reasons. There were problems *within* the 'week' and *between* 'weeks':[28]

> Much too much had to happen on that 'Monday'! And ... I was really at a loss how to deal with the further problem of how to string my 'weeks' and my 'Mondays' together.

Getting from one 'week' to the next required both a theory of capital accumulation and a theory of the revision of expectations. The first problem by itself was forbidding at the time; only the later development of modern growth theory made it manageable. Forty years have not brought us much advance on the second problem.[29]

In his retrospective evaluation, Hicks does not point to the problems that the temporary equilibrium method would have to overcome in order to provide a 'continuation' theory; instead, he focuses on how the method dealt with events 'within the week':[30]

> I tried to go further [than to work with *given* expectations], to allow for the effects of current transactions on expectations; supposing that these effects could (somehow) be contemporaneous with the transactions themselves... That however was nonsense ... It does deliberate violence to the *order* in which in the real world (in *any* real world) events occur ... It was this device, this indefensible trick, which ruined the 'dynamic' theory of *Value and Capital*. It was this that led it back in a static, and so in a neo-classical, direction.

What an extraordinarily harsh judgement this is! Why? Because in obliterating the *sequence* in which things happen, the model comes to ignore the structure of markets. It matters, for instance, whether people commit themselves on quantities and discover their mistakes through price change 'surprises' or set their prices and see their errors revealed in the behavior of quantities.[31] It matters, in Hicks's terms, whether the markets in the system are mostly of the *flex-price* or the *fixed-price* variety. In this century, 'the unorganized flexprice market, the old type, is on the way out ... modern markets are predominantly of the fixprice type.'[32] In Hicks's view, this historical transformation is of major macroeconomic significance. The change in the predominant market form is a change in the way that impulses are propagated through the system. The harsh language becomes understandable for, of course, Hicks sees the 'indefensible trick' still being practised all over!

## IS–LM

The younger Hicks may have had somewhat different reasons for abandoning his temporary equilibrium method. One of them surely was that Keynes had come up with an alternative method of short-period analysis. It was a rough and ready sort of short-period method and Hicks the Younger would have realized better than anybody else how rough it was. But it seemed to be adequate for Keynes's purposes and Hicks agreed that Keynes's purposes were the supremely important ones.

Soon after his original review, Hicks returned to the *General Theory* and wrote 'Mr. Keynes and the "Classics": A Suggested Interpretation'. The *IS–LM* apparatus of this immensely influential paper was not a Walrasian (or Paretian) construction but a hybrid. Keynes's macrotheory was built with Marshallian microcomponents. But the modeling idea was, as Hicks has himself explained,[33] borrowed from *Value and Capital*, where he had worked out a two-dimensional representation of the equilibrium for a Walrasian system of three markets.

The *IS–LM* model summarized numerous features of the *General Theory* with admirable economy, and it was to serve in the deduction of numerous Keynesian comparative statics propositions that Keynes had not thought of. The model became the backbone of instruction in macroeconomics for forty years. Nonetheless, something was just a bit askew with it. In later years, Hicks has several times come back to reassess it and the uses to which it has been put. In brief, (a) he has remained fairly content with it as a synopsis of Keynes's theory;[34] (b) he has become less satisfied with it as a way of portraying the 'classics' and hence as a tool for isolating Keynes's contributon by *IS–LM* comparisons;[35] and (c) he has grown somewhat sceptical about it as a general purpose framework for macroeconomic analysis.[36] His several commentaries on *IS-LM* all focus on the problem of time.

From the early 1950s to the mid-1960s, Hicks did not participate much in ongoing developments in economic theory.[37] When he returned to theoretical work full-time, he was eager to learn what had been accomplished in growth theory but found himself out of sympathy with the directions taken in macroeconomics and monetary theory. The trouble was that these directions had been set by Hicks the younger – in those parts of his work that the American economists had chosen to cultivate. Hicks's first dismaying confrontation with his own brain-children – now fully grown and so independent! – came, it appears, in 1957, when he was asked to review Patinkin's first edition. Patinkin's work had been systematically and rigorously built on the basis of the Hicks–Allen 'Reconsideration', the paper 'simplifying' monetary theory, 'Keynes and the Classics', and the first eight chapters of *Value and Capital* (together with some closely related works by Oscar Lange).[38] But the theoretical structure that Patinkin had erected on these foundations, Hicks thought, threatened to emasculate Keynesian economics.[39] Never a whole-hearted Keynesian, Hicks was nonetheless too much of a Keynesian to stand idly by under the circumstances.

Patinkin's basic model was a Walrasian general equilibrium model, built up from choice-theoretical individual experiments, via aggregation, to equilibrium market experiments. It allowed no Marshallian distinctions between short-run and long-run equilibria. It was either in 'the' equilibrium or not in equilibrium at all. Patinkin used the Hicksian technique for portraying the equilibrium of an aggregative version of the system as the intersection of two reduced forms in interest/income space. It 'looked' exactly like *IS–LM* – except that this version would not allow for unemployment.[40]

Hicks set out to show that 'classical' and Keynesian theory 'do not overlap all the way' – that all the Keynesian furore had not been pointless. His point of departure was the right one:[41]

> The crucial point, as I now feel quite clear, on which the individuality of the Keynes theory depends, is the implication ... that there are conditions in which the interest-mechanism will not work.

In the original Patinkin review, Hicks tried to show this in two ways. His first argument, however, amounted to a reassertion of the liquidity trap explanation of unemployment and Patinkin had only to repeat his demonstration of how, with flexible wages, the Pigou effect would restore full employment. Within the *IS–LM* context, the explanation of unemployment is thus thrown back to the 'rigid wages' postulate.[42] Hicks's second and surviving argument attempted to clarify the relationship between Keynes and the 'classics' by showing how the parameters of the *IS–LM* model depend on the length of period assumed. The extent to which wages are variable, Hicks pointed out, will depend not only on the magnitude of excess demand (or supply) of labour but also on the length of time allowed for adjustment. Over a sufficiently long period, the *IS* schedule should then be infinitely elastic (at the 'natural rate' of interest), while the speculative component disappears from money demand so that the *LM* schedule becomes quite inelastic. With a shorter period, the 'classical' dichotomy fails, and the shorter the period the more 'Keynesian' the picture: *IS* becomes very inelastic and *LM* exceedingly elastic in the very short run.[43]

This defense of Keynes (if such it was) could only focus attention on Keynes's own treatment of time, however. Hicks's reservations on this score (as well as those of other 'critical readers') went back all the way to the 1930s: 'but we have agreed to suspend our doubts because of the power of the analysis which Keynes constructed on this (perhaps) shaky foundation'.[44] It could not be left at that indefinitely. In his 1974 effort to address *The Crisis in Keynesian Economics*, Hicks left the matter to one side and simply made no use of *IS–LM* at all. But in *The Crisis*, he advanced the theory of liquidity as flexibility as one of the needed cures for the ailing Keynesian tradition. In contrast to how it emerges in static portfolio theory,[45]

> liquidity is not a property of a single choice; it is a matter of a sequence of choices, a related sequence. It is concerned with the passage from the known to

the unknown with the knowledge that if we wait we can have more knowledge. So it is not sufficient, in liquidity theory, to make a single dichotomy between the known and the unknown. There is a further category, of things which are unknown now, but will become known in time.

This, clearly, lends urgency to the question of how time is to be treated in Keynesian models. Immediately afterward, therefore, Hicks turned to re-examine the compromises of Keynes's method and found them, on close inspection, less and less satisfactory:[46]

> Keynes's theory has one leg which is in time, but another which is not. It is a hybrid. I am not blaming him for this; he was looking for a theory which would be effective, and he found it... but what a muddle he made for his successors!

In brief, the 'leg in time' is *LM*, the 'leg in equilibrium' is *IS*. (Clearly, this 'straddle', as Hicks called it, was a position that had to become uncomfortable with the passage of time! Hicks's own temporary equilibrium method[47]

> also was divided; there was a part that was in time and a part that was not. But we did not divide in the same place. While Keynes had relegated the whole theory of production and prices to equilibrium economics, I tried to keep production in time, just leaving prices to be determined in an equilibrium manner.

Production will not be equilibrated in a 'week'. Hicks's (1983b) 'IS–LM: An Explanation' carries the argument forward:[48]

> If one is to make sense of the *IS–LM* model while paying proper attention to time, one must, I think, insist on two things: (1) that the period in question is a relatively long period, a 'year' rather than a 'week'; and (2) that, because the behaviour of the economy over that 'year' is to be determined by propensities and such-like data, it must be assumed to be, in an appropriate sense, *in equilibrium*.

Product markets are in flow equilibrium throughout the 'year'; production plans are being carried through without disappointment or surprise; this, in Hicks's view, is how we must interpret the *IS* curve. What about the *LM* curve? It is a stock-relation and, by itself, could apply simply to a point in time. But to be consistent with the *IS* construction, Hicks points out, a more restrictive equilibrium condition should be applied, namely maintenance of stock equilibrium throughout the 'year'. Expectations and realizations must be consistent within the period. But at this point of his 1983 argument, we are suddenly back facing the dilemma of that 1933 paper: 'disequilibrium is the disappointment of expectations' – and in equilibrium processes there is no place for money! The 'Equilibrium method, applied to liquidity over a period, will not do'.[49]

Within the *IS–LM* construction itself, therefore, we find this tension between equilibrium and change which I see as a *Leitmotiv* through five decades
of Hicks's work. Hicks is 'quite prepared to believe that there are cases'
where we are 'entitled to overlook' the potential inconsistency between the
ways that the *IS* and the *LM* have been constructed. But he clearly no longer
regards it as a robust tool for the analysis of almost all macroeconomic
questions.[50]

*IS–LM* served us well for so long (didn't it?). How could we not have run
into obvious problems with it, if it teeters on the brink of conceptual inconsistency? *IS–LM* exercises produce the right answers (most of us will agree)
to a large number of standard macroquestions. Yet, it produces the wrong
conclusions (some of us insist) on some issues. Hicks leaves us with a
general scepticism about the method that does not help us much in determining what uses are safe and what uses are not.

In an attempt to find out what was the matter with *IS–LM*, I came to a
conclusion very similar to Hicks's judgment on the temporal equilibrium
method: as with all equilibrium constructions, *IS–LM* ignores the sequence of
events *within the period*. The result can be nonsense:[51]

> IS–LM, handled as if it were a static construction … produced a nonsensical
> conclusion to the *Keynes and the classics* debate: namely, that Keynes had revolu-
> tionized economic theory by advancing the platitude that wages too high for full
> employment and rigid downwards imply persistent unemployment. It failed to
> capture essential elements of Keynes's theory: namely, that the typical shock is a
> shift in investors' expectations and that it is the failure of intertemporal prices to
> respond appropriately to this change in perceived intertemporal opportunities that
> prevents rational adaptation to the shock. The same 'as if static' method produced
> the conclusion that *liquidity preference versus loanable funds* was not a meaning-
> ful issue; that it does not matter whether the system is or is not potentially capable
> of adjusting intertemporal prices appropriately in response to changes in
> intertemporal opportunities.[52]

Ignoring sequencing becomes a source of trouble in particular in connection with comparative statics uses of the *IS–LM* model, that is, the uses that
are the stuff which macrotexts have been made of for several decades, but
which Hicks did not consider in reassessing the model.

Consider, for illustrative purposes, the analysis of an increase in the supply
of money in the common textbook context where the money supply is simply
an exogenously fixed $M$. Full adjustment to this parametric disturbance requires a proportional rise in all money prices, with no effect on output,
employment or other real magnitudes. In an *IS–LM* diagram with money
income on the horizontal axis, both schedules have shifted the same distance
rightwards. In a Lucas model, if $M$ is observable, the system goes to this
position immediately. In a Friedman model (of, say, ten years ago), on the

other hand, nominal income responds strongly in relatively short order, but part of this is an increase in real output and employment, and full adjustment to the neutral equilibrium takes 'longer'. In a Keynesian model (of twenty years ago?), finally, the 'short-run' reactions are that the interest rate falls, velocity declines, investment and employment increase a bit, while the price level stays about the same.

All three possibilities can be demonstrated with the same basic model. How, then, do they differ? To Friedman, the Phillips curve is vertical only over the 'long run', not already in the 'short run' as in Lucas. In Friedman's short run, the monetary disturbance has output effects because the people temporarily miscalculate real wages. To the Keynesians, the (approximately) proportional increase in nominal income occurs only over the 'long run', not already in the 'short run' as in Friedman. In the Keynesian short run, the monetary disturbance has only weak effects on nominal income now, because people fail to anticipate the effect that it must have on nominal aggregate demand sooner or later; hence the short-run effects on income occur only in so far as some firms are induced by a fall in the interest rate to increase their investment, even though their expectations of future nominal aggregate demand have not improved.[53]

So, Lucas's people are assumed to know something that Friedman people do not, and Friedman people something that Keynesian people do not.[54] The temporal order of decisions matters when information is incomplete, when people have to react to situations they did not foresee, and when they learn from realizations they did not anticipate. Such learning can be slow or fast or, in some cases, not needed.

Note how these knowledge or learning assumptions are reflected in the mechanics of manipulating the *IS–LM* diagram. In the Keynesian exercise, *LM* shifts right, *IS* stays put, and the short-run effects depend on the elasticities of the two reduced forms. In the Friedman case, *IS* also shifts, although perhaps not quite all the way; the elasticities then are practically irrelevant. In the Lucas case, both reduced forms shift in parallel fashion. The *IS–LM* modeling strategy would seem to presuppose that we have to deal with a Keynesian world of slow learners. Otherwise it does not seem to make sense to adopt the two-stage procedure of, first, deriving the two reduced forms and, second, getting the answers by shifting one and keeping the other constant. The use of *IS–LM* as if it were a comparative static apparatus involves the lag-assumption that one schedule shifts before the other and that there will be a well-defined 'short-run' solution halfway in the equilibrating process. This sequencing or lag structure rests on assumptions of incomplete information on the part of various agents in the model.[55]

This conclusion we have derived from an illustrative case where Monetarist assumptions are made about the supply of money. There is, however, another possible interpretation of Keynesian *IS–LM* analysis which we will come to later.

## MONEY AND HISTORY

In the most exciting chapter of his *Critical Essays in Monetary Theory*, Hicks (1967a) sought to structure two centuries of monetary writings in a simple, striking and informative way. His 'Monetary Theory and History – An Attempt at Perspective' was critical of ahistorical monetary theorizing and insisted on the necessity of doing monetary theory in historical and institutional context. It also suggested that the history of monetary controversy could be understood as a running battle between two traditions, a 'metallic money' tradition and a 'credit money' tradition.

The 'metallic money' theorists, in Hicks's schema, focused on equilibrium propositions in their theorizing, dealt analytically with money 'as if' it were a commodity, and strove to reduce monetary policy to obedience to some 'mechanical rule'. Credit theorists, on the other hand, saw money as part of the overall system of debits and credits that extends beyond the banking system to encompass the entire economy. Credit expansions and contractions were central to their conception of the subject and so obliged them to try their luck at disequilibrium analyses, always aware that credit rests on confidence. Finally, writers in this tradition saw monetary policy as an exercise in judgment of contemporary conditions. Hicks named Ricardo the patron saint of the 'metallic' tradition and gave Thornton the same status in the 'credit' school of thought. He saw the currency school and, later, Hayek, Pigou, Rueff and Friedman as Ricardo's followers and put the banking school, Bagehot, Wicksell, Hawtrey, Robertson and Keynes, in line of descent from Thornton.

In insisting on the close link between monetary theory and history, Hicks thought above all of the evolution of credit markets and financial institutions: 'In a world of banks and insurance companies, money markets and stock exchanges, money is quite a different thing from what it was before these institutions came into being.'[56] The metallic money theorists (including the modern Monetarists) seemed determined to ignore this historical development. Consequently, Hicks's analysis suggested, time had put an ever increasing distance between their theory and reality.[57]

The 1967 'Perspective' helps one understand what Hicks regards as the important themes running through his own contributions to monetary theory.[58] Consider, once again, what aspects of the work of Hicks the Younger came to be influential and what aspects ignored. For decades, all graduate students have learned that the modern choice-theoretical money demand function stems from his 1935 'Simplifying' paper. Most will know that Hicks already had the demand for money depending on wealth, on anticipated yields on alternative placements and on the cost of asset transactions. Some may recall that his analysis was anything but reassuring on the stability of the function in terms of these arguments. Few (I am guessing) will remember that, in Hicks's hands, the theory immediately suggested the beginnings of a theory of financial structure, of the composition of balance sheets and of intermediation. Balance sheet equilibria, he noted,[59]

> [are] determined by subjective factors like anticipations, instead of objective factors like prices, [which] means that this purely theoretical study of money can never hope to reach results so tangible and precise as those which value theory in its more limited field can hope to attain. If I am right, the whole problem of applying monetary theory is largely one of deducing changes in anticipations from the changes in the objective data which call them forth. Obviously, this is not an easy task, and, above all, it is not one which can be performed in mechanical fashion.

In our textbooks, Hicks's paper is remembered for a money demand function with which any latter-day Monetarist could be comfortable. But, clearly, he was in the credit tradition from the beginning!

Moreover, it is the neglected themes of Hicks the Younger that the Elder has taken up and carried forward. The first step beyond his 1935 position came three decades later with the sketch in *Capital and Growth* (1965) of a simple financial system, consisting of a bank, household savers and firms:[60]

> Savers can hold their assets in bank money, or in securities (loans or equities) of the producing firms ... Firms have real assets, and they may have bank money; they have debts to the bank, and to the savers. The bank has debts owing to it from the firms; it owes debts (bank money) to the firms and to the savers.

The 'Two Triads' of 1967 introduced the classification of assets into running asset, reserve assets and investment assets; the specific assets that served these functions would differ between the balance sheets of households, firms and banks; for each type of transactor, the three classes of assets could be matched up with Keynes's transactions, precautionary and speculative motives; in Hicks's treatment, however, these three were no longer just motives for holding money but for preferring balance sheets of a certain structure. In 'Monetary Experience and the Theory of Money' (1977), the financial structure of Keynes's world was envisaged as three concentric sectors: (1) a banking 'core' with monetary liabilities and financial securities as assets; (2) a financial 'mantle' owing financial securities and holding industrial securities; and (3) an outer 'industry' owing the industrial securities and holding (the hard crust of?) the economy's productive assets (and some financial assets and money). In 'Foundations of Monetary Theory', Hicks added to this 'monocentric' credit economy model, some analysis also of a 'polycentric' world of multiple central banks (and flexible exchange rates).

What do we get out of this 'credit' approach that a Monetarist supply and demand for 'money' apparatus would not provide with less trouble? Hicks, of course, uses his financial structure model routinely in the analysis of a broad range of questions. In my view, however, the significant advantage of his approach is that it gives a better picture of the financial and monetary consequences of 'real causes': a rise in the anticipated yields on real capital will change the configuration of balance sheets desired by the business, household and banking sectors; the financing of investment will in part be intermediated by the banks; consequently, an increase in income due to a rise in marginal efficiency of capital will normally be associated not only with a rise in velocity but also with an *endogenous* increase in the money supply.

Hicks's insistence on linking monetary theory to monetary history has been echoed in recent years by rational expectations theorists, who insist that we must link short-run monetary theory to *monetary regimes*. These modern writers, however, have come to their preoccupation with the conditional nature of monetary theory from an entirely different angle. Their concern has been to keep track, not of slowly evolving financial institutions and markets, but of rapidly changing nominal (price-level) expectations. A 'monetary regime' may be defined as a system of expectations that governs the behavior of the public and is sustained by the consistent behavior of the monetary authorities.[61] Since the short-run effects of particular policy actions, for example, depend upon the expectations of the public, it follows that we need a different short-run macromodel for each monetary regime. A regime change occurs when the behavior rules followed by the monetary authorities change. This 'regime approach' directs our attention to the history of monetary standards, viewed as methods for controlling the level of nominal prices, and to the system of nominal expectations that would (rationally) go with each such method.

Historically, we find two basic but contrasting conceptions of how price-level control can be accomplished. I have labelled them the 'quantity principle' and the 'convertibility principle'. Briefly (and perhaps a bit too simply) we may say that the quantity principle dictates that the government should control the 'quantity of money' while the private sector sets the price level; the convertibility principle, in contrast, dictates that the government set the nominal price of some 'standard commodity', while the private sector determines the quantity of money.[62] The logically tidiest version of the first would be a fiat standard with flexible exchange rates, and of the second, a commodity standard with 'hard money' still in circulation. Price expectations on the fiat standard are almost entirely a matter of beliefs about what the government might choose to do; price expectations on the commodity standard (conditional on the belief that the standard will be adhered to!) are almost entirely a matter of forecasting 'real' business developments.

The two contrasting systems give the extremes on a more or less continuous spectrum of monetary regimes. The last fifty-odd years have taken us from a position rather close to the commodity standard end (in 1929) all the way to the extreme fiat standard end (after 1971). We could proceed to classify macrotheories according to the segment of the regime spectrum over which they might claim validity.

This classification of theories according to control regime differs from the Hicksian schema of metallic money theories versus credit theories and may be a useful complement to it. This may be seen, for instance, by considering how the American Monetarists fit into Hicks's schema. In a metallic money world, money is a produced commodity and thus not neutral; the price level is determined (in the long run) by the cost of producing the metal; the money stock is endogenous and not subject to policy control; the 'mechanical' policy rule is to maintain the metallic standard. The 'mechanical' rule of the Monetarists is to fix the growth rate of some $M$; it is predicated on the belief that $M$ is neutral and controllable (and 'more or less' independent of endogeneous real factors); the object is to control nominal income in the short run and the price level over the longer run; fixed exchange rates are readily sacrificed to this end. When Hicks includes both Ricardo and Friedman in the same 'metallic' tradition, these points of contrast are obscured (even as the contrasts between Ricardo and Friedman, on the one hand, and Thornton and the Radcliffe Report, on the other, are brought into focus). Similarly, Hicks has come to prefer Wicksell's 'pure credit' model (of an economy without 'hard money') as his vehicle for explaining the central theoretical message of the 'credit tradition'.[63] But to a Monetarist audience, for instance, the main lesson of Wicksell's cumulative process is simply that, on a fiat standard, interest targeting of monetary policy produces nominal instability. A model of a system where convertibility anchors the price level – and, therefore, anchors rational price expectations as well – does a better job of fitting credit as a real magnitude into monetary theory. It is easier, in such a model, to show both how banking policy can influence investment and employment via the price and volume of 'real' credit and how real income movements can influence the supply of nominal money via the demand for 'real' credit.

Keynesian theory, to take a case in point, seems suited to regimes that behave as if monetary policy were constrained by the requirements of external, if not also internal, convertibility. The real quantity of money varies endogenously over the cycle in such regimes; nominal price level expectations should be inelastic, and the numeraire component of prices correspondingly sticky. This brings us back to *IS–LM*. Clearly, the old textbook repertory of *IS–LM* exercises will pass muster much better if interpreted as applying to an economy which retains some significant vestiges of convertible money systems. (An open economy with fixed exchange rates will do, for instance, as long as we are not thinking of the dominant reserve currency country.) But the textbook should not have specified $M$ as a given parameter, controlled by the central bank.[64] Under convertibility, the monetary authorities do not have the powers to regulate nominal income assumed by Friedman or by Lucas. The Keynesian picture (of *LM* shifting, *IS* staying put) of relatively modest effectiveness of monetary policy, transmitted via the price and volume of credit, is nearer to the mark. Keynesian theory should do fairly well, I have argued elsewhere,[65] as long as the monetary system still resembles the kind of system that Keynes strove for as a monetary reformer. Its lack of attention to inflationary expectations was on the whole appropriate to the Bretton Woods world. When the last vestiges of Bretton Woods were swept away, its neglect of inflationary expectations became a critical flaw. We should not have been so surprised!

## CONCLUSION

In some quarters, Hicks is routinely blamed for the paths we have taken from his ground-breaking early contributions. Those who do so blame him have not studied him very closely. 'One of the best reasons for studying the elder Hicks, in fact, is precisely that he is less a prisoner of the younger Hicks's constructions than are most of us.'[66] Among the lessons that Hicks the Elder would impress on us, I have tried to bring out two:[67]

> One must assume that the people in one's models do not know what is going to happen, and know that they do not know just what is going to happen. As in history!

Monetary theory, especially, has to be developed 'in time [with] future becoming present, and present becoming past, as time goes on'.[68] And 'it belongs to monetary history in a way that economic theory does not always belong to economic history'.[69]

## NOTES

1. I have made one previous attempt. 'Monetary Theory in Hicksian Perspective' (Leijonhufvud 1981c) was written in 1968 but not published until 1981, at which time I was still reasonably content with the paper. Once it was in print my understanding of some of the issues began to change – as I shall explain below.
2. Cf. Hicks, *The Crisis in Keynesian Economics* (1974), Chapter 2, and the antecedent by Hart (1942).

3. In stressing this particular distinction between neoclassical and Keynesian theory over others, I am following G.L.S. Shackle more than my own earlier work. See especially Shackle (1972).
4. Quoting my own review (Leijonhufvud 1979, p. 525) of *Economic Perspectives* (Hicks 1977).
5. Cf. the 'Commentary' to *The Theory of Wages* (1963), p. 306. 'Plutology' and 'catallactics' are discussed in Hicks's 'Revolutions in Eonomics', in Spiro Latsis (ed.) (1976), reprinted in Hicks (1983a).
6. See Hicks (1977), pp. v–vi.
7. The foreseen consequences may of course be probability distributions of outcomes. This does not alter the problem.
8. Cf. Clower (1975), p. 134.
9. See Hicks, 'The Formation of an Economist' (1979b, p. 199), now reprinted in Hicks (1983a).
10. See Shackle (1972), Preface.
11. Hicks (1965, pp. 47–8) quotes Marshall (1928, p. 379, n. 1): 'A theoretically perfect long period ... will be found to involve the supposition of a stationary state of industry, in which the requirements of a future age can be anticipated an indefinite time beforehand ... and it is to this cause more than to any other that we must attribute that simplicity and sharpness of outline, from which the economic doctrines in fashion in the first half of this century derived some of their seductive charm, as well as most of whatever tendency they may have had to lead to false practical conclusions'. Of course, the second half of the 20th century takes a generally more permissive attitude to 'seductive charms' than this most eminent Victorian among economists. Shackle's aptly titled chapter 'Marshall's Accommodation of Time', in Shackle (1972), gives a sample of other remarks of Marshall's indicating his preoccupation with the issue.
12. Cf. Hayek (1928).
13. Robbins (1932), p. 79.
14. See Hicks (1933). This remarkably modern, historically important paper was finally translated and published in *Economic Inquiry* (November 1980) thanks to its then editor, Robert Clower. It is now reprinted in Hicks (1982).
15. Myrdal's 'Geldtheoretisches Gleichgewicht' (1933) was reviewed by Hicks in *Economica* (November 1934). The review is reprinted in Hicks (1982). Shackle, also a member of the Robbins circle, testifies to the great influence and importance of Myrdal's contribution in Shackle (1967), Chapters 9 and 10. Of Lindahl's temporary equilibrium concept, Hicks first learned through personal acquaintance. He has discussed temporary equilibrium methods repeatedly, for example, in *Value and Capital* (1939), especially Chapters 9–10 and 20–22, in 'Methods of Dynamic Analysis' (1956) now reprinted in Hicks (1982), and in *Capital and Growth* (1965), Chapter 6.
16. Hicks (1965), p. 60.
17. Hicks's 1936 *Economic Journal* review is reprinted in *Money, Interest and Wages* (Hicks 1982) as 'The General Theory: A First Impression'.
18. Surely Hicks was thinking of Marshall when (*Value and Capital*, pp. 115–16) he declined to follow 'the usual course of economists in the past ... and give one's static theory some slight dynamic flavouring, [so that] it can be made to look much more directly applicable to the real world ... But it will still be quite incompetent to deal properly with capital and interest, or trade fluctuations, or even money'.
19. *Value and Capital*, p. 115.
20. *Capital and Growth*, p. 47.
21. See especially his 'Time in Economics', as reprinted in Hicks (1982), for example, p. 291: '[Steady-state economics] has encouraged economists to waste their time upon constructions that are often of great intellectual complexity but which are so much out of time, and out of history, as to be practically futile and indeed misleading. It has many bad marks to be set against it'.
22. It is for this reason that I have proposed changing the Hicksian definition of dynamics to 'those parts of economic theory where *decisions* must be dated' (cf. Leijonhufvud (1983b)).

23.  *Value and Capital*, p. 137. Of course, this way out of the predicament ultimately requires us to formulate a theory of the behaviour of agents who know that they are likely to 'foresee their own wants incorrectly' (p. 134). This problem Hicks did not tackle in 1939. It is in his *Crisis in Keynesian Economics*, Chapter 2, 35 years later, that we find it addressed (Hicks 1974). Decision-making by agents who know that they will know better later (but don't know, even probabilistically, what it is they will learn) will not fit naturally into the usual constrained optimization apparatus. For a comprehensive attack on the problem, cf. Heiner (1983).

24.  Cf. *Value and Capital*, p. 131: 'There is a sense in which current supplies and current demands are always equated in competitive conditions. Stocks may indeed be left in the shops unsold; but they are unsold because people prefer to take the chance of being able to sell them at a future date rather than cut prices in order to sell them now. The tendency for the current price to fall leads to a shift in supply from present to future. An excess of supply over demand which means more than this is only possible if the price falls to zero, or if the commodity is monopolized, or if the price is conventionally fixed'.

25.  *Value and Capital, loc. cit.*

26.  It took more than thirty years for the profession to catch on to what Hicks had been up to in 1939. Grandmont's survey (1977) shows how the crisis of Keynesianism, which was in part a crisis of Keynes's method, had produced a more profound appreciation of the difficulties that the temporary equilibrium approach had been designed to address.

27.  'The 'traverse' problem that Hicks set himself in *Capital and Growth* and analysed at length in *Capital and Time* adds a forbidding burden of capital theory to the difficulties discussed in the text.

28.  Cf. 'Time in Economics', in Hicks (1982), p. 290. In 1956 ('Methods of Dynamic Analysis'), Hicks distinguished between the problems of *single-period theory* and those of *continuation theory*. Cf. the reprint in 1982.

29.  A 'Robertson lag' in income is yet another possible bridge from 'week' to 'week'. In Leijonhufvud (1968c), I tried to get to the *General Theory* by this route: I had a first period in which sales declined because sellers had inelastic price expectations and thus did not cut prices fast enough; in the next week, demand was then 'income-constrained' with consequent Keynesian multiplier effects, and so on. I thought at the time that I had, in effect, got over from *Value and Capital* to the *General Theory* in fairly good order and it puzzled me why Hicks had not tried this route. But Hicks had defined his temporary equilibrium in such a way as to preclude unintended shortfalls in sales. See his comments below on the 'indefensible trick'.

30.  Hicks (1977), p. vii. The sentences in quotes are from *Capital and Growth*, Chapter 6, where the matter is also discussed. Compare also Clower (1975) and Clower and Leijonhufvud (1975).

31.  See Hicks (1956), section 4.

32.  *Economic Perspectives*, p. xi. Cf. also *Capital and Growth*, Chapter 7, and *Money, Interest, and Wages*, pp. 226–35, 296–9, 320–24.

33.  Cf. 'IS–LM: An Explanation', in Fitoussi (1983) and also included in Hicks (1982).

34.  Cf., for example, *The Crisis in Keynesian Economics*, p. 6, and 'Recollections and Documents' in *Economic Perspectives*. This paper also records Keynes's detailed and favourable reaction to the *IS–LM* representation of his theory.

35.  Cf. *Critical Essays in Monetary Theory*, p. vii: 'But as a diagnosis of the 'revolution' [IS–LM] is very unsatisfactory. It is not a bad representation of Keynes; but it does not get his predecessors (the 'Classics' as he called them) at all right.'

36.  Cf., for example, 'Time in Economics', in Hicks (1982), pp. 28–90: 'All the same, I must say that the diagram is now much less popular with me than I think it still is with many other people. It reduces the *General Theory* to equilibrium economics; it is not really *in* time. That, of course, is why it has done so well.'

37.  Approximately, from *A Contribution to the Theory of the Trade Cycle* (Hicks 1950) to *Capital and Growth* (Hicks 1965). Or, perhaps, for the duration of his tenure as Drummond Professor (1952–65). For his preoccupations during this period, cf. Hicks (1979b), p. 202.

38.  Lange (1942) and (1944).

39. The book, he said, was written not 'to elucidate the "Keynesian Revolution", but to deny that it is a revolution at all'. Cf. Hicks (1957). This judgment was not fair to Patinkin as Hicks has acknowledged. Cf. Hicks (1979c), n. 5.

40. Patinkin understood, of course, that this model would produce unemployment only if one imposed the restriction of rigid (and too high) wages. He also was quite clear on the fact that Keynes had assumed neither rigid wages nor a liquidity trap. (Patinkin 1948 had in any case demonstrated already that a liquidity trap would not by itself lead to unemployment in this type of model.) Consequently, he chose to deal with Keynesian unemployment informally, discussing the unemployment dynamics of the system 'off the curves' of his formal model. Cf. Patinkin (1956), Chapter 13.

41. Cf. 'The "Classics" Again', as reprinted in Hicks (1967), p. 143. My reasons for judging this to be the right point of departure are spelt out at great length in Leijonhufvud (1981b).

42. Cf. Hicks (1957); Patinkin (1959).

43. Coddington (1983, pp. 68–73) discusses this Hicksian analysis in somewhat more detail.

44. Cf. *Capital and Growth*, p. 65. The particular difficulty ('now lulled to sleep by long familiarity') mentioned in this context was that '[Keynes's theory] works with a *period* which is taken to be one of equilibrium ... and which is nonetheless identified with the Marshallian 'short period', in which capital equipment ... remains unchanged. The second seems to require that the period should not be too long, but the first that it should not be too short ... It is not easy to see that there can be any length of time that will adequately satisfy both of these requirements' (pp. 64–5). One notes that this observation would seem to threaten the legitimacy of Hicks's accordion playing with the period in his 'The "Classics" Again'.

45. *Crisis in Keynesian Economics*, pp. 38–9.

46. 'Time in Economics', in Hicks (1982), pp. 288–9.

47. Ibid., p. 290.

48. '*IS–LM*: An Explanation', in Fitoussi (1983), p. 57.

49. *Causality in Economics*, p. 85.

50. Cf. '*IS–LM*: An Explanation,' pp. 60–62. The brief summary in the text fails, I am afraid, to do justice to the subtlety of Hicks's argument. The reader who would appraise it should consult also his *Causality in Economics* (Hicks 1979a), Chapters 6 and 7.

51. Leijonhufvud (1983b), p. 86 (p. 108 in this volume). But the *IS–LM* interpretation of Keynes still has backers who feel that the algebra cannot but lead us right. Paul Samuelson (who has, of course, advocated the sticky wages view as preserving the essentials of Keynes's theory) sees preoccupation with the model's conceptual foundations as revealing some sort of anti-mathematical obscurantism. See his Keynes centennial article in *The Economist*, 25 June 1983.

52. The equivalence of the liquidity preference and loanable funds approaches to interest determination was argued by Hicks the Younger in his 1936 review of Keynes and in *Value and Capital*, Ch. XII. There the argument was made in a temporary equilibrium context but it has been carried over to *IS-LM* by others. The argument is, I think, misleading except possibly in the context of rational expectations models: if the general equilibrium consequences of some parameter change are 'rationally anticipated', all markets would 'open' with the new equilibrium prices already 'posted'. For such a conceptual experiment, it indeed does not make sense to ask which excess demand was responsible for the change in which price. One must (to make sense) consider instances where, once price setters have posted prices based on their best forecasts, actual trading produces excess demands and supplies, thus revealing the 'errors' in the forecasts. The issue of the liquidity preference versus loanable funds squabble is how this error-activated feedback control of price works in the case of the interest rate – specifically, whether the interest rate is 'governed' by the excess demand for money or by the excess supply for securities. To discriminate between the two hypotheses, one must then consider states of the economy which do not have ED for money and ES of securities (or vice versa) at the same time. In a Keynes model, a 'decline in MEC' produces an example, namely a state with an ES of commodities and a corresponding ED for securities while – at this stage of the sequence – the ED for money is still zero. If the loanable funds hypothesis is true, it is possible that

the intertemporal prices mechanism will take care of the intertemporal coordination problem (without a recession); if the liquidity preference hypothesis is true, it is inconceivable.

53.  For a more careful and detailed discussion, cf. Leijonhufvud (1983b), pp. 69–70, 76–80.
54.  This sounds suspiciously like an IQ ranking for Lucasian, Friedmanian and Keynesian economists. This Keynesian didn't mean it that way!
55.  Cf. Leijonhufvud (1983b), p. 87.
56.  Cf. *Critical Essays*, p. 158.
57.  I have made a previous attempt at getting Hicks's 'Attempt at Perspective' (1967b) into perspective – and pretty much failed. Cf. Leijonhufvud (1981c). My review shows how influenced I then was by Friedman and Schwartz, Brunner and Meltzer, and particularly by their work on US monetary history since 1929. (In 1968, American Monetarists had hardly begun thinking about small, open, fixed-exchange-rate economies yet.) This made me critical, for instance, of Hicks's insistence on the 'inherent instability of credit'. The piece also shows my great fascination for Hicks's daring attempt to put 200 years of tangled controversies in order; for various reasons, the way I saw it, several important writers just would not fit neatly into Hicks's scheme – but I failed completely to suggest a scheme that would do better.
58.  The main line of Hicks's work in monetary theory runs as follows: 'A Suggestion for Simplifying the Theory of Money' (1935); Ch. XXIII, entitled 'Keynes after Growth Theory' in *Capital and Growth* (1965); the three chapters on 'The Two Triads' in *Critical Essays* (1967a); the chapter on 'Money, Interest and Liquidity' in *The Crisis* (1974); the 60-odd-page-long 'Monetary Experience and the Theory of Money' that is the backbone of the *Economic Perspectives* collection (1977); and 'The Foundations of Monetary Theory' in *Money, Interest and Wages* (1982).
59.  Quoted from reprint in *Critical Essays*, pp. 75–6.
60.  Hicks (1965), pp. 284-5.
61.  I have used this rather informal definition repeatedly. Cf, for example, Leijonhufvud (1983c).
62.  Cf. Leijonhufvud (1982, 1983a) and Chapter 6 below for rather more careful explanations.
63.  Cf. 'Monetary Experience and the Theory of Money', op. cit., pp. 61–73, and 'Foundations of Monetary Theory', op. cit., pp. 237, 264ff.
64.  On which Hicks can rightly say: 'I may allow myself to point out that it was already observed in "Mr. Keynes and the Classics" that we do not need to suppose that the curve is drawn up on the assumption of a given stock of money. It is sufficient to suppose that there is (as I said) "a given monetary system – that up to a point, but only up to a point, monetary authorities will prefer to create new money rather than allow interest rates to rise. Such a generalized (*LM*) curve will then slope upwards only gradually – the elasticity of the curve depending on the elasticity of the monetary system.' Cf. *Money, Interest and Wages*, p. 328.
65.  Leijonhufvud (1983c).
66.  Leijonhufvud (1979), p. 526.
67.  Hicks (1977), p. vii.
68.  Ibid.
69.  Hicks (1967b), p. 156. But this too is an old Hicksian theme. One finds it in his 1943 review of Charles Rist's *History of Money and Credit Theory*. Cf. Hicks (1982), pp. 132ff.

# PART II

# Monetary Regimes and Inflation

# 6. Monetary policy and the business cycle under 'loose' convertibility

> Monetary theory is less abstract than most economic theory: it cannot avoid a relation to reality, which in other economic theory is sometimes missing. It belongs to monetary history, in a way that economic theory does not always belong to economic history.
>
> Sir John Hicks[1]

In recent literature, the Hicksian lesson that we must develop monetary theory in historical context has re-emerged in the stress that the rational expectations literature puts on 'monetary regimes'. This development has even made the old subject of monetary standards fashionable again and an object of some genuine theoretical excitement. While this paper is not strictly speaking on the monetary economics of John Hicks,[2] I hope it will be recognized as doing monetary economics in a distinctly Hicksian vein.

In some previous papers,[3] I have sketched a simple framework for developing a macrotheory conditional on the monetary regimes deemed to be in effect. This approach distinguishes between regimes that stabilize the nominal scale of the economy by convertibility and those that do so by controlling the quantity of money. It suggests that actual monetary regimes may be ordered, as a first approximation, on a one-dimensional spectrum from pure 'convertibility control' at one extreme to pure 'quantity control' at the other. This paper aims to develop this conception a bit further.

## A SPECTRUM OF REGIMES

Over the last hundred years, our monetary system has evolved from one relying on commodity convertibility to one depending on state control of the quantity of fiat base money for the stability of nominal values. For each period or episode in our business cycle history, the question arises whether the theory of convertibility-controlled or that of quantity-controlled monetary regimes provides the more nearly appropriate interpretation of events. Among the many important issues that have become part of the Monetarist–Keynesian controversy, for instance, these historical questions are, I believe, quite central.[4] Whether the gold exchange standard of the 1920s or the Bretton Woods system in its different phases approximated more closely to one or the other type of monetary theory are not easy questions to answer. Answers require not just a determination of institutional arrangements in effect at the time but also an understanding of how monetary policy was in fact conducted within these arrangements and of how this conditioned the rational expectations of the public.

The theory of quantity-controlled fiat money systems is familiar to all. From Patinkin through Lucas, this case has dominated the literature of our time.[5] The theory of convertible money systems may bear some review, however. We have not seen much of commodity convertibility since the outbreak of World War I – except for that brief and in the end disastrous episode of the late 1920s – and most economists have come to neglect the theory of such regimes.

The main outlines can be stated quite simply. Whereas under quantity control the monetary authorities fix the quantity of some $M$ and let the private sector find the equilibrium nominal prices of commodities, under convertibility they fix the price of some commodity, $G$, and leave it to the private sector to create the equilibrium stocks of liquid assets, including 'money'. If it were feasible to make money redeemable in some basket of commodities, convertibility would fix the corresponding price level, with the money stock adjusting so as to maintain it. This hypothetical case of a price-fixing, quantity-taking monetary authority would be the logical counterpart to the usual quantity-fixing, price-taking story.

It is obvious that the monetary theory (or central banking doctrine) appropriate to the one pure case is very different from the one fitting the other. A commitment to convertibility relinquishes the option of controlling $M$. If maintenance of convertibility serves to control the nominal scale of the economy, on the other hand, the central bank is – within bounds – free to worry about credit conditions and their effects on real activity. If convertibility is indeed seen to guarantee the price level, rationally expectant agents will have inelastic nominal expectations, so that the central bank gains some leverage over real magnitudes: changes in bank rates change a real price; changes in bank reserves change the real volume of credit supplied. Banking policy affects the liquidity (again in real terms) of the private sector, but it is unlikely that any particular $M$ will provide a perfect or stable indicator of the effect on aggregate demand.

In all these respects the monetary policy theory appropriate to the convertible regime has been the target of persistent Monetarist criticism. Monetarist theory is itself best suited to the quantity control extreme on the spectrum. Control over some nominal stock must be the focal point of policy theory in order to provide a nominal anchor for an economy on a pure fiat standard.

The monetary authorities should, if possible, avoid disturbing the nominal scale of the economy. Attempts to fine-tune credit conditions are likely to detract from the primary task of providing nominal stability, and interest rate targeting, in particular, threatens nominal instability.

## THE WORLD WE HAVE LOST[6]

The drawing of these contrasts (and there are others) will not tell us, however, which theory applies midway, say, between the extremes. The pure cases are convenient analytical constructs but historical regimes will seldom approximate either the 'quantity-fixing, price-taking' or the 'price-fixing, quantity-taking' extreme. In particular, actual convertible regimes leave more scope for price-level movements and some room for discretionary control of the quantity of money in the short run. Much of the best monetary literature was written in an attempt to come to grips with regimes in which convertibility was becoming an increasingly 'loose' constraint on the price level. Consider briefly some closed economy and open economy variants of the basic convertible money model.

Take first the closed system case where gold currency is still in circulation. The regime fixes the nominal price of gold. If the market price of the metal were to rise above the legal conversion rate, non-bank transactors would cash in their notes for gold at the banks to profit from the arbitrage; if the gold price were to fall below this value, the banks would buy gold and expand their lending. If the banks were to 'over-issue', causing nominal aggregate demand to rise, the increased demand for gold currency would quickly check the inflation. Once the price of gold in the bullion market is at the legal conversion price, the banks cannot replenish their reserves by bidding gold away from non-monetary uses any further without triggering note redemptions. Except when convertibility is suspended or in the wake of major bank failures, therefore, the price level of commodities in terms of gold would vary only within relatively narrow limits. Under these conditions, convertibility is a tight constraint on the nominal scale of the economy.

Suppose next, however, that gold coins become strictly inferior to sound bank notes as a medium of exchange and disappear from circulation. Nothing but the fear of bank failure will now make the public decide to hold monetary gold. Rising aggregate demand will then no longer pull gold out of the banking system. This brake on inflation has been lost. There are two other possible ones. If the rising prices of commodities in terms of gold were to make people substitute gold for other metals in 'real' uses, increasing demand might eventually put pressure on the nominal price of gold and thus threaten redemptions. But it is one of the 'essential properties' of monetary metals *not* to be good substitutes for other things, so this will not be a dependable brake. The remaining possibility is that the banks maintain 'prudential' ratios of gold reserves to deposits that, while varying inversely with the loan rate, will still make them call a halt to expansion at some point. Even if the prudence of banks could be depended on,[7] it is clear that the price level can nevertheless vary within fairly wide limits in this system. We might term this a 'loose' convertibility case in comparison with the previous 'tight' one. It sets the stage for a managed (or mismanaged) gold standard.

This kind of analysis seems quaintly old-fashioned nowadays. The open economy cases, on the other hand, are only about a dozen years out of date. Here we are considering external convertibility at a fixed exchange rate. Whether convertibility will be a 'tight' or 'loose' constraint on nominal magnitudes depends on how well integrated into the world economy the country is – and also, to some extent, on how much resources it is willing to tie up in foreign exchange reserves. If price elasticities of the excess demands for tradables are relatively low and if capital mobility is slight or effectively restricted, the country can exercise some significant policy discretion in the short run and have its price level vary relative to the world price level (also in the short run). With excess demands for imports and exports very elastic or with a high degree of capital mobility, world prices and interest rates rule, of course, and the money stock is determined by demand rather than by supply.

In the 'tight' version of the gold standard, the theory of price-level determination becomes almost altogether a matter of the world supply and demand for the monetary metal. Because of their importance in the development of monetary theory, our memory of the 19th century tends perhaps to be dominated by the episodes of suspension of convertibility. But the history of price levels in that century is largely a story, on the supply side, of gold discoveries and of the innovation of the cyanide process and, on the demand side, besides real income growth, first, of the public and the banking system learning to economize on gold by changing payments practices and by pyramiding of reserves, and second, of countries previously on silver or bimetallic standards deciding to join the international gold standard.

Nonetheless, convertibility must surely have become a steadily 'looser' constraint, allowing greater cyclical variability of prices around the longer-term trend set by gold production, real income growth and so on. When the non-bank public's 'normal' demand for gold reached zero – when? – the link between the price level and the stock of the monetary metal would have become elastic in the extreme. In the short and medium run, it would seem price-level determination from that point onward (if not sooner) must have become much more a matter of banking policy than of gold production.

Is this the point at which we should trade in the model of convertible money for one of exogenously determined fiat money? Much of the more purely theoretical literature from Patinkin to Hahn and Lucas (who in this respect have to share the same taxonomic quarters) obviously takes it for granted that the theory of convertible money can simply be ignored. Nonetheless, it seems to me that this unresolved, and often unrecognized, question underlies much of the controversy swirling around the field of applied Monetary theory. The appropriate context in which to begin examining it, however, is not general equilibrium theory but business cycle theory.

## BUSINESS CYCLES AND MONEY

The theory of monetary standards, I am arguing, has considerable relevance for business cycle theory and, especially, for interpretations of business cycle history. In order to establish this relevance – or at least make it plausible – some general remarks on the subject of business cycle theory are required by way of preparation.

It is useful, I think, to classify business cycle theories[8] by the hypotheses they make about, on the one hand, the type of disturbance that normally starts a fluctuation and, on the other, the type of maladjustment (if any) that typically comes in the way of immediate optimal system adaptation to the disturbance. In the present context, I want to concentrate on two theories. The first one I classify as 'real/real', but 'intertemporal' should be understood as implicitly attached to each term. In what follows, I will call this theory 'Keynesian', although today's standard usage would attach the term to a rather different animal. The second theory, I classify as 'nominal/nominal'. I will refer to it as 'Monetarist', although it is perhaps not the only type of Monetarist theory that we have seen.[9]

Two hybrids are simply left out of account in what follows, despite their importance in the literature. One is the standard Keynesian 'real–nominal' theory, which combines real disturbances to investment with rigidity of nominal wages. The other is the type of New Classical 'nominal–real' theory which postulates nominal disturbances that are supposed to lead, somehow, to intertemporal labor–leisure misallocations.

We can now contrast the lines of causation typical of the two theories. The Monetarist $N/N$ theory is the most straightforward. The nominal shock is a change in an exogenously determined fiat money stock. With a stable demand function for money, there will follow a roughly proportional change in nominal income. The appropriate system response to a nominal shock, however, is simply a proportional scaling up or down of nominal values with no change predicted for aggregate real magnitudes. A nominal maladjustment hypothesis, usually inflexibility of money wages, is added, therefore, so as to make the theory capable of accounting for output and employment fluctuations.

The case of purely nominal disturbances, however, could not apply to convertible regimes (except to suspension episodes). 'Monetary' theories of the business cycle can still be consistent with convertibility, but would more appropriately be termed 'credit cycle' theories in that context.

The textbook version of Keynesian *R/R* theory starts with a 'shift of the marginal efficiency of capital'. Some event causes entrepreneurs to take a dimmer view of the profitability of employing present factor services to augment future output. Relative to the initially given prices and activity levels, therefore, they decide to reduce their rates of investment. At initial intertemporal prices ('market rate exceeding the natural rate'),[10] this creates an excess supply of present resources and an implicit excess demand for goods in the future (saving exceeds investment). The appropriate system response entails a change in the relevant relative prices; in this instance real rates of interest should fall. The Keynesian maladjustment hypothesis is that they do not fall sufficiently but are instead stabilized by speculation based on inelastic expectations about the normal rate of return. The result of this intertemporal maladjustment is a decline in present output and employment.

This hypothesis has fallen completely out of favor in recent years and is scarcely discussed any longer. It is not very clear why. A no doubt incomplete catalogue of arguments against it runs as follows.

1.  The real impulse hypothesis leaves unexplained the positive correlation between money and income (which is the central empirical regularity in Monetarist theory).
2.  If real *aggregative* impulses ever occurred, they should show up in the data as episodes with output and money prices inversely correlated.
3.  The notion of aggregative real impulses is suspect, because there is no reason why real disturbances to different sectors or industries should be systematically correlated.
4.  Even if real impulses to different industries were preponderantly of the same sign on occasion, the resources required for these sectors to expand (for example) would have to be bid away from others, which would consequently be seen to contract.

There may be various ways in which to answer these objections. I would stress four points. First, the level of activity in the system depends on the prospective real rate of return on investment. (This is true also in equilibrium business cycle theory, as Lucas has taught us.) If the perceived value-productivity of present inputs in terms of future outputs increases, while that in terms of present outputs remains the same, it will pay to expand employment. (Farmers work longer hours in the planting season.) The sectors that first see improved intertemporal prospects ahead may expand, therefore, without forcing corresponding contractions elsewhere.

Second, the money stock should be endogenous in this story – as pre-Keynesian 'real' business cycle theorists normally had it, although Keynesians have on the whole not followed this lead.[11] We may suppose that increasing output in the business cycle upswing is financed by producers getting trade credit from their suppliers and bank credit for their larger wage-bills. Bank lending may be based, in effect, on 'real bills'. The banks may be aided and abetted by a central bank 'leaning against the wind' to moderate fluctuations in interest rates. Velocity, bank deposits and base money all vary procyclically.[12] Thus rising investment and employment do not put downward pressure on money prices.

Third, the prevalence of increasing returns throughout the manufacturing sector is probably an important factor in accounting for the gradual spread of the expansionary impulse from the sectors first affected to the economy in general. Consider a simple but graphic example. Suppose the typical manufacturing firm runs two assembly lines in parallel, but that the two lines have certain work stations in common. In recession, the firm shuts down one assembly line but cannot lay off half its workers – the operators who man both lines have to stay. Suppose also the firms form an input–output system in which this non-linear technology prevails everywhere: Firm A buys an intermediate input from B, which buys from C, which buys from A and so on. Each firm experiences higher unit costs in recession, but cannot charge higher prices since its customers are in the same position. Everyone makes losses and further retrenchment will not eliminate these losses. When the turning point comes, however, this all works in reverse and all firms can rationally expect 'improving factoral terms of trade' from expansion.[13]

Fourth is the Wicksellian theme: for the economy not to overshoot the equilibrium adjustment to the improved intertemporal prospects in a couple of its sectors, the real rate of interest should rise to its new 'natural' level. But what that level should be is difficult or impossible for market participants or government policy-makers to diagnose. If, for instance, the central bank stabilizes interest rates by giving the banking system free rein to rediscount at the initially prevailing interest rate, the sectors that should expand will expand too far and pull other sectors and consumers into a general boom.

## MONETARY STANDARDS AND THE PHILLIPS CURVE

Either the *N/N* or the *R/R* story can be made to fit the stylized facts of the cyclical behavior of money supply, nominal income, real income and employment (although the *R/R* story has less trouble than the *N/N* one with the cyclical behavior of interest rates). It is of some importance to keep the distinctions between the two clear. The line between the *N/N* and *R/R* hypotheses has become more muddled than necessary in the literature by the prevalence of a common macroanalytic practice – or, really, malpractice. The practice has been to do most problems in two stages, focusing first on how shocks of either kind influence nominal income in order, second, to go on to the problem of how nominal income changes break down into nominal and real changes. ('First, shift *IS* or *LM* and find out what happens to *Y*. Then check your short-run Phillips curve.')[14] This procedure loses track of the elementary but crucial difference between nominal and real shocks. A nominal shock requires a change in the nominal scale of the economy but does not require real adjustments. A real shock requires reallocation of resources but no adjustment of the general price level. How a given change in nominal income should be expected to decompose into price and quantity changes depends therefore on which causal chain we are following: (a) the *N/N* chain from nominal shock to nominal income and via wage/price inflexibilities to real income and employment, or (b) the *R/R* chain from shocks to investment expectations via inflexibilities of intertemporal prices to output, employment and the real money stock. There is no reason to suppose – as it was our common mental habit to suppose[15] – that the short-run Phillips 'trade-off' should be the same in both cases. If a change in money income of given magnitude was due to a nominal disturbance, we would expect a larger price-level effect and a smaller employment effect than if it was caused by a real disturbance. A sequence of *R/R* episodes occurring within a stable nominal framework might leave a more or less stable and regular Phillips pattern of counterclockwise loops of successive observations as part of the historical record. A sequence of *N/N* episodes – as we know by now – will generate a largely unpredictable trail of jumbled clockwise loops in the data.

Of the two hypotheses, which one is the more likely to account for most cyclical episodes? The answer will depend on the nature of the prevailing monetary regime.

To see how the monetary regime question comes in, it is easiest to start with the extreme cases. It is clear, to begin with, that tight convertibility precludes the pure *N/N* cycle. It rules out purely nominal shocks, and purely nominal inflexibilities, therefore, are not of much immediate consequence. At this extreme of our spectrum of regimes, therefore, we get all *R/R* and no *N/N* cycles. At the opposite extreme of discretionary quantity control, on the other hand, the *R/R* story is not at all precluded. Discretionary manipulation of a fiat standard sets the stage for the *N/N* story – although one should note that systems experiencing frequent and sizeable nominal shocks are not apt to retain much nominal inflexibility. At this end, therefore, we are likely to have both kinds of problems.

It is obvious enough that we have been at this fiat quantity control extreme for the last fifteen years or so. But how should one characterize the Bretton Woods period? For those countries that pegged their currencies to the dollar, Bretton Woods was a convertible regime getting tighter with time as world markets for tradables and capital became increasingly integrated.[16] For the United States itself, the question does not have an obvious answer.

My own tentative view, in brief, is the following. Fixed exchange rates were not by themselves an effective constraint on the key currency country. The United States could have inflated the Western world long before it blundered into doing so. Instead, of course, the monetary authorities of the United States gave priority to stabilizing the domestic price level. In so doing they sustained, by quantity control, a system of nominal expectations appropriate to an economy with convertible money. This gave the US Phillips curve the appearance of stability up until the late 1960s – in those good old days, the nominal expectations of the public did not respond to every wiggle in the time path of the money stock. This relative stability of nominal magnitudes was shared by those countries that basically accepted the discipline of fixed dollar exchange rates. Thus, for about twenty years, the world economy at large functioned in fair imitation of a convertible standard system.

This may sound paradoxical to those who recall the persistent criticisms of the United States, as long as it was still running a balance of payments surplus, for 'breaking the rules' of a convertible standard. Sterilization of current account surpluses by the United States, it was argued, unfairly put all the adjustment burden on the deficit countries. In this sense, admittedly, the United States was not mimicking a convertible standard during the period in question. But if, in the immediate postwar years, when its main trading partners had a very high propensity to spend out of international reserves, the United States had followed a rule of expanding domestic aggregate demand as long as net gold inflows continued, the result would have been cumulative world inflation. Bretton Woods was not a gold standard regime. On the whole, the banking systems of the world no longer had a demand for gold, and the world price level could no longer be anchored by the gold stock. Bretton Woods was basically a key currency standard and required the key currency country to control its money supply and to stabilize its own price level. Thus breaking the rules of a commodity convertible standard was necessary if the world economy was to function as if it were on such a standard.

Despite the complaints over sterilization and the distribution of adjustment burdens, the system implicitly required restraint in the management of the key currency. Other member countries would find little incentive to stay pegged to the dollar if this exposed them to erratic nominal shocks originating in the United States. When the United States went into its 'random walk inflation' (and refused to be disciplined by the loss of gold), Bretton Woods was doomed. Japan and West Germany, in particular, could not possibly see it as in their national interest to follow this dance of the dollar.

This view of the Bretton Woods regime runs counter to the *N/N* interpretation of US business fluctuations during the period in question. Shifting the emphasis back onto the *R/R* hypothesis in this way does not necessarily entail rejection of all the Monetarist lessons. It is still consistent, for instance, with the belief that the central bank reaction function may play a very important role in determining the amplitude of fluctuations in real aggregates. But it interprets the historical time path of $M_2$ (say) as reflecting mainly endogenous movements in real money demand rather than exogenous shocks to the economy's nominal scalar.

## BANKING POLICY AND THE PRICE LEVEL

Consider the real cycle story from the monetary point of view. For simplicity, assume an economy with a financial sector consisting on the whole of a late 19th century banking system. Begin the story roughly at full employment and suppose that some entrepreneurs discover investment opportunities promising above normal returns. With these improved prospects, the economy as a whole should adapt by increasing labor inputs and saving. But those who do the additional labor will in general not be those who are going to do the additional saving. Nor will the entrepreneurs in general have the equity capital in liquid form that is required to exploit the new opportunities. The financial market serves to bring together the labor, the savers and the entrepreneurs. In the case supposed – where the banks make that market – expansion of real activity entails expansion of the real volume of inside money.

If the monetary system were to be 'inelastic', so that the banks were unable to expand, this would interfere with the acceleration of growth that is the appropriate system response to new Schumpeterian opportunities.[17] This is the kernel of truth in the 'real bills' argument – and recognizing it as such need not entail the belief that the real bills policy doctrine is right, safe or non-inflationary. What it means is that a measure of accommodation by the banking system in response to real cyclical growth impulses is appropriate. But there is no easy criterion for exactly what measure of accommodation is appropriate. Hence Central Banking as an Art.

John Hicks's favorite monetary writers saw the point:[18]

> Thornton accordingly held that a credit system must be *managed*. It must be managed by a Central Bank, whose operations must be determined by judgment, and cannot be reduced to procedure by mechanical rule.

Mill is unable to follow Ricardo in looking for mechanical rules by which credit is to be controlled: it can only be controlled by quite subtle appreciation of the 'feel' of the market, by monetary *policy*.

Look at the problem from the standpoint of a central bank. We may suppose that the economy's entire gold reserve has been pyramided into the central bank, so that we have 'loose' convertibility. To what extent should it let the volume of bank rediscounts fluctuate? Alternatively, to what extent should it try to stabilize the real rate of interest? Its success, or lack of success, in tracking the 'natural rate' determines the extent to which the central bank is, in effect, adding nominal impulses to the real impulses here assumed to initiate the fluctuations. The narrower the band of interest variation that the bank tries to maintain, the larger (*ceteris paribus*) the fluctuations in the nominal money stock that real shocks will induce.

Money varies endogenously in this model. The real cycle has a 'monetary' aspect to it – if the banking system were constrained to obey a Friedman rule, for instance, observed real fluctuations might have smaller amplitude (and real interest rates larger amplitude). In an equilibrium real cycle, the co-movement of money would reflect only the (non-inflationary) adjustment of real bank credit. With a Wicksellian 'cumulative' overlay, part of the variation in money becomes a nominal amplification of the cycle.[19] The first differences of monetary time series, therefore, reflect a mixture of real and nominal impulses.

A central bank might well have a tendency to be somewhat too expansionary on the average over the cycle, leaning a bit too much with the wind in expansion or against it in contraction. It is an easy (and popular) error to make but not an easy (or popular) one to correct. The result, over a complete cycle, is a price level a bit higher and a banking system a bit less liquid than it should otherwise have been.[20] This can be corrected through a policy of contracting credit – but deflationary pressure tends to be costly given the inelastic nominal expectations in a regime of this sort. The alternative is to find new ways to economize on the monetary metal. By various measures the demand for gold by domestic residents and banks can be reduced (or, in the end, prohibited). Eventually, however, the problem becomes global, and economizing on reserves becomes a matter of negotiation between nations.

The metallic standards are often affectionately recalled by economists as 'automatic' and 'non-political'. And it is true of course that the monetary metals served very well to govern trade in a world of warring princes. But the modern history of fixed exchange rate regimes shows them evolving into highly politicized, ceaselessly negotiated systems.

# TRANSMISSION AND THE EFFECTIVENESS OF MONETARY POLICY

The transmission of monetary impulses and the effectiveness of monetary policy were central issues in the Keynesian–Monetarist controversy from the start. Much of the impetus of early Monetarism stemmed from a reaction toward Keynesian 'ineffectiveness' doctrines of the time. Transmission theory is a good example of a subject that has often been debated in general terms but would benefit from being reworked in particular terms, that is, from working out the transmission mechanism for each particular monetary regime. A quick inventory of transmission mechanisms in the literature of recent decades turns up at least six candidates (T1–T6 below).

It is useful first to distinguish two ineffectiveness doctrines from the 1940s and 1950s. I tend to think of one as American and the other as European, although I am not altogether certain that such a systematic pattern in the views of economists on the two sides of the Atlantic can be documented.

T1.    The American view argued that high interest elasticities of money demand prevented increases in the money supply from depressing the rate of interest by much and that, besides, the interest elasticities of investment and the other major spending categories were very low. Monetary policy was ineffective because each link in the main transmission chain was weak and unreliable. A secondary transmission route, the real balance effect, was recognized, but hardly seen as having practical relevance.

The textbooks of the 1950s and 1960s taught this view of the matter as Keynesian economics. (It was one of those things that were not the economics of Keynes.)[21] In the standard *IS–LM* exposition, *M* was independent of endogenous variables and determined by the authorities. Whether *M* could be controlled was not a focal issue.

T2.    The European view was more pessimistic on the question of whether the monetary authorities could control *M* by open market operations and discount policy. In the 1950s, many European countries tried to escape the discipline of their external convertibility by exchange controls, and similarly tried to give their internal monetary policies more bite by various and sundry measures of credit rationing and capital market controls. In Britain, still trying to play the role of a major reserve currency country, the Radcliffe report did not so much dispute controllability as argue that quantity control of any particular aggregate was pointless in view of the many alternative sources of liquidity in a financially highly developed economy.

The Monetarist challenge to these ineffectiveness doctrines has often been met with the complaint that Monetarist theory did not explain why or how monetary impulses were transmitted so strongly and so reliably. The secret to the effectiveness of Monetarist transmission, so the quip went, was hidden from unfriendly inspection in a 'black box'.

This particular criticism seems a bit unfair, for one can count at least four Monetarist theories of the transmission mechanism.

T3.   The first is the account from the early 1960s by Friedman and Schwartz.[22] This story, as Okun also commented at the time, was qualitatively indistinguishable from the view of monetary transmission taught by such Keynesians as Tobin or Modigliani. The main channel is the substitution effects rippling through financial markets to finally reach and affect the demand prices of producible assets. At this time, Friedman and Schwartz differed from the Keynesians (or I suppose one should say, the 'pro-money' Keynesians) mostly in being more optimistic about the strength of each link in the causal chain from monetary impulse to real sector response.

T4.   Somewhat later, Brunner sharpened the issue by stressing the difference between two interpretations of the term 'the interest rate' in this context.[23] On the one hand, the concept of the interest rate as a borrowing cost had often been used to argue that firms financing investments out of retained earnings would not respond to monetary policy. On the other hand, Brunner advanced the concept of the interest rate as expressing the relationship between the (often implicit) rental value and the market value of all types of assets, real as well as financial. A decline in the interest rate, for instance, raises the demand price of an income stream relative to its rental. (This had basically been Keynes's concept also.)

As Brunner explained it, Monetarists saw these relative price effects as reaching into every nook and cranny of the economy to raise the demand price of all kinds of reproducible durables. Consequently, they believed monetary policy to be more effective than did Keynesians. Note that monetary policy is so 'effective', in this account of the transmission mechanism, because it is so *all pervasively non-neutral* in the short run.

T5.   Towards the end of the 1960s, there was a significant shift in the transmission story told by Chicago Monetarists. It occurs in works by William Gibson and by Friedman.[24] In this third Monetarist theory, the liquidity effect on interest rates is downplayed as relatively weak and evanescent. The central bank is regarded as having no significant influence on real rates of interest. (The relative price mechanism, therefore, is fading out of the picture.) The emphasis is shifted, instead, to market anticipations of the growth in nominal income or of rising prices as the present incentive to increased nominal expenditures.

T6.    The final version is, of course, the New Classical one of Lucas, Barro et al. Here, there is no systematic liquidity effect or indeed any other real effect except in so far as economic agents are temporarily misinformed. Transmission is entirely via rational expectations. The credible announcement that the money stock is about to be increased will suffice to raise prices and increase nominal spending. When monetary policy is anticipated, it is effective immediately and without fail. And, in the absence of significant distribution effects, it is neutral – also in the shortest run.

Six stories and a wide variety of beliefs! It is particularly noteworthy that the four Monetarists' transmission stories are not a straightforward sequence of successive clarifications of the same doctrine. In Brunner's story (T4), monetary policy is effective because it is so pervasively non-neutral; in Lucas's (T6), it is instantly effective, although neutral. Effectiveness in the New Classical case is purely a matter of nominal scale, however. New Classical monetary policy is totally ineffective (apart from possible surprise effects) when it comes to real variables. In the (T3) and (T4) stories, money stock policy can have persistent, though not truly long run, real effects. The contrast between the early Monetarists and the later New Classical theories is stark.

Which transmission mechanism then is the *true* one? That will *not* be a good question to ask if the answer might focus on one to the total exclusion of the remaining five. We are better off, I think, asking in each instance whether there are regimes (or just states of the world) to which each particular transmission story might apply. When the answer is affirmative, that transmission hypothesis ought not to be discarded and forgotten, even if it is not the currently most applicable one. My own views on the above six are in brief as follows.

T1.    The liquidity trap and interest-inelastic spending story applies in the wake of a great monetary and financial collapse.

T2.    The ineffectiveness story that stresses the lack of control of the money stock applies in tight convertibility regimes. In recent decades this means small open economies on fixed exchange rates.

T3,4.    The non-neutral effectiveness stories should apply in loose convertibility regimes where agents have inelastic price-level expectations. Not so small countries and the large one under Bretton Woods are cases in point.

T5.    The story that combines an evanescent liquidity effect and a strong nominal income expectation effect while still attributing to monetary policy considerable predictable short-run influence on real income may be the most plausible in the transition from loose convertibility to inflationary quantity control. In my judgment it is doubtful, however, whether one could conceive of a regime, in the proper rational expectations sense, that would have a stable transmission mechanism of this kind.

T6.    The story of neutral transmission via rational expectations could only be true for a quantity-controlled fiat regime. It is not obvious, however, that it is a good theory of how such regimes work in practice. The period by period exercise of discretionary policy means that transactors face a future random walk in the nominal price level but a random walk with unstable coefficients. This 'random walk monetary standard'[25] is far from neutral compared to a regime of stable nominal values. It entails great economic costs and serious social consequences. It is one of the disappointments of the New Classical literature that it has done so very little to deepen and extend our understanding of conditions of monetary instability.

## NOTES

1.    Hicks (1967b), p. 156.
2.    I have two excuses for thus straying from the theme of this conference ('The Monetary Economics of Sir John Hicks', held at Brasenose College, Oxford, Sept. 1986). They are entitled 'Monetary Theory in Hicksian Perspective', and 'Hicks on Time and Money' (Leijonhufvud 1981c and 1984c).
3.    Cf., Leijonhufvud (1982) and also (1983c).
4.    For an illustration, see the section on 'Transmission and the Effectiveness of Monetary Policy', below.
5.    In the course of the Patinkin debate, the theory of quantity-controlled fiat money systems was often used in the characterization of 'classical' monetary theory. But there have been at least a few voices protesting that the 'classics' must surely have had a better guide to the gold-standard world of the 19th century than that! See, for instance, Thompson (1974) and Glasner (1985).
6.    With apologies to Peter Laslett (1973).
7.    The fear that the prudential ratio of the gold reserves of banks to their demand liabilities might not be stable (or always larger than zero!) will prompt government monopolization of note issue and, perhaps, imposition of legal reserve requirements.
8.    For a somewhat more detailed discussion, see Chapters 1 and 2 above.
9.    A strict *N/N* model would be a straightjacket for Friedman and Schwartz's *Monetary History* (1963a). While they insisted that money was an exogenous factor in some critical episodes, they did not maintain that all changes in the money stock should or could be so interpreted. Subsequently, the 'natural rate of unemployment' hypothesis was added to Monetarist doctrine, however, which pretty much forces one to interpret it in *N/N* terms.
10.    For detailed exposition, see Leijonhufvud (1981b).
11.    James Tobin (1963) might have turned Keynesian economics in this direction. But the

ensuing discussion (it seems to me) has not always distinguished clearly between the two propositions, (a) that the money stock varies endogenously in fluctuations caused by real disturbances, and (b) that the central bank (in an inconvertible fiat regime) is unable to control the money stock and, ultimately, determine the nominal scale of the economy. The latter proposition, which became a favorite target of Monetarist polemics, is one that Tobin would not advocate. To Gramley and Chase (1965), the central bank's influence on M1 is only indirect, and the relationship between the base and the money stock subject to variations due to a number of factors not controlled by the authorities. While money stock control, therefore, is portrayed as exceedingly difficult, they are more concerned to argue that money stock is an unreliable indicator for monetary policy than that money stock control is impossible. The more extreme position is taken (and with some vehemence) by Kaldor (1982).

12. Note that, in this *R/R* story, employment co-varies with money income for reasons that have nothing to do with either nominal misperceptions or other institutional or contractual maladjustments of money wages. Money income co-varies with money, for the non-Monetarist reason that movements in real income cause endogenous movements in the real money stock.

13. Two other objections to the 'shifting MEC' hypothesis should perhaps be mentioned (1) One asserts that the average rate of profit has been approximately constant secularly; agents with rational expectations, therefore, would not react to things that go bump in the dark, since they know that the economy-wide MEC does not shift about. The response to this one, of course, is that agents that have absolutely inelastic expectations about the real rate of return that can be earned, some place, in the economy will act so as to put all of the adjustment on the rate of capital accumulation and none of the adjustment on the real rate of interest when they perceive their own individual investment prospects as having changed. (2) The other argues that real interest rates show too little variation over time to be capable of explaining the actual amplitude of business fluctuations. But this, of course, is entirely consistent with a Wicksell–Keynes explanation wherein the more the interest rate is stabilized by speculation, the larger will the variations in the rate of investment be, *ceteris paribus*.

14. For an attempt to sort this out, see Leijonhufvud (1983b). For *IS–LM* considered in relation to quantity-controlled and convertibility-controlled regimes, see Leijonhufvud (1984c), pp. 33–9, 43–4.

15. Thus, for example, James Tobin in his Fall 1986 Jacob Marschak lecture at UCLA mentioned that he used to explain this to undergraduate classes as the 'common funnel hypothesis'. In his blackboard illustration, separate 'monetary' and 'fiscal' impulses feed into the 'common funnel' of nominal GNP changes and then separate again into quantity- and price-effects.

16. Bretton Woods, of course, was only 'tight' as long as one followed the rules. It was always possible for these countries to assume control of their money in order to conduct stabilization policies with some independence from the dollar. But doing so would force either devaluation (sometimes postponed by borrowing of reserves) or, as in the case of Japan, the more or less indefinite accumulation of dollars.

17. For an explicit general equilibrium model exhibiting the properties suggested here, see Mossetti (1986).

18. Quotations from Sir John Hicks, (1967b, p. 164 and 166 respectively). I have quoted these passages before – and that time with critical intent (Leijonhufvud 1981a, p. 212). Live and learn!

19. This nominal amplification of the cycle under a convertible regime still does not make a very Monetarist story. In Monetarist theory, the real rate of interest is assumed to coordinate saving and investment more or less continuously; the market rate tracks the natural rate. In the above story, nominal amplification comes in only in so far as the two Wicksellian rates diverge. When market rate equals the natural rate, so that the system is in intertemporal equilibrium, changes in the money stock are 'real'.

20. Recall Wicksell's objection to the 'needs of trade' doctrine: it implies no automatic tendency for the system to return to the original price level once prices have risen through

too much accommodation by the banks to the needs of trade.
21. See Leijonhufvud (1968c).
22. Friedman and Schwartz (1963b).
23. Brunner (1970; 1971).
24. See Gibson (1970a, 1970b), Friedman (1968) and his discussion of the matter in Gordon (1974). See also the reaction of Brunner and Meltzer to this latter statement of Friedman's in their contribution to the Gordon volume, pp. 72 ff.
25. See Leijonhufvud (1984a, 1984b – Chapters 8 and 9 below). In the interpretation of the Bretton Woods and the subsequent regime given here I have been much influenced by the work of my colleague Benjamin Klein (see especially Klein 1975). For some time-series evidence consistent with the contrasts drawn between these two regimes, refer to Crabbe (1988).

# 7.  Theories of stagflation

The occurrence of stagflation came as a nasty shock to a great many economists. Evidently, the economics profession has gotten so much into the habit of teaching that unemployment and inflation are alternating or alternative phenomena that their actual conjuncture seemed at first to be a riddle to which received theory might not supply an answer. A few writers of some note indeed went so far as to proclaim that stagflation proved the bankruptcy of standard theory.

Well, stagflation is not a riddle. Far-fetched or ad hoc explanations are not required. Instead, theories of unemployment and theories of inflation can be combined in a variety of ways that avoid contradiction. I want to discuss a few of these. It seems easiest to start by considering different theories of unemployment.

## STAGFLATION I: THE CASE OF THE MISSING MARKET MECHANISM

The first theory of unemployment that needs to be mentioned is based on the notion that labor markets do not have functioning market mechanisms. Wage rates are not governed by demand for and supply of labor. In particular, an excess supply of labor does not constitute a 'market force' that will set in motion adjustments that could result in its own elimination. Wage determination is to be explained by institutional factors, exogenous to the market.

A common version of this theory has wage rates independent of the excess demand for labor at all values of employment below full employment, with inflation in wage rates setting in at overfull employment. This version has been often cited by people who find stagflation a paradox and regard it as proof that the world has left 'Keynesian' economics behind on the scrapheap of no longer useful social theories.[1]

This theory draws a sharp line between deficient and excessive aggregate demand. You have either one or the other, and the one gives you unemployment and the other inflation. So how can you have stagflation consistent with this view of the world?

The answer given is that you have to relinquish the exclusive preoccupation with aggregate demand that characterizes most of received business cycle theory, and bring in aggregate supply. If the aggregate supply price were to rise at a faster pace than the rise in nominal aggregate demand, the observed consequence should be a contraction of output in the midst of inflation. A wage push of a magnitude larger than what the monetary authorities will validate is one possibility – and the one most often adduced, of course. The second possibility for getting unemployment and inflation at the same time in this framework is to have cost–push emanating from an important factor of production complementary to labor – say, energy. Needless to say, this one has been rather popular since 1974.

I would like to make two observations about the missing market mechanism theory before we proceed.

1.  The theory suggests that stagflation is the result of a rather fortuitous concatenation of events: 'too big' a factor-price rise just happens to impinge on an inflation that is already going on for other reasons. There is no intimation here that recessions must be expected to occur in inflationary regimes as well as in regimes of monetary stability.
2.  The theory does suggest that monopolistic or collusive price-setting in input markets is critical in the explanation of stagflation – that with competitive markets the phenomenon would not occur.[2] Economists who accept this theory therefore tend to advocate income policies or price controls as supplements to aggregate demand management policies.

## STAGFLATION II: THE CASE OF THE NATURAL RATE OF UNEMPLOYMENT

This theory, of course, starts from a position directly opposite to the previous one. Here we assume a well-functioning labor market mechanism that functions 'as if competitive', and sets corrective forces in motion when employment differs from its equilibrium level. It does not necessarily work with great speed, however, for it must work on the basis of less than complete information.

Theories with the natural rate feature are not necessarily Monetarist for the rest. Here, however, I have a Monetarist theory in mind and will use the label accordingly. In the present context this will be taken to mean two things:

1.  all impulses disturbing the time path of the economy are money supply impulses; and

2.  the assumption that the labor market does work is supposed to suffice by itself to guarantee convergence, even if delayed, to the natural rate of unemployment.

The trick here, obviously, is to explain both the inflation and the simultaneous unemployment in a stagflation episode as due to the same kind of disturbance rather than as consequences of the concatenation of two different shocks. It can be done by suitable assumptions about the system's lag structure: inflation is caused by monetary expansion, while deviations of unemployment from its natural rate reflect delayed adjustments to past monetary shocks.

The most familiar version of Monetarist stagflation explanation stems directly from Friedman's original critique of the Phillips curve. Suppose we start the story with the economy in a state of zero inflation and equilibrium unemployment. Then let the monetary authorities increase the rate of money stock growth by, say, 10 per cent. Nominal aggregate demand accelerates correspondingly but, in the first stage, not all of the increase in nominal income comes in the form of price rises. There is also an increase in employment and output, as the volume of search unemployment temporarily decreases. Later on, as workers overcome their initial 'bamboozlement' (as Tobin called it),[3] unemployment would rise back to its natural rate; with the growth in nominal income proceeding at a constant rate, inflation would actually accelerate at this stage as prices that initially lagged behind the rate of monetary expansion now catch up. [4]

If, next, we suppose that the monetary growth rate is again reduced by 10 per cent, an initial stage of quantity adjustments would find unemployment growing beyond the natural rate as inflation decelerates. If the story is graphed in Phillips space, successive 'observations' would describe a clockwise loop around the vertical long-run Phillips curve. Two parts of the loop are of interest in the stagflation context: (A) the 'NW' segment where inflation is accelerating and unemployment below its natural rate but increasing; and (B) the 'NE' part where inflation starts to decelerate and unemployment increases beyond the natural rate.

From this story (as far as we have taken it) we would, however, not expect to observe a stagflation phase (C) where inflation is rising with unemployment in excess of its natural rate and growing. Is an inflationary recession of this type excluded by Monetarist natural rate theory? Not really. In principle, the theory is flexible enough that 'anything' may happen. But the story it might tell of a C-type episode is, perhaps, not altogether plausible. It is instructive to consider how it would go.

The immediate objective is to change the lag assumptions so as to obtain a process that loops counterclockwise. That is easily done. The lag structure, however, is not a merely mechanical matter. The lag reflects important behavioral assumptions regarding 'who knows what, when'. Movements of real output and employment away from their equilibrium levels reflect information differentials between two sets of agents in the model. In the standard, Friedman-loop exercise, entrepreneurs learn the truth about the inflation before workers do; observing demand prices for their output going up in relation to money wages, firms find that they can hire labor at a reduced real wage; workers whose perceptions of the inflation rate are lagging believe they are being hired at unchanged or somewhat improved real wages. It is this inconsistency in beliefs that produces the disequilibrium with market clearing. Firms and workers only contract for a volume of employment different from the natural rate because of it. If both types of agents had the same beliefs about the inflation rate, they would agree on the equilibrium volume of employment – even if both were wrong about the rate of inflation in prospect.

For the clockwise loop, entrepreneurs perceive what the rate of inflation is going to be before workers do. To get the counterclockwise loop, we should assume that labor catches on before firms do.[5] When the inflation rate is stepped up and workers, perceiving it correctly, demand unchanged real wages, firms (incorrectly) see a rise in the real supply price of labor and, consequently, offer less employment. It is a possible story but, intuitively, it seems somewhat contrived.[6]

Models of the type just discussed are so simple in structure that there is hardly anything else than the real wage that agents can be wrong about. It is not something one should be wrong about for very long, moreover, for the missing information should be gained quickly if not immediately: workers bamboozled into accepting jobs at apparently attractive remuneration will find out the price level that goes with their money wage 'by next period' at the latest. Persistent and large-scale disequilibria are unlikely in this setting, therefore. A single relative price to worry about and a one-period time horizon make for a coordination problem simple enough that adjustments in the money wage responding to the excess demand for labor are all it takes to ensure a quick return to equilibrium activity levels.

The missing market mechanism theory, as we have seen, leads its proponents to wish for more policy instruments. Monetarist natural rate theory will make one wish for less. Both unemployment and inflation are results of monetary mismanagement. The policy implication of it all, of course, is just to cease and desist.

## STAGFLATION III: THE MYSTERY OF SAVING AND INVESTMENT

Although we have not heard much about them in recent years, there is a whole class of older business cycle theories that made investment the villain of their plots. Let us call these 'real' business cycle theories to distinguish them from 'monetary' (or Monetarist) ones where the causal impulse always stems from the money supply. Keynes's theory was a 'real' one in this sense. It will be of particular interest here because of its central contention that a functioning labor market mechanism would not by itself suffice to guarantee full employment if the system failed appropriately to coordinate saving and investment. If, at full-employment real income, there is an *ex ante* 'gap' between saving and investment, reductions in the money wage will not restore equilibrium.

Could the recession phase of such a cycle coincide with inflation? Or, to express the same question from a different angle, was the 'real' business cycle a problem that could all along have been wiped out by inflationary policies?

Consider how a recession develops from a 'real' disturbance. Suppose we start with the economy on a full-employment equilibrium growth path. Next, there is 'a decline in the marginal efficiency of capital' (as it used to be called in Keynesian analysis), perhaps due to a slackening in the rate of technical progress. If all agents perceive correctly what has happened, the system as a whole should adapt rationally to changed circumstances and traverse to a lower growth path. Resources should be transferred from capital goods producing industries to consumption industries. This should not entail any reduction in aggregate employment, nor need that the amount of labor demanded necessarily be less even if money wage rates stay unchanged. The interest rate should fall, so that desired saving will not exceed the new lower level of investment.

But all agents will not in general correctly assess what is happening. Information on the decline in prospective yields on new investment is dispersed piecemeal among entrepreneurs, each of whom is concerned primarily with the prospects of his own firm, and most of whom have limited confidence in their own forecasts. No one has a complete overview of the investment outlook in every industry. Each firm that cuts its investment spending will, however, also reduce its demand for external funds. Information on the reduced supply of new securities will be pooled in financial markets, where investors will, in effect, have to take a position on what they believe has happened to the economy-wide real rate of return. If they underestimate the decline, that is, if they overestimate the real rate that can be earned at a full-employment investment level, there will emerge what Keynes called a 'speculative' demand for money. On balance, the financial markets take a bearish stance, with most investors going liquid, hoping to buy back into the market later at lower securities prices. The speculative demand is a net increase in the aggregate demand for money relative to an unchanged supply. The resulting excess demand for money, coupled with the excess supply of commodities (due to the cut in investment spending), means that nominal aggregate demand will fall.

In our natural rate of unemployment analysis, deviations from employment equilibrium stemmed from inconsistent beliefs on the part of firms and workers with regard to the real purchasing power of the agreed upon money wage. This problem does not arise in the saving–investment case. Here, the discoordination stems instead from the inconsistent belief of firms and security markets investors about the realizable rate of real profit in the economy. This inconsistency is revealed in the decline of money income below its equilibrium value. Prevailing money wages are in line with equilibrium money income. If there had been no misunderstanding between entrepreneurs and investors, the system would have continued at full employment without any change in money wage rates. Once these groups have failed to reconcile their beliefs about the prospective return to capital (leaving, in Wicksellian terms, a market rate in excess of the natural rate), there is nothing that labor can do by adjusting their wage demands that will restore the economy to general equilibrium.[7] We may suppose that the one thing workers will not do immediately is to auction off their services for the day at whatever wage employers will pay in total disregard of their own beliefs about what the equilibrium rate is. If, consequently, money wages fail to fall in proportion to the decline in nominal aggregate demand, the result will be unemployment.

This story can be summarized in the form of the following excess demand table (Table 6.1):

*Table 6.1*

|  | Labor | Commodities | Securities | Money |
|---|---|---|---|---|
| Initial equilibrium | 0 | 0 | 0 | 0 |
| MEC declines | 0 | ES | ED | 0 |
| Interest rate declines | 0 | ES | 0 | ED |
| Money income and employment fall | (ES) | 0 | 0 | 0 |

The question is: Can unemployment arise in this way in the midst of an inflation? The notion that it well might would seem to run into trouble in the third row of the table. It shows an excess demand for money arising at one stage of the process.[8] But inflation is supposed to be fueled by an excess supply of money. So how could we have both at once?

## Two Questions

We now have two questions about stagflation. First, could one simultaneously observe unemployment, excess capacity and other excess supply phenomena together with rising money prices if markets generally were competitive?[9] Second, if in the traditional aggregate demand theories of business cycles – whether Monetarist or Keynesian – it takes an excess demand for money to produce a recession and an excess supply of money to produce inflation, can these theories provide a sensible explanation for stagflation?

Those who see a riddle in the coexistence of excess supplies and rising money prices in competitive markets are, I think, led astray by an ambiguity that has long been tolerated in theoretical accounts of how the market mechanism is supposed to work.

The usual story that we tell in the classroom (if indeed we go beyond just pointing to the intersection of supply and demand) might go like this: 'if good $i$ is in excess supply, competition between dissatisfied sellers will make the (money) price of $i$ fall'.

I believe we will have to get used to putting it a bit more carefully than that. For example: 'if good $i$ is in excess supply, competition between suppliers of good $i$ should make them reduce the amount of purchasing power over other goods that is demanded when a unit of good $i$ is offered'. It is helpful, at least at first, to try to peer through the veil of money. If the suppliers of a good cannot sell all that they would like to sell, they will have to offer better terms, that is, better real terms. This does not necessarily entail asking for less money.

The ambiguity of the first short-hand statement used not to matter. 'Back in the good old days', whenever we were not talking about some hypothetical barter exchange in the first place, we were talking about monetary exchange in the presumed setting of a monetary standard so constructed as to assure the approximate constancy of the purchasing power of money over the longer run. In that setting, of course, a seller who wants to offer better terms for what he is selling has to ask for less money per unit.

Imagine, then, if you will, a monetary standard so constructed that money as a claim on real resources 'wastes away' at 15 per cent per year. In that setting, if excess supply prevails in a market, theory makes us expect to observe sellers offer buyers gradually better terms – which is to say, the money price in that market should rise at a pace less than an annual rate of 15 per cent. That much is straightforward. This good is then getting cheaper in terms of those goods whose money prices do rise at a rate of 15 per cent or higher.

But can we have this happening to all non-money goods at the same time? If all non-money goods are in excess supply, then money must (by Say's principle) be in corresponding excess demand. And that, of course, is quite possible. The assumption, in the present case, that money is a depreciating asset does not exclude the possibility of a generalized excess demand for money – for real cash balances.

### Gesell Money

The conceptual experiment of the 'depreciating standard' is not a perfect analogy for a real world inflation. If it is spelled out in some more detail, we can then see where it fits and where it does not fit.

Consider a case of 'ordinary' inflation where the government causes the money stock to grow by 15 per cent per annum. For simplicity, let us suppose that 15 per cent money growth produces a 15 per cent inflation. We ignore the growth in real GNP.

The analogical case suggested above, is one of stamped money. All government-issued money is dated. At the date of issue, a one-dollar bill will legally discharge a debt of one dollar. One year later, we suppose, it will only discharge a debt of 85 cents. The legal tender law is redrawn to make legal tender depreciate in its purchasing power at 15 per cent per year. Banking laws can be rewritten so that checking deposits are compelled to behave similarly. Money issue might be handled as follows. We may imagine that the initial money issue was distributed over all the days of the year. Subsequently, every day the monetary authorities retire the money issued one year earlier and reissue money to the same face value amount, 85 cents of each reissued dollar goes to the citizens who are returning old dollars to the central bank. Fifteen cents to the dollar is the seigniorage that is available for resource absorption by the government.[10] If operated in this manner, this Gesell money scheme[11] will keep the nominal stock of money constant and thus stabilize the price level.

So it is not a case of inflation at all. In fact, all that this conceptual experiment has in common with a real world inflation are the consequences of inflation exhibited by a neoclassical monetary growth model of constant, foreseen inflation – which is to say, very little. People will hold less of this taxed money than they would if it was not taxed; their attempts to economize on the holding of real balances will be associated with certain, rather trivial, efficiency losses. But that is all.[12]

Suppose, then, we have an economy in equilibrium with a given stock of Gesell money. Assume some event that produces a decline in the marginal efficiency of capital. If now, on balance, securities market investors underestimate the decline in real rates of return that the maintenance of equilibrium requires, there will emerge a speculative demand for money (even as it continues to depreciate), putting downward pressure on money income. From this juncture on, the recession would develop according to the standard Keynesian scenario.

In real terms, the analysis should come off exactly the same if we change the setting to that of a system which is initially in equilibrium on a 15 per cent 'foreseen' inflation time path. For concreteness, assume that all agents watch the actual rate of money creation and gear their price setting directly to this 'anticipated' magnitude. In that case, prices will be rising at 15 per cent per annum, but the Keynesian intertemporal coordination failure will not allow nominal aggregate demand to expand commensurably. The result would be unemployment in excess of the equilibrium rate of unemployment.

This type of stagflation – if it occurs – may be more persistent than the type of unemployment under inflationary conditions that we analysed under the natural rate heading. Recall that in the Monetarist analysis of deviations from the natural rate of unemployment, the errors in employment resulted from inconsistent beliefs about the real value of the money wage being paid. Since experience should in short order reveal erroneous expectations about this magnitude, we do not expect these deviations to be of very large magnitude or of long duration. In the Keynesian case, we have an error in the demand price for reproducible durable physical assets. At first, the demand prices are too low because the market rate of interest at which future expected earnings are discounted is too high. This error will be rectified as the recession develops. But the experience of the recession will at the same time erode expected future earnings, and this effect will not be falsified by experience in short order.

The Gesell-money analogy teaches us that the statement that 'inflation is caused by an excess supply of money' is misleading. Money stock growth in excess of real output growth is necessary to sustain an inflation. But the rate of money growth just sufficient to sustain inflation at the rate (firmly) expected by the public will correspond to a zero excess supply of money.

**Inflation and Allocation**

Friedman, in his Nobel lecture, warned that stagflation may be the inevitable outcome of persistently inflationary policies. High rates of inflation will make the economy increasingly inefficient. This, I have no doubt, is true. But it is not clear that these inflation-induced inefficiencies will predominantly be of a kind that reduces the demand for labor. Nor does it seem particularly plausible that persistent inflation will produce a predominant and persistent inconsistency of beliefs between firms and workers of the particular kind that will generate unemployment in excess of the natural rate according to our earlier analysis. So a strictly Monetarist monocausal explanation of stagflation is not very convincing.

Is inflation likely to turn into stagflation? My earlier analysis showed that we should not expect inflationary policies to erase the business cycle. It did not show that inflation would produce recession. On the contrary, the kind of inflation presupposed in that analysis – the kind of inflation for which the stable Gesell money system makes a close analogy – comes so close to being neutral with regard to resource allocation that it makes the possibility of inflation producing its own recession seem utterly far-fetched. An inflation of the constant, predictable rate variety should not affect the marginal efficiency of capital (in real terms). Unless it does, a Keynesian (saving–investment) theory is not going to produce a conclusion at all different from Monetarist theory.

So where do we stand now? We have taken three different theories of unemployment and shown that each of them is consistent with simultaneous inflation. It is certainly useful to know that one must not expect inflation to eliminate unemployment problems – important people have been confused about that – but neither Stagflation theory I, nor II, nor III seem adequate to an understanding of the American experience of the last fifteen or so years. We need not, I think, look around for a fourth theory of unemployment. It is the theory of inflation presumed in each of our three stagflation theories that is no good.

## Anticipated Inflation Examined

Current inflation theory poses two polar cases, unanticipated and anticipated inflation, and would have us characterize an inflationary economy as located somewhere on the spectrum of possibilities defined by these two extremes. The analysis of unanticipated inflation assumes that people do not know what is going on. It will not help us explain stagflation, because it implies overemployment. The theory of anticipated inflation assumes that people do know what is going on and, consequently, are able to predict inflation accurately enough so as very nearly to neutralize its effects. This is a perfectly logical model. But as a theory of inflation, it is nonsense. It is important to understand why it is nonsense.

Implicitly, the theory of anticipated inflation asserts that inflation can be cured overnight, with the benefits of so doing in no measure offset by the social costs usually thought to accompany disinflation. It implies, to put it plainly, that the problem that we have agonized over for a decade and a half could be gone tomorrow.

Recall once more that our Gesell money exercise is a perfect real-terms analogue for the anticipated inflation case. It is obvious that the Gesell world can be restored to 'non-inflationary conditions'[13] very easily. First, you simply abolish the 15 per cent tax on its money – a matter of a stroke of the pen. Second, recognizing that Gesell denizens will demand larger real balances when money is not taxed, you increase the stock of nominal money sufficiently to avoid creating deflationary pressure on the economy. That is all. Naturally, one does not expect any unemployment to develop as a consequence of these measures.

How do you do it when you have to deal, not with the Gesell analogue, but with a 'real' anticipated inflation of 15 per cent? The trick is a currency reform which I will call the 'blueback' scheme. Assuming that the inflation rate has been fixed at 15 per cent in terms of 'greenback' dollars, the government should issue 'bluebacks' that by law appreciate at a rate of 15 per cent per year relative to greenbacks. On the day of the currency reform, $T$, the exchange rate of bluebacks for greenbacks is unity but, from that day onward, bluebacks grow in their legal capacity to extinguish debt contracted in greenbacks in this manner:

$$\$_{\text{blue}} = \$_{\text{green}} e^{(-.15)(t-T)}$$

This means, for instance, that a debt of 1000 greenback dollars due and payable at $T=10$ years can be discharged by handing over (approximately) 192 blueback dollars. Note that, under the assumed conditions, neither debtor nor creditor would be at all upset by the passage of the blueback currency law. Both already knew, on day $T$, that 1000 greenbacks ten years hence would have the purchasing power of no more than 192 'constant $T$-date dollars'. No one will object.

Greenbacks will rapidly disappear from circulation, since they are taxed and bluebacks are not. To avoid deflationary pressure in the transition to price stability, therefore, somewhat more bluebacks have to be issued than the greenbacks retired. If this is only done right, the unemployment rate should be quite unaffected by the currency reform. We now have a zero inflation rate in the blueback currency.

Anyone who will accept the blueback scheme as a solution for the world's inflation problems is welcome to it. If real world inflations were adequately represented by the anticipated inflation model, the blueback scheme would be the perfect cure. But the conclusion to draw, I believe, is that the anticipated inflation model should be rejected as a theory of inflation.

On what grounds?

The initial conditions assumed for the exercises fail to replicate the conditions relevant to the present inflation in essential respects. The model assumes a believable precommitment by the government with regard to future rate of money growth, a precommitment which extends, moreover, into the indefinite future. (In our example, we assumed a constant rate of money creation, to be guaranteed for at least ten years beyond date *T*.) Such precommitments must entail significant constraints on the discretionary monetary policy choices in future periods. In the case that we have analysed, the monetary authorities are bound to create money at a 15 per cent rate – neither more nor less. The anticipated inflation model presumes what amounts to a monetary constitution so restrictive as to leave virtually no room at all for discretion by the money-creating authorities. The model *must* assume this, for rational agents will not anticipate a rate of inflation that no one is trying to maintain.

As a theory the model is plainly wrong. No one is trying to produce any particular rate of inflation. People who do know what is going on will not 'anticipate' the inflation. People who know what is going on will know that the future rate of inflation cannot be predicted (or its effects neutralized) because the relevant political authorities have refused to commit themselves to any particular future pattern of money growth. They are in effect asking private sector agents to make their long-term commitments first while reserving their own options. Among these will be, in particular, all the possible 'unanticipated' monetary policies that will falsify any assumptions about monetary policy on the basis of which private contracts may have been concluded. The only commitment of which policy-makers (and their economic advisors) have given evidence is that of playing the short-run Phillips curve, one period at a time, as that curve shifts, and tilts, and loops the loop.

This maximization of the short-period discretion of the policy authorities does not add up to a framework for monetary stability. It is not a rational regime. But it is what we have ended up with.

Standard inflation theory focuses our attention on the rate of inflation. The blueback scheme shows that the inflation rate, within an otherwise stable and predictable monetary regime, can be brought down overnight. The rate is not our problem, the regime is.

### The Riddle of Random Monetary Mismanagement

A useful theory should match its assumptions about what people know and can predict to the policy regime with which they have to live. Regimes that significantly constrain the future exercise of discretion by the monetary authorities will be called *constitutional*. Commodity standards, fixed exchange rate systems and systems obeying Friedman rules exemplify constitutional regimes. The present policy regime of the United States does not belong in this set. In analysing the consequences of inflation, the alternatives to be compared are not price stability on the one hand with constant, predictable inflation on the other – or a stable with a depreciating monetary standard. Instead, we should contrast a stable monetary regime with what may be described as a random walk monetary standard (RWMS).[14]

Under the RWMS, the authorities decide one period at a time whether to accelerate, keep constant or decelerate the rate of money stock growth. They are assumed to take only present period economic conditions and immediate political pressures into account and not to be constrained by concern with the more distant future. The rate of money stock growth at some future date $t$, $M_t$, will not even be seriously contemplated until the last minute – and then chosen on the basis of what seems most pleasant and convenient under the exigencies of that moment to those who happen to be in charge. The identity of policy-makers a few years down the road cannot be predicted, nor do we know what kind of economic theory they will be guided by. To complete the picture, add that this random walk has shown upward drift in the past and that we have little reason to trust the stability of its coefficients.

If we look ahead only one period at a time, the RWMS theory will not differ much from a Monetarist model with comparable short-run uncertainty. Unanticipated monetary policy will cause rates of output and employment to differ from 'natural' activity levels. A Keynesian habit of mind will make one pay particular attention to saving and investment. This means looking several periods ahead. Under the RWMS, the uncertainty attaching to forecasts of future price levels increases very rapidly as one tries to peer further into the future.

Real earnings on the existing capital stock, as well as prospective real rates of profit on new investment as perceived by producers, will be reduced in a RW inflation for the following reasons.

1. A purely nominal increase in earnings will be taxed as a rise in real profits. This, of course, is a feature of any inflation, as long as the tax code remains nominally defined, and has nothing to do with its randomness.

2. Whenever producers fail to anticipate short-term monetary policy, they will fail also to choose the right activity levels. In the RWMS environment, rational producers know that they must look forward to an indefinite sequence of short runs, in the course of which failures to produce at the rate where marginal revenue equals marginal cost are likely to be more frequent and the errors larger than they would be in a regime providing monetary stability

3. In the RWMS environment, private contractual agreements become more uncertain as to their real outcomes. With contracting a less effective and

reliable strategy, economic agents will try supplementary strategies for controlling the real terms on which they can obtain or dispose of resources. These supplementary strategies are apt to be political and, when successful, to result in price controls and other forms of costly governmental regulation.[15] To the extent that increasing union activism in the RWMS environment may lead to a worsening of labor relations in industry, this too should be listed among the factors contributing to reduced prospective profits.

On these grounds, then, we predict that investment, and hence the rate of economic growth,[16] will be reduced under RWMS conditions. But from this inference one should not jump to the further conclusion that the reduced investment should also be predicted to produce a Keynesian increase in unemployment. One must first ask what is likely to happen to saving.

Consider first the returns on financial assets that savers might demand. On stocks, real earnings per share have fallen. On bonds (free of default risk), the maximum real rate of interest that can be found must have fallen by as much as has the general rate of profit in the economy. In addition, short real rates of interest can be expected to fall, not only by as much as the rate of profit, but also relative to it.[17] This is so because the RWMS creates a strong incentive to postpone irrevocable commitments. The uncertainty that agents face concerning the price level at any future date $T$ can be sharply reduced simply by waiting. If it is possible to delay committing money to a project until one is closer to $T$, the final decision can be made with considerably less uncertainty about the money returns. Meanwhile, the resources awaiting definitive placement will have to be held in short-term, money-denominated assets. The flexibility premium that the market is willing to pay for the privilege of carrying resources over time without having them committed may be high enough, if the real rate of profit is also quite low, to cause real short rates of interest to be persistently negative.

These conditions should discourage the accumulation of financial assets by households and cause a redirection of saving into tangibles, such as consumer durables and housing. Household accumulation of tangible assets is, of course, itself a part of aggregate demand. For a Keynesian analysis of aggregate demand, we should compare changes in investment to changes in savers' demand for financial assets.

In principle, a Wicksell–Keynes recession might occur in the course of an inflation. We may well imagine that, along an inflationary time path, there develops a situation where the market 'real' rate of interest exceeds the natural rate of interest (as in Wicksell); with investment exceeding full-employment saving, the economy will then respond (as in Keynes) with a contraction of output and unemployment. It is a possible stagflation scenario.

Hypotheses of this class have hardly been explored at all in the stagflation discussion. One reason for this may be that everyone knows that *ex post* real rates have been consistently very low, and short ones even negative – which makes it seem implausible that market rates are also 'too high'. But one should not underestimate the extent to which RW inflation increases risks and undermines the prospective real rate of profit. Real rates of interest have fallen far, but the marginal efficiency of investment perceived in American manufacturing has obviously fallen farther – for investment has declined. Although real rates of return are abnormally low, the possibility of an inflationary recession of this kind cannot be ruled out. But I do not think that it is in fact relevant to recent experience.

A random walk inflation does reduce the marginal efficiency of capital and will keep it persistently low. Yet, it is obvious that this has not led to persistent Keynesian unemployment. In fact, the American economy in the 1970s proved itself capable of generating new jobs at an unprecedented pace. Apparently, the RWMS discourages saving even more than it does investment.[18] US investment is low, but US saving does not suffice to finance it. Foreign capital inflow into the United States has become substantial.


## STAGFLATION IV

The random walk monetary regime depresses economic growth, both by reducing capital accumulation and by slowing down productivity increases. It will also exacerbate social tensions and undermine popular confidence in inherited political institutions and social arrangements. The last decade and a half of monetary mismanagement has been a self-imposed disaster for the United States, the dimensions of which most American economists have only begun to recognize.

The recessions that have been superimposed on this trend – in 1970–71, 1975–76, 1980–? – are probably best to be explained in standard Monetarist fashion as due to decelerations in money growth that were 'unanticipated' at least in the sense that the authorities' perseverance in pursuit of their stated goals was generally doubted.

This view of the macroeconomic problems of the United States uses a RWMS version of Stagflation III to explain the persistently disappointing performance of the American economy in this period, and Stagflation II to account for the sharper recessions that punctuate this depressing story. But it does not make use of Stagflation I at all. One does not need the 'new supply-side economics' to explain the stylized facts.

What makes the energy problem a crisis is precisely what has turned the inflation problem into a crisis, namely our persistent inability to look at the facts squarely and then do what must be done. What must be done with the inflation is to return to non-inflationary conditions within a new framework for monetary stability.[19] To the extent that 'new supply-side economics' is used to conceal this or serves to divert attention from it, it is a harmful doctrine.

# NOTES

1.  Economists who insist that this version of the theory is strictly Keynesian make a needless puzzle of the initial victory of Keynesianism in the United States. The period 1933–37 in the United States had large-scale (albeit shrinking) unemployment combined with considerable inflation.
2.  See, for example, Haberler (1977).
3.  Tobin (1972).
4.  Darby (1976, pp. 159–60, 334–49).
5.  Assuming that, when firms know what is going on, labor has an exaggerated notion of the inflation rate that will produce the same consequences.
6.  When Friedman considered stagflation in his Nobel lecture, he did not take this tack. Instead, he argued that high rates of inflation render the economy increasingly inefficient (see Friedman 1977). Agreed. It is not obvious, however, that the inefficiency will be of a kind that reduces the demand for labor.
7.  For detailed discussion, see Leijonhufvud (1981b, especially section 6).
8.  This excess demand for money, moreover, is a necessary part of the story. If no excess demand for money emerges as the interest rate declines, the market rate will fall until it coincides with the natural rate; full employment saving will equal investment on a lower growth path; there will be no deflationary pressure on the price level – and the equilibrium volume of employment will be offered at prevailing money wages.
9.  By 'competitive', I do not here mean suppliers facing infinitely elastic demand curves', but suppliers engaging in, and finding themselves subject to, rivalrous behavior.
10. Some economists believe that an optimizing government will make use of the inflation tax on money and that this explains why we have inflation. I do not subscribe to that theory but believe rather that politicians, economists and central bankers tend to make a sorry mess of things and thus create outcomes that few of them really desire. At any rate, if the motive for persisting in inflationary policies were indeed the revenues they provide, then my depreciating money standard is a much preferable manner of going about it. See note 12 below.
11. Silvio Gesell's stamped money scheme is today remembered chiefly because of Keynes's fascination with it at the time that he completed the *General Theory* (Keynes 1936, especially p. 357). My main argument in the text is, of course, that Gesell money would not eliminate the business cycle or, more to the point, prevent the occurrence of recessions of a Keynesian type. Keynes's delight with the Gesell scheme was not well founded, therefore, but due rather to his characteristic failure to distinguish between nominal and real interest rates.
12. Compared to a 15 per cent steady inflation, the depreciating standard introduced the transactions cost of constantly updating the legal exchange value of money balances. But it removes the costs of intermittently revising prices. When prices of different goods are changed on different dates, changes in relative prices that tend to misdirect resources occur. The inflation becomes 'ragged' (Leijonhufvud 1977). This is avoided altogether by the depreciating standard method of taxing money balances. This method also avoids, of course, disrupting the intended outcome of private contracts concluded prior to the governmental decision to raise revenues in this peculiar manner.

13. Admittedly, this is a somewhat paradoxical expression since the price level is already constant in the Gesell money exercise. But it is nonetheless precise, in context.
14. Or, more accurately, random walk monetary growth-rate standard. My UCLA colleague, Benjamin Klein, whom I would credit with the basic idea of approaching these problems from the standpoint of a theory of monetary standards, has suggested what amounts to a random walk in the price level (rather than inflation rate) as a suitable analytical characterization for the US policy regime from the mid-1930s to the early 1960s (Klein 1976).
15. This argument is developed at length in Leijonhufvud (1977).
16. Productivity growth will be lower in part because investment is lower. But productivity is also apt to be reduced because the 'raggedness' of an RW inflation makes it more difficult to combine resources optimally. There is apt to be less in the way of productivity improvements, moreover, because managerial talent is absorbed in all the various ways of playing the inflation.
17. The short real rate is compared to the profit rate here because it is not clear what deflator should be applied to nominal long rates in order to calculate real long rates under RWMS conditions. In addition, the RWMS is bound to cause a thinning out of long-term markets, since borrowers and lenders alike can be counted on to be averse to the enormous price-level uncertainty that the RWMS creates over the long run.
18. The facts are not as uncomplicated as in my text. Over the period 1965–78 Fellner's study shows a large rise in the ratio of tangible wealth to income and a large drop in the ratio of financial wealth to income. Financial wealth in real terms has indeed declined absolutely. But the proportion of current income allocated to the acquisition of financial assets has actually increased somewhat (Fellner 1979). The reason for this rise in the ratio of financial saving to disposable income is that households cannot allow their real holdings of money, savings deposits and the like to shrink at the rate of their negative yield during the inflation. Once the volume of real cash balances demanded has been adjusted to their negative yield, for example, what is taken out by the inflation tax has to be replenished through saving each period. The portion of financial saving that is undertaken to offset the inflation tax on financial assets should be compared with the spending done by the government out of the proceeds of the tax in order to see what happens to the overall savings 'leakage' out of the circular flow. As indicated by the text, it is my conjecture that this leakage has declined by at least as much as has the investment 'injection' in the course of the American inflation.
19. What must be done with the energy problem is even more obvious. Real oil prices in the United States must sooner or later be brought to the level where the price elasticity of demand (net of domestic supplies) is about unity. This can be done by imposing our own taxes, with the revenues staying in the country. Or it will be done by the OPEC cartel, with the revenues going abroad. Obviously there will never be any strain on the cartel at prices much below this level – any disagreement between its members can be resolved by a 'positive sum' move. For seven years. American policy has been based on the hope that a monopoly can be sweet-talked out of charging a monopoly price. When one cartel member lets his price lag a few months behind the rest, this is apparently regarded as proving this hope well founded.

# 8.    Inflation and economic performance

A *monetary regime* is defined as a system of expectations that governs the behavior of the public and that is sustained by the consistent behavior of the policy-making authorities. The effects of the great inflation on American economic performance, in my view, are very largely attributable to a change in regime. The conventional story of the welfare costs of inflation, in contrast, analyses the consequences of a rise in the rate of depreciation of real balances within an otherwise unchanged policy regime.[1] In so defining the problem, it misses the boat.

One important class of misallocative effects of inflation, namely those that are due to the nominal rigidity of taxes, subsidies and sundry laws and regulations, will be slighted in what follows. I do not slight their importance. They are obviously of major significance. They are avoided here, however, because in that direction lies a bottomless swamp of public finance problems, from which one could not hope to extricate oneself in half a paper. The current inflation poses problems that go to the very core of monetary theory. These problems need to be addressed, have not been addressed, and deserve priority.


## THE ANTICIPATED INFLATION MODEL

To have a willing audience among economists for a discussion of inflation's effects on economic performance, one must first deal with the following syllogism:

Inflation is a monetary phenomenon.
Money is neutral.
When people adapt to it rationally, inflation becomes neutral.

What is wrong with that?

The anticipated inflation model is a most useful analytical tool. Yet for too many of us, it has been a snare and a delusion. It is a good model that makes bad theory.

To see why this is so, imagine a constant-rate, fully anticipated inflation to which the economy has had time to adjust completely. All existing contracts have been concluded on the presumption, shared by both parties, that the inflation will continue at this pace forever. For concreteness, let the inflation rate be 15 per cent. Ignoring the inflation tax on real balances or, alternatively, assuming that competition among banks will keep the real rate of return on money unchanged, suppose that this economy functions in real terms exactly as if the price level were constant. By this assumption (and for present purposes only), the inflation is strictly neutral. We want to contrast two ways of getting from this 15 per cent inflation to a constant price level.

The slow and painful way is *disinflation*. Under the assumed conditions, reducing the rate of growth of the money supply by 15 per cent should bring on another Great Depression. Nobody expects the deflationary shock. It violates firm and universally shared expectations and will, therefore, bring about the worst possible contraction of output and employment. It changes the real terms of all outstanding contracts and forces a massive transfer of wealth from debtors to creditors. It is unlikely that all of this wealth could in fact be transferred; widespread bankruptcies are bound to occur, and an 'implosion' of the financial system similar to that of 1929–33 is probable.

This analysis of disinflation from a firmly anticipated inflation verges on self-contradiction. One poses a hypothetical inflationary process that has minimal social cost because it is fully anticipated; one juxtaposes a mode of ending the inflation that incurs maximal social costs because it is totally unanticipated. Less starkly drawn, this contrast is often painted by economists who want to suggest, (1) that inflation is not so bad, and (2) that the time to deal with it is never now. But the game is rigged. One should not assume that people who live in a regime where a 15 per cent deceleration might happen at any time are going to plan confidently on the continuation of inflation at a constant rate. If they do not so plan, however, the costs of inflation are not necessarily minimal, and the entire matter needs to be re-examined.

The quick and painless way to end an anticipated inflation is the currency reform that I call the 'blueback' scheme. Since, under the assumed conditions, 'greenback' dollars depreciate in real purchasing power by 15 per cent per year, one should create a new blueback currency and make it, by law, appreciate relative to greenbacks at 15 per cent per year. On the initial date the exchange rate between the two monies is one for one, but from that day onward bluebacks grow constantly in their legal capacity to extinguish debts contracted in greenbacks. One year later, 85 blueback cents will pay off a one-dollar greenback debt; two years later, it takes about 71 blueback cents; ten years later, 19 cents.

If the originally held expectation of a constant 15 per cent greenback inflation of indefinite duration were indeed rational, then the blueback reform would ensure perfect price-level stability indefinitely. The scheme has two advantages over disinflation. First, employment is entirely unaffected. It is not necessary to suffer through a recession to get back to constant prices.[2] Second, no one is swindled in the process. The real terms of contracts remain to be fulfilled as originally envisaged. Creditors who after ten years received 19 blue cents instead of one green dollar are getting exactly what they expected to get in real purchasing power. Both of these advantages of the currency reform over disinflation stem, of course, from the fact that *nothing is really done* about the greenback inflation. The rate of greenback inflation is not reduced at all; it is only made subject to an arithmetical conversion. It is a cheap trick, if you will. But it does not evade the real issue. On the contrary, 'really doing something' about the greenback inflation would be an irrational, destructive policy under the conditions assumed. It is assumed that we start from a quite stable *monetary standard*, which happens to have the peculiar property that money depreciates in real purchasing power at 15 per cent a year. The public firmly expects this regime to continue. To disinflate is to adopt a policy that is inconsistent with this system of expectations. It would break the prevailing regime and wreak havoc. The blueback scheme, by contrast, merely removes the peculiar property of this otherwise stable regime.

## THE RANDOM WALK MONETARY STANDARD

The wrong way to get rid of an anticipated inflation is to disinflate. The right way is to convert to bluebacks. Nothing could be simpler, or politically easier, than to cure an inflation that conforms to the assumptions of this model. But it does not follow that the blueback scheme is preferable to disinflation in coping with the great American inflation. What follows is only the conclusion that the assumptions of the anticipated inflation model evade the real issue.

The model presupposes the government's believable precommitment to future rates of money growth. This precommitment extends into the indefinite future. It binds the authorities to create money at the requisite rate so as to keep the 15 per cent inflation rate absolutely steady. Only a firm commitment of this sort could sustain the expectations assumed in the model. Rational agents will not anticipate a rate of inflation that no one is even trying to bring about. This, then, is a system where policy-makers have either relinquished or been deprived of all short-run discretionary authority. The system operates, in effect, under a *monetary constitution*, and a very restrictive one at that. What could be less descriptive of the policy regime that has been allowed to develop in the United States during the last twenty years?

How, then, should we characterize the current monetary regime of the United States? Our definition of the concept of 'monetary regime' had two parts to it: it is (1) a system of expectations governing the behavior of the public, and (2) a corresponding set of behavior rules for the policy-making authorities that will sustain these expectations. We choose among possible regimes by choosing behavior rules for the policy-making authorities. In the example above, the public unanimously predicts a particular constant inflation rate and the authorities are rigidly bound to produce it.

In 1984 the monetary authorities of the United States – that is the Administration, the Congress, and the Federal Reserve System – do not obey *any* reasonably well-defined set of policy rules that would tend to produce some particular, reasonably predictable path of the price level over the long haul. There is no monetary constitution in effect that limits the short-run options of the authorities for the purpose of providing long-run stability.

In order to have a label for the present regime, I will refer to it as the *random walk monetary standard*. This should be understood as a metaphorical name rather than a technical description of the regime. The metaphor captures some of the relevant properties, but the system is not as neat and tidy a money supply process as a random walk in the technical statistical sense.[3] Under the random walk standard, the policy-making authorities decide one period at a time whether to accelerate, keep constant or decelerate the rate of money supply growth. Only current economic conditions and immediate political pressure are taken into account in making this decision. It is not constrained by concern with a more distant future. What the rate of growth of the money stock is going to be at future dates will not even be discussed until the last minute – and then it will be chosen on the basis of what seems, under the exigencies of the moment, most pleasant and convenient to those who happen to be in charge. Short-run discretion is maximized. It is constantly exercised. The result is a monetary regime for the United States that is thoroughly bad, albeit not the worst imaginable.

If we look ahead only one period at a time (whatever length of calendar time this might refer to), the theory of a random walk standard does not seem to introduce anything new. Unanticipated monetary policy will, in familiar fashion, cause rates of output and employment to diverge from 'natural' activity levels. But it is not obvious that monetary policy over the next six or twelve months is significantly harder to anticipate today than it was twenty years ago. The public knows the people in office, knows the current economic and political conditions they have to cope with, and knows a little something about what economic theories they tend to be guided by. The educated guesses about what actions the authorities will take that rational people make from such information inputs will differ. But in this respect, things have not changed much.

What is harder to anticipate is the cumulative effect of random walk monetary management over several periods. The 1981 price level may not have looked much more uncertain in 1980 than the 1961 price level looked in 1960. But in 1960, reasonable people thought the 1970 price level could be predicted within reasonable bounds. In 1980, putting a number on the 1990 price level could only be a joke. Under a random walk monetary standard, the uncertainty of future price levels increases rapidly the further one looks into the future. It is especially the long-term commitments of the private sector, therefore, that will be adversely affected by the refusal of the monetary authorities to precommit themselves over the long run.

Over the long run, monetary policy is unpredictable because we do not know what people will be in charge, what conditions they will face or what economic theories they will believe in. Successive growth rates of the money stock are not the results of coordinated decisions at each separate date; rather, they are the outcomes of the confused and unprincipled interaction of Administration, Congress, and Federal Reserve. The rules of this interaction have been more or less designed to dissipate the responsibility for monetary policy in the way most comfortable for all parties. Each can with reason blame the other two. But note that none of these uncertainties would matter very much if some set of constitutional constraints were in force that would prevent the rapid cumulation of moves in one direction. A useful constitution need not be as restrictive as a Friedman rule. A measure of short-term discretion can be allowed if reversion to some mean is built into the system.

## THE RATE OF INFLATION AND ITS VARIABILITY

Our examination of the anticipated inflation model taught us that it takes as much monetary discipline to keep an inflation going at precisely 15 per cent as it takes to maintain price stability. (By 'discipline' we mean simply the narrowing down of the range of otherwise available discretionary policy options.) Discipline is something you accept for the sake of long-run stability or predictability.[4] Conversely, constitutional constraints are relinquished in order to 'buy' more scope for short-term discretionary policy.

These considerations help us explain the relationships between rates of inflation and various measures of the uncertainty associated with it.[5] It is not obvious why highly inflationary environments should be in some significant sense more uncertain. But we do not expect to see inflation rates of 15 per cent or 50 per cent combined with strict monetary discipline. A polity willing and able to uphold a monetary constitution, with all the self-denying ordinances necessary to guarantee a constant inflation rate with only moderate errors, might as well also accord itself the additional benefits of a stable price level.[6] At the same time, we expect to observe double-digit inflation as a frequent occurrence or as the normal order of business in polities that have decided to throw off the shackles of monetary discipline to enjoy the 'kicks' of monetary discretion. Inflation rates of 50 or 100 per cent are most likely to occur in countries where the stability of the political constitution is in doubt – and a monetary constitution cannot be guaranteed where the political constitution is not. In a sample of low-inflation countries, we expect to find an 'undisciplined' one only by the odd coincidence. In a sample of high-inflation countries, we do not expect to find any member proving its willingness and ability to forgo future discretionary options or to guarantee a stable inflation rate.

## RATIONAL EXPECTATIONS UNDER A RANDOM WALK STANDARD

In the anticipated inflation model, the state of expectations can be represented by a single number, namely the expected rate of inflation. We could replace the constant rate of inflation in that model by a more complicated anticipated time path. Similarly, we could allow for some uncertainty owing, for instance, to the technical difficulties of obeying the constitution to the letter. These generalizations would not introduce anything of significant novelty. To keep in the spirit of the model, one should, however, stick to the assumption that the overwhelming majority of agents have the *same* probabilistic beliefs about future price levels. When this is the case, we will call the state of expectations 'coherent'. Incorrect expectations are systematically punished by losses, and correct expectations rewarded by profits. The tendency is strong, therefore, for individual subjective expectations to converge on the constitutionally dictated, objective time path of prices.

If our present regime were a random walk in money growth rates in the proper statistical sense, agents would also learn its objective properties and thus converge on the same expectations. This would be the case, for instance, if the central bank were required (note the 'constitutional' language that unavoidably creeps in!) to have a 'drawing', at fixed temporal intervals, from some normal distribution with zero mean of accelerations and decelerations of money growth rates. Today's actual inflation rate would then be everybody's expected inflation rate for all future periods.[7] Similarly, the variance of every agent's forecast of future price levels would blow up exponentially with distance from the present in the same way. But the statistician's 'drunkard's walk' requires someone who is very drunk – more so than central bankers normally allow themselves to be during working hours.

The actual process does not obey such rigid statistical laws. It is reasonable for rational observers to hold quite different opinions about what is the likely future time path of the price level. States of expectation are then 'incoherent'.

The variance of an individual agent's forecast will be relatively small for the immediate short period: as in the true random walk process, it will grow exponentially with distance from the present. The distribution over agents of expected one-period inflation rates should show a fairly strong central tendency: the 'expected rate of inflation' of current macromodels is perhaps best thought of as the modal current one-period expected rate. But the distribution of expected price levels by agent for dates two, five or ten years into the future is likely to be widely dispersed. It may even be bimodal, for example.[8] Continued experience with living under a random walk standard, moreover, will not make individual long-term price-level forecasts converge. The random walk process will each year reward with profits those who guessed the one-period inflation right; it will chastise with losses those who guessed wrong. But it will not teach either group how to make a more 'objective,' improved two-year or five-year price-level forecast. The profits and losses produced by frequent turnarounds in monetary policy serve no social function of improving collective economic performance.

## THE REDISTRIBUTIVE IMPLICATIONS OF ABANDONING THE RANDOM WALK

At any time, the hangovers of past states of expectation will also be present in the form of outstanding contracts that were concluded at various dates in the past. Inflation expectations are different at different times. Hence we have dollar contracts today, the terms of which are still to be carried out fully, that embody inflation expectations ranging from zero per cent on up into double digits. Many of these contracts, moreover, will owe their existence exclusively to the difference in inflation expectations between creditor and debtor on the date that they were signed. (These, as we will see, are associated with inefficiencies in resource allocation.) Picking an agent at random, we might come up with someone who is in a pension plan presuming zero inflation, has a mortgage embodying a 5 per cent inflation premium, presently expects a 10 per cent inflation rate over the medium term, but is still paying off a loan embodying a 15 per cent expected inflation, and so on.

Why are these hangovers relevant? Past states of mind, one would think, should surely belong in the category of 'bygones that are forever bygones'. What counts for individual private agents is indeed only the forecasts they make now. But the monetary authorities are obliged to take the legacies of the past into account.

To see why this is so, consider the reasons why bluebacking is not unambiguously preferable to disinflating as a means of bringing down the US inflation rate. A return to monetary stability starts with the decision to accord legitimacy to one particular expectation about the time path of prices. Monetary policy will seek to validate the legitimate expectation and, correspondingly, to disappoint all others. Disinflating all the way back to constant prices means that debtors who expected a continuation of inflation will have to pay much larger real sums to their creditors. At the other extreme, stabilizing the greenback inflation rate at 15 per cent, preparatory to bluebacking down to zero per cent, means that all creditors who expected the inflation rate to be brought down from 15 per cent will see part of their wealth transferred to their debtors.

Whichever way you go, the redistributive consequences are complex and colossal. Any decision to commit government policy to the realization of some constitutionally generated price path implies a certain pattern of such redistributions. A governmental precommitment to a particular inflation rate – of zero per cent, 15 per cent or any other number – is politically easy to uphold in an economy that already has a long history of monetary stability around the inflation rate in question. When all agents hold the same expectations, the choice of what expectations to validate is not going to be difficult. The other easy case occurs in the wake of hyperinflation. Hyperinflation reduces the real value of outstanding nominal contracts to next to nothing. The new constitutional framework for monetary stability can be written on a clean slate.

A random walk inflation in the low double digits may be the most difficult to escape from and the most tempting to let continue.[9] To announce a constitutional rule is to propose a pattern of redistributions that, although largely unknown to the authorities, can be calculated by those affected. A continuation of random walk monetary mismanagement will, it is true, cause at least as many unanticipated gains and losses. But these unfold one period at a time. There is never a point in time when their entire present value is focused on the present. Therefore, an unanticipated return to monetary stability will be highly controversial. It also carries risks of a recession the magnitude of which cannot, because of the incoherent state of expectations, be accurately predicted. Consequently, it is more convenient not to decide today. This daily refusal to decide today is the basic feature of the random walk monetary standard.

## Politicization of Central Banking

The redistributive implications of any move toward monetary stability lead to one additional conclusion. The Federal Reserve cannot be expected to decide what expectations are legitimate and should be validated. It is out of the question that the non-elected members of the Federal Open Market Committee (FOMC) should on their own make and enforce decisions with such vast redistributive consequences. The concept of an independent central bank, staffed by professional bankers and standing apart from politics, necessarily requires political agreement on a monetary constitution in order to be practicable. Professional central bankers could be held responsible for managing a gold exchange standard, a Friedman rule or a price stability rule, for example. Given a constitution, the independence of a professional central bank is desirable. In the absence of political agreement on a monetary constitution, however, a non-political central bank becomes impossible. A fiat money-producing bank, under those conditions, can only bend with the day-to-day shifts in the political pressures on it. It may be staffed with people of unquestionable courage, integrity and competence, but they will have no legitimate basis on which to resist these shifting short-term pressures.

It is largely pointless, therefore, to blame the Fed for the erratic course of monetary policy over the last twenty years. The responsibility for monetary stability lies of necessity where the US Constitution puts it – with Congress.

## ECONOMIC PERFORMANCE IN INFLATIONARY REGIMES

We now turn from the theory of inflation to an analysis of its effects on economic performance. An anticipated constitutional inflation, we know, has only trivial social costs – of the order of milk subsidies, perhaps, or tariffs on foreign shoes. The costs and consequences of random walk inflation make a lengthy litany, not all of which can be recited here.[10] I will discuss three categories of effects. The first concerns mistakes in resource allocation due to the inability to predict the inflation rate. The second concerns distortions in resource allocation that are the consequences of individually rational adaptations to the random walk regime. The third concerns the social and political consequences of random walk inflation.

### Expected Forecast Errors: Production and Investment

The dispersion of inflation rate expectations under the random walk monetary standard will lead to inefficiencies in resource allocation that could be avoided in constitutional regimes.[11] Production takes time. Producers commit money today to earn revenues at future dates. For resources to move consistently into their highest valued uses, all agents must be guided by the same relative prices. Agents whose inflation forecasts differ will be guided by inconsistent intertemporal relative values.

The simplest illustration runs as follows. Imagine an industry of numerous identical firms all with the same U-shaped average cost curve. The firms have to buy variable inputs at today's prices to produce output that will be sold at next period's prices. Pick a firm whose expected inflation rate happens to correspond to the inflation premium that the financial market has incorporated into the nominal interest rate. Suppose further that our hand-picked firm chooses to produce at the minimum average cost. At this output, its current marginal cost equals the discounted value of next period's price. Firms that expect more inflation will produce more; those expecting less will produce less. In either case, they incur higher unit costs. The average cost for the industry, consequently, is higher than it should be by an amount that varies positively with the dispersion of inflation expectations.

More generally, today's production decision is a commitment to money expenditures to be made at several dates in the expectation of revenues at (mostly) more distant dates. Again, for resources to move into their socially highest valued uses, all agents should be guided by the same real rate of interest in making their intertemporal allocation decisions. The problem caused by the dispersion over agents of expectations is most easily seen by rewriting the familiar Fisher equation as follows:

$$(\dot{r}_i^e + \dot{p}_i^e) = i = (\dot{r}_j^e + \dot{p}_j^e)$$

where subscripts $i$ and $j$ denote individual market participants. Competition will ensure that all transactors face the same nominal rate, $i$. But for both our agents to use the same real rate in their economic calculations, $\dot{r}_i^e = \dot{r}_j^e$, their inflation expectations would have to be uniform, $\dot{p}_i^e = \dot{p}_j^e$. The dispersion over agents of inflation rate expectations is likely to increase as we consider dates further removed from the present. We conclude, therefore, that long-term investment is particularly likely to be inefficiently allocated.

The volume of investment will also be reduced. The expected return on investment is reduced, and its variance is increased. Both factors will tend to depress the demand price for capital goods, and thus the rate of capital accumulation.

Consider a firm representative of the industry in our previous illustration. It will make mistakes in choosing its output rates with some representative frequency. Under the random walk monetary standard, such errors will be more frequent and larger than they would be in a regime providing monetary stability. To the extent that the cost of these inefficiencies is born by the firms themselves and not transferred to customers or suppliers, profits on capital are reduced. So are prospective earnings on new investment. This tendency is reinforced when the tax law treats an increase in nominal earnings as if it represented growth in real profits. It is further reinforced by price controls and other forms of governmental intervention that random walk inflation tends to induce.

## Expected Forecast Errors: The Negative Real Rate Riddle

In the financial markets, the most obvious consequence of the random walk regime is the thinning out of the long-term bond markets. Since the dispersion of price levels fans out rapidly the further one looks into the future, lenders and borrowers will be equally reluctant to commit themselves to long-term nominal contracts. Neither side can get a risk premium from the other. Consequently, we expect the volume of such contracts to shrink (and the volume of investments that are normally financed in this way to decrease even further than implied above).

A more interesting problem is posed by the fact that, until recently, nominal rates of interest on short and medium-term placements did not in general rise sufficiently to compensate for the inflation. Such assets continued to be held year in and year out in large volume at *negative* real rates.

A clue to this problem may be found in the strong incentives to procrastinate created by the random walk regime. Agents will try to postpone commitments beyond the time when they would normally be made in a stable money regime, and also to reduce the volume of commitments that are difficult or impossible to postpone until late in the game. This incentive affects not only long-term investments and financial contracts, but relatively short-term ones as well.

As an example, consider from the standpoint of date $t = 0$, an expenditure of funds that will produce sales receipts at some later date – for instance, $t = 3$. If we take as our example of a constitutional regime one that operates on a Friedman rule, the variance of the $t_3$ price level looks much the same from $t_1$ as it does from $t_0$. One would pay only a very modest sum for the privilege of postponing the commitment to reduce the uncertainties stemming from monetary policy. Under the random walk monetary standard, the perceived uncertainty of the $t_3$ outcome will be very much reduced if it is possible to wait until $t_1$ before making an irrevocable decision.

Haste makes waste. There will be some social cost in the inefficiencies of trying to live with shorter lead times. But the more interesting aspect of this inducement to procrastinate is the increase in *flexibility preference* that it implies.[12] Short-term money-denominated assets will carry an increased flexibility premium; that is, they will earn a real rate of interest that is lower than normal relative to the yield on long-term placements.

The *real* term structure of interest becomes more of a speculative notion than an empirically operational concept under random walk monetary conditions. The dispersion of expectations (which are largely unobservable) makes it unclear how one would deduce a number with a good claim to being *the* real long-term rate of interest. But we have argued that real corporate earnings will be reduced under the random walk standard. This is consistent with the behavior of stock markets. The low real rates of return in prospect on long-term fixed investments should put a ceiling on the long-term real rate of interest that people are willing to pay in order to finance such investments. We conclude, therefore, that the entire real term-structure schedule shifts down. In addition, the increase in flexibility preference will push down short rates relative to long rates. In the random walk regime, consequently, fully foreseen negative real rates can be a steady-state phenomenon. Note that the analysis hinges on the increase in the perceived uncertainty of the price level with distance from the present. The flexibility premium could disappear without any reduction in either the present rate of inflation or in the perceived uncertainty about its immediate future. What it takes is a diminution in the ratio of the variance of long-term price level forecasts to that of short-term forecasts.

## Social Selection

The market economy is, among other things, a system for selecting people for fame and fortune – mostly fortune. The system is supposed to award material wealth for hard work, for thrift, for alertness to the wishes of the sovereign consumer and for inventiveness. Reasonable people may disagree about how 'deserved' the distribution of wealth is that emerges in this way. What is indisputable is that monetary instability must change the rules of this natural selection and hence promote a different breed.

Under a random walk monetary regime, being efficient and competitive at the production and distribution of 'real' goods and services becomes less important to the outcome of socioeconomic activity. Forecasting inflation and coping with its consequences becomes more important. People will reallocate their effort and ingenuity accordingly.

Survival and prosperity under a competitive regime require the capacity to adapt to changing conditions. Inflation brings a marked change in the relative significance of two broad types of adaptive skills. The product designer who can come up with a marginally improved or more attractive product, the production manager who in a good year can increase the product per man-hour by a per cent or two, the vice-president of sales who might reduce real distribution costs by some similar amount, are all examples of roles that have become less important to the stable functioning or survival of a corporation. Other functions requiring different talents have increased in importance. The vice-president of finance with a talent for adjusting the balance sheet to minimize the real incidence of an unpredictable inflation is one example. The creative financing artist floats to the top in real estate. But the wise guy who does a good job at second-guessing the monetary authorities some moves ahead is the one who really counts. Smart assessments of the risks generated by the political game in Washington outweigh sound judgments of conventional business risks. Other roles gain in importance also (for reasons that we will come to); among them is the lawyer capable of finding ways to minimize the impact of sudden new governmental interventions and the operator who is quick to spot ways of making a profit (or avoiding a loss) from new subsidy, quota or price-control schemes.

In short, being good at real productive activities – being competitive in the ordinary sense – no longer has the same priority. Playing the inflation right is vital. In the 1960s and 1970s, this has been the way for ambitious Americans to get rich. But an entire people cannot improve their living standards by playing this game.

## The Political Consequences of Inflation

In this inflationary environment, the real outcome of private contractual agreements becomes more uncertain. Unpredictable inflation redistributes wealth indiscriminately, producing results that by generally accepted standards are unjust and unfair. Inflationary redistribution is a peculiar injustice in that the injured party cannot seek redress in the courts. The courts cannot deal with inflationary injustices because what is basically at issue in disputes of this kind is what expectations the parties *ought to have had* in signing the contract. In a system with a monetary constitution, legitimate inflation expectations are defined and monetary policy seeks to validate them. In our old illustrations of an economy with a 15 per cent constitutional inflation rate, for instance, the courts would have no problem; a creditor who expected a lower rate (or a debtor who expected a higher rate) would have to bear the consequences. In the absence of such a constitution, however, the courts have no norm that could be applied to restore justice to contracts disrupted by inflation.

Contracting is a means of controlling the future activities of others in order to reduce uncertainty to manageable proportions and to make it possible to pursue a course of action with a reasonable prospect of success. Inflation renders contracting a less effective, less reliable strategy for controlling the real terms on which one can obtain or dispose of resources. When private contract fails, political compact becomes the substitute strategy. It is predictable, therefore, that random walk monetary policy will bring in its wake an upsurge of efforts by all sorts of groups to obtain by public compulsion what private cooperation will not achieve. Legislatures will be swamped by demands to control X's prices, to regulate Y's way of doing business, to tax Z – and to subsidize *me*.

Finally, the consequences of the American inflation do not stop at the nation's boundaries. The inflation must be judged also as a momentous foreign policy fiasco, one of far greater consequence in the long run than the sundry setbacks that have so exercised the public. It is in the long-run interest of the United States that as many countries as possible opt for the Western model of economic development and allow themselves to become integrated in the world economy. The performance of the Soviet-type command economies has been anything but impressive. But the rapid and irregular depreciation of the world's leading key currency and the stagnating growth of the major trading nations have obviously reduced the apparent advantages of the pro-Western course. And the inability of the United States, demonstrated over a decade and a half, to put its own house in order makes it seem very doubtful that the conditions will be restored under which free market economies will be able to resume healthy growth.

No one would wish to argue that inflation has been the only factor in the disappointing performance of the American economy in recent years. Yet, in my opinion, the last decade and a half of monetary mismanagement constitute a self-imposed disaster for the United States the dimensions of which the economics profession has only begun to realize.

## NOTES

1. The standard theory of welfare costs of inflation is surveyed in Part 4 of Barro and Fisher (1976), They indicate their own dissatisfaction with it: 'An urgent order of business remains clarification of the reason for the public's dislike of inflation: if it is merely unanticipated inflation that is objected to, is the public under some illusion, or are economists under some illusion?' (p. 146).

2. In the text above, I ignored the inflation tax on real balances and its allocative effects. In the case where greenback money is being taxed at 15 per cent per annum, the blueback scheme introduces a new, untaxed money that will therefore immediately displace the old currency. Since the demand for real balances will be larger once money is no longer taxed, a larger nominal supply must be provided in order to avoid deflationary pressure on the blueback price level and the associated probable consequences for employment.

3. Two points on which the metaphor is technically inaccurate should be mentioned. First, the public will not think of *today*'s money stock growth rate as something simply 'picked from an urn' with a known statistical distribution. For dates very close in time, information will be available or obtainable at some cost that, although subject to varying interpretations, will make educated guesses about the near-term inflation rate possible. On the other hand, for money growth rates two, five or ten years into the future, the individual investor can hardly do better than to assume that they will be drawn from an urn. Second, however, there is no theoretical reason to expect stability over time in the coefficients of this random walk. It has shown drift in the past – that is how we wandered into the double digits – and may well drift again in the future.

4. This, obviously, is as true for democracies as for other types of political systems. Constraints on the short-term discretion of elected authorities are regarded by some people as 'anti-democratic' – an argument that reveals a failure to understand why democracies adopt democratic constitutions.

5. In the last few years, quite a literature has accumulated on this topic. See, for example, Vining and Elwertowski (1976); Klein (1977); Jaffee and Kleiman (1977); Parks (1978); Cukierman (1979); Blejer and Leiderman (1980); Cukierman and Wachtel (1979); Logue and Sweeney (1981).

6. Such a polity would not inflate for taxation purposes. *If* real balances are at all suitable objects for taxation, inflation is *not* the right way to tax them under 'constitutional' circumstances. It is far preferable to raise the same revenue by taxing bank deposits and instituting a Gesell currency, that is, a dated currency valid, for example, only for a year, so that it has to be exchanged at the central bank at the end of the year at the rate of one old dollar for 85 'updated' cents. This arrangement allows taxation of the money stock while maintaining a constant price level. It will not disrupt contracts between private parties, avoids the costs of changing prices and the like, and is therefore preferable. Inflation remains, of course, a matchless tool of taxation (and debt repudiation) without the consent of the governed. But then we are back, surely, in a setting without effective constitutional constraints on the authorities.

7. This statement assumes, of course, that everyone expects constant real growth and a constant time trend in velocity and that these expectations also agree.

8. The state of expectations relevant to economic decisions with a two, five or ten-year horizon cannot, then, be summarized as a single number for econometric purposes. Indeed the state of expectations becomes practically impossible to measure and one is forced to consider it largely unobservable.

9. Fortunately, one of the otherwise undesirable consequences of random walk inflation may prove a saving grace: contracts will be concluded for shorter terms or with call features or renegotiation options. This will reduce the redistributive problems discussed here.

10. For more on the subject, see Leijonhufvud (1977).

11. Note, however, that it is not always possible to guarantee political agreements on a particular monetary constitution. The Great Deflation under the emerging gold standard during the last third of the 19th century, for instance, would have been a fairly painless affair if all individual deflation rate expectations had converged on the deflation rate that the system actually produced. But the development of the international gold standard did not follow some obviously preordained course. The decisions of countries to abandon silver or bimetallism and join the gold standard were not foregone conclusions: the dates of these decisions could not have been predicted very far in advance. In the United States, free coinage of silver – which would have turned the trend of prices around – remained a live political issue until Bryant's final defeat in 1896.

12. For the concept of flexibility preference, see Hart (1942) and Hicks (1974), Chapter 2.

# 9. Constitutional constraints on the monetary powers of government

In a memorable Peanuts cartoon of quite some years ago, Peppermint Patty was shown in school struggling with a true/false examination. Her efforts to divine the malicious intent of capricious authority went something like this. 'Let's see, last time he had the first one False. So this time it should be True.' 'He wouldn't have just one False, after a single True. So: False, False.' 'OK, now we've got True, False, False, True ... ' 'Looks reasonable so far', she says with a contented smile.

If this sounds vaguely familiar, it may be because you read the business and financial pages. 'This quarter should be GO, because they want interest rates down before the election.' 'Next quarter will be STOP again, though, because otherwise we risk a revival of inflationary psychology.' 'Quarter after that is probably STOP too, but then it is bound to be GO because something will have to be done about unemployment.' 'So, now we've got GO, STOP, STOP, GO ... Looks reasonable so far.'

But not much farther. It is possible sometimes to muster considerable confidence in Peppermint Patty divination for the first few steps into the future. But a few more steps and it falters and then disappears altogether. You cannot build up a firm expectation of the price level in 1985 in this way. Your price-level expectations for 1990 or 1995 will be so diffuse that, if possible, you would rather not write contracts the real outcome of which will depend significantly on your guesses being in the right ballpark.

In order to understand the case for constitutional constraints on the monetary authorities, we need first to understand what is wrong with the monetary regime that we have allowed to evolve in the US over the last twenty years.

## CONSTITUTIONAL MONETARY REGIMES

A *monetary regime* is, first, a system of expectations governing the behavior of the public. Second, it is a consistent pattern of behavior on the part of the monetary authorities such as will sustain these expectations. The short-run response to policy actions will depend on the expectations of the public, which is to say, on the regime that is generally believed to be in effect. A policy designed to slow down the growth rate of nominal aggregate demand may, for example, drastically increase unemployment without much effect on inflation or, with different expectations ruling, it may slow down inflation without much effect on unemployment. Since the predicted consequences of the same action may differ between regimes, we need a different macromodel for each regime.[1]

Different monetary regimes will show different patterns of macroeconomic behavior. We can choose among different possible monetary regimes by choosing behavior rules for the fiscal and monetary authorities. By choice of regime, it is possible to select systems with more or less desirable macroeconomic performance.

A *constitutional regime* is one in which the discretion of the policy-making authorities is constrained, at least in the short run.[2] The scope for discretionary policy allowed by a monetary constitution may be wide or narrow. The 'constitutional' requirement to defend a fixed exchange rate, for example, leaves a rather wide choice of permissible policies in periods when foreign reserves are adequate. The requirement to follow a Friedman rule, in contrast, leaves hardly any discretionary authority of consequence (unless the privilege to fiddle with regulation Q be so regarded). Most monetary constitutions will have *escape clauses*. Under the gold standard, for instance, the temporary suspension of convertibility in the face of banking panics or in case of a major war escapes the constitutional rules of the standard. Misuse of escape clauses, of course, will destroy the system of expectations characteristic of the regime in question and, consequently, spell its abandonment.

Why then should we put constraints on the exercise of discretion in monetary management? Opponents to monetary constitutions make two major points that need to be answered. First, they argue, a binding rule is 'undemocratic' if it prevents elected officials from responding as best they can to the wishes of the electorate. Second, a constitutional constraint such as a Friedman rule means that policy will not take current information on the system's behavior into account (but, the critics object, control theory tells us that it will always be possible in such cases to find a feedback-governed rule that will improve on the system's performance).[3]

The answer to both objections is at bottom the same. Consider the control theoretic point first. It assumes that the system that is the object of control is structurally 'the same' whether run on a constitutional basis or on an unconstrained discretionary basis. Systems exist for which this is a valid presumption. Rational expectations theory has made it a familiar point to us, however, that it is not a valid assumption for economic systems. Discretionary policy will not just 'correct the course' of the same system using the latest available information on its performance; it will impinge on a system that behaves differently from a system under a monetary constitution. Consequently, one cannot be confident that relaxing previously existing constraints on discretionary policy-making will bring a net social benefit.

Consider how the systemic interaction between public and policy-makers might deteriorate. Suppose an economy already such that the private sector resorts to Peppermint Patty divinations of future monetary policies. Transactors have to base their decisions (especially their investment decisions) on highly unreliable guesses about future money prices. These expectations that will guide the public's behavior are in turn unobservable to the policy authorities. Since the expectations are unreliable, they are also likely to be volatile and to change in ways that are difficult for policy-makers to infer. But the results of policy actions depend on these expectations. Thus, both parties rely on unreliable information and consequently their decisions are vulnerable to error. Macroeconomist observers would find that their ability to predict the path of the system has deteriorated. Policy-makers, the business community, the general public – and, not to forget, the economists – all do badly in a regime of this sort.

What is required to improve the situation is that the policy-making authorities change over to a simpler, less complex pattern of behavior. This will improve the private sector's ability to forecast future price levels. Economists will be able to assume that the public's expectations bear some stable relation to the pattern of policy in effect. Better economic predictions mean that policy-makers can at least know what they are doing, although their choices of what to do are more circumscribed.[4]

One of the arguments for constitutional constraints on democratically elected officials is exactly the one just given. By restricting 'arbitrary' actions (even when majority support can at least temporarily be mustered for them), a more reliable framework is created for private activity.[5]

## COST OF INFLATION

The argument for constitutional constraints on the discretionary powers of the monetary authorities that was sketched above puts much stress on the unreliability of price-level forecasts when the pattern of monetary policy becomes difficult to foresee. A constitution could make future values more predictable. Many advocates of unbridled discretion would certainly see this argument as a very weak one. The simple truth is that economists have had trouble figuring out why unstable or unpredictable nominal values should be damaging. 'Inflation is a monetary phenomenon.' 'Money is neutral.' 'When people adapt to it, inflation probably becomes very nearly neutral.' ('So, why worry?'). Those who do not see a significant social cost in inflation also will not find the case persuasive for constraints on discretion.

In order to understand the case for a monetary constitution, therefore, one needs first to understand the costs and consequences of inflation.[6] The problem comes in two parts: (a) the effects of inflation, given predominantly nominal contracting in the economy in question, and (b) the reasons why the private sector does not eliminate nominal contracting and neutralize erratic inflationary policies by generalized indexing. This paper will not resolve this second part of the problem.

The usual analysis of the costs of inflation starts from the neoclassical anticipated inflation model. This is a seriously misleading model which assumes that we know how to make future price levels predictable and that a credible constitution fixing the price path is in effect. The question asked of it is how the social cost of inflation would vary with the rate of inflation *under such a regime*. The answer is that since, under the conditions assumed, inflation is nothing more than a tax on real money balances, the social costs are those of the various little inefficiencies that occur as a consequence of the attempts that people make to avoid the tax by economizing on real balances. This puts inflation as a social problem in the class of milk subsidies or sundry excise taxes. Another conclusion to be drawn from the model is that an inflation of this sort could be cured overnight with no more trouble or disruption of the economy than usually accompanies changes in taxes.[7]

A corollary of that point says that it is not the rate, but the regime, that is the relevant inflation problem. The anticipated inflation model is a bad model precisely because it misdirects our attention to the rate of inflation (which is easily changed) and away from the inflationary regime (which is not easily reformed).

What kind of regime will make people engage in Peppermint Patty prediction? What are the consequences of making people live under such a regime?

Elsewhere, I have called the present American regime the random walk monetary standard (RWMS). I should add that this is meant metaphorically, not as a technical, statistical description. Under the RWMS, the authorities decide one period at a time whether to accelerate, keep constant or decelerate the rate of money stock growth. Only current economic conditions and immediate political pressures (and, perhaps, the latest macroeconomic fad to reach public notoriety) enter into the decision. Future money growth rates are left to the future. Whoever will be in charge when the time comes will accelerate or decelerate as he sees fit. The only 'rule' governing the process is that at each point in time one chooses what seems the most convenient and expedient thing to do.

There is no 'scientific' way to forecast future price levels in this system. For price levels relatively close to the present, I may generate expectations by telling myself some Peppermint Patty tale, reassured by the hope that the system will not wander too far away from where it is today.[8] Other people will tell somewhat different Patty tales, so even short-term expectations are likely to be somewhat incoherent.[9] The uncertainty attaching to any individual forecast of the price level will grow exponentially with distance from the present. The price level ten years into the future is a subject for joking, not for rational discussion. Yet, of course, in an economy such as ours *people are forced to bet on it all the time*.

What will be the consequences? I have written on this at length elsewhere, and detailed discussion would take us away from my assigned topic. The effects may be grouped in somewhat rough and ready fashion into three categories.

1.  Long-term bond markets will thin out and markets for some types of contracts might even disappear. The raggedness of price adjustments in an inflation puts 'noise' into the relative price mechanism and makes it more difficult to coordinate current resources efficiently. Frequent turnarounds in monetary policy will mean more frequent mistakes in output decisions. Such mistakes affect current profits adversely, and the expectation of their continuance under this regime reduces the incentive to invest in long-term capital. The increased risk of long-term nominal financing reinforces this tendency. So, we expect that both productivity and capital accumulation will be adversely affected by the RWMS.

2.  Under the random walk standard, the ability to forecast inflation and to hedge against it when it cannot be forecast with any accuracy becomes more important to the success and survival of firms than efficiency and competitiveness in the production and distribution of goods and services. The rules of the economy's 'natural selection' of individuals for fame and fortune change: finance people are favored over marketing people, lawyers over product designers, accountants over production managers. People, especially ambitious people, will reallocate their efforts and ingenuity accordingly.

    In the 1960s and 1970s playing inflation right has been the way for ambitious Americans to make it big. But an entire people cannot improve their living standards by playing this game. Who takes care of making productivity growth happen while the rest of us take care of our real estate deals and inflationary tax shelters?

3.  In the RWMS environment, the real outcome of private contractual agreements becomes more uncertain. Contracting becomes a less effective, less reliable method for reducing the risks, particularly of long-term ventures, to manageable proportions. When contracting increasingly fails, political lobbying becomes a substitute strategy for many groups. Random walk monetary mismanagement will bring in its wake efforts by all sorts of groups to obtain by public compulsion what private

cooperation failed to achieve. Legislatures will be swamped by demands to control this price or that rent, to regulate his or her way of doing business, to tax X and subsidize Y. In trying to cope with it all, they will themselves become less efficient, just as the economy has become less efficient, in carrying out their proper business. The political system thus loses legitimacy. And a generation of politicians will come to face the *ultimate indignity*: the public demand for *new* constitutional constraints on government – constraints not imposed on a previous generation of legislators.

## MONETARY CONTROL

If you are persuaded by the case for a monetary constitution, the big question becomes, of course, what kind of monetary constitution we ought to strive for. The proposals that recent debates have made familiar to us all are: (a) to adopt a Friedman rule fixing the growth rate of some monetary aggregate, or (b) to return to the gold standard. These two are examples of constitutions built on the basis of contrasting conceptions of how price-level control is best to be accomplished. For brevity, we may refer to these as the *quantity principle* and *convertibility principle*, respectively.

The quantity principle aims at control of the price level through control of some monetary aggregate, usually referred to as the 'quantity of money'. In its logically tidiest form, such a system will be on a pure fiat standard. It requires central banking. It is not a system, therefore, that you would leave in private profit-motivated hands. It virtually implies government control of the banking system. With some oversimplification, perhaps, we may say that the government sets the quantity of money and the private sector then decides the level of prices.

The convertibility principle, in contrast, requires the government to set the legal price of a commodity (such as gold) and let the private non-bank sector decide the quantity of paper money and bank deposits it desires to hold. If overissue of bank monetary liabilities were to raise the market price of the standard commodity above the legal conversion rate, the commodity would be more cheaply obtained at the banks. Redemptions of bank money would eliminate the overissue. The non-bank public, rather than the government, polices the banking system so as to protect the economy from inflation.

Early banking history shows us systems relying altogether on convertibility for monetary control. Until recently, modern monetary systems have generally been compromises between the two principles. The present American system, however, retains no shred of convertibility. We rely completely on governmental quantity control. This system has already failed us badly.

It is important to understand the reasons underlying the gradual movement away from convertibility as the main regulating principle of nominal values. Aggregate demand in a gold reserve standard system (for example) is subject to monetary disturbances: (a) through changes in world gold production and through the decisions of countries to join or secede from the international gold standard, (b) through balance of payment deficits or surpluses, and (c) through expansions and contractions of bank credit and, most particularly, banking panics. From the first two, we used to protect ourselves by sterilization of reserve flows. More recently, of course, the final elimination of gold from our monetary system and the move to flexible exchange rates have perfected our 'protection' against disturbances from these sources. But the main motive behind the historical trend away from convertibility control to pure quantity control has been the desire to insure the monetary system against runs on fractional reserve banks.

The method of monetary control does not complete the description of a monetary regime. A corresponding characterization of the nominal expectations of the public is also required. In a gold standard system, the public would learn to expect some long-term drift of the price level, determined basically by the growth of the world gold stock in relation to the growth in output. Cyclical fluctuations of the price level around this trend are also to be expected, but their amplitude would be confined to that of the relative value of gold in terms of other commodities.[10] In this system, finally, transactors must be prepared for occasional threats to the solvency of banks.

Nominal expectations under a pure fiat system depend entirely, of course, on how it is being run. The most important question in this regard is probably whether or not the desideratum of monetary stability is allowed to dominate government fiscal requirements. Virtually all the worst inflations of this century have been the result of making monetary policy subservient to the public finances rather than vice versa. The random walk monetary standard is a less virulent form of the fiat-quantity control system – or at least the first fifteen years make it seem so to us.[11] The entire evolution of the fiat system has been a story of striving for added discretionary powers, so that a very restrictive constitutional version of it may not be a very realistic political possibility. But, in principle, a Friedman rule could stabilize price-level expectations and reduce the uncertainty attaching to them much as would a convertibility system, and with the important added advantage of a very much reduced risk of banking collapses.

The systems of public expectations associated with the respective regimes determine what can be expected from central bank policy. Consider the effects of monetary policy *when the public knows perfectly well what is going on*. Under the fiat-quantity regime, a fully anticipated increase in the monetary base should have no effects on real aggregate demand, if 'distribution effects' can be ignored. Admittedly, the qualification can be important.[12] But it is to invite confusion if one lets possible exceptions obscure the rule: that exogenous fiat money is basically neutral. A central bank controlling only a nominal quantity cannot normally expect to exert much control over real magnitudes. A history of volatile fiat-quantity manipulation will give the private sector strong incentives to watch the central bank closely at all times. This causes the effectiveness of monetary policy to diminish and, in the New Classical limit, to vanish.

Under the fiat quantity regime, the authorities can sooner or later make nominal income whatever they want (although to little constructive purpose). This is altogether outside the powers of a central bank constrained by convertibility on a commodity standard. It has no control at all over the price level in the longer run. By the same token, however, it can within the limits of the standard operate on real magnitudes.

This becomes most obvious if we imagine the logically extreme (and correspondingly impractical) case of a multi-commodity standard such that convertibility would ensure not just the fixity of the price of gold but the virtual fixity of the price level. Variations in central bank credit change the volume of 'real' credit in such a system. If, despite the absence of exogenous nominal shocks, the economy experiences business cycles, the central bank can play a useful role by restricting its credit in booms and extending credit in recessions. It is likely to use the 'price of credit' (the bank rate) as its main instrument. The interest rate is, of course, a 'real' rate in this setting, and reducing it and keeping it low does not carry the imminent danger of an explosion of nominal values, since the price level and *price expectations* are kept in check by convertibility.

The analysis is considerably more complicated for the gold standard case[13] and will not be carried through here. The point remains that a central bank, operating within the constraints of convertibility, can affect the price and availability of 'real' credit and, thereby, also real activity levels. The effectiveness of stabilization policy of this brand is no doubt rather limited, but it depends for its effects neither on redistributing wealth arbitrarily nor on fooling everybody by doing the unanticipated. This kind of central banking is at its most effective when fully anticipated.

Monetary regimes constructed on the convertibility principle in the manner just discussed have been gone for fifty years. It is an even longer time since we had a well-functioning regime of this type. In discussing monetary reform today, it would be dangerously irresponsible to forget that the attempt to restore a world monetary order after World War I on a gold standard basis was relatively short and absolutely disastrous. For the understanding of our own times, the compromise regime that emerged after 1933 and at Bretton Woods is much more important.

This regime removed gold convertibility for the public and retained it only between central banks. This not only reduced the risk of banking panics directly, it also made feasible a system of deposit insurance that virtually guaranteed that they would not recur on the scale of 1931–33. But without the redemption privilege, the private sector could no longer protect itself against 'debauchment of the currency'. This, in effect, put the United States on governmental quantity control (while small open economies did not gain much scope for autonomous policy unless they restricted the international convertibility of their currencies). The Bretton Woods system was a perennial target of academic criticism. What seems most interesting about it in retrospect is that a system of expectations basically appropriate to an economy with convertible money was sustained by quantity control and with the central convertibility mechanism removed.

A system of price-level expectations consistent with the convertibility principle means, most importantly, that people expect prices to revert to the longer-term trend if and when they go above or below trend. For such expectations to be maintained when the economy is not in fact on a commodity standard, the central bank must, in effect, 'mimic' the behavior of such a standard, that is, contract above trend and expand below it. It must also maintain the faith that this pattern of behavior will be continued indefinitely. An (at least implicit) constitution will be of help in this regard. For small open economies, a habit of defending a fixed exchange rate may be the way to accomplish this task.

In the United States, monetary stability was maintained in this way for twenty years. With the private sector firmly expecting a quite low, and not very variable, rate of inflation, the Federal Reserve System could affect the availability and price of 'real' credit to some extent. Thus monetary policy could play a limited, but constructive, role in attempts to stabilize aggregate employment. The continuance of this regime depended, however, upon the authorities not overreaching themselves. The old Keynesian doctrine of the 'ineffectiveness' of monetary policy – a doctrine fitting a true commodity standard – may have served, inadvertently, as a myth protecting the regime. When the Monetarist doctrine that the quantity of money was an effective regulator of nominal income gained acceptance, it was inevitable that advocates of discretionary policy would put it to use. This was particularly so in so far as they also believed in the stickiness of nominal wages, for this suggested that the stock of money (if Friedman was, perchance, right?) would serve as an effective regulator of employment. But vigorous manipulation of the supply of nominal money will destroy the system of expectations that makes nominal prices relatively inflexible. When the private sector comes to watch the central bank's base figures Friday by Friday, even the limited usefulness of monetary policy under the dollar exchange standard would seem destroyed. We then end up in a situation where a time path of base money not much more volatile than in the stable regime can produce price-level movements of far greater amplitude than before, as the market attaches extrapolative rather than mean-reverting expectations to various short-run wiggles in the base.

## CONSTITUTIONAL PROPOSALS

What kind of constitution should we then aim for? I do not come fully armed with my own proposal for the monetary order of the 21st century. I have, however, two suggestions for discussion – and more public discussion is exactly what we need.

### A Peel–Friedman System

For the time being, I think, we are stuck with the problem of getting some order back into a monetary system relying on fiat-quantity control. From the previous discussion, I conclude that discretionary quantity policy will do us little good when the price level is perceived as having no constitutional anchor. For providing an anchor, I see no substitute for a Friedman rule. Of the several possibilities, a rule imposed on the monetary base seems prefer-able. The previous discussion also suggests, however, that when the price level does have an anchor, central bank 'credit' policy might have a quite limited, but still potentially useful, role to play. With unlimited discretion, we want a rule; given a rule, we want discretion. Combining the two is the trick.

We might borrow a leaf from Peel's Bank Act of 1844. You will recall that it divided the Bank of England into an Issue Department and a Banking Department. The Issue Department operated on a rule, albeit on a gold standard rule (as understood by the Currency School) rather than a Friedman growth-rate rule; it issued Bank of England notes as a simple linear function of its gold holdings. The Banking Department could then engage in discre-tionary stabilization policy with the note issue as the base for the rest of the banking system. The total amount of Issue Department note liabilities would set the upper limit on feasible Banking Department expansionary ambitions at any time.

Veterans of the 'rules versus authority' battles on both sides will detest such unprincipled compromise. But if some advocates of discretion could bend this far, perhaps we could muster enough support in the profession for monetary reform with some constitutional stability built into it.

A Peel–Friedman system would split the Fed into an Issue and a Stabilization Department.[14] The Issue Department makes base money grow according to rule. This determines once and for all how much government debt is permanently monetized in any given year. The Stabilization Department treats this base money as if it were foreign reserves in a fixed exchange rate world. It could pursue an expansionary policy only as long as it had excess reserves on hand, and it would have to build up reserves before it could do it again.

Two problems with this approach may deserve brief mention. First, as has been pointed out with some frequency, we cannot choose a growth rate of some monetary aggregate from today until the end of this century with much confidence that we will be satisfied with the consequences. Financial innovation is proceeding at a great pace and with unpredictable consequences for the future demand for base money. I would approach this problem by amending the Federal Reserve Act so as to make price-level stabilization over the longer term *the* basic and overriding responsibility of the Federal Reserve System. Other goals of social policy should be eliminated from the Act. This provision of the Act should then be seen as stating the basic intent of the monetary constitution and would serve as the escape clause under which changes in the Friedman rule could be made. If, for instance, the originally chosen growth rate for the base turns out to be quite inflationary in a few years, it could be adjusted downward for this reason – but for this reason only.

Second, the unilateral decision of the United States to stabilize the purchasing power of the dollar will create an incentive for other countries to fix their exchange rates with the dollar. A possible transitional problem would be a 'dollar shortage' for them and a deflationary excess demand for base dollars for us. The United States might agree to limited issues by the IMF of Special Drawing Rights convertible into dollars to cope with this problem.

### A System Based on Convertibility?

My second suggestion can be made more briefly. It is simply that monetary economists should start seriously to study the possibility of constructing a new system of monetary control based essentially on the convertibility principle. The reason for this suggestion is simply the fear that unchecked financial innovations and computerization of the payments mechanism will eventually (indeed, before too long) make monetary control on the quantity principle no longer feasible.[15] An illustrative nightmare will make the point. Suppose that all debits and credits in the economy arising from current resource transfers are fed into a clearing house computer programmed to hunt for closed loops of indebtedness and to clear all such loops up to the largest common numerator. Debts and claims are systematically settled without the use of a medium of exchange. The monetary base might become the 'small change' of such a system. Contracting the supply of small change will not stop an inflation; it merely creates a 'coin shortage', as we know.

The convertibility idea, to repeat, is to fix a price and let the private sector endogenously determine monetary and financial aggregates. If quantity control becomes increasingly tenuous and unreliable, some sort of composite-good convertibility system might offer a preferable alternative. Some schemes of this sort have been discussed in the literature, but I have not come across any that are *obviously* workable. The subject deserves more thorough exploration.

## CONCLUSION

I have not committed myself to a particular constitution. One reason for this is that I am not certain what the best scheme would be. But I also happen to believe that we need a monetary constitution. What type of constitution we would individually prefer is a secondary matter and should be kept in the background. If too many of us start peddling our own favorite schemes, we will fail as a group in helping to get an effective movement for monetary reform off the ground. The late lamentable Gold Commission should convince us of this, if we did not know it already.

The Reagan administration has done as much as could be hoped to bring down the rate of inflation in this country. Some would say it has done more. But the administration has done *nothing at all* to ensure for us a future of relative monetary stability. Indeed, if those looming future deficits will have to be monetized, the present government will be seen as having taken us farther down the road toward South American monetary arrangements.

Reducing the current rate of inflation and building a new framework for monetary stability are two distinct tasks. Doing one's utmost on the first does not necessarily contribute to the accomplishment of the second. It is more than just plausible that the failure to tackle monetary reform has already been a costly one. Disinflation undertaken and understood as an orderly transition to new and stable monetary arrangements should be less costly in terms of unemployment than disinflation, the pace and persistence of which must be the object of speculation. If, moreover, 1984 were to bring us another government bent on reflation, then 1980–82 will be remembered (as Nixon's first years, or Ford's) as just another bad lurch in the drunkard's walk that has become the American system of monetary policy.

The President ought to appoint a National Monetary Commission. But this one had better be a worthy successor to the Commission that laid the groundwork for the Federal Reserve System and to the Commission on Money and Credit of twenty-odd years ago.

# APPENDIX 9.1   RULES WITH SOME DISCRETION[16]

The main part of Barro's (1986) paper discusses earlier work by himself and David Gordon. That work models the behavior of the monetary authorities and is concerned with such questions as the incentive compatibility of monetary rules, that is, whether it is possible to find rules that are credible because the authorities will have no incentive to break them.

In 'Rules, Discretion and Reputation in a Model of Monetary Policy', Barro and Gordon (1983a) considered a model of monetary policy under full discretion. The rational expectations equilibrium of this model gave a high inflation rate on the average combined with (futile) attempts at countercyclical policy. A policy rule, if binding, would improve matters.

In 'A Positive Theory of Monetary Policy in a Natural Rate Model', Barro and Gordon (1983b) showed that a reputational equilibrium for the model yields a solution halfway between this full discretion case and the rule-bound case.

These attempts to model the behavior of the policy-making authorities and their interaction with the public are an interesting branch of the recent literature. We will see more work along these lines; indeed, I am afraid that we will see more of it than is instructive, for it is possible to ring almost endless changes on models of this kind.

Yet, interesting as these incentive compatibility problems are, it is difficult to know whether they are the first thing we should worry about in discussing the choice (or design) of a monetary regime. In Barro's model, the policy-makers are assumed to have an incentive to break the announced rule in order to create surprise inflation and, therefore, an increase in employment. Unanticipated inflation makes the representative consumer work more than he would like to if he knew what was going on. But why should the representative consumer, in his role as the representative voter, reward the policy-makers for swindling him into working too much? (The policy-maker expects to be rewarded, and in Barro's model, this is a rational expectation.) Barro asks us, in fact, to consider a world in which inflation is to be deplored but unanticipated inflation encouraged. But why should rational agents dislike anticipated and like unanticipated inflation in a world where the first is basically neutral while the second fools them into behaving inoptimally? The Kydland–Prescott–Calvo–Barro line on this question is that the representative voter has already made the mistake of imposing an income tax on himself, which has induced him to goof off, so that he is actually grateful to be fooled into working more. It is a clever answer – too clever by half, maybe. It tells us that we should stop looking for policies that might result in stable money and predictable nominal values, for if we found one and used it, it would thwart the representative person's rational desire to be fooled into not working less than he truly wants to.

This conclusion would spell a somewhat pitiful and inglorious end to monetary theory as we have known it. Before abandoning the time-honored enterprise, we might ask how we got ourselves painted into this particular corner. Two sets of interrelated issues are important:

1. The choice of monetary regime, I agree, has to be discussed as a choice between rational expectations equilibria that yield different time paths for inflation and unemployment. That said, however, the question becomes how much understanding of the system the rational expectations approach obliges us to impute to agents.
2. The analytical setting not only of Barro's paper but of most of the recent discussion is a model world in which, in the absence of nominal shocks, unemployment stays at its natural rate and in which monetary policy can be effective only in so far as it generates nominal surprises. The second issue is whether this is the appropriate model for the choice of regime question.

On the first issue, it has come to be regarded as naive to suppose that economists might understand the economy better in some respects than economic agents – so naive, in fact, that if you want to earn top dollars as an economist, you must profess to know nothing of value, for if you claim otherwise, both your colleagues and the representative agent will infer that you must think you know some things that certainly ain't so. A marginal social product of zero is the upper bound. Everyone has tired of the old anecdote about the two economists and the bill on the sidewalk: 'Look, there lies a $100 bill!' – 'No, there doesn't'. The modern version would go: 'I think I've learned something useful.' – 'No , you didn't!' Barro's paper ends on this note: 'If an economist labels the actual institutional selection as inferior to other arrangements, what does that labeling mean? Conceivably the economist may have unearthed new knowledge, but other possibilities are more likely.'

My own old-fashioned view on all this is by and large the naively optimistic one that people are not terribly smart and tend to bungle things. I also believe therefore that economic performance, like most things, might be improved upon. I admit a slight complication to this rosy view of the matter – namely that economists belong to the set of people who tend to bungle things. In particular, I see the inflation and monetary instability of the last twenty years as one big muddle created by people who did not understand what they were messing with, aided and abetted by an economics profession that did not – and still does not – understand the economic and social consequences of monetary instability.

On the second issue, Monetarist natural rate of unemployment models have received far more attention than they merit. The evidence is, of course, overwhelming that the Phillips curve shifts with inflationary expectations. At the time of the controversy, the Monetarist natural rate model was the perceived alternative to the stable Phillips trade-off models; it was lent too much credibility by their demise. The actual evidence *for* it does not, I think, compel us to take it seriously.

In particular, we do not have strong reasons to believe either that aggregative fluctuations occur only in response to nominal shocks or that all changes in money (however measured) should be interpreted as exogenous nominal shocks that should have no real aggregative consequences as long as only nominal prices adjust appropriately. Consider, for instance, convertible monetary standards. External convertibility will suffice – open economies with fixed exchange rates. Here the monetary authorities are powerless to change the nominal scale of the economy by pumping money into it. The money supply is essentially endogenous, so purely nominal shocks will at least not come from this direction. Rational nominal expectations are inelastic with respect to both the current price level and the current money stock. Business fluctuations occur primarily in response to real shocks (such as the old Keynesian standby, the 'shift in the marginal efficiency of capital') and are characterized by the endogenous co-movement of money and trade credit with real activity. Employment varies with the perceived real rate of return. The central bank, although unable to make nominal income any number it might want since it does not control the nominal scale of the system, does have some limited, short-run ability to affect real income through its influence on the real price and availability of credit. This potentially useful power to influence real magnitudes is at its maximum when fully anticipated and at its minimum when unanticipated. Economists who look, instead, for a useful role for the central bank based on its capacity, under an inconvertible fiat standard, to create nominal surprises have, I am afraid, gotten the whole subject of monetary stabilization policy backwards.

Consider, then, our use of rules in some other areas of endeavor. Most team sports, such as basketball for instance, are played subject to a set of rules large enough to make a small book. Why do we let a group of middle-aged, out-of-shape men impose constraints on the actions of these superb athletes? The rule books go far beyond merely forbidding deliberate mayhem. Why not leave the rest to the discretion of the people who will be in the best position to judge what is the best thing to do?

Imagine experimenting with the game by successively tearing the pages out of the rule book (starting at the back) and observing the caliber of play as the structure of the game is loosened up. Pretty soon the play will deteriorate and get sloppy as the allowable options open to each player in any given situation multiply. The interaction between players on the floor becomes increasingly unreliable, and the game will be less fun to play and less fun to watch. Gradually, unintentional injuries will become more frequent. Eventually, when the last page is gone, if not sooner, the players will no longer know what game they are supposed to be playing. (You might also consider tightening the rules until the game becomes a ceremony prescribed by strict protocol: each team takes turns marching in slow procession up the court to deposit the ball in the basket and so on.)

Presumably all basketball players optimize all the time, and presumably they have better information in any given situation than the rule-makers. Yet we have no philosophical difficulties in discussing the pros and cons of changing the rules at the margin. And we have a good idea of why we do not leave professional basketball to be determined as a reputational equilibrium among players without imposed rules and without umpires.

The monetary regime that we have allowed to develop in this country is (in some relevant respects) like a ballgame with rules much too loose to permit fast, reliably coordinated, relatively injury-free play. Private sector agents do not know what to expect in the way of nominal shocks from the monetary authorities in the future; consequently, they are unable to make reliable inferences about the real outcome of present longer-term commitments. The policy-makers cannot infer the expectations of a public that does not know what to expect; consequently, they are unable to make reliable inferences about the effects of their own actions. And economists, finally, find that they do badly trying to predict the sequential outcomes of this unreliable interaction between policy-makers and the public. *Everyone does badly.* And everyone stands to gain by changing the game. Even middle-aged, out-of-shape economists might be able to draft rule changes that improve the game and are incentive-compatible all round.

Now if business cycles occur also for non-monetary reasons and if central banks have some power, even if limited and temporary, to change the real cost of credit, then we might want them to have the discretion to use this power for stabilization purposes. On the other hand, the monetary authorities must also simplify their behavior if they are to be able to use their 'real' powers at all reliably. In particular, we want them to cease creating nominal surprises. How can these desiderata be combined?

Congress should legislate a *maximum* for the monetary base that the Federal Reserve could have in existence at any given time (Leijonhufvud 1984d). This ceiling on the base should be made to rise (like the Friedman rule) $x$ per cent per year, $x$ being computed as the difference between some long-run average for the growth rate of real output and the trend in the velocity of base money. On the date that the legislation goes into effect, the initial legal maximum base should be set 10, 15 or perhaps even 20 per cent above the actual base as of that date.

This rule leaves some room for discretion. It also leaves open the choice of short-term policies and operating procedures. As long as the Federal Reserve finds itself well below the ceiling, it can expand or contract, and it can execute either policy by using either quantity or interest targets. But while the authorities would retain short-term discretion as long as they are below the ceiling, the possibility that US monetary policy might come to follow a long sequence of predominantly inflationary moves is eliminated.

A central bank operating under a law establishing a ceiling for the monetary base would have to treat the difference between the maximum legal base and the actual base as if it were its foreign exchange reserves and the bank were operating in a fixed exchange rate system. It could pursue an expansionary policy (or step in as lender of last resort) only as long as it had excess reserves. If, in trying to help the economy out of one recession, it were to go so far as to hit the ceiling, it would have to plan on a prolonged period of expanding at less than the permissible Friedmanian rate in order to accumulate the ammunition needed to be of help in another.

The longer-term nominal expectations of the public in the resulting monetary regime should come to approximate the expectations that are rational under a gold standard – with the added benefit that the public does not have to worry about the vagaries of world gold production and the like. Although the main purpose of my proposal is to reduce the long-term nominal uncertainty that is surely the major problem with our present 'random walk monetary standard', it may have the added benefit of reducing the amount of short-term speculation on the course of monetary policy. The market's intense fascination with month-by-month, or even week-by-week, variations in the money supply is a recent phenomenon. Once it is clear that Friday money supply announcements do not signal changes in the stance of the authorities over the longer term, short-term inflation expectations should also become less volatile and more coherent. To the extent that this is achieved, our ability to predict the consequences of macroeconomic policy measures will improve. And everyone will be better off for it.

## NOTES

1. That the predicted consequences of the same action may differ sounds slightly paradoxical perhaps. But the consequences of policy actions depend on how they are *interpreted* by the public and on how the public therefore reacts.
2. The US Constitution is far too difficult to amend for the purposes here discussed. A more appropriate degree of constraint on short-run discretion is that common in European constitutions, where a constitutional article can only be changed or amended by majority votes in two consecutive sessions of the legislative body, usually with the proviso that the two sessions be separated by a general election.
3. Most monetary constitutions, of course, do not eliminate short-run discretionary policy totally. But all must have constraints that are sometimes binding – and when they are, behavior governed by feedback is ruled out.
4. On the last two paragraphs, see Heiner (1983).

5.  An example (also due to Ron Heiner) from another sphere may help illustrate the general principle involved. Consider some team sport, such as basketball. Some of the rules of the game have been imposed to prevent intentional injuries. Leave those intact. But imagine successively abolishing more and more of all the others, leaving behavior to the 'discretion' of finely tuned athletes. At some point the quality of play will begin to deteriorate. In the absence of rules restricting their behavior, sufficiently reliable interaction is not possible and the athletes will not be able to show their skills to best advantage.

6.  What I have to say on this subject simply paraphrases what I have written elsewhere. See Leijonhufvud (1977, 1980, 1984a).

7.  The way to do so is by a type of currency reform that I have called the 'blueback scheme', and described in 'Inflation and Economic Performance' (Leijonhufvud 1984a).

8.  Suppose a new monetary authority comes in determined to be 'tough' on inflation and starts braking it down more abruptly than has been tried by previous authorities. If this is interpreted as a return to constitutional money, all may go well. But if nothing is done to actually institute a constitution, it is really rather more likely that the 'tough' policy is perceived (a) to increase the 'step size' of policy changes in the RWMS process, and (b) to increase the probability of a near-future reversal of disinflation. *That* would not be a good way to go!

9.  See Leijonhufvud (1983d), where the term 'coherence' (of the state of expectations) is used to denote a situation where everybody has the same expectations (although the variance of individual expectations might be large).

10. Cyclical expansions in an old-fashioned gold standard system would be financed by expansions of bank and non-bank trade credit. There is a limit to how far nominal income can be bid up in such fashion. When the process begins to put upward pressure on the market price of gold, redemption of paper money will put an end to the banking system's ability further to extend credit.

11. A particularly interesting hybrid is the one investigated by Sargent and Wallace (1981). They deal with the timely example of a system that is under some monetary discipline presently but is committed to fiscal deficits so large that they will have to be monetized later. They show this to be a recipe for very high current real rates of interest.

12. Indeed, quite a bit of old-fashioned Keynesian theory could be hidden behind this innocuous phrase. If, for example, in a recession, important sectors were 'liquidity constrained' because they had ended up with larger than anticipated real debt burdens, inflation might stimulate these sectors to increased real activity. It would do so by redistributing wealth, of course; that is, by swindling others.

13. See Fremling (1982).

14. Compare Niehans (1978), Chapter 12, pp. 286 ff.

15. As I was writing this paper, Philip Cagan came to the UCLA Money Workshop with a paper arguing the same point. See Cagan (1982).

16. Comment on Barro (1986).

# 10. On the use of currency reform in inflation stabilization*

A successful deceleration of inflation will not by itself promise a future of monetary stability. That requires fiscal balance over the longer run and monetary discipline in each short run. The macroeconomic literature on inflation stabilization nonetheless tends to devote more attention to the problems of bringing down the inflation rate than to those of keeping it down – perhaps because the former seem more technocratic and less fundamentally political than the latter.

In attempts to stabilize very high or hyperinflations, currency reforms are frequently a component of the stabilization plans. The most common type of such reform, namely the one that simply 'sheds zeros' from a nominally inflated standard of value, is also of minimal interest. A second type subjects part of the stock of money (and of money substitutes) outstanding to simple expropriation or else to forced conversion into bonds of more or less long term. Such measures simplify the stabilization task if price controls have effectively prevented the price level from catching up to the stock of money that has been created. From the standpoints of individual property rights or of distributive justice, however, they will almost inevitably be arbitrary. This kind of currency reform was used in the West German stabilization following World War II, has been imposed in the Soviet Union in the past and seriously considered again in the present. Neither of these two common types of currency reform will be discussed further in this paper.

The problem under consideration here is neither the bookkeeping cost of writing so many zeros all the time nor the more substantive danger of taking the lid off a hitherto suppressed inflation. We are concerned, rather, with the potential real consequences of bringing about a deceleration of the price level that may accord neither with the present expectations of the public nor with previous expectations embedded in still existing contracts.

Since the rational expectations approach became prominent in the 1970s, credibility has become a central concept in almost all discussions of disinflation strategies. If the policy-making authorities have or can establish credibility, it is often argued, they will be able to bring private-sector inflation expectations into line with their policy targets and thus avoid the contractionary consequences of a disinflationary policy that is less than fully anticipated. Credibility, therefore, seems to hold out the prospect that inflation might be quickly and drastically reduced without serious unemployment consequences. This prospect is at its most alluring for countries suffering such high inflation rates that policies of gradual disinflation in any case seem hopeless – even though under those conditions the credibility of the authorities has very likely already been expended.

Even with credibility, however,[1] disinflation will redistribute wealth from debtors to creditors on outstanding contracts and give rise to unemployment through pre-existing labor contracts and through 'debt-deflation' disruptions of credit. To abandon gradualism for a 'shock policy' remains a gamble, therefore, even if the shock can be made credible, for one can never depend upon all private contracts being by mutual consent renegotiated so as to eliminate these consequences. The 'memory' of past inflation embedded in contracts thus imparts inertia to the ongoing inflation.

In its 1985 'Austral Plan', Argentina included a type of currency reform which, under certain conditions, can be quite helpful in overcoming these problems. Variants of this reform have subsequently been tried by Brazil and by Peru, and its possible use has been discussed also elsewhere. The conditions under which this type of currency reform can be recommended are not generally well understood, however. They are explored in this paper.


## BLUEBACKING

The particular kind of currency reform considered here we call the 'blueback' scheme, referring to an example previously used to illustrate the idea.[2] This illustration may as well be made to serve once more.

Imagine an inflation corresponding in all essential respects to the assumptions of the neoclassical model of a fully anticipated inflation. For simplicity, take the case of a constant inflation rate. The aggregate price level increases at the same rate as the money supply; individual prices grow at the same rate on average, although relative prices may show somewhat larger variability since nominal price adjustments need not be synchronized. Apart from possible effects of this kind, the inflation simply constitutes a $\pi$ per cent tax on cash balances, and it has no other social or economic consequences than those attributable to this tax. We may refer to it as a 'quasi-neutral' inflation.[3]

In this imagined economy, a variety of contracts will exist but they will have one feature in common: all have been concluded on the firm expectation, shared by all parties, that the inflation will continue at the $\pi$ per cent rate indefinitely. In this setting, the parties are able to calculate the anticipated real value of a future dated nominal payment without ambiguity.

Call the existing monetary unit the 'greenback'. The real purchasing power of greenbacks depreciates at the perfectly stable rate of $\pi$ per cent per period. A stable money of constant purchasing power, therefore, would appreciate relative to the greenback at $\pi$ per cent per period. Consider then the simple expedient of introducing a new currency (the 'blueback') which *by law* grows in its capacity to extinguish greenback debt at $\pi$ per cent per period.

On the day of this reform, bluebacks and greenbacks exchange at a one-to-one rate. But one period later, one blueback legally discharges a debt of $1+\pi$ green units, and $t$ periods later, of course, the relationship is:

$$B = G/(1+\pi)^t$$

Thus, if the inflation rate is 15 per cent, for instance, a debt of one green dollar due ten periods hence will be extinguished at that time by the payment of approximately 19 blue cents. *If* the purchasing power of blue money has been kept constant in the interim, the creditor is then receiving in real purchasing power exactly what he expected to receive before the currency reform was put into effect.

What that would mean, of course, is that nothing at all is done about the depreciation in the greenback's purchasing power. The greenback inflation continues as before (although it will eventually become unobservable). And this is as it should be for, under the assumptions of the neoclassical antici-pated inflation model, it would be irrational, destructive policy to force the green inflation rate down. All agents have fully adjusted to it; all contracts and agreements embody a firm belief in its continuance. A policy of disinflation that goes against these firmly and unanimously held expectations can only wreak havoc of the worst kind.

What the blueback scheme aims to accomplish, therefore, is simply to replace the green money that is subject to the $\pi$ per cent inflation tax with blue money that is not to be taxed in this way. If the exercise is to succeed, however, not only must prices stabilize at once, but the generally shared expectation, after the reform is announced, must be that they will remain constant indefinitely. For this to be possible, several requirements have to be met.

First, since the reform is predicated on elimination of the inflation tax, the government must either replace its inflationary seigniorage with other taxes or else reduce expenditures so as to produce a budget that is consistent with the indefinite pursuit of a non-inflationary policy.[4] If nothing is done about the pre-existing deficit, so that it has to be covered by printing bluebacks, this would contradict the announced stabilization. If, then, the blueback goes to an inflation rate of $\pi$ per cent, greenback claims (having been subject to the conversion) will depreciate in real purchasing power at a $2\pi$ per cent rate, implying a redistribution of wealth in favor of debtors equally as arbitrary and equally as large as the redistribution in favor of creditors that the blueback reform is intended to prevent.

Second, since green money is taxed and blue is not, the green money will very quickly disappear from circulation. But the amount of real balances demanded of the non-taxed money is going to be larger. The authorities must accommodate this increased real demand by allowing the nominal money supply to increase in order to avoid deflationary pressure on the blue price level and consequent adverse effects on employment.

Another requirement for the scheme to be successful, namely government credibility, is built into the initial conditions of the model. For an inflation to be 'fully anticipated', the government must be committed to maintaining it at the anticipated rate, and this commitment must be utterly credible not only as to intent but as to result. In this context, therefore, we may suppose that agents redefine their expectations immediately to match the announced new fiscal and monetary policies, and that each agent is perfectly confident that all others will do likewise.[5] This behavior of private sector expectations, in turn, will be confirmed by the simultaneous, coordinated halt to price increases that is itself compatible with the government's new stabilization program.

In this somewhat abstract context, the blueback idea serves mostly as a conceptual tool to diagnose the crippling limitations of the anticipated inflation model. If real world inflations were 'like' the inflation model, they could be cured overnight by bluebacking. All the agonizing over the dangers of various disinflation strategies would be pointless. Reducing the inflation rate is as simple as cutting an excise tax. Within the model, things are that simple because it represents the inflation process as a peculiar form of absolutely perfect monetary stability – peculiar in that it does not offer stable purchasing power but instead a stable rate of depreciation of purchasing power. Implicitly, it assumes a completely believable precommitment by the government – indeed, a precommitment extending to future governments – to produce a particular inflation path and not to deviate from it.

The blueback trick works because we start from a policy regime of the most exacting discipline and only the rate of inflation needs changing. Under the conditions assumed this is easily done. The scheme has the virtue of making it clear that in actual inflations it is not the *rate* but the *regime* that is the problem.

At the same time, the regime of the anticipated inflation model, which makes the blueback scheme work, bears so little resemblance to actual inflationary regimes that it comes as a surprise that the scheme would ever be of any real use.

## INDEXED CONTRACTS

The 'fully anticipated' inflation would not give agents reason to avoid nominal contracts. It is only a small step in the direction of real world inflations, however, to admit sufficient uncertainty so that at least some indexed contracts are concluded. Because price indices are compiled only at discrete intervals and published with some delay, indexed contracts will tend to have an inertial component, since payments will be adjusted using lagged rather than fully contemporaneous changes in the index in question. For low or moderate inflations, this inertial component of index contracts will be of quite minor consequence. In the case of very high inflations – the inflations for which a currency reform is most likely to be part of a stabilization plan – the proportion of the real value of a contract that is not corrected by the index can be quite substantial.[6]

The blueback scheme can be extended in a relatively easy way to indexed contracts. Let $t$ be the date of the currency reform and consider a contract arranged at date $t-i$ calling for payment at $t+j$. In writing the contract, we suppose, the parties were trying to arrange a payment of agreed-upon *real* 'base value'. Let the corresponding nominal value at $t-i$ be $V_0$ 'green dollars'. The contract specifies a certain price index, $I$, as the means by which the nominal payment is to be adjusted for inflation so as to maintain its real base value. At date $t-i$ the latest available value for $I$ was $k$ 'days' old[7] and we may suppose that the same length of lag was anticipated to occur at $t+j$. Thus the contractual payment in greenbacks will be

$$G_{t+j} = V_0\left(\frac{I_{t+j-k}}{I_{t-i-k}}\right).$$

The currency reform should seek to preserve the real value of contracts as of the date of the reform. Just before the stabilization, at $t$, this payment will have an *expected* real value (at time $t$ prices) of[8]

$$E_t(V_f) = V_0\,\frac{E_t(I_{t+j-k})}{I_{t-i-k}}\,\frac{1}{(1+\pi)^j}.$$

Note that for some contracts outstanding at $t$, the date $t+j-k$ on which the index used in the adjustment of payments was last measured can be earlier than $t$ (that is, $j-k < 0$). In this instance, the payment $G_{t+j}$ is treated as a predetermined sum in greenbacks which is to be converted into blue money at the factor for date $t+j$, namely $1/(1+\pi)^j$. The blueback payment would then be

$$B_{t+j} = \frac{G_{t+j}}{(1+\pi)^j}$$

with a real value of

$$B_{t+j} = V_0 \frac{I_{t+j-k}}{I_{t-i-k}} \frac{1}{(1+\pi)^j}.$$

The conversion thus corrects for the unforeseen shift in the inflation rate at $t$ and makes the real payment equal to the value expected at that date.

The second case is somewhat more complicated. Suppose that, since the date of the reform, price indices are measured in stable monetary units (that is, the indices are computed from collected prices quoted in bluebacks). If, then, the reform failed to require a correction for the lag in the indices, the contract would require a payment of

$$B_{t+j}^u = V_0 \frac{I_{t+j-k}}{I_{t-i-k}} = V_0 \frac{I_{t+j-k}}{I_t} \frac{I_t}{I_{t-i-k}}.$$

The right-hand expression makes clear the consequences of the indexing lag: the adjustment formula is based on the movements of the index over $i+k$ 'days' of high inflation (between $t-i-k$ and $t$) and $j-k$ days of low inflation (between $t$ and $t+j-k$), while between the original date of agreement and the payment date, there were actually $i$ days before the reform and $j$ days after. Thus the lag 'carries forward' the correction for the pre-reform inflation rate to payments to be made after prices have been stabilized. More precisely, the real value of the payment that was originally expected can be written:

$$E_{t-i}(V_f) = V_0 \frac{E_{t-i}(I_{t+j-k})}{I_{t-i-k}} \frac{1}{(1+\pi)^k}$$

because the inflation expected to take place between $t+j-k$ and $t+j$ was $(1+\pi)^k$.

If, therefore, the reform specifies that the payment in bluebacks is to be calculated as

$$B_{t+j}^c = \frac{B_{t+j}^u}{(1+\pi)^k}$$

(that is, making the conversion into the new currency using the blue/green exchange rate for date $t+k$, since $k$ is the lag of the indexing formula), the sum due will be:

$$B^c_{t+j} = V_0 \frac{I_{t+j-k}}{I_{t-i-k}} \frac{1}{(1+\pi)^k}$$

and the correction made will prevent an unintended real wealth transfer from the debtor to the creditor.

The calculation assumes that the authorities imposing the reform know what inflation rate is generally expected at time $t$: $E_t(\pi)$. They use this rate for the conversions. If this rate were different from the one originally anticipated, $E_t(\pi)$ $\neq E_{t-i}(\pi)$, the correction will, of course, not restore the originally anticipated real value to the contract. This illustrates a general feature of the blueback reform, namely that capital gains and losses incurred prior to $t$ are treated as 'bygones' – the reform only prevents those that would be brought about by the abrupt stabilization.[9] Similarly, if the index chosen by the contracting parties has diverged from some more generally accepted deflator for 'real purchasing power', the reform treats this as a realization of a relative price risk accepted by the parties at the outset, and a feature of the contract, therefore, that should not be interfered with. Finally, the actual and originally expected real values of the payment may fail to coincide because of relative price changes that occur due to the stabilization itself. A correction for these is almost certainly not feasible in practice.

## CREDIBILITY

The assumption of complete credibility on the part of the monetary authorities may fit naturally into the neoclassical model of fully anticipated inflation, but it seldom if ever fits the actual circumstances surrounding very high inflations. We have used this assumption above in explaining the elemental principles of the blueback reform, but as we proceed (ever so cautiously) in the direction of greater realism, it needs to be reconsidered.

To see how it enters in, consider some of the features of the conversion mechanism:

The reform predetermines the 'crawling exchange rate' between the two currencies – or, equivalently, the proportional discount to be applied to previously contracted nominal payments – for dates beyond $t$.[10] In practice, the conversion rate need not be announced in advance for all time to come; leaving the conversion rate beyond some horizon date 'to be announced later' offers some protection against the risk that a later resurgence of inflation will distort the real outcome of the reform. Still, the rate must initially be set for some period ahead. The conversion, then, only acts 'neutrally', as intended, if the price level effectively stops rising during the time for which the conversion rates have been pre-announced.

As long as price-level stability is maintained, the conversion will act only on nominal values of payments, irrespective of the nature of the originating contract. The uniform deflation of nominal values does not otherwise modify agreements previously made – the 'real' provisions of contracts are left unchanged. Note, in particular, that interest rate differentials are maintained.

Whether the price level can be stabilized, even if only for a transitional period, depends in large part on whether people believe it will be stabilized. In order for the blueback scheme to be viable, it is probably necessary that the public is confident that large wealth redistributions will in fact be avoided. This can only be the case if it is quite clear that inflation will stop, at least for some time.[11] The stabilization of expectations is obviously a condition for spot prices (and other prices not fixed by earlier contracts) to stabilize. But it is also required in order to deal with already outstanding contracts if strong public resistance to the conversion scheme is to be avoided.

The announcement of credible fiscal and monetary measures that will be seen to avoid the monetization of fiscal deficits over the conversion period is, in all probability, a necessary condition for private-sector nominal expectations to stabilize. But such measures may not be sufficient. In the actual circumstances of high inflation, people are apt to use a variety of inflation 'theories' as bases for forming their inflationary expectations; the government may need to provide a corresponding variety of 'anchors' for their expectations. Some kind of transitional incomes policies – even a general price freeze – may be required in order to signal the strong commitment of the authorities to 'enforce' a period of price stability to match the conversion that it is imposing on private contracts.[12]

## CONTRACTS IN HIGH INFLATIONS

High inflations are not steady processes. Typically, the 'average' inflation rate and relative prices are both highly variable. Although people spend much time and effort gathering information, they are unable to anticipate price movements with any precision. Their uncertainty about the real value of nominal sums blows up very rapidly with distance from the present. Effective planning horizons become very short. They know that their best inflation forecast for the month ahead can very easily be off by several percentage points. The very meaning of 'the' inflation rate is blurred for them by the volatility of relative prices. The likely forecast error cumulates to much larger figures[13] as they look further ahead, so that nominal contracts made over anything but very short periods appear forbiddingly risky.

In high inflations, agents have several options: they can simply avoid certain transactions; they can choose to make shorter contracts; or they can rely on indexing clauses. In fact, all of these strategies are to be observed, in different combinations depending upon the concrete situation. But no matter what strategies are adopted, the real effects of price instability cannot be eliminated.

For some kinds of transactions, renegotiations are particularly costly. In the case of housing rentals, or recurrent customer–supplier relationships or, in particular, labor contracts, the parties will normally want an agreement that covers more than just a few weeks or months.[14] Since, in a high inflation, expected errors in predicting the price level over periods of such length are large, there is practically no alternative to indexing for 'long' contracts of these types.

There are several problems with indexing, however. One of them, obviously, is the choice of the basket of goods whose price will be used to adjust the value of payments, when there are several available proxies for 'the' price level. People are then led to take implicit bets on the performance of indices, a 'speculative' activity most often unrelated to the main purpose of the transaction. Although most contracts are linked to indices such as the CPI, a variety of other formulas are also found in use; this diversity may reflect the existence of inconsistent forecasts of relative price movements.

The reporting lag is another complication. Indexing is backward looking, which means that the purchasing power of payments changes when the inflation rate fluctuates. There are, of course, prices (such as the exchange rate) that are almost continuously measured, so that contemporaneous indexing could be obtained by linking to those prices. But 'dollarization' of contracts has drawbacks since the real exchange rate is apt to be volatile in high inflations. For most people, maintaining constant purchasing power over a basket of foreign goods is of little or no help if, in so doing, their command over the domestic goods that are the stuff of daily existence is rendered more variable.[15] Typically, dollarization only becomes a more or less universal practice in the limiting case of true hyperinflation, when the variability of inflation has become extreme, and when the prices of domestic goods also tend to be quoted in terms of foreign currencies.

Shortening the length of contracts is a natural response when information about future conditions is very unreliable. For short horizons, indexation is of little use since (given the lags in obtaining and using the indices) a simple adjustment using the past inflation rate will do as well. Short contracts, then, are written in nominal terms, and incorporate the price expectations of the transactors. In erratic inflations, individuals are likely to form quite different expectations from one another. There is then no clear-cut way to establish what 'real' result was anticipated by the parties to a contract and no possibility of establishing an objective standard of fairness that could be imposed by the courts. Given the heterogeneity of expectations, the real outcome cannot possibly fulfil them all.

Some contracts take a 'mixed' form, in which payments are index-adjusted at relatively long intervals, and remain fixed in nominal terms between the moments when these adjustments are made. A common practice in some countries is that of quarterly or half-yearly wage rises linked to the past increase in the CPI, with constant money wages in the meantime. This produces a sawtooth pattern in the real value of payments and can, when the index adjustments are not synchronized, give rise to large differences in the real price of the same good or service on the same date.

High inflation economies differ from one another with regard to the way in which contracts are typically made. What contracting strategies will predominate depends on the magnitude of the inflation, on the institutional structure of the country in question and also on its previous experience with monetary instability. For example, in Brazil and Israel, indexation was formally introduced in a wide variety of financial contracts (see Simonsen 1983; Fischer 1985). In Argentina, although indexing was often used,[16] it was much less widespread. Instead, financial assets were held mostly in the form of very short-run nominal instruments or foreign currencies.[17] Also, while in Brazil (with an inflation rate on the order of 15 per cent per month at the beginning of 1986) non-synchronous wage adjustments based on an explicit indexing formula were made every six months, the practice in Argentina by early 1985 (when the inflation rate oscillated between 20 and 30 per cent per month) was of monthly increases, often without any explicit linkage to the CPI.

Irrespective of these differences, contracts will carry a 'memory' of past conditions, be it in the form of backward-looking indexation or of expectations formed at a previous date. At any given moment, there is a stock of outstanding agreements; the real value of the payments resulting from them will be affected by the history of price-level changes from the dates the respective contracts were concluded. In high inflations, this memory shortens, as the length of contracts shortens; only in hyperinflations does it reach the vanishing point.

## CURRENCY REFORMS IN PRACTICE: ARGENTINA

The first monetary reform of the type discussed here was that implemented as part of the Argentinian 'Austral Plan' in June 1985. The system used to convert debts was directly inspired by the 'blueback' scheme (Heymann 1986, 1987). The Austral Plan's shock stabilization also included, among other measures, a general price–wage freeze and an end to Central Bank credits to the Treasury. The announcement of the stabilization program was by and large unexpected; private decisions made before the reform reflected the general belief that inflation would continue to run at a very high rate at least for some time to come.[18] The inflation rate (measured by the CPI) had averaged 26 per cent per month in the first half of the year, with a minimum of 21 per cent in February and a maximum of 30.5 per cent in June. The stabilization attempt achieved an abrupt deceleration: through the second half of 1985, CPI growth averaged 3 per cent per month.

The monetary reform was established by a government decree, later confirmed by Congress. Its main features were the following.

1. A new monetary unit, the austral, was created to replace the peso argentino. Currency, bank current accounts and savings deposits payable on demand were converted into the new unit at a rate of 1000 pesos per austral. Since all prices were also divided by the same factor and immediately expressed in australes, this simply took zeros off the currency. The peso became no more than a transitory unit of account for debts originally defined in that currency.

2. Nominal obligations denominated in pesos and due after the reform date were to be settled in australes at a conversion rate that depended upon the date of payment. Initially, these rates were announced for the first 45 days following the reform and were based on a monthly depreciation rate for the peso relative to the austral of 29 per cent.[19] (Later, new conversion rates were announced that tried to approximate the pre- versus post-reform inflation differential.) The initial conversion table was based on the assumption that, since most outstanding contracts were of quite recent origin, it was appropriate to make the peso price of the austral grow at approximately the inflation rate of the period immediately preceding the reform. The conversion scheme was to be applied to all payments resulting from contracts outstanding at the date of the reform, irrespective of the nature of the agreement, with the exception, however, that wages and pensions were to be adjusted in June and settled in australes (at the 1000 to 1 rate).[20] For time deposits (antedating the reform) and other obligations with an explicit interest rate, the sum payable in pesos was to be calculated as stated in the contract and then converted into australes according to the conversion scale. Thus the interest rate in australes (for the post-reform part of the time span of a contract) would equal the difference between the nominal peso interest rate and the 29 per cent per month growth rate of the peso/austral conversion factor. In some instances, this calculation could result in interest rates in the new currency becoming negative; since negative real rates were often observed during the inflation, no provision was made to prevent this from occurring.

3. The reform maintained all indexing clauses as they stood in the respec-

tive contracts. Payments calculated on the basis of index values meas-ured prior to the reform[21] were to be treated as peso values and be subject to conversion into australes by the factor of the payment date. The last payment determined in this fashion would serve as the basis for future adjustments to be made according to the escalation formula incor-porated in the contract. This was designed to eliminate the 'carry-over' of past inflation due to indexing lags (in the way outlined above), with-out otherwise modifying the contents of the specific contract.[22]

As could be expected, the currency reform provoked lively debate. Inter-estingly enough, however, neither the general design of the conversion scheme nor the specific rate of depreciation of the old currency implicit in the conver-sion scheme met with much objection. In the main, the reservations raised concerned the neutrality (or lack of it) of the conversion as applied to specific types of transactions and also the difficulties, as perceived in some quarters, in applying the mechanism to indexed contracts.[23] Among the issues raised[24] were arguments challenging the fairness of the conversion scheme for certain types of nominally determined payments. For example:

1. The reform specified that the conversion to australes be made using the factor corresponding, not to the date when payment was due, but to the date when payment was actually made (after adding interest or punitive charges as specified in the contract). Many creditors found this provision to their disadvantage.
2. Some holders of time deposits complained that, while a reduction in interest rates could have been appropriate, it was unfair to 'deflate' the capital value (including accumulated interest) of deposits as was done by the reform. This complaint was more insistent in the (relatively few) cases where the conversion resulted in a negative nominal rate of re-turn.[25]
3. Some creditors claimed that the sums they were due to receive 'did not incorporate inflationary expectations' and, therefore, should not be sub-ject to 'deflation'. This argument was made for a variety of payments including, for instance, lawyers' fees (see for example, Alterini 1985).
4. Similarly, some debtors complained that 'exorbitant' nominal interest rates charged before the reform remained as high in real terms after the conversion.

Quite possibly, some objections were motivated simply by 'money illu-sion'. In general, however, the theme running through the complaints voiced was a different one, namely that the reform was 'blind' and did not attempt to restore justice to contracts and agreements distorted by the previous inflation. Implicitly, what was demanded was a new legal avenue for the case-by-case 'reopening' of contracts.[26] But the conversion scheme was not designed to enforce some independently defined standard of fairness on the outcomes of contracts but to replicate, as closely as possible, the real outcomes that would have resulted had the pre-reform inflation continued as expected.

The longer-term, indexed contracts did present a problem,[27] since the sharp acceleration of inflation in the years preceding the Austral Plan had caused significant distortions which the conversion scheme simply perpetuated. Whereas these distortions were already present before the reform, it is equally obvious that the actual terms of these contracts did not match those originally intended. This is one area in which a case-by-case redefinition of contract terms might possibly be attempted.[28] Actually, many contracts of this type were voluntarily renegotiated so as to more or less synchronize price adjustments with payments dates and thus avoid indexing lags. This was done, in particular, with public-sector purchasing contracts.

Despite these problems and reactions, the Austral conversion was on the whole uneventful and proved useful in avoiding the redistributive effects of the abrupt stabilization that would otherwise have occurred. The debate surrounding it faded away rather quickly, leaving no great legacy of dispute or litigation.[29]

## BRAZIL AND PERU

Shortly after the Argentine program, Brazil and Peru also attacked their inflations with 'heterodox shock' programs; in both cases a conversion scheme was put into effect.[30] In Peru, the conversion scale was used only for obligations that did not carry explicit interest charges; interest rates on bank deposits and loans, on the other hand, were reduced by government dictate as from the day of the start of the plan, without resort to conversion. The Brazilian scheme was more comprehensive (see, for example, Pelaez 1986). Nominal obligations were converted into the new currency (the cruzado) using a scale similar to that used in Argentina. The main difference was that the conversion factor (by which the cruzado value of the old cruzeiro declined at 14.5 per cent per month, which approximated the inflation rate previous to the reform) was pre-announced in Brazil for a period of one entire year – with the implicit presumption that cruzado inflation would be zero over this long a period! All indexed debts (with the exception of savings accounts), most notably government bonds, were converted into cruzados at the date of the reform, with their value adjusted to that date according to the corresponding formula, and were then to remain fixed (without further indexing) in nominal terms; furthermore, indexation was forbidden for new contracts of less than one year's duration.

Wages and housing rentals, which prior to the Cruzado Plan had been adjusted through 'mixed' indexed-nominal formulas, were to be converted so that their cruzado amount came to approximate in real terms their average values over the latest pre-reform period of length equal to the interval between index adjustments. Thus, for example, wages stemming from contracts more than six months old were converted as follows: the earnings of the six months previous to the reform were expressed in prices of the date of the reform by 'inflating' the sums in question by the CPI change since the date received; the average of the values thus obtained was established as the new wage in cruzados.[31] It may be noted that this system left open the possibility of nominal wage reductions, for contracts that had just undergone an indexing adjustment and for which, therefore, real earnings were near their peaks.[32]

The various conversion schemes differed in their specifics, in part because the concrete problems that had to be faced were not the same: Brazil, for example, had to find a formula suitable for its system of half-yearly non-synchronized wage adjustments whereas Argentina had to deal with monthly, simultaneous increases. But although the reforms were of the same general type, some conceptual differences can also be identified. The Argentine scheme was more concerned to define a uniform mechanism that could be used independently of the nature of the transaction and to leave unchanged the main features of the terms established by the parties in the contracts, while the Brazilian reform, for example, suspended most indexation clauses.

## THE PRECONDITIONS FOR REFORM

The programs of which these reforms were a part did not achieve sustained stabilization: after some time, inflation rates returned again to high levels; some years later, the countries in question had bouts of hyperinflation. The eventual failures have no bearing on the appraisal of the conversion schemes, however. Monetary reforms of this kind can do no more than smooth the initial transition. Experience has now shown that they can play a useful role for this purpose. The Latin American 'heterodox shocks' could hardly have been attempted without them. Monetary reforms are neither magical solutions nor irrelevant gadgets: in the right circumstances, they can help to bring down the inflation rate with dramatic swiftness and thus make stabilization less difficult to achieve.

What then are the right circumstances? They do not make a broad class. After one is done defining the wrong circumstances, what remains is a rather narrow class of cases.

Both backward and forward-looking conditions need to be considered.[33] The backward-looking questions are as follows. How many past states of expectation, embodied in still outstanding contracts, do we have to deal with? How coherent were they (that is, to what degree were individual expectations consistent)? By how much did they diverge from one another? Looking forward, the questions are as follows. How far into the future do people at present have well-defined and reasonably consistent price expectations? Can we infer what they are with reasonable reliability? What future price path will the government be able to 'guarantee'? For how long?

Consider, first, the two opposite cases of hyperinflation and quite moderate inflation. For hyperinflations, the blueback idea is simply irrelevant. A hyperinflation leaves no surviving legacy of the past monetary regime. A scheme designed to cope with inflationary 'inertia' is superfluous when contract-embodied memory and foresight both become 'the ghosts of departed quantities' (as Bishop Berkeley said about derivatives). In this respect, stabilization efforts in a hyperinflation start with a clean slate.[34]

For moderate inflations – in the lower double (annual) digits, say – memory and expectation are both likely to be too long. Contractual rights and obligations acquired or entered into many years ago and/or with many years still to run will exist in large volume. Contracts that have a long term to maturity require a 'greenback-to-blueback' conversion scale that extends far into the future. That prospect raises two problems. First, the government may not be able to hold any given trend of blue prices indefinitely. Of course, the rate of depreciation of green money need not be announced in advance for more than a limited period. This would retain the flexibility to adjust later for changes in the post-reform inflation rate. But a system that necessitates dictating an officially sanctioned inflationary expectation to be applied to 'old' contracts long after the reform would create an unrequited focal point for political pressures of every kind and become a source of endless recriminations and disputes. Second, the choice of which inflationary expectation to legitimate becomes more and more difficult the farther into the future it has to be projected. Using the blueback scheme entails projecting a particular 'expected' time path of 'green' inflation forward as the basis for calculating the real outcomes of contracts in terms of 'blue' money. A monetary policy to stabilize the blue price level will then validate this particular expectation *and disappoint all others*. The question whether this can or cannot be justified is a quintessentially political one.

The blueback scheme takes the state of expectations as of the date of the reform as the one which is to be legitimized. This entails treating the capital gains and losses due to past inflation as bygones. But what people now expect and what they think they have *a right to expect* are not always the same.[35] Any government that itself strives for legitimacy cannot treat people's beliefs about what they may legitimately expect as 'bygones, forever bygones'. Some past state of expectation, embodied in a substantial volume of still outstanding contracts, may have a better claim to legitimacy than today's expectations. People on nominal pensions, for example, may be resigned to the expectation of continued inflation but still feel strongly that they have a right to expect that the erosion in the real value of 'green' pensions be stopped rather than made permanent. The heavy, complex overhang of past states of expectation will mean that gradual disinflation is preferred to shock stabilization in dealing with moderate inflations.

Between moderate and hyperinflations we are left with the high inflations which have shortened contracts and, therefore, shortened both the past and the future that has to be taken into account. But the erratic variability of high inflations that has this effect also increases the chance that agents form inconsistent expectations of the real value they agree to pay or to receive through a nominal contract. It also causes more frequent changes in these expectations as the parties re-evaluate their beliefs of yesterday. For certain types of agreements, they will then resort to index clauses, but swings in the inflation rate will cause the real outcomes of such contracts to vary as well (since the adjustment formula hardly ever uses fully contemporaneous prices). In an erratic high inflation, therefore, the status quo at the time of the stabilization does not have well-defined expectational properties. It is then unclear what standard should be applied to correct contracts – or if this should be tried at all.

This leaves a type of high, but not too high, inflations (in the range of two digits per month, say). In addition, one needs an inflationary 'plateau' of moderate variability in the inflation rate for some period before shock stabilization is tried. This period of some stability in the inflation rate has to be fairly lengthy in relation to the contract lengths that remain common.[36] This was – more or less – the starting point of the three Latin American stabilization attempts in which blueback reforms were used.

# NOTES

*    **Co-authored by Daniel Heymann.**
1.   Government credibility by itself does not necessarily solve all problems of coordinating a simultaneous and consistent deceleration of all prices. But this complication can be deferred at this point.
2.   For previous expositions of the 'blueback' idea, see Leijonhufvud (1980, 1984a). The idea is also used in the discussion following Leijonhufvud (1977), cf. p. 323.
3.   To speak of 'stabilizing' a quasi-neutral inflation is, indeed, self-contradictory. It is more accurate, as we will argue, to think of the experiment simply as abolishing the tax on cash balances.
4.   Under the very strong foresight assumptions made in the particular context of the antici-

pated inflation model, this consistency requirement can be stated simply in present value terms. A commitment by the incredibly credible government to raise the requisite tax proceeds at some future time, however distant, will suffice to convince agents that the present values of government expenditures and taxes are balanced. In more realistic situations, governments with a history of inflation behind them had better bestir themselves and close their flow deficits without much delay!

5. The 'expectations of expectations' problem of Phelps, in other words, should not be of concern in the postulated context. Cf. Phelps (1983a, 1983b).

6. Consider an inflation running at a monthly rate of 30 per cent, for instance. Let the price index be compiled at monthly intervals and suppose that a contract calls for payment in mid-month. If both parties expected the inflation to continue at the 30 per cent per month rate at least up to this mid-month date and had agreed to terms embodying a correction for this, then an abrupt stabilization would entail a redistribution from debtor to creditor amounting to 15 per cent of the real value of the contract.

7. Some indices do not reflect prices at a particular date but rather time averages. For these indices, we will assume that they give values equivalent to instantaneous measures at the mean date of the reporting period.

8. $E_t(I_t+j-k)$ denotes the value of $I$ that the index is expected at time $t$ to take at $t+j-k$; with the exceptions noted in the text (where $k>j$), the realization of this index cannot possibly be known at $t$, of course. Indeed, if the reform goes through, an index value for 'green prices' will never be recorded for $t+j-k$.

9. It is possible that under certain conditions it might be found preferable to attempt to take into account the state of expectation at the original date of contract. As will become clear, however, this would not only create horrendous complications in procedure but, in most instances, also leave a legacy of disputes that could threaten the legitimacy of the entire stabilization plan.

10. Other schemes to deal with contracts through monetary reform have been proposed. In particular, Arida and Resende (1985) propose the issue of a new currency whose price in terms of old money would be defined by indexing to the price level in the old currency. In principle, this makes the exchange rate between the two types of money a variable rather than a predefined constant. This might seem to hold out the promise of escaping the need to guarantee price-level stability after the reform (although it would reintroduce the indexing lag problem if the inflation rate of the old money does not remain constant). But, since it is likely that the old (taxed) money will very quickly disappear from circulation, making the corresponding price index meaningless, the conversion rate thereafter would have to be established by fiat – just as in the blueback scheme.

11. At this point the reader should go back and resume reading at the beginning of the paragraph!

12. The public will be bound by law to accept the conversion of private contracts. If this is enforced without an equally 'binding' guarantee of stable 'blue' prices, the reform will sow dissension and resistance. Since controls are both costly and obviously difficult to sustain for prolonged periods, this limits the length of the transition period over which the conversion scheme can be applied. Hence, the scheme is better suited for high than for moderate inflations since, in the former, contracts will be for shorter durations (see below). We are dealing here only with the conditions under which a 'blueback' reform may be successful – not with the more general problem of the conditions for successful stabilization. The point that incomes policies may be required in order for the currency reform to be applicable is rather incidental to the case to be made for their use in 'shock' programs, which rests mainly on their role in coordinating the expectations and thus pricing behavior of the public. See, for example, Heymann (1986) and Machinea and Fanelli (1991).

13. To quote inflation rates in percentages per year strikes people living under these conditions as meaningless. When the Austral Plan was first announced, European and North American newspapers and news magazines tried to explain to their readers what the situation immediately prior to the reform was like. In so doing, most of them chose to

translate Argentinian inflation rates into annual figures – and produced estimates that were up to 2000 percentage points apart!

14. However, in hyperinflations, wage negotiations, for example, are also very short term (for the German case, refer to Bresciani-Turroni 1937 and Schacht 1927). This is presumably due to the difficulty of finding indexing formulas that share the risk in a mutually agreeable manner. Nonetheless it remains true that, as inflation increases, some types of contracts shorten much less readily than others.

15. The markets that are first dollarized, in fact, are not the ones in which the continuous availability of an index measure would be particularly beneficial. Dollarization tends to spread first in the sale or purchase of housing, for instance, that is, in markets where people are making major wealth placements for some length of time.

16. Frenkel (1984) found that, in many cases, wages followed an (implicit) backward-looking monthly indexing rule. By mid-June 1985, salaries in the government were being adjusted by 80 per cent of the CPI increase in the previous month.

17. By mid-1985, 20 per cent of interest-bearing deposits in banks were indexed; the other 80 per cent consisted of savings accounts and time deposits, mostly with 30 days maturity or less. One year later (during a period of relatively low inflation), the share of indexed deposits had declined to 3 per cent but time deposits for 45 days or longer were still only 4 per cent of the total. Most loans made outside the banking system carried a fixed nominal interest rate and had very short maturities (often 7 days, and almost always less than one month).

18. General discussions of the Austral Plan can be found, for instance, in Heymann (1986), Machinea and Fanelli (1991) and Gerchunoff and Bozalla (1987).

19. The widely circulated schedule tabulated the peso/austral rates as follows:

*Appendix to para. 4 of decree No. 1096/85*

| Date | Australes per thousand pesos argentinos | Thousand pesos argentinos per austral |
|---|---|---|
| June 15 | 1.000000 | 1.000000 |
| June 16 | 0.991548 | 1.008524 |
| June 17 | 0.983167 | 1.017121 |
| ……… | | |
| July 31 | 0.676751 | 1.477648 |

20. Note, however, that wages were frozen following this adjustment, while for other contracts subject to conversion, indexing clauses remained in effect after the reform.

21. These included adjustments made using the June 1985 price indices, on the presumption that most of that month's inflation would be due to price movements before the start of the stabilization program.

22. As mentioned above, some contracts have a mix of nominal and indexed features. In Argentina, a common example was that of rental agreements adjusted by indexation every three months but with nominally fixed payments in the intervening months. Under inflationary conditions, such contracts acquire a sawtooth pattern of real payments. The Argentinian conversion scheme for these contracts was such that, after the indexing lag was taken care of, the real payment at the 'sawtooth peak' (that is, immediately after the escalator clause had been applied) would be equal to that of the previous peak. With a lower inflation rate between indexation adjustments, this meant that the average value of payments would be higher. This matter was not crucial in Argentina; it was quite important in Brazil, where this kind of contract was much more common and included most labor contracts (see below).

23. Shortly after the reform announcement, the government had to issue clarifying norms that specified more explicitly how the adjustment lag for any given index contract should be determined and what conversion factor should be used for the resulting payments.

24. Much of the subsequent literature has dealt with the reform from the legal point of view. See, for example, Adrogue (1985), Eilbaum (1985), Moisset de Espanes et al. (1985) and Trigo Represas (1985).

25. The minimum interest rate for time deposits in banks just before 15 June was 28 per cent per month, that is, less than the 29 per cent per month depreciation rate of the peso relative to the austral. Deposits made at the 28 per cent rate would end up having earned negative nominal interest *ex post*.

26. Contracts could, of course, be renegotiated or challenged in court, both before and after the reform. Through its previous experience with volatile inflations, the Argentinian judicial system had in fact evolved a *doctrina de imprevisibilidad* that allowed for the revision of contracts in the event of unforeseen price-level changes. Argentine law, therefore, was not completely insistent that 'a peso is a peso'. This 'unforeseeability doctrine' had been applied mostly in cases of inflationary accelerations. The point of the austral reform, however, was to avoid triggering widespread litigation. The conversion scheme defined a general rule for dealing with contracts of different types which could be used as a basis either for direct agreement between the parties or, if necessary, for decisions by the courts.

27. Initially, some people objected that since escalation clauses simply reflected price changes, indexed sums should not be converted. This objection, of course, neglected the lags built into the indexing formulas.

28. An alternative conversion scheme might have made the conversion factor correspond, not to the inflation differential between the reform date and the payment date, but to that between the date of origin of the contract and the payment date. This kind of scheme, however, would not only be complicated by the proliferation of conversion scales (that is, one for every contract origination date) but also by disputes over the dates at which specific obligations would be considered as having originated. Contracts that undergo partial revisions while in effect will present this kind of ambiguity, and such revisions are apt to occur frequently in high inflations. Neither the conversion scheme that was actually used nor this hypothetical alternative is entirely satisfactory for these long-lived contracts. This demonstrates again that a more or less steady inflation rate for some period prior to the reform is a condition for the scheme to be viable. How long this period of steadiness needs to be depends on the extent to which the age distribution of outstanding contracts has been shortened by the inflation. A currency reform of the 'blueback' type had better not leave more than a small subset of 'long' contracts as special cases.

29. The Argentinian inflation remained relatively low for about a year following the 1985 stabilization program. Subsequently, it accelerated sharply on several occasions. These later spurts seldom affected the contracts covered by the reform, which had mostly expired. None of the later attempts to get inflation under control again used a 'blueback' scheme. There were two strong reasons not to do so. First, these later efforts were less likely to achieve stability over some significant period than was the 1985 program. Second, they were in each instance preceded by periods of highly variable inflation rates so that a uniform treatment of contracts would have been far less appropriate than in the original case.

30. The Brazilian plan is described, for example, in Cardoso and Dornbusch (1987) and in Modiano (1991). Israel disinflated abruptly in 1985, but the program did not provide for the correction of contracts. It may be that the small volume of nominal assets and the importance of dollar-linked instruments (which are in effect indexed to the exchange rate so as not to be subject to index-lag problems) made a conversion scheme more or less superfluous in this case. For a discussion of Israel's asset structure in recent years, see Fischer (1985).

31. More precisely, this meant setting the wage in the new currency at the value

$$B_t = \frac{1}{6}\sum_{j=0}^{5} G_{t-j}\left(\frac{P_t}{P_{t-j}}\right),$$

where

$$\left(\frac{P_t}{P_{t-j}}\right)$$

approximates the ratio of the CPI at the moment of the reform (1 March 1986) to that at the date of the payment $t-j$. Wages resulting from contracts less than six months old were converted by taking the last nominal payment (made around the date of the reform), adjusting for an estimate of the price increase between the month the contract started and 1 March 1986 and then estimating the average real value that this nominal sum would have had in an interval of six months if prices grew at a constant rate of 14.4 per cent per month. That is:

$$B_t = G_t \left(\frac{P_t}{P_{t-k}}\right) \frac{1}{6} \sum_{j=0}^{5} \frac{1}{(1+\pi)^j},$$

where $t-k$ was the time of origin of the contract, and $\pi$ the inflation rate just before the program used in the calculation. In all cases, the values obtained for wages through the conversion were increased by 8 per cent, as a separate measure.

32. The special increase of 8 per cent (see the previous note) reduced the number of cases in which nominal wages actually ended up lower.

33. Recall that the setting in which bluebacking works perfectly is the artificial one of the fully anticipated inflation model. In that context, it is assumed that the same inflation rate was expected at all past dates (relevant to contracts still outstanding at $t$), for all (relevant) future dates, and that all these past states of expectations were 'coherent' in the sense that individual agents held the same beliefs. Constancy of the inflation rate is not necessary as a matter of logic, of course. As long as the hypothetical economy evolves along some path of perfect nominal foresight, however complicated, a blueback scheme could be devised for it.

34. From a less narrow standpoint, of course, the hyperinflationary process which eliminates 'inertia' as a 'technical' problem is seen to destroy other elements of continuity as well, and thus to generate a dangerous mix of social anomie and political extremism.

35. Refer also to Leijonhufvud (1984a), pp. 28–9.

36. In the Argentinian case, the inflation rate had stayed in the high 20s (per cent/month) for about half a year prior to June 15, 1985 – a long period compared to the 30 to 45 day deposits which were the longest purely nominal contracts existing in any substantial volume that were to be bluebacked.

# 11. High inflations and contemporary monetary theory

In this paper, I am drawing throughout on joint work with Daniel Heyman[1]. Our interest is in economic behavior under conditions of extreme monetary instability, that is, in deep depressions and very high inflations. Only the inflations will be discussed in what follows.

The first part of the paper describes some of the salient features of high inflations. The remainder will discuss some of the issues that high inflation behavior poses for contemporary monetary theory.

## VERY HIGH INFLATIONS

By very high inflations, we mean inflations that are higher than 'moderate' but below hyperinflation. We consider an inflation to be in the 'moderate' range as long as the people who have to live through it generally remain content to quote the inflation rate in percentages per year. In 'high inflations', people measure inflation in percentages per month and consider annual figures meaningless except for historical purposes. When the effective horizon for quoting money prices or agreeing on nominal contracts falls below one month, the economy is considered to be in hyperinflation. The conventional criterion for hyperinflation since Philip Cagan's now classic study of post-World War I German inflation has been a rate of price rise of 50 per cent per month.[2] This appears to be in rough accord with our behavioral definition. Those who would prefer having approximate numerical boundaries for our 'high inflations' might think of them as in the range between, say, 8–10 per cent per month and Cagan's 50 per cent.

High inflations, in contrast to hyperinflations, can be sustained for many years. They are more interesting also in that the distorted remains of a financial structure survive in high inflation, whereas hyperinflations burn it out altogether. The effects of inflation on financial structure will be of particular interest because finance theory has come to loom large in the most modern work in monetary theory.

These inflations are all associated with the monetization of large, persistent fiscal deficits. In standard neoclassical theory, they are modeled as general equilibria with a fiscal distortion due to the inflation tax but, on the whole, not otherwise different from how the economy would function under conditions of monetary stability. The reality is quite different.

High inflations are pathological processes, the products of sociopolitical persistence in negative sum games. The losses are large. In a period of rapid growth of the world economy, Argentinian real per capita income declined 26 per cent over the 1980–89 decade, for instance.


## THE FINANCES OF THE GOVERNMENT

We regard high inflations as processes of 'unreliable interaction' between the public and the private sector. Let me take the sectors one at a time, beginning with the government. If we describe high inflations from the private sector's point of view as random walk standards[3] of a particularly virulent variety, the obvious question becomes why any sane government would behave in such unpredictable fashion, given the economic costs and social consequences of so doing. The general answer is *loss of control.* That generalization made, it remains to give it some specific content. What follows is intended to be (as that all too useful evasion goes) 'stylized facts'. I cannot guarantee that they apply to every high inflation country episode.

The main features of government finances in high inflation regimes are the following.

1. A ramshackle tax structure and a poorly functioning tax collection system.
2. No systematic and comprehensive budget process to allocate planned expenditures 'rationally' and to control the actual ones. Government departments, nationalized industries and other organizations operate under 'soft budgets'.[4]
3. A significant portion of government revenues are allocated to extraordinary expenditures (wars, reparations, foreign debt service).
4. Government debt cannot be marketed in significant volume.

The high inflations are also highly variable inflations and the variations in the rate are fairly unpredictable to the private sector. One major reason for this is *the impossibility of debt management* (4); the government cannot smooth transitory disturbances to its cash flow deficit, but must monetize them as they come. The immediate result is a high-frequency nominal impulse.

The market for government debt is at best very thin and may not exist at all. In the latter case, the government finds itself in effect in the position of an insolvent debtor – despite its ability to print legal tender. How is this possible? Consider a fiscal deficit, net of interest, which is large enough to be near the maximum point on the inflation tax Laffer curve. If the market perceives the government as unable to reduce this primary deficit, the demand for public debt will vanish. The government cannot, by offering higher nominal interest rates, induce the private sector to finance the postponement of the monetization of deficits any further, because increased real interest payments cannot be financed, not even through the inflation tax.

### Erosion of the Tax System

It is not the case that the Latin American high-inflation governments necessarily spend more. But they tax less. If the general taxes – VAT and the income tax – were actually collected across the board at the legislated rates, they would be in good shape. But they are shot through with exemptions and loopholes and are widely evaded. Collection is erratic, inefficient and sometimes corrupt. As a result they only yield perhaps 3–5 per cent of GNP each. Much government revenue stems from a crazy quilt of excise taxes and the like that, although they individually yield little, are imposed at very high rates and thus cause significant distortions.

The lag between tax accrual and tax collection causes a large decrease in real tax revenues. High inflations add a powerful incentive to pay late to all the standard incentives to avoid taxes. This Olivera–Tanzi lag effect is reversible – even temporary stabilization improves the fiscal picture considerably.

### Lack of a Structured Budgeting Process

Budget projections for periods as long as a fiscal year become impossible under conditions of high and erratic inflation. The allocation of expenditures, therefore, cannot be settled for the coming year in one comprehensive political negotiation. Instead, the *de facto* budget is constantly revised without the benefit of parliamentary legitimation, and various political pressure groups negotiate their demands sequentially (rather than simultaneously). Governments will find such sequential negotiations difficult to handle, for each successive interest group feels itself 'the last to be compensated' and does not have to moderate its demands because of countervailing pressures from other groups. So, not only will expenditure allocation be inefficient and inequitable, but it will be extremely difficult to control total expenditures.

The whole thing is obviously a negative sum game. Why then the persistence? Escape from high inflation requires the creation of an efficient tax machinery. But if others will come to control it in the future, should I support its creation today? Mutual suspicions of this sort among parties and interest groups keep these countries ungovernable, independently of who is in power. These suspicions feed on the frequent changes and sharp reversals of relative real incomes that are characteristic of these high inflations.

Once in this situation, government policy-makers find it just as difficult as people in the private sector to take the long view. Rather than attempting to implement some social optimum or other, they find themselves making the best of a bad situation from one day to the next. The result will be policies that are time-inconsistent in almost every area – and correspondingly difficult for the private sector to predict.

## LIVING WITH HIGH INFLATION

Standard inflation theory would have us concentrate attention on the inflation tax and the various distortions that it causes.[5] These effects may be passed by with but two brief observations.

First, the social costs of the inflation tax do become quite substantial in the range of inflation rates considered here. The amount of time and effort spent economizing on cash balances is really very large.

Second, the incidence of the inflation tax is very uneven. For a variety of reasons it is strongly regressive. The well-to-do are generally better able to avoid the inflation tax than are low-income people – except in so far as the very poor live outside, or fall out of, the market nexus altogether. In Brazil or Argentina, furthermore, not much of the proceeds of the tax go to lower-income people. In those cases, at least, inflation does not benefit the poor. It is important to emphasize this, because the prejudice is deeply ingrained in the literature that anti-inflationary policies hurt the working class.

The phenomena *not predicted* by standard inflation models are more interesting. In particular:

1. The staying power of domestic money. It continues in general use even at extremely high rates of inflation taxation.[6]
2. The disappearance of markets. High-inflation countries end up with an extremely impoverished structure of intertemporal markets.
3. The excess variability of relative prices.

### Contracts and Asset Markets in High Inflations

High inflations are not steady processes. Typically, the 'average' inflation rate and relative prices are both highly variable. Although people spend much time and effort gathering information, they are unable to anticipate price movements with any precision. Their uncertainty about the real value of nominal sums blows up very rapidly with distance from the present. Effective planning horizons become very short. They know that their best inflation forecast for the month ahead can very easily be off by several percentage points. The very meaning of 'the' inflation rate is blurred for them by the volatility of relative prices. The likely forecast error cumulates to much larger figures as they look further ahead, so that nominal contracts made over anything but very short periods appear forbiddingly risky.

Long-lasting physical assets tend to have their markets dollarized. For the most part the alternative wealth placements considered by owners are also abroad.[7] The ownership of housing is the most important case here. Note, however, that the stock markets tend not to survive. There is then no organized market in manufacturing capital.

With regard to contracts,[8] people have three options: (a) they can simply avoid certain transactions, (b) they can choose to make shorter contracts, or (c) they can attempt to control the added uncertainty by means of contingency clauses. In practice, the latter means indexing. In fact, all of these strategies are to be observed, in different combinations depending upon the concrete situation. But no matter what strategies they adopt, people are unable to negate the real effects of price instability.

For some kinds of transactions, renegotiation – or the threat of having to renegotiate – is particularly costly. In the case of housing rentals, or recurrent customer–supplier relationships or, in particular, labor contracts, the parties will normally want an agreement that covers more than just a few weeks or months.[9] Since, in a high inflation, expected errors in predicting the price level over periods of such length are large, there is practically no alternative to indexing for 'long' contracts of these types.

There are several problems with indexing, however. One of them, obviously, is the choice of the basket of goods whose price will be used to adjust the value of payments, when there are several available proxies for 'the' price level. The reporting lag is another complication. Indexing is backward looking, which means that the purchasing power of indexed payments changes when the inflation rate fluctuates. There are, of course, prices (such as the exchange rate) that are almost continuously measured, so that contemporaneous indexing could be obtained by linking to those prices. But 'dollarization' of contracts has drawbacks, since the real exchange rate is apt to be extremely volatile in high inflations. For most people, maintaining constant purchasing power over a basket of foreign goods is of little or no help if, in so doing, their command over the domestic goods that are the stuff of daily existence is rendered more variable.[10] Typically, dollarization only becomes a more or less universal practice in the limiting case of true hyperinflation, when the variability of inflation has become extreme, and when the prices of domestic goods also tend to be quoted in terms of foreign currencies.

Shortening the length of contracts is a natural response when information about future conditions is very unreliable. For short horizons, indexation is of little use since (given the lags in obtaining and using the indices) simple extrapolation of the immediately past inflation rate will do as well. Short contracts, then, are written in nominal terms and incorporate the price expectations of the transactors.

High-inflation economies differ from one another with regard to the way in which contracts are typically made. What contracting strategies will predominate depends on the magnitude of the inflation, on the institutional structure of the country in question and on its previous experience with monetary instability. For example, in Brazil and Israel, indexation was formally introduced in a wide variety of financial contracts.[11] In Argentina, although indexing was often used, it was much less widespread. Instead, financial assets were held mostly in the form of very short-run nominal instruments or foreign currencies. Also, while in Brazil (with an inflation rate on the order of 15 per cent per month at the beginning of 1988) non-synchronous wage adjustments based on an explicit indexing formula were made every six months, the practice in Argentina by early 1985 (when the inflation rate oscillated between 20 and 30 per cent per month) was one of monthly increases, often without any explicit linkage to the CPI.

In sum, high-inflation economies tend to end up operating on a *multiple standard*. The Argentinian economy of the 1980s, for example, had a triple standard roughly as follows:

1. spot markets for long-lasting assets were dollarized;
2. housing rentals and wages were indexed or partially indexed; and
3. wholesale and retail markets for consumer goods and services, intermediate products and so on continued to use domestic money.

Such multiple standards are shot through with problems and inconsistencies of various kinds. The real estate market is in dollars, but there is no mortgage market in any currency. When the exchange rate moves, it changes the relative price of dollarized houses and indexed rentals, causing huge excess demands in one market while the other dries up completely.

The general picture to have in mind is one of the intertemporal structure of markets shrinking, starting in the long end. In moderate inflations, it may be only the markets for 30-year bonds and fixed-rate mortgages that disappear. In an economy mired in high inflation, the bank loans and trade credit of a few weeks maturity may be the longest-term instruments surviving in the private sector. The limit of this process is revealed in the signs seen in many stores during Argentinian bouts of hyperinflation: 'Closed for the lack of prices'. At the limit, all transactions become speculative. Retailers do not know at what prices they will be able to restock tomorrow. A wrong move and their working capital is wiped out – and they cannot borrow to start up again.

At this point, the sociopolitical consequences of high inflation are dramatized. When the 'Closed for the lack of prices' sign goes up, the riots start and the police powers of the state have to be mobilized to halt the slide into generalized anarchy. But this is also the point where the survival of the state hangs by a hair – for what the government can offer the police or the military is just newly printed paper money. And if the police complain that it isn't worth anything, the government is reduced to its final promise: 'OK, OK we'll double that.'

## Relative Price Variability

Here I am relying on the work of Angel Palerm (1990), whose detailed study is based on monthly data for the least aggregative subcomponents available of the Mexican WPI (1940–84) and CPI (1969–84).

There has been some recent discussion of the statistical fact that the positive relation between the inflation rate and relative price variability gets very weak at high rates of inflation. The impression that beyond some point additional inflation 'doesn't matter' is almost certainly completely false, however. Palerm finds that the variance of the price change distribution decreases dramatically as frequency of observation is decreased. Also, the ratio of the variance based on monthly observations to that based on longer intervals increases with the inflation rate. Thus we infer that the 'flat portion' of the relationship hides a dramatic rise in intramonth price variability. This is in accord with abundant anecdotal evidence.

Numerous papers modeling excess relative price variability have been published. Most of them are built on the 'Keynesian' presumption that the phenomenon is due to the 'stickiness' of a subset of prices. They tend to take for granted that *flex-prices* closely follow 'the' inflation rate (that they determine what it is, really) and that the infrequent, discrete step-adjustment of *fix-prices* 'is to blame'. The picture that we get from Palerm's study is more complicated.

Palerm studies subsets of prices with high and with low adjustment frequencies, respectively. Call them, 'flex-prices' and 'fix-prices'. He finds: (a) that fix-prices 'conform' better to the time path of the respective indices than do flex-prices; (b) that in devaluation episodes, fix-prices respond more promptly and strongly than flex-prices; (c) that accelerations of inflation are associated with a larger than average number of fix-prices being moved (the positive skew of the distribution of price changes also increases when inflation accelerates); and (d) that similarly, deviations of current inflation from trend do not reflect the faster response of flex-prices but rather the bunched adjustment of fix-prices.

## HIGH INFLATION AND CONTEMPORARY MONETARY THEORY

The simple fiscal–monetary model of inflation depicts an economy in a Solow growth equilibrium somewhat distorted by the 'tax' on money. Except for the distortions caused by the tax (one is to infer), everything is as it would be under monetary stability: the set of markets operating is the same, relative prices are roughly the same, and the activities are coordinated to precisely the same extent.[12]

A more up-to-date theory takes an Arrow–Debreu complete markets theory as its starting point. As in all neoclassical theory, money hangs in there less by hook than by crook. The modern insistence on staying as close as possible (or closer) to complete markets puts a sharper edge on the old paradoxes of having money in general equilibrium. This monetary theory is merging with finance theory. Modern finance theory is formally carried out entirely in real terms – conversion to money asset prices is entirely ad hoc (this is the appropriate term of opprobrium, isn't it?). From finance, we import Modigliani–Miller in generalized form: financial structure does not matter (by and large). Among its lemmas: (a) Ricardian equivalence, and (b) irrelevance of open market operations.

How should high inflations be handled within a contemporary monetary theory of this sort? The natural approach to take is to assume that the Arrow–Debreu dated goods/natural contingencies space expands to encompass also the various probable 'states of the State' for each date/state of nature. But it can be shown that in trying to calculate the optimal allocation in Arrow–Debreu space, the representative agent has posed a problem for himself that is *not computable*.[13] Expanding the space further to take in conditional fiscal strategies of the government will not make this theoretical line any more plausible. But, apart from such methodological doubt, this brand of theory *would multiply markets* – and that is exactly the wrong implication.

In relation to this literature, then, what do we do with the high-inflation problem of *disappearing markets*? I see three strands in the literature on 'missing markets':

1. The first is the idea that the rational expectation of the future price will substitute for the market clearing price in each of the missing markets, and that, drawing up their plans on the basis of these expected prices, agents will end up acting exactly as they would with complete markets.

This tack obviously is of no help, since it gives us a theory in which it does not matter how large the set of actually operating markets is.

2.  Another strand starts from the recognition that the substitution of rationally expected prices for market-determined prices as·in (1) easily results in the multiplication of equilibria. But all of them are supposedly perfectly coordinated (although exactly how agents achieve this when they do not know which one will be realized is unclear) and are thus of no more relevance to the high-inflation inquiry than the previous strand.

3.  A third presupposes that agents are Arrow–Debreu planners and asks whether they will be able to insure themselves fully or achieve Pareto optimality if deprived of some markets and so on. In cases where the answer is negative, we may get some clues to the consequences of disappearing markets. But the reasons given (if any) for why the markets are missing (for example, information asymmetries) are often such as to make their relevance doubtful to the high-inflation case where first they do exist and then they don't.

I am not an expert in these areas but my impression is thus that at present we have no help to hope for from any of these strands of the recent literature.

*The economic performance of high-inflation economies is far worse than in economies with monetary stability.* The line between order and disorder in the system is shifting as an economy moves into high inflation, and the shrinkage of the set of actually operating markets is a symptom of this. Theories of perfect and/or unchanging coordination offer little help. The economy will not be able to grope its way behind the fluttering 'veil of money' to find that all-but-unaffected 'real' equilibrium which, defined by technology and tastes alone, is merely somewhat distorted by the inflation tax. Instead, labɔring under extreme monetary instability, it moves into far less well-coordinated states.

Models that collapse to a social planner's optimal program, whenever not prevented from so doing by utter artifice, hold no promise – it seems to me – of throwing light on these high-inflation problems.

## A DIFFERENT APPROACH

There is an ongoing controversy in the field of artificial intelligence between those who advocate the traditional 'top-down' and those who favor a 'bottom-up' approach. The 'top-down' approach relies on the sheer crunching power of a centralized processor eventually to replicate whatever human intelligence can do.[14] The 'bottom-up' approach relies on interacting networks of relatively simple processors and attempts to make 'neural nets' evolve that will handle tasks far beyond the capacities of the components.

Neoclassical monetary theory is quintessentially 'top down'. More perhaps than other branches of economics, it suffers from the curse of the methodological commandment to cast all behavior description in terms of optimization. Having once assumed the typical agent to be an optimizer, neoclassical theory is hard put to find an acceptable way of stopping short of the perfectly coordinated 'rational' system. It is of course possible, within that theory, to change the assumed environment so that the equilibrium will be worse than it otherwise would be. This can be done in innumerable ways. But the equilibrium will always be 'as good as you allow it to be'.

I do not see how we are ever going to get a handle on ill-coordinated processes such as high inflations (or, for that matter, Keynesian depressions) in this way. To that end, two conjectures:

1. For that purpose, one has to conceive of the economy as a network of interacting processors, each one with *less capability* to process information than would be required of a central processor set to solve the overall allocation problem for the entire system. In other words: *bounded rationality*.
2. We should move on, eventually, from forcing money into theoretical systems that will function perfectly well without it to consider the possibility that money is used in the economy *because* people lack the kind of rationality presupposed in complete markets models.[15] Monetary calculation, nominal contracting, and monetary payments practices, I conjecture, are *essential* to the integration of the computations of the boundedly rational processors of local information.[16] Money, therefore, is not a veil in any meaningful sense. Disturb its functioning sufficiently, and the economy will not achieve as 'rational' and finely coordinated an equilibrium as it otherwise would.

## BACK TO HIGH INFLATION

*Why do markets disappear?* There are a couple of lines that might be pursued, including some recent work on 'Knightian uncertainty' by Truman Bewley, in trying to explain why transactions cease in some part of the space. Here I follow that of Ron Heiner.[17] Heiner notes that as we ascend the hierarchy of the more or less standard decision problems posed in economics, the competence of the assumed decision-maker is always increased so as to be fully adequate to the added complexity. This leaves out the question of what happens when the complexity of the environment increases relative to the competence of the agent.

Heiner maintains that the implication of standard theory, that added complexity always results in commensurably more sophisticated decision strategies, is *false*. His 'theory of reliable interactions' shows agents *simplifying* their strategies instead. In settings too complex for reliable control of outcomes, they 'don't try to be too smart' but adopt rules of thumb that entail ignoring information that would actually be useful to someone trying to calculate the optimal decision.

In high inflations, I believe, people withdraw from various intertemporal markets and contract forms where they cannot reliably control the real outcomes of their actions.

## Why Should It Matter?

### Calculation

Consumers require knowledge of intertemporal equilibrium prices in order to evaluate their wealth correctly, just as firms do to calculate the value of investment opportunities. Consider how the errors and inconsistencies that they are likely to commit increase as we deprive agents of information in stages.

1.  Take away the Arrow–Debreu future markets prices. This we are used to in all realistic macroeconomics.
2.  But we usually assume that people are guided by a market-determined real interest rate. That requires knowing the nominal interest rate and having *identical* inflation expectations. Inflation expectations become incoherent even in moderate inflations, so that the relevant 'law of one price' ceases to hold in the main intertemporal markets.
3.  In the high-inflation economies, nominal market-determined interest rates beyond the next month or two also disappear. Not much is left of a rational basis for decentralized economic calculation.

### Commitment

The production theory that totally dominates in macroeconomics still has the Ricardian farm as the representative production unit: featuring constant returns when both land and labor can be varied, smoothly diminishing returns when labor is varied with land constant. Suppose, instead, an economy made up of Smithian factories.[18] Here 'the division of labor depends upon the extent of the market'. Increased division of labor is productive so that the average product of inputs increases with the rate of output. A highly articulated division of labor, moreover, tends to be associated with a high degree of complementarity between inputs. Picture the extreme case of an economy that is an interlocking input–output structure of assembly lines where a whole line comes to a halt if one machine breaks down, if one worker leaves his work station or if one intermediate goods supplier fails to deliver. Markets for many of these inputs will be thin, moreover.

A structure of this kind requires the support of innumerable *credible pre-commitments* to reduce the risks faced by individual producers to manageable proportions. When Heiner-type agents decide that high inflation makes intertemporal *contracts* into independent sources of risk so dangerous as to outweigh their prospective benefits, they will also retreat into a less special-ized, more nearly linear, less productive structure and everyone will be poorer as a consequence.

### The Excess Variability of Relative Prices

When considering departures from perfect coordination, the Keynesian habit is to look for sticky prices and violations of market-clearing conditions. When the object of study is inflation, the more appropriate focus is inefficien-cies associated with violations of the law of one price.

Excess relative price variability reflects fragmentation of individual mar-kets and transitory but ever-renewed inconsistencies of relative prices. It stems from increased variability in the rate of inflation of individual prices and lack of synchronization between these prices. This means, of course, that the 'market forces' normally keeping them in line must have weakened in some sense. Relative prices are not being arbitraged.

The weakening of arbitrage starts with the disappearance of intertemporal markets. In their absence, intertemporal smoothing does not occur to the normal extent. What we normally would think of as 'riskless arbitrage' be-comes highly speculative whenever the chain of transactions cannot be closed instantly. The 'Closed for the lack of prices' sign is a case in point. While the increased variance of prices for individual commodities initially encourages increased consumer comparison shopping, the information produced by such searching depreciates so rapidly in high inflations that the incentive is much weakened. Spatial as well as temporal violations of arbitrage pricing occur everywhere.

## TENTATIVE CONCLUSIONS

The modern economy is complicated, as Hayek would put it, 'beyond human comprehension', too complicated by far for individual agents to confront 'directly' in their planning. The typical (albeit not representative) agent could not begin to cope with all the opportunities and options that the economy offers, let alone with a goods–dates–contingency decision space of the dimensionality of the Arrow–Debreu model.

The system has evolved to this degree of complexity, not because it is populated by agents typically endowed with commensurate cognitive skills, but, on the contrary, because ways to simplify individual decisions and to simplify the coordination of individual activities have gradually evolved. The modern economy has not evolved so as belatedly to exploit in full the cleverness that its inhabitants possessed all along. Rather it has evolved to a complexity beyond human understanding, because people with limited cognitive capabilities have devised ways of getting along without dealing with the full complexity of the system.

These simplifying strategies are a combination of collective institutional arrangements and individual cognitive short-cuts, adapted to one another. We view both money and organized markets as belonging to these institutional arrangements.

It is odd that economists routinely recognize this when discussing the division of labor, that is, specialization in production. In that context the representative agent is not supposed to know and master everything. In the theory of exchange (and finance), cognitive limitations have traditionally been more or less ignored. And monetary theory from Patinkin onwards has been discussed in the framework of exchange theory, with production (and specialization of knowledge) eliminated as an inessential complication.

High inflations destroy social institutions and arrangements that would not have existed in the first place if economic agents were not subject to cognitive limitations. By relying on a monetary theory that assumes such 'unbounded rationality' in agents, we fail to understand the social and economic consequences of inflation and the benefits of monetary stability. So, such theory is dangerous.

## NOTES

1. While this is my own summary and he has no responsibility for errors, much of the material I have learned from Heymann. Our book, *High Inflations*, was published by Oxford University Press (1995). Earlier versions of this paper were given as lectures at the Fourth Summer Workshop of the Siena International School of Economic Research, at Universität Hohenheim (Stuttgart) and at the Bank of Uruguay.
2. See Cagan (1956).
3. For the concept of 'random walk monetary standard', refer to Leijonhufvud (1984a).
4. See Kornai (1986) and also the earlier treatment in Kornai (1980).
5. The view that the economic costs and social consequences of inflation are by and large confined to the effects of the inflation tax on cash balances had become the prevalent one among American and Western European economists already more than twenty years ago. For a critique that may have been too intemperate and hostile in wording – characterizing

the prevalent view as one of 'profound and appalling naiveté' and so on – but from which I would not otherwise detract, see Leijonhufvud (1977). It should perhaps be acknowledged that the standard model referred to in the text also predicts the so-called Tobin effect: that people will hold less money but titles to more real capital in inflationary situations. We see no empirical evidence whatsoever for this implication in the high inflations.

6. Strictly speaking, of course, modern monetary theory has nothing to say about the conditions under which the use of domestic money might be abandoned. It cannot, since it provides no satisfactory account of why it is used in the first place. We feel nonetheless that the staying power of money deserves to be listed as one of the riddles posed by the evidence on high inflations. That riddle, however, will not be explored in this paper.

7. Brazil was, however, for a long period an exception in this regard.

8. The paragraphs immediately following repeat material from Chapter 10 above.

9. However, in hyperinflations, wage negotiations, for example, are also very short term. This is presumably due to the difficulty of finding indexing formulas that share the risk in a mutually agreeable manner. Nonetheless, it remains true that, as inflation increases, some types of contracts shorten much less readily than others. For the German case, see Bresciani-Turroni (1937) and Schacht (1927).

10. The markets that are first dollarized, in fact, are not the ones in which the continuous availability of an index measure would be particularly beneficial. Dollarization tends to spread first in the sale or purchase of housing, for instance – that is, in markets where people are making major wealth placements for some length of time.

11. See especially Simonsen (1983) and Fischer (1986).

12. Besides, any other tax by which public expenditures could be financed would cause distortions too. So, whether the inflation is a 'bad thing' is an open question – from the standpoint of this literature.

13. K. Velupillai (1999).

14. Uncomputable problems pose a threat to this line.

15. A subsidiary conjecture for good measure: that, in general equilibrium theory of that sort, we will never achieve a model of money that captures all four of the traditional functions of money at once.

16. Also, that markets are essential as compilers of information in this process. How can we conceive of aggregate demand functions as having any operational significance without corresponding markets actually in operation?

17. Heiner (1983) and Bewley (1989).

18. See Leijonhufvud (1986b – Chapter 13 below).

PART III

# Markets, Firms and the Division of Labor

# 12. Notes on the theory of markets

## I

In a 20-year old paper that has not gotten the attention it deserves, Richard Goodwin[1] dealt with the market as a servo-mechanism or homeostat. A homeostat is a control device that regulates the behavior of a 'machine' on the basis of information about, and evaluation of, its actual past performance, that is, on the basis of feedback. The purpose of control is to bring actual performance into line with desired performance and this is done, in effect, through a process of trial and error. The application of these concepts to the question of the stability of the equilibrium of an isolated market is quite straightforward, but still worthwhile, I think, if you go slow – just throwing it out as a loose analogy, obviously, does not do anything for us. We will regard, then, the market as a device for 'solving' demand and supply equations by trial and error, that is, through an iterative process.

It will help if we consider first the very simplest kind of device. The illustration familiar to all is that of the thermostat (Figure 12.1).

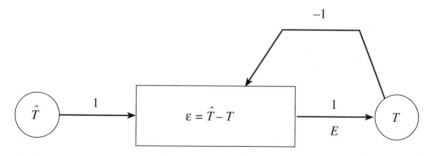

$\hat{T}$ = desired temperature (*input* into control device)
$T$ = actual temperature (the *output*)
$\varepsilon$ = observed error (to be brought to zero)
$E$ = 'shift operator' (marks the response of the control device)

*Figure 12.1   Diagram of a thermostat*

In Figure 12.1, we have to the left an exogenous input – a desired value for the controlled variable is given from outside. This input is received, in the middle, into a receptor which also records the actual value of the variable and measures the error – the difference between the two. (The error depends positively on $\hat{T}$ and negatively on $T$; to indicate this, the corresponding arrows are marked 1 and –1 respectively.) The effector, to the right, is 'error-actuated' – whenever the receptor finds a non-zero error, it transmits an order to the effector to have the output changed according to rules given by some response function:

$$\Delta T = T_1 - T_0 = f(\varepsilon_0).$$

Even the most unsophisticated thermostat should have built into it at least the rules that:

1.   it quits when the desired temperature prevails;
2.   the temperature is raised when the room is 'too cold'; and
3.   vice versa.

That is:

$$f(0) = 0$$
$$f(\varepsilon > 0) > 0$$
$$f(\varepsilon < 0) < 0$$

But these properties of the response function are only in the nature of mini-mum requirements and do not ensure a satisfactory mechanism. Lags in either link of the feedback loop or strong responses to small errors, for example, would produce oscillatory behavior.

On this we do not elaborate, but turn instead to the market.

## II

We are going to regard the market as a servo-mechanism that continually feeds back the discrepancy between its actual and 'desired' state and (hopefully) adjusts the actual state in the direction required to reduce the 'error' towards the appropriate zero value. But we are now dealing with a mechanism that is a good deal more subtle and complicated than the simple thermostat.

First, there are two variables, and not just one, to be controlled, namely *price* and *rate of output*. For reasons that will become clear as we proceed, we will not invoke duality of price and output as an excuse for dealing explicitly with the control of only one of the two. There are two feedback loops and, to begin with, we will take them one at a time. Second, the market mechanism is subtler than the thermostat. The thermostat has the desired value of the controlled variable given to it from the outside (and from the outset). As economists, we are wont to put ourselves in the role of outside observers who, knowing the demand and supply functions, are able to calculate the equilibrium values for price and output. But we should not permit ourselves to assume that the inside observers – the actual market participants – possess and act on this knowledge. The 'market machine', consequently, cannot operate on the basis of known target values for the variables it is designed to control. In outlining the feedback control of price, therefore, we cannot assume a receptor constructed to measure the actual–desired price discrepancy. *Mutatis mutandis*, the same applies to the rate of output – decisions to change output are not based on the discrepancy between actual and equilibrium industry rates of output, because we do not assume that there is any decision-maker in the market who is in a position to measure this output 'error'.

I will discuss the homeostatic control of price and rate of output under the headings that have become conventional, namely 'Walrasian stability' and 'Marshallian stability' respectively.


## III   WALRASIAN STABILITY

The iterative process assumed in this case, Walras called the *tâtonnement* – literally 'groping' – process. In the Walrasian case, we look at the market as groping for the market-clearing price.

The standard static equilibrium, we identify with the solution to equations (12.1)–(12.3):

$$q^d = D(p) \tag{12.1}$$
$$q^s = S(p) \tag{12.2}$$
$$x = D(p) - S(p) = 0 \tag{12.3}$$

We have two familiar diagrammatic representations of this little system. Either we graph functions (12.1) and (12.2) with the equilibrium state represented by their intersection, or we simply graph $x(p)$ with the equilibrium price, $p$, given by its intersection with the price axis.

How is this equilibrium established? The usual answer (presuming the stable case) is that, if $p > \hat{p}$, supply exceeds demand and competition between unsuccessful sellers will tend to drive the price down. The process comes to a halt when $x = 0$ and $p = \hat{p}$. If $p < \hat{p}$, competition between frustrated buyers ...

and so on. The three equations by themselves, however, say nothing about the process – they only assert the ultimate solution.

As pointed out before, the market homeostat is not provided with the 'desired' price, so the feedback mechanism cannot rely on observed errors in the value of the controlled variable. Instead, the *observable* error is that between quantities demanded and supplied. The Walrasian receptor registers the value of $x$. The response by the effector is given by

$$\Delta p = p_1 - p_0 = f[D(p_0) - S(p_0)],$$

a function embodying the following 'rules of search':

$$f(0) = 0$$
$$f(x > 0) > 0$$
$$f(x < 0) < 0.$$

The first rule tells the market when to quit – although, so to speak, it does not know what it is looking for, it will know when it has found it.

Suppose, following Goodwin and, at one remove, Walras, we start at $t = 0$, with $p_0$ – a price *crié au hasard*. We can then simulate the adjustment process by the following iterative search for a solution to equations (12.1)–(12.3):

| | |
|---|---|
| 1st try: | $p_1 = f[D(p_0) - S(p_0)] + p_0;$ |
| 2nd try: | $p_2 = f[D(p_1) - S(p_1)] + p_1;$ |
| .......................................................................; |
| $t$-th try: | $p_t = f[D(p_{t-1}) - S(p_{t-1})] + p_{t-1};$ |

The search is for the 'zero error', that is, for the price that, when tried, 'gives the same answer back'. Thus, to illustrate, suppose $p_{t-1} = \hat{p}$. Then, on the right-hand side of the '$t$-th try', we would have $D(p_{t-1}) - S(p_{t-1}) = 0$, and consequently $\Delta p = f(0) = 0$. The last line above would read $p_t = 0 + p_{t-1}$, that is, the same answer back.

When, and *if*, the solution is found, the process repeats itself until disturbed. What about the 'if'?

Whether an iterative procedure will lead to the solution or not will depend on:

1.  the form of the equations, and
2.  the type of search process used.

Put more generally – and more loosely – success depends upon the 'environment' in which the search takes place and on the rules of search followed. A simple set of rules may work in one setting but not in another. Similarly, a search may be successful in a given setting with one set of rules but not with another.

Since we have so far described only one set of rules of search, we are not in a position as yet to illustrate the last proposition. That will have to wait until the Marshallian homeostat has been described. For a demonstration that the success of a given iterative procedure depends upon the form of the equations, we have only to remind ourselves of the familiar possibilities illustrated in Figures 12.2 and 12.3.[2]

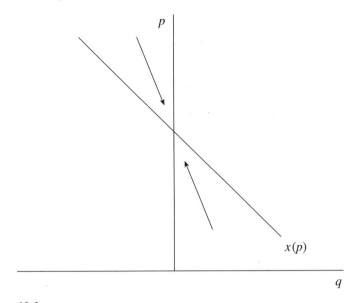

*Figure 12.2*

The type of search process or search rule built into the Walrasian homeostat presumes that whenever $D > S$, price is 'too low' and whenever $S > D$, price is 'too high'. When, as shown in Figure 12.3, the equations are such that this presumption is false, the servo-mechanism will not work; it will not 'zero in'. Instead of having a *deviation counteracting* control, we will find that the feedback effects are *deviation amplifying*; the system departs further and further from the solution.

For the system to work properly given this search process, therefore, the Walrasian stability condition must be fulfilled. The excess demand curve must slope downward to the right where it intersects the price axis. The form of the equations must be such that we have:

$$\partial x / \partial p < 0.$$

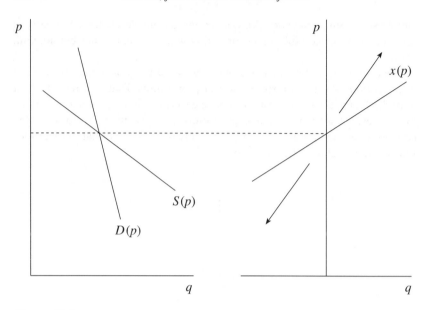

*Figure 12.3*

Although our primary interest is in the dynamics of the market *per se*, we recall that the system must 'obey' this condition for us to be able to draw meaningful conclusions from comparative static experiments with it.

The standard market diagram is the best one to use in order to exhibit the role of the 'form of the equations'. If the adjustment process is not known, however, that diagram alone does not tell the whole story. It may be complemented with a diagram of the sort used to discuss the thermostat described earlier, showing the type of feedback mechanism that is involved (Figure 12.4).

Here we have the receptor to the left, the effector to the right. The gross properties of the function relating observed error to response we have already discussed. The mechanism as a whole is seen 'to observe' quantities and to regulate price. Price changes are fed back via two loops, that is, via demand and via supply decisions separately. As indicated by the question marks, the figure does not contain sufficient information by itself to enable us to determine whether the control mechanism will be deviation counteracting. If you are willing to rule out the Giffen-good possibility, one of the question marks can be dropped. If you dare also disregard the ability of a backward-bending supply curve, the other one goes as well. The homeostat is then seen to be operating with unambiguously *negative* (error-reducing) *feedback*. If we can presume this reassuring case, we can also choose a somewhat simpler repre-

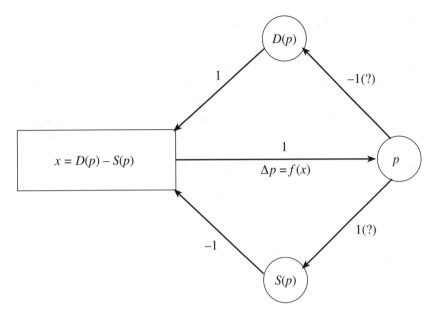

*Figure 12.4*

sentation that makes both the similarities and the differences with the thermostat more obvious (Figure 12.5)

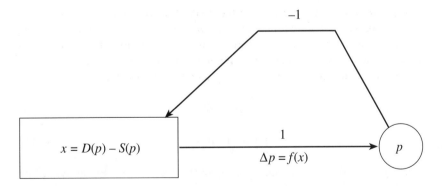

*Figure 12.5*

## IV   MARSHALLIAN STABILITY

In the Walrasian case, the iterative process dealt with the problem of arriving at the 'right' price. At each step of the process a price was regarded as given – as an independent datum for each 'price-taker' to react on. 'Higgling and haggling' in the market would produce a new price if, at the prevailing price, $x \neq 0$.

In the Marshallian case, we deal with the problem of finding the 'right' rate of *output*, that is, the right *quantity*. The solution is found by a trial and error process involving rates of supply. Again, we start off from an arbitrary rate of output – a quantity *crée au hasard*, as it were. At each successive step, a new 'trial' quantity is taken as given. The reaction of consumers and producers to the value of this 'independent' variable, we describe in terms of:

1.   the *demand price* – the maximum price at which consumers are willing to absorb this rate of output, and
2.   the *supply price* – the maximum price required to induce producers to continue this rate of output.

The rate of output is the 'output' (controlled variable) of this 'machine'. The feedback mechanism relies on the response of producers to discrepancies between their *supply price* and the *actual price*.

At this point, we sneak in an assumption that we will have to come back to later, namely that the *actual price* that will prevail when the quantity is given *equals the demand price*. The rationale – however inadequate – for so postulating is that suppliers always seek to get the maximum price possible and that we have competition between buyers.

Equilibrium is characterized by the equality of demand price and supply price. I choose to work with the *excess supply price*, $\pi$, as the 'error' that this homeostat is to eliminate.[3] Alternatively, then, the equilibrium condition may be expressed as $\pi = 0$. (For the individual firm this implies $MC - MR = 0$.) The static equilibrium, we thus identify with the solution to:

$$p^s = s(q) \tag{12.4}$$
$$p^d = d(q) \tag{12.5}$$
$$\pi = s(q) - d(q) = 0 \tag{12.6}$$

For this system, too, we have our choice of diagrams. Either we graph functions (12.4) and (12.5) with the equilibrium quantity and price given by their intersection, or we graph $\pi(q)$ with the equilibrium output, $\hat{q}$, given by its intersection with the quantity axis.

The static picture, again, tells us nothing about how the solution is arrived at. To quote Cliff Lloyd in context: 'Knowledge of where a man is buried tells us little of the life he led.' How is this rate of output determined? The usual answer (presuming stability) is that, if $q > \hat{q}$, then $\pi > 0$, implying *losses* on the margin that will induce producers to cut back the rate of output. And vice versa.

Thus the groping for the 'normal' rate of output proceeds, it is suggested, according to rules of search embodied in the response function:

$$\Delta q = q_1 - q_0 = h[s(q_0) - d(q_0)],$$

with the properties

$$h(0) = 0$$
$$h(\pi > 0) < 0$$
$$f(\pi < 0) > 0$$

Again, the machine does not know what it is looking for, but its built-in rules of search tell it to quit when the right output rate has been found. Just as the Walrasian homeostat based its regulation of price on information about quantities, the Marshallian homeostat regulates quantity on the basis of information about 'prices' – or, more exactly, marginal valuations on both sides of the market. To show the successive trials and errors that the Marshallian homeostat goes through is very simple and, therefore, superfluous.

Having outlined a different search process, it is of course true that the results of search depend upon the form of the equations. The Marshallian stability conditions must clearly be that:

$$\partial\pi/\partial q > 0$$

so that we avoid the case illustrated in Figure 12.6.

With a downward-sloping excess supply price schedule, the postulated mechanism will lead the market participants astray. The feedbacks will turn out to be deviation amplifying rather than counteracting (negative).

The feedback-controlled 'governor' is outlined in Figure 12.7.

Once more, a simpler representation is sufficient if one is allowed to presume that the demand price schedule slopes downward and the supply price schedule upward (Figure 12.8).


# V

We have now sketched two different search processes and are thus prepared to show that, with the form of the equations given, success may depend upon

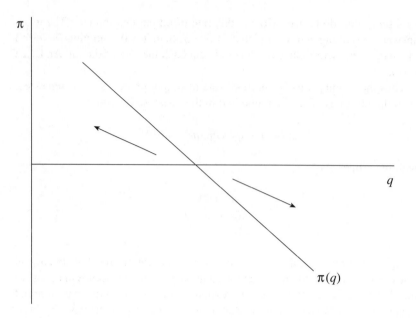

*Figure 12.6*

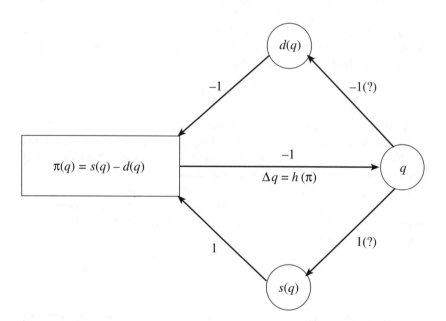

*Figure 12.7*

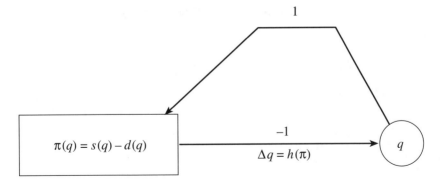

*Figure 12.8*

the process used. A variety of more or less weird possibilities where one or the other process will not find the answer can be easily constructed. The one with some claim to our attention is the case of the decreasing cost industry (Figure 12.9).

In Panel A, we have marked one of the schedules both *s* and *S*, and the other both *d* and *D* – thereby warning of one potential source of confusion in the discussion of this case. Supply price and supply, demand price and demand, are concepts that should be kept clearly distinct.

In Figure 12.9, the hybrid *sS* schedule has been drawn less steeply sloped than the *dD* schedule. As seen in Panels B and C, this yields the case where the Walrasian dynamics do not work but the Marshallian do.[4]

One reason why we did not invoke the duality of (the equilibrium values of) price and output as an excuse for elaborating on only one of the processes – the *tâtonnement* would be the standard choice – is now becoming apparent. What should be the conclusion – stable or unstable? It depends. It depends on assumptions that remain hidden if all we have to go on are the algebraic coefficients of the two schedules. These alone do not tell us what kind of conceptual market experiments are supposed to apply to the situation under study. Clearly, the interpretation to be put on the *sS* schedule is crucial.

Following Professor Viner, it has become the convention to distinguish between cases of 'backward-bending' and 'forward-falling' *supply* schedules. A more informative terminology, I would suggest, would distinguish simply between 'backward-bending *supply*' and 'downward-sloping *supply price*'.[5] If *sS* is really a supply schedule, Walrasian dynamics apply and the situation is unstable. If it is a supply-price schedule, we have a Marshallian stable case.

Even this, however, falls somewhat short of clarifying the matter completely. One sometimes sees the statements just made paraphrased in the following fashion: 'It depends on whether it is a Walrasian or a Marshallian

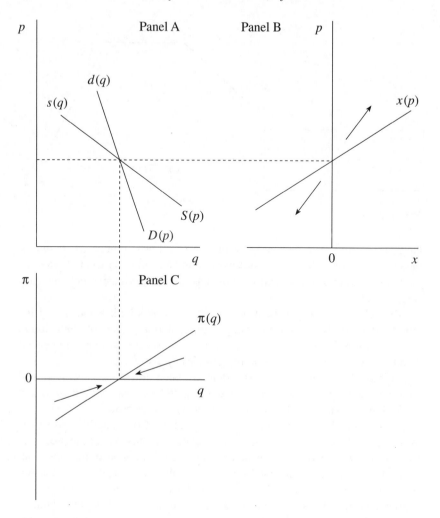

*Figure 12.9*

world we are considering.' The suggestion of a simple dichotomy that such a statement carries is inappropriate.[6] The two sets of possible worlds overlap. Indeed, if we keep strictly within the traditional treatment of the Marshallian homeostat, the 'worlds' to which it applies constitute a subset of those in which the Walrasian homeostat is operative.

To see this, consider the 'sneaky assumption' made when we first introduced the Marshallian case. Producers' decisions on changing output are geared to the relationship between their supply price and the *actual* price.

That is the way we *must* formulate it.[7] The assumption made earlier, however, was that actual price always equals the demand price for the output rate prevailing at the moment.

How can this be? The assumption, of course, must be that the Walrasian homeostat is in operation and brings it about – and is operating 'very fast' (very fast indeed) to bring the *observable*, actual price into line with the demand price associated with the output of the moment. On every 'market day' a price is established that clears the market of the output forthcoming on that day, whereas the quantity-regulating feedback takes a whole 'short run' to do its work.[8]

Consequently, the Walrasian feedback mechanism is *contained within* the Marshallian. So, a more complete representation of the latter than that provided in Figure 12.8 should look like Figure 12.10. Note that in linking the two mechanisms together (in this 'classical' fashion), the inputs into the respective receptors are not represented exactly as before. Figure 12.10 makes it explicit that the Marshallian receptor 'observes' the market-clearing price for the output of the moment. The Walrasian receptor picks up, *not* the horizontal distance between the demand and supply price schedules,[9] but the discrepancy between the quantity demanded at the ruling price and actual output. Since the demand schedule is negatively sloped, the 'environment' in which the Walrasian search process takes place, on any given market day, is characterized by an $x(p)$ function having the desired negative slope. The $x(p)$

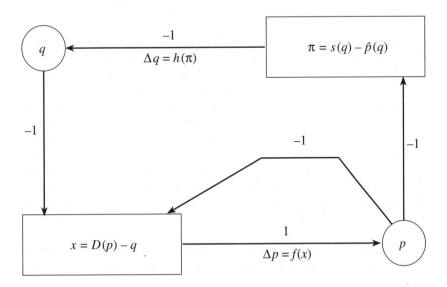

*Figure 12.10*

function of Figure 12.9 is never operative. So even though we have the functioning of the Marshallian market mechanism dependent upon the Walrasian homeostat nestled within, the machine will work.

## Summary

In the third and fourth sections, we gave illustrations of the proposition that, given a specified iterative procedure, success will depend upon the form of the equations. In the fifth section, the decreasing cost case was used to illustrate the proposition that, given the form of the equations, success may depend on the rules of search being used. Whether the market depicted by Figure 12.9(A) would be stable or unstable is a question that cannot be answered unless the relevant market mechanism is specified. To specify the mechanism requires not only description of the homeostats regulating price and quantity separately but also description of the exact manner in which they are *coupled*. The coupling of the Walrasian and Marshallian homeostats is shown in Figure 12.10.

## VI

With relatively minor modifications, the control device illustrated in Figure 12.10 may be used in expositing a number of other pieces of standard classroom analysis. For example:

1.  The analysis of markets for stock–flow goods and the explanation of simple accumulation processes are rather easily handled.[10]
2.  A time lag in the quantity-adjustment link of the system in Figure 12.10 produces the 'cobweb' model. While this model rests on rather silly behavioral assumptions that make it of limited economic interest, 'oscillatory malfunction' is an extremely important topic in the study of self-regulating systems and some of the elementary principles involved are very conveniently explained with the help of the cobweb model. The explosive cobweb case, for example, shows that the coupling of two homeostats, each one of which appears stable when viewed in isolation, may – due to lags in communication – produce a mechanism that is not at all 'well behaved'.

At this point, however, it is best to cease and desist. The reader's patience with elementary exercises in demand and supply analysis has no doubt been tried enough. Few price theory texts devote as much space to market processes as this paper has already consumed, and without getting very far at that. The present-day tendency both in theoretical work and (I believe) in the teaching of theory is to concentrate on the choice problems of individual economic units. The *interaction* of these economic units – the theory of markets – is, in contrast, most often cursorily treated. Once demand and supply functions have been carefully built up, the model is quickly 'slapped together' and one jumps directly to the properties of its equilibrium solution. The present approach seeks to complement the standard classroom geometry with diagrams that clearly portray the communication 'network' on which the coordination of the activities of individuals depends. Careful scrutiny of such networks may reveal to students some unexpected twists to even the most familiar and elementary model. It becomes apparent, for example, that the market mechanism portrayed by Figure 12.10 is *at no point dependent on input of information on what quantity producers would like to supply at the given price.*[11]

At the point where we have left it, however, the analysis is merely a modest beginning. Pedagogical claims for the approach will have to rest not so much on what has been accomplished by the analysis above as on what it reveals is yet needed in order to provide an adequate analysis of even the simple isolated market case. Consider the following.

1. By the explicit inclusion of the Walrasian homeostat, Figure 12.10 gives a fuller description of the Marshallian market than did Figure 12.8. But it is not a complete description of the information that has to be generated for the market to work as assumed by the model. Price is assumed to be *unique* at each point in time; Jevons's 'law of indifference' is assumed to be in continuous and instantaneous operation. But the elimination of price discrepancies through competition is in itself a communication process, the nature of which ought to be explicitly represented. We ought to have a 'Jevons's homeostat' within the Walrasian.

2. *Tâtonnement* models are notorious for their use of the contrived assumption that all market participants are price-takers. Although the model of Figure 12.10 is not a pure Walrasian one, it nonetheless retains this objectionable feature: no one sets price.

3. The model does not allow for the rate of sales to differ from the rate of output, nor for the rate of consumption to differ from the rate of purchase. Giving up the interrelated assumptions that all of output is always sold (even in disequilibrium) and sold at a price no lower than the demand price will lead in the direction of real world problems – the analysis of which proves much less manageable than what has been attempted here.

All three of these limitations point to the desirability of developing models with an explicitly stochastic treatment of prices and quantities. All three limitations, also, have to be overcome before a rigorous treatment of Keynesian dynamics can be accomplished.[12]

## NOTES

1. See Goodwin (1951).
2. The adjustment process has been described above as taking place in discrete steps. This means that it is obviously possible for the process to *oscillate*. As described in the literature, the *tâtonnement* process usually is assumed to involve continuous registration of the error and continuous price adjustment, with no time lags in either link of the feedback loop; these assumptions remove the possibility of oscillatory behavior. I am (somewhat inconsistently) following convention here in not worrying about oscillations at this stage.
3. I am aware that it is more common to choose the *excess demand price*. I go against common usage in the frail hope that some student sometime will thereby be prevented from confusing excess demand price with excess demand.
4. With the $sS$ schedule cutting the $dD$ schedule from above, of course, the stability conclusions are reversed. No other justification than expository convenience is offered here for using the other case of the two in the discussion.
5. With backward-bending supply, as price is raised, the (*maximum*) quantity supplied decreases. With downward-sloping supply price, as output is increased, the price required to induce producers to maintain that output rate falls. What does such a supply price schedule tell us about suppliers' behavior consequent upon a rise in price? The answer, which interprets this as a comparative statics question, becomes of course singularly uninformative: that the *minimum* quantity that producers will consent to supply decreases! The inference, on the other hand, that the rate of change of output increases if positive, decreases if negative, makes more sense. What pursuit of such exercises will sooner or later do, however, is to uncover a most embarrassing question: who is supposed to set prices around here anyway?
6. Also, of course, there are other possible 'worlds', that is, types of market adjustment behavior that cannot be classified either under the Walrasian or the Marshallian heading. Cf. footnote 8.
7. At this point the temptation to recast personal preference as a methodological imperative (all too often sinned against) becomes too strong to bear: our theoretical conclusions in economics are sound only in so far as the economic choices asserted to be made are made on the basis of information that can, within the model itself, be shown to be available to the decision-makers in question.
8. See Leijonhufvud (1968c), Chapter 2.
9. Compare footnote 5.
10. See Clower (1954) and Witte (1963).
11. Since Figure 12.10 has a fair claim to representing *the* 'classical' (Keynes's sense) market mechanism, the observation in the text suggests an exam question (asked only half in jest): what good are supply functions in classical economics? Apart from the fact that supply functions have their place in the asset markets, labor markets and so on, of Marshallian economics, one obviously cannot deny Walras his place as a 'classical' economist, and in the Walrasian tradition all markets do, of course, have their supply functions. This tradition has come to predominate almost totally in pure microtheory since Hicks's *Value and Capital* (1939) and Samuelson's *Foundations of Economic Analysis* (1947). One consequence of this is worth noting: the study of the stability properties of general equilibrium systems has come to be almost completely confined to that of the *tâtonnement* stability of pure exchange models. The presumption has apparently been that the conclusions thus reached would carry over to exchange *cum* production systems and that the regulation of output rates would pose no additional problems. As far as I am

aware, the literature does not even contain any systematic attempts to justify this tenuous (not to say untenable) presumption.

12.  See Leijonhufvud (1968) Chapter 2.

# 13. Capitalism and the factory system

Economic theorizing utilizes, on the one hand, mathematical techniques and, on the other, thought experiments, parables or stories. Progress may stagnate for various reasons. Sometimes we are held back for lack of the technique needed to turn our stories into the raw material for effective scientific work. At other times, we are short of good stories to inject meaning into (and perhaps even to draw a moral from) our models. One can strive for intellectual coherence in economics either by attempting to fit all aspects of the subject into one overarching mathematical structure or by trying to weave its best stories into one grand epic.

This chapter attempts to revive an old parable, Adam Smith's theory of manufacturing production, which has been shunted aside and neglected because it has not fitted into the formal structure of either neoclassical or neo-Ricardian theory. The discussion attempts to persuade, not by formal demonstrations (at this stage), but by suggesting that the parable can illuminate many and diverse problems and thus become the red thread in a theoretical tapestry of almost epic proportions.

The subject may be approached from either a theoretical or a historical angle. Regarding the theoretical starting point, it is possible to be brief since the familiar litany of complaints about the neoclassical constant-returns production function hardly bear repeating. The one point about it that is germane here is that it does not describe production as a process, that is, as an ordered sequence of operations. It is more like a recipe for bouillabaisse where all the ingredients are dumped in a pot, $(K, L)$, heated up, $f(\bullet)$, and the output, $X$, is ready. This abstraction from the sequencing of tasks, it will be suggested, is largely responsible for the well-known fact that neoclassical production theory gives us no clue as to how production is actually organized. Specifically it does not help us explain: (1) why, since the industrial revolution, manufacturing is normally conducted in factories with a sizeable work force concentrated in one workplace; (2) why factories relatively seldom house more than one firm; or (3) why manufacturing firms are capitalistic in the sense that capital hires labor rather than vice versa.

# REVOLUTIONS: AGRICULTURAL AND INDUSTRIAL

The story of the industrial revolution has often been told around the theme of technical invention and innovation in spinning and weaving, steel-making and power generation, freight transportation and so on. Similarly, the agricultural revolution that preceded it sometimes seems just a long catalogue of new crops, new rotations, new ways to drain or fertilize land, new techniques of selective breeding and the like.

If one looks at the two revolutions from the standpoint, not of technological history, but of a new institutional history, the agricultural revolution becomes primarily the story of enclosures and the industrial revolution the story of the coming of the factory system and, eventually, of the joint stock corporation.

It is customary in standard treatments of 18th century English economic history to hail both these organizational developments as obvious examples of progress. Carl Dahlman (1980, pp. 209–10) has pointed out that the juxtaposition of the two poses something of a paradox, for one process seems to be almost the reverse of the other. The reorganization of agriculture, known as the enclosure movement, was a move away from the collective 'team' working of village land. Each family ended up working its own farm. Correspondingly, it required the unscrambling of joint ownership rights in land held in common (and of obligations owed to the collective). In the somewhat later reorganization of manufacturing we have the reverse. The coming of the factory was a move toward collectively organized modes of production. It replaced the family-firm craftshop and the putting-out system. The craftshop run by a master craftsman with a couple of journeymen and apprentices and with family helpers had been the dominant type of manufacturing business since the early Middle Ages. Under the putting-out system, an entrepreneur 'put out' materials for processing at piece rates by workers who usually worked at home. The factory pulled the work force in under one roof. Later on, the limited liability manufacturing corporation arose to pool individual titles to physical capital in the joint stock arrangement.

Thus the Dahlman paradox: what is progress in manufacturing is backwardness in agriculture and vice versa! The open field system and enclosures are admirably analysed in Dahlman's book. The present inquiry concerns the factory system.

# THE FACTORY SYSTEM

Contemporaries tended, of course, to marvel at the new inventions and to be deeply impressed by the (very visible) role of fixed capital in the new factories. The most prominent features of the factories were (a) the size of the work force in one and the same workplace, and (b) the new machinery. The impulse has been to explain (a) by (b), that is, to take for granted that the novel spinning frames, weaving looms, steam engines and other new machinery made the explanation for factory organization of the work almost too obvious to require explicit comment.

Some histories of the industrial revolution have taken the line that the new machinery explains the factories. The point has been made, for example, that the early steam engines, with their low thermal efficiency, were very large, stationary ones; consequently, if one wanted to utilize steam power, one had to pull a sizeable labor force in under one roof and run the various machines of the factory by belt transmission from a single source. The answer suggested in this sort of illustration is that the new technologies introduced obvious economies of scale (for example, in power generation) that led quite naturally to large-scale factory production.

Economies of scale were obviously one aspect of the story. But they do not make the whole story. Some 150 years later, small-scale electrical motors removed the basis for the particular type of scale economy just adduced – but did not, of course, thereby undermine the factory system. (At the same time, the economies of scale in generating electricity were even more formidable than they had been in steam power.) We might also check some centuries earlier. The 14th-century arsenal of Venice was one of the wonders of the world for the size of the labor force concentrated in it. Yet, the organization of ship-building in the arsenal was not that of a single firm; instead, numerous craftsmen, owning their own tools, each with a few journeymen and apprentices, operated within the arsenal and cooperated via exchange transactions in the building and outfitting of ships. In short, the famous arsenal was not a factory and not a firm.[1]

There are other examples of large work forces in one location before the industrial revolution. Large woolen manufacturing workshops existed in England since at least the beginning of the 16th century. Their size would not have been dictated by machine technology.[2] Although medieval mining was in general organized as independent partnerships of miners, by the 16th century deeper mineshafts with dangerous ventilation and drainage problems raised the capital requirements in mining beyond the means of artisan miners. The mines became capitalist firms. Alum, bricks, brass and glass were 17th-century examples of technology dictating production in sizeable establishments.[3] In these instances, the workplaces *were* factories and *were* firms.

The putting-out system was also replaced by the factory system. It exemplified capitalist control of production, often without capitalist ownership of the means of production.[4] The organization could be large but the workplaces were, of course, small.

It is not all that obvious, therefore, what role should be assigned to indivisible machinery in explaining the emergence of the factory as the dominant form of manufacturing enterprise. Some questions remain. Why, for example, did not the steam engine simply lead many independent masters to locate in the same workplace (and, perhaps, pay rent for the right to attach their newfangled machines to the overhead steam-powered shaft)?[5]

## THE CLASSICAL THEORY OF THE DIVISION OF LABOR

There is one contemporary observer whom economists might be particularly inclined to pay attention to, namely Adam Smith. *The Wealth of Nations* is, of course, a bit early (1776) for the mechanized, steam-powered, relatively fixed-capital-intensive factory system to have become established as the wave of the future. Even so, it is worth remembering that Smith did *not* dwell much on machinery as one of the 'causes of wealth'. Instead, of course, he made the 'division of labor' his grand theme. In fact, Smith (1937, p. 9) does treat the role of machinery as important but secondary and subsidiary to increasing division of labor in his account of economic progress:[6]

> Every body must be sensible how labor is facilitated and abridged by the application of proper machinery. It is unnecessary to give any example. I shall only observe, therefore, that the invention of all those machines by which labor is so much facilitated and abridged, seems to have been originally owing to the division of labor.

The classical theory of the division of labor was greatly advanced by Karl Marx in *Das Kapital*.[7] In his day, of course, the factory system was the wave of the present. Marx made the use of machinery the criterion of modern industry, which he associated with factories. At the same time, however, he emphatically agreed with Smith that mechanization followed from the division of labor.[8] In Marx's (1906, p. 969) historical schema, capitalism was subdivided into a manufacturing period ('from the middle of the 16th to the last third of the 18th century') and the subsequent modern industrial epoch. Manufacturing, in Marxist terminology, resulted from applying the principles of the division of labor to as yet unmechanized industry.

In Smith's famous pin-making illustration of the benefits of the division of labor, two modes of organizing production were contrasted. Prejudging matters a little, let us call them crafts production and factory production, respectively.[9]

In *crafts production*, each craftsman sequentially performs all the operations necessary to make a pin. In *factory production*, each worker specializes in one of these operations so that 'the important business of making a pin is,

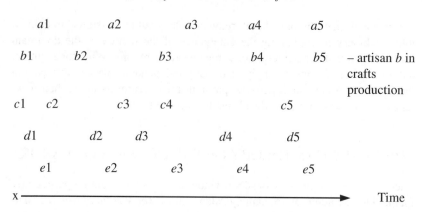

*Figure 13.1    Crafts production*

in this manner, divided into about eighteen distinct operations which, in some manufactories, are all performed by distinct hands' (Smith 1937, p. 4–5).[10]

Suppose, for illustration, that we have five craftsmen producing a product that requires five successive operations. These must be undertaken in temporal sequence, running from left to right in Figure 13.1. Here each artisan is working at his own pace and the individuals differ in (absolute and comparative) skill across the different operations.

Suppose, next, that we simply rearrange the work in some given workshop as indicated in Figure 13.2. People who previously worked in parallel now work in series. Worker *b* now performs only operation 2 but does so on all units of output produced by the team. Each individual now has to work at the pace of the team. This, obviously, makes supervision of work effort easier. Note, however, that we do not change the engineering descriptions of the operations performed, we do not change the tools used, and we do not change the people involved. We might expect output to be unchanged as well, there-

| *a*1 | *b*2 | *c*3 | *d*4 | *e*5 | | |
|------|------|------|------|------|------|------|
| | *a*1 | *b*2 | *c*3 | *d*4 | *e*5 | |
| | | *a*1 | *b*2 | *c*3 | *d*4 | *e*5 |
| | | | etc… | etc… | | |

x ──────────────────────────────────────────────►
    Time

*Figure 13.2    Factory production*

fore. Yet both Smith and Marx would tell us to expect a large increase in productivity from this reorganization of the work.

The sequencing of operations is not captured by the usual production-function representation of productive activities; nor is the degree to which individual agents specialize. A production function simply relates a vector of inputs to one or more outputs without specifying the method by which the tasks involved are coordinated, Thus Smith's division of labor – the core of his theory of production – slips through modern production theory as a ghostly technological-change coefficient or as an equally ill-understood econo-mies-of-scale property of the function.[11]

The economies achieved by switching from crafts to factory production arise from increased division of labor. In the above example, labor was entirely undivided to begin with, so that the conversion takes us from indi-vidual production to *team* production. There are three aspects to this that deserve comment. First, the specialization of labor in team production will require *standardization of production*. Under crafts production, in contrast, the skills and care of individual artisans will be reflected in non-standard output. Second, serial production requires coordination of activities in the sense of the *time phasing* of the inputs of individual workers. Third, the labor of individual workers becomes *complementary* inputs. If one work station on an assembly line is unmanned, total product goes to zero.

So far we have supposed that the number of workers and the tools are unchanged and that the only change arises from their improved coordination. But it is obvious that the conversion from crafts to factory production will present opportunities to economize on inputs.[12]

The switch is *capital saving*. This is an aspect easily missed. The reorgani-zation of production undertaken to increase the division of labor will very often also create opportunities for mechanizing some stage of the process. Hence what we tend to observe is that an increase in fixed capital takes place at the same time. The impression we are left with is that productivity in-creases are normally due to more capital-intensive technology being adopted.[13] But the pin-making illustration is a counterexample.

In crafts production, each artisan would be equipped with a full comple-ment of pin-making tools. Suppose, for simplicity, that there is a different tool for each of the five stages in the series. Then, four out of five tools are always idle when artisans work in parallel under crafts production.[14] In factory production, only one complement of tools is needed, not five.[15]

It is possible that the more decisive capital-saving incentive may be the opportunity to economize on goods-in-process inventories. Suppose that, under crafts production, considerable time (and concentration) is lost in switching from one task to the next. A master craftsman with a thick enough market to allow him to produce in batches would then perform operation 1 $x$

times, before moving on to operation 2 and so on. If his dexterity (as the classical writers used to say) at each task were equal to that of the specialized factory worker, the factory's competitive edge would lie mainly in its lower working-capital requirements. Economizing on goods in process is likely to have been particularly important in the evolutionary struggle between the factory and the putting-out system.

The switch to factory production will also save on *human capital*. No worker need possess all the skills required to make a pin from beginning to end. Under crafts production, each individual has to spend years of apprenticeship before becoming a master pin-maker. In factory production, the skills needed to perform one of the operations can be quickly picked up. The increased productivity resulting from specialization in simple, narrowly defined tasks is the advantage arising from increased division of labor most emphasized by the classical economists. Correspondingly, the decreased investment in human capital is the disadvantage that most concerned them.

## HORIZONTAL AND VERTICAL DIVISION OF LABOR

There are two dimensions along which the division of labor may be varied. Adam Smith drew examples from both (without, however, making the distinction clear). The manufacture of pins illustrates what we will call *vertical* division of labor. Recall his observation that 'in so desert a country as the Highlands of Scotland, every farmer must be butcher, baker and brewer for his own family'. When the growth of the market turns slaughtering, baking and brewing into specialized occupations, we have examples of *horizontal* division of labor.

The distinction is seldom drawn in the literature. This may be in part because those authors who see the advantages of division of labor as deriving primarily from the concentration of time, experience and ingenuity on the part of individuals in a narrower range of tasks, are looking simply for *all* the differentiations of functions that the expansion of markets will allow. Charles Babbage (1833, pp. 175–6) improved on Smith's statement of the division of labor by making clear how functional differentiation brings comparative advantage into play also inside the individual firm:[16]

> That the master manufacturer, by dividing the work to be executed into different processes, each requiring different degrees of skill or force, can purchase exactly that precise quantity of both which is necessary for each process; whereas, if the whole work were executed by one workman, that person must possess sufficient skill to perform the most difficult, and sufficient strength to execute the most laborious, of the operations into which the art is divided.

But there are reasons for making the proposed distinction. An increase in the vertical division of labor requires less skilled labor at the various stages of the manufacturing process. Increased horizontal division of labor does not in general carry this implication and is perhaps more likely to mean an increase in human capital per worker. Furthermore, increased horizontal division is a question simply of *minimum economical scale*, whereas vertical division of labor results from an increasing-returns-to-scale technology.

This implication of pin-making technology may be another reason why the distinction is most often fudged, particularly in the neoclassical literature. Stigler (1951, p. 185), in his famous article on the subject, notes the dilemma bequeathed by classical to neoclassical theory:[17]

> Either the division of labor is limited by the extent of the market, and, characteristically, industries are monopolized; or industries are characteristically competitive, and the theorem is false or of little significance. Neither alternative is inviting.

Marx saw the significance of the distinction very clearly. The consequences of expansion of the market for a branch of manufacturing, he pointed out, would depend upon the technology. He distinguished two 'fundamental forms', namely 'heterogeneous manufacture' and 'serial manufacture'. The latter, of course, was exemplified by Smithian pin-making and offered opportunities for vertical division of labor. As an example of the former, Marx used watch manufacturing. All the parts of a watch could be separately manufactured for final assembly. This 'makes it ... a matter of chance whether the detail laborers are brought together in one workshop or not'. Heterogeneous manufacture might be carried out under the putting-out system, therefore (Marx 1906, pp. 375ff).

## SOCIAL CONSEQUENCES

The competitive impetus to exploit the economies afforded by vertical division of labor would seem to explain, therefore, many of the social consequences of the 19th-century factory system that have been the object of so much adverse sociological commentary:[18]

1. When labor is subdivided vertically, less skill is required, and less versatility as a producer is acquired by the individual worker. The use of child labor at some work stations often becomes feasible.[19]
2. No normal prospect of promotion or improvement in social status is to be expected; the unskilled workman does not become a master of his guild by sticking to his job for many years.

3.   More discipline is required of a sort that most people will find irksome and that most rural emigrants would have to be taught; you cannot work at your own pace; you have to be on time; random absenteeism must be subject to relatively severe sanctions.
4.   'Alienation from the product': no worker can take personal pride in the output or its quality.

Considerations of this sort do not give one grounds for blundering into the much controverted subject of the development of standards of living during the industrial revolution in Britain. The point to be made is simply that the competitive pursuit of the productivity gains afforded by the vertical division of labor will explain many of those conditions in industry that were criticized by contemporary observers.

## THE EXTENT OF THE MARKET

In our simple five-worker example, a doubling of output under crafts production will require a doubling of all inputs. Under factory production, some economies of scale will normally be present. In factory production, 'the division of labor depends on the extent of the market' – and so, therefore, do the scale economies that can be realized. These will be of two kinds.

### Parallel Series Scale Economies

Suppose, in the example, that one of the workers (worker $d$ at work station 4, let's say) is idle half the time after conversion to factory production. Then double the output that can be had with nine workers, and the flow of work would be organized as in Figure 13.3.

This is the source of increasing returns emphasized by Georgescu-Roegen (1972) as almost universally present in manufacturing – but not, as all the classical economists agreed, in agriculture. Even on the sophisticated assembly lines of a large-scale factory, some factor ('fund' in Georgescu-Roegen's terminology) is almost bound to have an input stream that is not perfectly continuous. Babbage's 'master manufacturer' cannot always divide the work so as to 'purchase exactly that precise quantity' of the services of the factor that is technically required to produce his output. A machine that is idle half the time cannot be replaced by half a machine employed all of the time. But it may be possible to double its utilization rate if, say, the machine can be shared between two parallel assembly lines and the firm can sell twice the output.

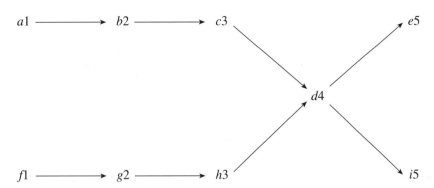

*Figure 13.3    Parallel assembly lines*

These parallel scale economies are probably never totally exhausted. In our five-stage example, it might be found, for instance, that worker $b$ is busy only 80 per cent of the time, in which case a quintupling of output can be had with only a quadrupling of stage 2 workers. And so on. But it is clear that, if we keep the number of serial stages constant, these economies of parallel replication become less and less significant as output is increased. It can in fact be shown that this is a case of asymptotically constant returns (although with a non-monotonic approach to the asymptote).[20]

**Longer Series Scale Economies**

Smith, Marx and Mill, however, were thinking more of another source of economies of scale, namely increased vertical division of labor. As the extent of the market grew, opportunities would arise, they thought, for further efficient subdivision of the production process into a greater number of serial tasks. This vertical differentiation would not only be efficient in itself but, as it proceeded, would open up new possibilities for exploiting scale economies of the Georgescu-Roegen kind.

## MECHANIZATION AND DIVISION OF LABOR AS A 'DISCOVERY PROCEDURE'

As one proceeds with the analysis of this classical division-of-labor theory, it increasingly escapes the analytical categories of static neoclassical production theory. The classical theory becomes a theory of an *evolutionary process*, rather than a theory of the rational choice between known alternatives.

Recall that Smith and Marx both insisted that the new division of labor *preceded* the mechanization of industry. They also thought that one led to the other, and they thought it rather obvious what the causal link was: as one subdivides the process of production vertically into a greater and greater number of simpler and simpler tasks, some of these tasks become so simple that a *machine* could do them. The mental task of analysing the production process so as to carry through the division of labor leads to the *discovery* of these opportunities for mechanization. Once the principles of the division of labor are mastered, the discovery of how industry can be mechanized follows.

Mechanization, in turn, will renew the sources of economies of scale. Suppose each stage of what was previously a five-stage process is subdivided into two. Suppose further that it is then discovered that stage 4b can be mechanized. But at the old scale of the enterprise, the 4b machine may be idle 90 per cent of the time. In that case, the most economical scale of production has multiplied tenfold.

**Differentiation of Function: Capital and Labor**

The process leads to increasing functional differentiation of both capital equipment and labor. But in one respect the consequences are quite different – and it turns out to be a socially important respect.

Although the tasks that become mechanized tend to be quite simple, completely standardized tasks, the machines very often will be extremely specialized to do just this one task (or series of tasks) in the production of just one product. This means that they may have no alternative employment. This differentiation of equipment can be observed also in simple handtools:

> [S]o soon as the different operations of a labor-process are disconnected the one from the other, and each fractional operation acquires in the hands of the detail laborer a suitable and peculiar form, alterations become necessary in the implements that previously served more than one purpose ... In Birmingham alone 500 varieties of hammers are produced, and not only is each adapted to one particular process, but several varieties often serve exclusively for the different operations in one and the same process (Marx 1906, pp. 374–5).

In the course of this vertical subdivision of the production process, *labor becomes increasingly unskilled*. The sociocultural consequences are disturbing. Adam Smith gradually became so convinced that the division of labor tended to produce an unskilled, illiterate, brutalized proletariat that in the end his *Wealth of Nations* contained two views of the division of labor (West 1964; Rosenberg 1965). In the early chapters, it was the source of the wealth of nations. Toward the end of the book, it became the ruination of the laboring classes. This outlook Marx took over.

From the more narrowly economic standpoint, the vertical subdivision of production makes the machines functionally more specialized or dedicated. A particular machine, as a consequence, may have few alternative uses but is also not easy to replace. With labor, the result is rather different. The individual worker becomes a detail laborer, that is, specialized in the sense that, when at work, he performs only one task. But the task is an unskilled one. The worker, consequently, can be easily replaced and can also easily qualify for alternative tasks. Thus, increasing specialization has quite different implications for the competitive position of capital and of labor, respectively. We will return to this point shortly.

## American and Japanese Traditions in Production Management

The American tradition in production management has made the most of the static advantages of the division of labor: minimal human capital requirements, maximum dexterity in the performance of individual tasks. and minimal time lost in switching between tasks – these are the principles stressed on Henry Ford's assembly lines and in Taylorite time and motion studies.

Apparently, Japanese production management violates all of these principles. Each member of a production team is supposed to learn every work station on the assembly line. Human capital input is maximized rather than minimized. But the dynamics of the Smithian evolutionary process are improved. The Japanese teams are better at discovering potential improvements in both products and methods.

## THE CAPITALIST FIRM

Consider next an idyllic thought experiment of so-called team production.[21] A number of individuals come together for the purpose of producing a particular commodity. In the 'original state', we suppose, there are no marked distinctions of wealth, power or status among these people. Some of them will contribute their skills and labor; others will commit themselves to bring machines to the joint enterprise.

We may assume that they will decide to take advantage of the Smithian economies of vertical division of labor and so set up production in the form of a single, long assembly line. For simplicity, let there be $n$ stages of production, machines and operatives – one per machine. The product could also be produced by $n$ individual artisans using a set of simple handtools or in $k$ shorter assembly lines of $n/k$ workers using less specialized machines. But we presume, with Smith and Marx, that by setting up on one long assembly

line, the collective effort will produce a larger output with the same resources.

The questions are: how many firms will there be, will the typical firm be a
capitalist one, and if so, why.

One can imagine the possibility of successive firms, each one buying the
output of the stage preceding and selling to the stage succeeding. In half of
these firms (one might also imagine), the owner of the machine hires the
operative and pays wages, whereas in the other half the worker rents the
machine he or she is working with. But these imaginings, of course, fit
singularly ill with the ways in which we find modern manufacturing to be
organized.

Since the team utilizes the economies of scale due to the division of labor,
the enterprise earns a joint rent (or a surplus, if you will). Total sales proceeds
exceed the sum of the earnings that the inputs would find in alternative
employments. The joint rent is a 'snake' in this paradise. For how is it to be
divided? In our illustration, all the inputs are assumed to be strictly complementary. If one machine is withdrawn from the assembly line, total output
falls to zero. If one worker is missing, the consequence is the same. Marginal
productivities will not supply the criteria for the distribution of product.

The division of the joint rent becomes a bargaining problem. Let the
members of the collective form coalitions among themselves and bargain
against the rest. How well might the various coalitions do? How stable would
we expect them to be?

Consider first how the bargain might go between the machine owner (capitalist) and the operative (labor) at one of the work stations on the presupposition
that the total sum going to this work station has somehow been arrived at.
Each can threaten the other to withhold input so that their joint income will
go to zero. But the bargaining situation is not symmetrical. There are plenty
of unskilled laborers in the market, but few if any substitutes for the specialized machine. This might make us suspect a tendency for the capitalist to
walk away with the joint rent, leaving the laborer with a wage equal to
alternative earnings. But there is also another asymmetry: the unskilled laborer
has many, the specialized machine few, alternative employment opportunities. If, therefore, the laborer could threaten to 'fire' the machine, the worker's
bargaining position would be very strong indeed. The question becomes who
can fire and replace whom? Or, who owns the work station, the machine
owner or the operative?

To get a clue to this question, consider the bargaining situation among the
capitalists. Each machine owner can threaten to reduce output and, therefore,
everyone else's earnings to zero[22] – until a replacement for the machine can
be found. But, again, the market for very specialized machines will be thin,
so replacements – and alternative employments – for them are hard to find.

Any agreement about the division of earnings among the machine owners would be extremely unstable.[23] So unstable, in fact, that some organization of production that avoids the complementarities between the highly specialized inputs of cooperating owners might be preferred – even at the cost of forgoing the advantages of the division of labor. To sink one's capital into these dedicated machines will not appear to be an attractive investment – unless some stable organizational form can be found.

The solution, of course, is to prevent individual capitalists from owning and controlling specific machines. Instead, a firm is formed and any capitalist who joins has to give up ownership of his machines and accept shares in the firm. Thus the assembly line is vertically integrated into one firm.[24] We might find a market gap between firms along the production chain at some stage where the market in the intermediate product issuing from the stage is thick enough so that firms on both sides of the gap are safe from hold-ups.

The formation of a firm as a solution to the machine owners' bargaining problem has one additional advantage (for them): it creates a cartel of capitalists that bargains as one unit against workers. This cartel will own the work stations. It can fire and replace workers; the workers cannot threaten to fire and replace the dedicated machines. The non-unionized worker is not going to come out of that contest with any part of the joint rent (unless, of course, he or she has some firm-specific capital). As long, at least, as unions can be kept illegal, the factory owners will continue to appropriate all the rent.

Unionization will look like labor's best bet in this situation. Workers cannot pool their labor power, as the capitalists pool their physical capital, in order to hire the machines at a rental that would leave the joint rent going to the workers of the labor-managed firm. Labor will not be owned, and specialized machinery is not for hire. The producer cooperative is a possible compromise form but, on the whole, successful enterprises started as worker partnerships are going to end up owning capital and hiring labor – which is to say, end up as capitalist firms. Unions that do succeed in capturing part of the joint rent, on the other hand, might thereby discourage capital accumulation and the further productive subdivision of labor and hence weaken the competitive position of the enterprise over the longer run.

The labor union is a subject on which economics has a less than secure grasp. In neoclassical economic theory, unions are just another pernicious form of monopoly. The alternative 'labor relations' tradition tends to reject economic theory and to draw lessons more friendly to unions from labor history. Perhaps the view of the manufacturing firm presented here might provide ground on which theoretical and historical analysis could finally meet?

## FLUCTUATIONS AND GROWTH

Our representation of the pin-making technology is so simple as to be little more than a metaphor. It is obviously capable of considerable formal elaboration.[25] But at this point the question is whether there are good reasons to prefer it to that other simplistic metaphor, the neoclassical production function. The Smithian production function may well have advantages in areas other than the ones discussed in this essay. It may be worthwhile, in conclusion, to indicate some of these potential applications.

One of the mainstay stylized facts of applied macroeconomics is that employment in manufacturing fluctuates less than proportionally to output over the business cycle. Most macroeconomic models assume a neoclassical constant-returns-to-scale technology, and most macroeconomists explain the Okun's Law phenomenon as reflecting the hoarding of labor, in particular workers with firm-specific skills, during recessions. According to this hoarding hypothesis, firms keep workers on during recessions, although they are not needed in production, in order to make sure their skills are available when business picks up again.

The Smithian increasing-returns technology suggests a competing hypothesis. Firms that utilize the scale economies of parallel series (Figure 13.3) will reduce output by shutting down, say, one assembly line of two. But the work station that the two lines have in common cannot be left unmanned. Thus, half the work force cannot be laid off when output is cut in half.[26] By the same token, the laid-off worker cannot, by cutting his or her own wage, get the line started up again. Individuals are not able by marginal wage cutting to expand the number of production jobs being offered at the factory in recession.[27]

When the extent of the market determines the division of labor, economic growth will bring productivity gains. The growing economy will show increasing division of labor not only within firms but among firms. The economy becomes more complex as it expands. When, in our simple illustration, the work of the five artisans was reorganized into a five-man factory, the production process became more complex in the straightforward sense that the number of people cooperating in making any given unit of output increased. It is this increasingly complex coordination (when it can be maintained) of larger and larger numbers of specialists that shows up as increasing productivity.[28] It is perhaps overoptimistic to hope that the exact modeling of division of labor production would give us an econometric handle on the Solow–Denison growth residuals. But it could give us a better qualitative understanding of how economic development differs from mere economic growth, which would be worth having. An economist used to thinking of production in terms of the Smithian division of labor model is likely to be more impressed with the dangers of protectionism, for instance, than colleagues whose thinking runs in neoclassical or neo-Ricardian channels. To the welfare losses arising from impediments to trade in constant (or diminishing) returns models, the Smithian economist[29] would add not only the static loss of scale economies forgone but also the dynamic losses of innovative discoveries forgone when the Smithian evolutionary process is stemmed. Although the loss of competitive improvements never made may be unquantifiable, comparisons between open and closed economies suggest that they are nonetheless the most significant category of welfare losses due to protectionism.

## CONCLUSION

The theory of the capitalist factory outlined here shares elements with other explanations that have been proposed. It is not to be expected, however, that the proponents of these other theories will be entirely happy with it. The present theory stresses the complementarity of inputs as a central problem, as do Alchian and Demsetz (1972), but it does not at all accept their insistence that the bargain between capital and labor is essentially symmetrical. My story has a great many points in common with Williamson's 'organization of work' (1980) but differs from his in seeing technological rather than transaction cost considerations as central. Finally, like Marglin (1974), I recognize an element of power in the capital–labor bargain as essential. Marglin would insist, however, that the capitalists' control of production has no technological or efficiency rationale, whereas I see the capitalists' power as rooted in the efficient, Smithian technology.

## NOTES

1. See Lane (1973, especially pp. 162–5). Production by small firms inside a larger facility remained an important organizational form in manufacturing into this century. A famous example is the Winchester Repeating Arms Company, which operated in this manner until the outbreak of World War I. See Buttrick (1952).
2. See Mantoux (1962, pp. 33–6). Mantoux was not willing to count the royal manufactories sponsored by Colbert in France as forerunners of the industrial factory system, mainly because they required royal subsidies or patronage for their continued existence.
3. Nef (1934). Nef also discusses large plants, such as cannon foundries, in various metallurgical branches.
4. That is, the individual weaver might own his own loom, for instance.
5. It was tried: 'In the Coventry silk weaving industry the experiment of "cottage factories" was tried. In the centre of a square surrounded by rows of cottages, an engine-house was built and the engine connected by shafts with the looms in the cottages. In all cases the power was hired at so much per loom. The rent was payable weekly, whether the looms

worked or not. Each cottage held from 2 to 6 looms: some belonged to the weaver, some were bought on credit, some were hired. The struggle between these cottage factories and the factory proper lasted over 12 years. It ended with the complete ruin of the 900 cottage factories' (Marx 1906, p. 509). Marx mentions other examples 'in some of the Birmingham trades'.

6. See also Smith (1937, p. 86): 'The greater their number, the more they naturally divide themselves into different classes and subdivisions of employment. More heads are occupied in inventing the most proper machinery for executing the work of each, and it is, therefore, more likely to be invented.' And, of course, the opening paragraph itself (p. 1): 'The greatest improvement in the productive powers of labor, and the greater part of the skill, dexterity, and judgment with which it is any where directed, or applied, seem to have been the effects of the division of labor.'

7. Marx (1906, Part 4, Chapters 14, 15, pp. 368–556). This is, of course, a far more extensive treatment than we find in Smith. It is far superior to that of J.S. Mill, who had little of any interest to add to Smith. See Mill (1964, Book 1, Chapters 8, 9:1, pp. 116–36). It is worth noting, however, that Mill (pp. 132, 135) too shared the opinion of Smith and Marx that the advantages of division of labor had precedence over 'the introduction of processes requiring expensive machinery' among the 'causes of large manufactories'.

8. Kenneth Sokoloff's (1984a, p. 556) study of a large 1832 sample of manufacturing firms in the US Northeast finds that 'the evidence serves to undercut the notion that the early period of industrialization was based on a proliferation of new, machinery-intensive technologies'.

9. Marx's distinction between 'manufacturing' and 'factory production' is a perfectly good and useful one. It is omitted here so as not to burden the discussion with too much terminological baggage.

10. Everyone recalls his calculation: 'Those ten persons, therefore, could make among them upwards of forty-eight thousand pins in a day.' Marx checked on pin-making in his own day: '[A] single needlemachine makes 145,000 in a working day of 11 hours. One woman or one girl superintends four such machines and so produces near upon 600,000 needles in a day' (Marx 1906, p. 502). The most recent report is Pratten (1980): Today, one operative supervising 24 machines, each of which turns out 500 pins per minute, will make about six million pins in a day.

11. Professor Georgescu-Roegen especially stresses the failure of neoclassical production theory to illuminate the fundamental difference between manufacturing processes and agricultural production processes where nature dictates the time phasing of operations. See Georgescu-Roegen (1972), which is reprinted (with several other essays germane to our subject) in Georgescu-Roegen (1976).

12. Sokoloff has mustered impressive evidence on the efficiency advantages of small, non-mechanized factories over craftshops in the early industrialization of the American northeast. His estimates of total factor productivity show 'factories' with more than five employees to be more than 20 per cent more productive than artisanal shops. See Sokoloff (1984b, sections 3, 4).

13. Events will sometimes challenge that impression. Swedish economists will recall the Horndal effect (so named by Erik Lundberg). Horndal was a steel mill considered outdated by its controlling corporation, which intended to concentrate production in its more modern plants. Investment in Horndal was therefore stopped altogether. The expectation, of course, was that in a couple of years the mill would not cover variable costs. To the consternation of observers, however, the rate of productivity growth in Horndal kept pace with that of the rest of the industry for many years (Lundberg 1959, pp. 663–4).

14. It was in fact normal for each craftsman (guild member) to own the tools he was using.

15. See John Rae (as quoted by Mill 1964, p. 129): 'If any man had all the tools which many different occupations require, at least three-fourths of them would constantly be idle and useless.'

16. Babbage found that priority for this statement of the advantages of division of labor belonged to Gioja (1815).

17. Compare Arrow (1979, p. 156): 'This dilemma has been thoroughly discussed: it has not

been thoroughly resolved.' But, surely, there is no genuine dilemma – just our obstinate collective refusal to draw the obvious conclusion and allow the empirical reality of increasing returns to displace the convenient construct of 'perfect competition'.

18. See especially Thompson (1967).

19. Goldin and Sokoloff (1984) find that, in the first half of the 19th century, even quite small factories (with five or more employees) were giving a greater share of jobs to women and children than did artisanal shops.

20. Sokoloff's data suggests that, for non-mechanized factories deriving their competitive advantage solely from the division of labor, economies of scale would tend to be very nearly exhausted already in the size range of six to fifteen employees and totally exhausted at twenty. (For the already mechanized textile industries, the scale economies were much stronger and remained significant up to a far larger scale.) See Sokoloff (1984b, section 3).

21. Inspired by Alchian and Demsetz (1972).

22. In the literature on vertical integration, this is familiar as the post-contractual 'opportunistic behavior' of Williamson (1975) or the 'hold-up' problem of Klein, Crawford and Alchian (1978).

23. Technically speaking, the core is empty since every distribution can be blocked. (It does not seem helpful to insist that the empty core is a transaction cost problem.) I am especially grateful to Dan Friedman for clarifying the structure of the bargaining situation for me.

24. That the integration should be vertical does not seem to be necessary in general. In Dahlman's theory of the open field system, avoidance of the hold-up problem explains why the scattering of strips was maintained over the centuries. With arable strips scattered, the individual farmer could not, in some dispute over communal production or distribution issues, threaten to withdraw and thereby to reduce the benefits of scale economies to the village as a whole (Dahlman 1980, pp. 120–30 and 135–8).

25. An attempt in this direction is made in Ippolito (1977).

26. Marshall's cost curves, which have managed to survive (at least in undergraduate teaching) in uneasy coexistence with neo-Walrasian theory, have a rather natural fit to the Smithian technology. In neoclassical production theory, we cannot be sure that there are any firms to talk about. With the Smithian theory, we at least have no doubts about their existence. Marshall tended to presume long-run decreasing cost for his firms; this property follows directly from the increasing returns of Smithian technology. Marshall's short-run U-shaped average cost schedule gets its downward-sloping segment by the same argument as used above in connection with Okun's law and its upward-sloping segment, quite conventionally, from the diminishing marginal product of variable factors when fixed factors are kept fixed. Pricing in the markets supplied by these firms, however, should be analyzed in Hicksian, rather than Marshallian, terms. We should expect them to be 'fix-price' rather than 'flex-price' markets.

27. I very much agree, therefore, with Martin Weitzman (1982) that the prevalence of these increasing returns technologies must be taken into account if one is to understand the situation of manufacturing workers in a recession. Unemployment theory, Weitzman argues, must as a first logical requirement explain why unemployed factor units do not set up in production on their own. In the Smithian division of labor case the answer is straightforward: the manufacturing worker simply does not have the skills and knowledge required to make the product as an artisan.

28. Another example of an important idea that has not found a home in neoclassical theory but would fit into a Smithian production theory is Erik Dahmen's 'development block'. In a growing economy, all the component sectors of a Dahmen block have to be completed before any one of them becomes economically viable (see Dahmen 1971).

29. This worthy, of course, expects countries with similar factor endowments to export similar products to each other and would not be surprised if trade of this description reached large volume.

# 14. Information costs and the division of labor

Economic development, as opposed to 'mere' economic growth, is a process of system evolution toward more and more *complex* patterns of coordinated activities. It entails, in Adam Smith's language, 'increasing division of labor'.

What drives economic evolution in the direction of increasing division of labor are economies of scale. *If* we can sustain more complex forms of cooperation, these scale economies will make us all richer. But to sustain increasingly complex economic structures requires us to maintain political and monetary stability as well as free trade – relatively free trade, at least – over large geographical areas.

'The division of labor depends on the extent of the market.' Product innovations create new markets, and an almost infinite variety of cost-reducing process innovations extend the markets for particular commodities. For the entire system of interrelated markets, the lowering of transportation costs, extending markets over space, has historically been the main technical force tending to increase the division of labor.

It is reasonable to believe that the costs of processing, transmitting and storing *information* have by now taken over the role in economic development that transportation costs played for so long.

## ECONOMIC DEVELOPMENT AS THE INCREASING COMPLEXITY OF ECONOMIC SYSTEMS[1]

Complexity, in ordinary discourse, is a vague notion. We have all heard complaints of the type 'modern life is so complicated' accompanied by contrasts drawn to a supposedly 'simpler' past. Often, it really isn't clear whether this kind of statement has any content at all; if one tries to give it content, one will discover that it may at least as easily be false as true.

Since the division of labor has been driven further today, people are apt to have a narrower range of productive skills so that, in this particular sense, their life is *simpler*, not more complicated. Most people would find life horribly difficult if they had to match Adam Smith's Scottish Highland's farmer who was 'butcher, baker and brewer for his own family'. Claude Levi-

Strauss found that people of a certain tribe had to learn 4,000 varieties of jungle plants and what, if anything, they were good (or bad) for. My own 'savage mind' packs a somewhat less extensive botanical knowledge. '[T]he intellectual advantage of civilization', observes Thomas Sowell (1980, p. 7), 'is not necessarily that each civilized man has more knowledge but that he *requires* far *less*.'

This kind of ambiguity is present, I suspect, because *complex structures require simple building blocks*. Just as you can build almost anything from Legoblocks, complex 'modern' economic systems can be built using simple people almost all of whom do not know how to butcher, bake, brew – or fix their own car.

The notion of 'complexity', in any case, needs to be firmed up. To insist on a formula for quantifying complexity may be overly ambitious – a fake scalar measure may be worse than useless. But we need to make the concept concrete enough so that it is possible to speak meaningfully of 'more' or 'less' complexity, even though a partial such ordering is the best that can be hoped for. To that end, a concrete example may be the best way to begin.

In her charming book, *Medieval People*, the distinguished economic historian, Eileen Power (1963) describes the life of a serf of the Abbey of St Germain-de-Près, by the name of Bodo.[2] We may suppose Bodo to have been a 'representative man' of the 10th century whom we could compare to some 'representative man' of 20th century Europe or North America in a variety of ways. Most obviously, Bodo had shorter life expectancy. His life was hard in various senses, one of which was that it was full of hard physical labor. His nutrition was inadequate by modern standards. He was not a free man. He was poor.

Why was he poor? The answers take off in different directions depending upon the economic theory one happens to have in mind. One theory of economic development might direct our attention to innovations: chemical fertilizers, the internal combustion engine and the tractor had not been invented yet. Another might single out the capital–labor ratio: Bodo had too little capital cooperating with him in production.

The aspect of the answer I want to emphasize is that Bodo was poor because few people cooperated with him in producing his output and, similarly, few people cooperated in producing his real income, that is, in producing for his consumption. The point is most easily made by focusing on the consumption side. Suppose we could make an accurate *value added* accounting of the consumption basket of the Bodo family. Far more than 50 per cent of it, surely, would be accounted for by the direct efforts of Bodo and family members. Almost all the rest would be due to other members of his village. Only a minute portion of it would be associated with an exchange transaction.

The point is made more vivid if we consider the spatial aspect. It is quite possible that Bodo spent his whole life within a radius of a few kilometers of St Germain-de-Près. Perhaps he had never been out of sight of the place. Similarly, almost all of the value added contributions to his consumption basket would have been made by people within that same radius. Perhaps he used a little salt from the Atlantic coast – that would be about the extent of his participation in interregional trade.

There is a similar temporal aspect where we would consider, so to speak, the 'location in time', rather than in space, of the people having contributed to the representative individual's consumption. Bodo probably used some inherited tools. He tilled land that had been cleared by his forefathers. Modest as his house certainly was, it may nonetheless have been generations old. Still, in the poor society, production involves less use of durable capital goods. It is less 'roundabout', as Böhm-Bawerk would have put it.

Our rich 20th century representative man, then, occupies a node in a much larger network of cooperating individual agents than did poor Bodo. His network, moreover, is of very much larger spatial extent. The average distance from him of those who contribute to his consumption or make use of his productive contribution is longer. Similarly, his network also has greater temporal depth – the number of individuals who $t$ periods into the past made a contribution to his present consumption is larger than in Bodo's case.

The debates around Böhm-Bawerk's 'roundaboutness' concept have left us with the lesson that a perfect index for it cannot be found. That conclusion is bound to carry over to the task of measuring the temporal complexity of production and thus to system complexity in general. Usable, though less than perfect, indices may be constructed, however.

Looking at the division of labor in the way sketched above will suggest that tolerably good measures for the 'complexity' of an economy could be borrowed from the literature on industrial concentration. For instance, instead of looking at the proportion of industry output represented by the $k$ biggest firms, we would look at the proportion of a representative family's consumption represented by the $n$ largest individual value added contributors. Or we might compute a Gini coefficient on a similar basis. In principle, such measures could then be used to substantiate some (not all!) statements about the increase or decrease in the complexity of the division of labor between different points in time.

We need not linger over the problem of the best such measure. One reason for not bothering, clearly, is that none of the borrowed concentration measures might be operational at reasonable cost in the suggested application. The point is simply that the notion of 'complexity' is not inherently vague – at least not hopelessly so. When the dates of comparison are a thousand years apart, at least, the results will not be ambiguous!

There are, of course, a number of other candidates for the 'strategic factor' in economic development. I am not prepared to take inventory. After the first oil shock, many writers looked back on Western economic development as characterized first and foremost by rising per capita use of inanimate energy. Old-style East bloc planning has heavy industry, particularly steel, as the strategic factor. The heavy industry model, in turn, is perhaps no more than a special case of the 'industrial revolution' conception of economic development which makes the growth of manufacturing industries the key in development.[3] This conception rules our thinking, for instance, when we become alarmed that the trend of employment in manufacturing may begin to behave the way we like the trend in agriculture to behave.

All of these conceptions of what economic development is about have something to recommend them – a context in which they fit – and there is little purpose in trying to make a general case against them. For many purposes, however, I believe that it is better to conceive of economic development as the creation of increasingly more complex structures of the division of labor. The standard of living of the average person is thus seen to depend on our ability to maintain the conditions – 'the extent of the market' – that make these complex patterns of cooperation feasible.

## THE DIVISION OF LABOR AND INCREASING RETURNS TO SCALE

In standard economic analysis, we usually work with models that will not at all generate the picture of economic development that I have just given. Neoclassical growth models, for instance, or Heckscher–Ohlin-based international trade models do not show this association between living standards and system complexity. Conventional economic wisdom has it that rich people demand more diversity in consumption and that economies of scale in production are commonplace, but conventional economic analysis usually assumes homothetic utility functions and constant returns to scale production functions. In economies that would conform to these assumptions, the division of labor in the system as a whole can be replicated in a system $1/n$th as large. Following Martin Weitzman (1982) in happily taking the theory to its *in absurdum* limit, one might imagine an economy where each worker produces his tiny share of every commodity in GNP in his own backyard. The Smithian 'extent of the market' is completely irrelevant in such a model.

The same is true in conventional international trade theory. Comparative advantage based on spatially immobile resources dictates that autarky will be shunned and trade take place, but the pattern of trade between two countries would be exactly the same if the two were $1/n$th their actual size.[4]

The reason why economists hang on to the constant returns models for bitter life is not only that the alternatives are more complicated to handle – that, after all, would just enlarge the employment opportunities for mathematical economists – but mainly that we lack a widely accepted theory of pricing under increasing returns, a convincing model of how competition operates between firms with increasing returns, and also a micro-founded theory of income distribution for systems of this sort.[5] I will supply none of these missing theoretical pieces but proceed on my merry way as if we could nonetheless discern some of the main outlines of a theory for such an economy.

The starting point is Adam Smith's famous pin-making example. The essentials of the case are familiar to all (see Smith 1776; Leijonhufvud, Chapter 12 above). Suppose we have a number of pin-making artisans (say ten), each of whom carries out the entire process of making a pin, using a number of tools in succession. It is then possible, Smith maintained, to reorganize work so as to increase greatly the productivity of labor. The way to do it is to define the production process as an ordered sequence of (ten) tasks and to have each artisan specialize in one of these tasks.

This reorganization of work will get more output from a given work force. Each task will be performed more expertly and much faster than before. In part, this is due simply to specialization on routine tasks, in part to assignment of people to tasks so as to exploit the comparative advantages of a non-homogenous work force. No time is lost switching from task to task, and so forth. In addition, the organization of work according to division of labor principles saves on human capital and perhaps also on tools. The original artisans can be replaced by factory workers with a much narrower range of skills.

Smith's example of the division of labor shows this organization to be more *complex* in the sense outlined previously: a greater number of people cooperate in the production of any given unit of output. I want to treat it, therefore, as my paradigmatic case.

## THE DIVISION OF LABOR AND THE FIRM: SCALE ECONOMIES

Smithian work organization will generally show increasing returns to scale. The structure of such a system changes as it grows: 'the division of labor depends on the extent of the market'.

The sketch of the superior pin-making technology does not tell us whether the increased division of labor takes place altogether within one firm or, perhaps, between several. The intermediate good resulting from the completion of the *i*th task might itself be a commodity with its own market. Since firm boundaries are thus indeterminate (at this point of our story), we cannot tell whether the scale economies realized from increasing division of labor are to be classified as internal or external. That said, it will be convenient to proceed as if we had to deal simply with a single firm, operating a single plant.

The (mimimum cost) structure of the plant changes in a number of dimensions as the market grows. The sources of scale economies usually interact, so that the realization of economies in one dimension opens up new opportunities in the others.

1. *Subdivision of labor.* As output expands, the firm will look for opportunities to subdivide the production process into a greater number of distinct tasks, realizing new Smithian economies.
2. *Parallel lines economies.* At low levels of output, some factor stocks capable of yielding a continuous stream of input services will be idle much of the time. If, for example, one operative on an assembly line is idle half the time, then output can be doubled without doubling employment, by building a parallel line and having him work on both.
3. *Mechanization.* The next step, often a short step, in the evolution that takes us from the handicraft of the skilled artisan to the chain of routine tasks of the factory hands is mechanization. The continued subdivision of labor results in operations so 'mechanical' that a machine can do them – and do them both faster and better. To keep such machines from being idle much of the time, however, will require a correspondingly wide 'extent of market', so mechanization normally entails a step up in the most economical scale.

The exploitation of the economies that open up as the extent of the market grows produces increased functional differentiation of both capital equipment and labor. But the implications for capital and for labor are not symmetrical. The roles of capital and labor in firm governance are not symmetrical either – capital hires labor, not the other way around. This suggests the possibility of a theoretical account of the capitalist manufacturing firm based on the type of technology sketched above. When the division of labor is highly articulated within the firm, this technology would result in a pattern of work organization well represented by Henry Ford's original assembly line. (It may be best, therefore, to think of our theoretical firm as located in time somewhere in the early part of this century.)

The technology enters the problem in the following ways:

1. Inputs tend to be complementary to one another (for example, the assembly line stops if one worker is missing or one machine breaks down).

2.  The typical machine is highly specialized, 'dedicated' to particular tasks in the manufacture of a particular product. It may have no alternative uses, but is, on the other hand, not quickly or easily replaced: it has a thin market.
3.  The typical factory worker works at a specialized task, but an unskilled one. There are lots of alternative jobs for which he could quickly and easily qualify, but he is on the other hand easily replaced: his market is a thick one.
4.  Because of the returns to scale, the enterprise typically earns a monopoly rent; because inputs are complementary, this is a joint rent.[6]

Naturally, this is a hard-drawn caricature. (Hopefully, the apologies do not have to be spelled out at length!) Using these assumptions, I argue the nature of the manufacturing firm as follows.

The joint rent creates a distributional problem which must be solved in order for the factors to exploit the returns to scale. Complementarities among inputs mean that marginal productivities are undefined and give no guidance to a 'fair' distribution. Division of the joint rent becomes a bargaining problem that is only partly determined by the cooperating inputs' alternative opportunities in outside markets.

Suppose the machines were owned by separate 'capitalists'. Each one of them can block any coalition among the others that tries to impose a particular distribution of income. In the extreme complementarity case, blocking is done by withdrawing one machine, reducing total output to zero. The core of this game is empty, therefore, which means very simply that this is not a stable social institution. Capitalists will not choose to freeze their wealth in the form of highly dedicated equipment unless a reliable institutional form is found.

To stabilize the cooperative arrangement required for the exploitation of the economies of scale, ideally no one should be in a position to threaten the withdrawal of a complement to other inputs. (In the end, of course, the best that can be done very often leaves us with management facing unionized labor in a bilateral bargain of this sort.) The firm, therefore, is created to control all machines that are complements and have thin outside markets.

In manufacturing, therefore, the normal solution to the organizational problem has been that 'capitalists unite' in a cartel called the 'firm' and hire labor. Labor will have strong incentives to unionize in this particular setting. 'Labor hiring capital' is not a feasible alternative to 'capital hiring labor' under the conditions assumed. In order for worker-managed firms hiring capital equipment to be feasible, either the capital inputs should not be highly complementary in the line of production in question or the market for such equipment should be thick enough for competition to guarantee reliable behavior.

In the literature on vertical integration, the boundary between firm and market is analysed along very similar lines. High degrees of 'asset specificity' (Williamson 1975, 1986) threaten inter-firm contracts with post-contractual opportunism or 'hold-ups' (Klein, Crawford and Alchian 1978) so that vertical integration within one firm becomes preferred.

# COMPUTERS, ROBOTS, AND THE DIVISION OF LABOR

How is computer-assisted manufacturing going to affect industrial firms of the type just described? It is a question to which answers will have to be frankly speculative, but it is at least possible to point out some of the dimensions that will require study.

### Factory Employment and Service Sector Employment

In recent discussions, it has become fashionable to express alarm at 'deindustrialization' and the growth of the service sector. Is alarm the appropriate response to the decline in employment in certain manufacturing sectors?

Adam Smith and Karl Marx both believed that the division and subdivision of labor was fated to turn industrial work into simpler and simpler, more and more mindless tasks. They both feared that the eventual result would be a proletariat of mindless simpletons. (Remember Charlie Chaplin working the assembly line in 'Modern Times'!) But the increasing mechanization, which they also saw as resulting from the division of labor, introduced an offsetting tendency. It has tended to replace workers with machines at precisely the most repetitive, mechanical tasks, while at the same time creating a range of new jobs that require the exercise of skill and judgment in the operation, maintenance, repair and refitting of machinery. During this century, this offsetting tendency has surely long since swamped the original one that so preoccupied Smith and Marx.

Computer-assisted manufacturing should complete this development, replacing virtually all routine production jobs with machines. Machine operators will tend to be replaced by a few production supervisors who may do their work at computer screens in a control booth. On-duty maintenance crews are also likely to provide more skilled jobs because of the nature of the new equipment.

The computerization of the traditional industries will create a range of new jobs in the repair, reprogramming and conversion of industrial robots. There does not seem to be strong reasons, however, why these jobs should be performed by employees of the manufacturing corporations. Many such jobs are likely to be done on contract by outside firms. Many of these might be quite small businesses, on the scale of your local plumber or electrical repair shop – firms whose prosperity and survival depend on the skills of a single owner.

If these conjectures turn out to be right, the 'old' jobs will disappear from the traditional manufacturing industries while many of the 'new' ones emerge outside. To the extent that the 'deindustrialization and growth of the service sector' is of this sort, it should simply be welcomed. (If the former is due to foreign competition and the latter to the growth of government employment, there is reason to be concerned.) 'Deindustrialization' is a word with frightening connotations, because we are so acculturated to associate 'industrialization' with economic development. That association is probably becoming misleading. Suppose our old manufacturing industries go the way of Western agriculture: very few jobs and embarrassing output surpluses! Why not?

## An End to Batch Economies?

The economies of scale of the traditional 'factory system' were associated with standardization of the product; that is, they were economies of turning out identical items in large volume. Large batch size will become less important with computerization. The automobiles coming off a Japanese assembly line, for instance, are no longer identical. Computers keep track of the color and various options that are wanted for each car and do so at very low cost.

Consumers, therefore, should be able to look to a future where they will not need to compromise as much as hitherto with the manufacturer's conception of the 'median taste'. This, of course, will be a clear gain – although the biggest gain will go to those with snobbish or otherwise idiosyncratic tastes.

This particular development should not be misunderstood. That smaller batches will become economical does *not* mean that the economies of large scale are weakened. It means, rather, that the economies of assembly line production can be had even while turning out differentiated products. At present, what we see in Prato or Taipei – and perhaps also in Canoga Park, where I live – is that these new possibilities to produce small batches economically, using industrial rather than artisanal methods, are being exploited most vigorously by relatively small newcomers. In lines of business where assembly line economies remain important, however, the long-run effect may be that large producers will be able to invade the narrow 'ecological niches' where the absence of potential batch economies has previously protected the small ones.

Benetton is apparently an example of this. They color their garments after they are sewn up, thereby obtaining economies of scale in the production of uniformly white garments, and are able to provide diversity of colors in small batches without suffering the diseconomies of the usual specialty shop.

Another possible example is single family housing. It has long been true that the quality of prefabricated housing can be controlled much better in various dimensions than is generally possible when houses are built, and not just assembled, on site. In Sweden, prefab housing has had a fairly extensive market; in the US it has not – presumably because of more diversity of preferences in the American market. If it becomes feasible to produce the elements of fabricated houses without standardizing the final output – by having computers keeping track of how the plumbing is connected and what lengths of pipe this requires where – then small construction contractors may find themselves driven out of business by larger corporations.

The reduction in the diseconomies of small batch size that is a likely consequence of the revolution in information processing will not create a general tendency toward decentralization and smaller units. But there are a number of other new trends to consider and some of them may be more promising for small business.

## The All-purpose Robot?

Suppose that someone eventually develops an all-purpose machine, a robot that with the proper software and optional attachments can do 'anything' (that is, everything that any machine can do). Not a likely story, of course, but the unrealistic assumption allows us to discuss in general terms the consequences of capital that can be converted from one use to another (that is, capital that is 'redeployable', in the terminology of Klein and Leffler 1981).

Smith, Babbage, Marx and Mill thought the division of labor in pin-making was efficient because the workman tended to lose concentration and dexterity if required to switch tasks all the time. Now the computer, supposedly, does not lose its concentration, but robots apparently do lose their 'dexterity' if asked to switch a lot. A workman can go back and forth between using a drill and a screwdriver, let us say, with little loss of time. To use robots to best advantage, I gather, you should not ask them to do that. Some production-planning principles learned in the organization of human work may, therefore, gain rather than lose in relevance once applied to robots rather than humans. In particular, the precise sequencing of tasks becomes a more rigid requirement. (Suppose, for instance, that a piece of sheet metal has to be cut a certain shape, have a number of holes drilled, be heated and bent, and then be enamelled or otherwise surface treated. With robots, you want to make sure that all the holes are drilled at the same stage and not at two different stages; with human workers on the assembly line, it might not matter much.)

The term 'assembly line' should be understood here, not concretely, but as a figure of speech to remind us that production is an ordered sequence of tasks. Now, the theory of the 'old' manufacturing firm sketched previously argued in effect that we should find these task sequences to be *vertically integrated* whenever it would otherwise be the case that owners of embodied capital at one stage of the production chain could be 'held to ransom' by those at one or more other stages. The conditions that set up a possible 'hold-up' situation include: (a) a high degree of complementarity between capital inputs at various stages; (b) specialized inputs, such as 'dedicated' machines, that cannot be converted to other uses at low cost; (c) thin markets for the specialized capital, which makes it time consuming and otherwise costly to replace a particular piece of equipment or to find alternative employment for it.[7]

The all-purpose robot, we may suppose, would eliminate conditions (b) and (c). It could be reprogrammed and refitted for some alternative use at relatively low cost. And the market for all-purpose machines should be pretty thick – although, admittedly, there may be problems with 'all-purpose lemons'.

The consequences would be two-fold. First, the rationale for large, vertically integrated manufacturing firms is much weakened. Here, therefore, we find that tendency favoring small firms which we did not find in considering batch economies. Second, the all-purpose robot might well have a rental market. This kind of convertible capital might, therefore, favor the development of firms that are 'non-capitalistic' in the sense that they rent, rather than own, most of their non-human capital.

### Return of the Putting-out System?

The putting-out system never disappeared altogether, of course. The 'jobbers' have been ever-present in the garment districts of the world. But as a mode of organizing industry it declined relative to the factory system with the coming of the industrial revolution. The system did allow the organization of production along Smithian division of labor lines; its evolutionary disadvantages probably had most to do with the amount of capital tied up in inventories and in costs of keeping track of inventories, including the losses due to theft. If so, these are the types of costs that have been radically reduced by computerized inventory control and the like.

As just noted, malleable capital, in the guise of our hypothetical all-purpose robot, would reduce or eliminate the difficulties of linking various stages of production by contract rather than by overarching ownership. If a production process involves several firms, however, a coordinating agent will still often be required.

'Putting-out' in the literal sense refers to a coordinating agent who owns the raw material or intermediate product that his subcontractors work on. No doubt this arrangement will survive here and there in the world where significant differences in the cost of capital prevail between the jobber and his subcontractors. But, in general, we should not expect a return of the practice in this particular form. In an industrial organization context where, as we have just argued, the coordinating agent might well choose not to own the capital equipment, the reasons are also weak for him to own the goods in process.

Subcontracting of most or all stages of production by a centrally placed coordinating agent is likely, however, to become of increasing importance. The coordinating firm may even stay out of manufacturing more or less altogether while specializing in trading and in final goods marketing.

## DIVISION OF LABOR IN THE MACROECONOMY

Let us move the focus of discussion from the firm to the larger system. Picture a non-linear input–output system, representing a manufacturing sector where each firm produces under increasing returns to scale. Every firm, we will assume, also uses at least one intermediate product that represents a significant proportion of value added in the firm's output and that is, of course, also produced under increasing returns by some other firm or firms.

### New Sources of Comparative Advantage?

A subsystem of interrelated firms of this sort will show increasing returns. That means, as before, that part of the total income of the system is in the nature of a joint rent and that the distribution of that rent, also as before, poses a problem. In the hypothetical system where, by assumption, the 'hold-up' problem no longer is present, it should be possible to rely on contractual agreements, governed by competition, to provide a solution. But, in general, asset specificity will not be altogether eliminated, and the contracting difficulties and transactions costs might well be formidable.

In an interesting recent paper, Julia Bamford (1987) discusses the sociological aspects of the economic growth of 'Terza Italia'. Her paper yields, among other things, some interesting insights on this problem. Stable, relatively tightly knit communities are seen to have, in effect, a comparative advantage in stabilizing patterns of cooperation among numerous firms that together earn joint rents. Such communities can bring shared cultural values to bear on the contracting parties so as to narrow the range at least of bilateral monopoly indeterminacies. They can also keep track of an individual entrepreneur's reputation for fair bargaining and post-contractual performance. By contrast, highly mobile, 'melting-pot' societies would have a comparative disadvantage in this setting.

## Costs and Benefits of Integration

Finally, some questions to which there are no easy answers. What are the costs and benefits of 'belonging to' such a structure? What are the alternatives? How will the costs and benefits change as a consequence of the new technologies?

The benefit, of course, is that the average standard of living will be higher the more thoroughly integrated the local economy is in the worldwide division of labor. This, at least, is true in long-run equilibrium.[8] But getting to the long run can be fatal, we have been told, and there are indeed serious risks in committing oneself to such integration. The necessary political conditions for a very high degree of international division of labor might fail, and usher in international financial disorder or protectionism. In addition, the local economy becomes more dependent upon international business cycle conditions which cannot be controlled by national stabilization policies.

The problem is that productive structures such as the one sketched above are incapable of proportional reduction in activities. Although there are other, more widely held explanations for it, I believe this is illustrated by Okun's Law, that is, the rather robust empirical regularity that output varies with an amplitude roughly three times that of employment over the cycle.

For concreteness, think of a 'representative firm' that runs two parallel assembly lines, with some machines and their operatives serving both lines. In recession, the firm shuts down one line, but it cannot lay off half the work force. To cover the higher unit costs at the reduced output, the firm would require a higher relative price paid for its product. But its customer firms are in the same position. Consequently, everyone is making losses in the recession, and most cannot get out of making losses by further output reductions at the margin. Furthermore, the individual worker who has been laid off cannot induce the firm to start up the idle assembly line by lowering his real supply price, nor can the individual firm induce an expansion in the entire input–output structure by reducing the supply price of its output.

To the extent that final demands for the net outputs of such a system are foreign, national monetary policies can do little to stimulate a real recovery from recession. It will be easy enough to inflate, but difficult to bring about expansion of the input–output structure. As the division of labor becomes increasingly complex and spreads across space with less and less regard for national boundaries, failures to coordinate macroeconomic policies become more costly.

Recessions in systems of this kind are more difficult to deal with, therefore, than macromodels with the usual constant-returns production functions would suggest. Large movements in real exchange rates are similarly seen to cause serious problems for production systems of this kind. To shrink a system with built-in economies of scale that has been adapted to one vector of exchange rates in order to re-expand in a new direction can be a horribly difficult process, quite different from the smooth adjustment along the production possibilities frontier suggested by models that abstract from indivisibilities, non-convexities and complementarities in production.

Conventional economics is not done with the kind of production theory discussed in this essay. Past neglect of it means both that one's intuition is not trained to go very far with the analysis and that there is little formal theory to fall back on when one's intuition runs out. For very practical reasons – 1992! – we need more theoretical work in this area.

## NOTES

1. The general view of economic development taken here has its *locus classicus* in Allyn Young (1928). After long neglect Young's ideas have become the object of promising formal development in Romer (1986, 1987). The present article, however, attempts to avoid entanglement in old and thorny questions of where the lines between external and internal economies of scale are to be drawn.
2. Basil Yamey tells me that Eileen Power was so fond of using Bodo in her teaching that her London School of Economics colleagues claimed she was inculcating 'bodolatry' in the students.
3. Note that the three ideas mentioned all fit comfortably into constant returns models of production. They tend to miss, therefore, the increasing returns–division of labor theme of this article.
4. It is, however, international trade theorists in particular who have taken up the subject in recent years and made some progress with it. That international trade predominantly consists of cross-shipments of similar products between areas with similar factor endowments is the apparent motivating fact behind this effort. See the excellent survey by Helpman (1984) and the book by Helpman and Krugman (1985).
5. For the possibility – doubted or denied by generations of theorists – of combining increasing returns with perfect competition, see Chipman (1965, section 2.8, 1970), Helpman (1984) and Romer (1986, 1987).
6. In exceptional cases, competition from producers of close substitutes might make profits non-positive. But the jointness problem would, of course, remain.
7. Again, 'machine' is a figure of speech. The argument applies whenever there are costs to dissolving a particular organization of inputs and finding alternative employments for them.
8. There is a tradition of citing increasing returns as a reason for protectionism (the infant industry argument). The hunch underlying the opinions voiced above is that the loss from the general decrease in the division of labor occasioned by protectionism would more than offset the gain in the more or less 'infant' sector. But this is not a demonstrated conclusion. Helpman and Krugman (1985, p. 265) end their book with an assessment of the state of our knowledge on this issue: 'Our analysis ... suggests an overall presumption that trade remains beneficial in a world characterized by economies of scale and imperfect competition. Indeed, the presumption is for extra gains over and above the conventional gains from trade.'

PART IV

Problems of Socialist Transformation

# 15. Inflation and reform in the USSR*

The impressions of an economist visiting the Soviet Union today are dominated by two acute dangers: the danger of the reform movement coming to a standstill and the danger of inflation.

The current economic situation is not one where it is possible to remain for any appreciable length of time. The command economy system has been undermined. The minimal institutional requirements for a private sector market economy have not been met. The state has yet to create for itself the public finance system of the mixed economy. It is, of course, possible *not to act* in the present situation, but it is not possible to sustain it. The current economy is in several respects an unworkable system and a stalemate in economic policy will, by default, make it increasingly so.

If this is a bad place to stand still, should one move back or go ahead? Western observers take it for granted that moving back is not an option. But in the Soviet Union it is not only conservatives, anxious to repair the military–industrial complex, who are talking retreat. There are also those who, professing a desire for market reform, think that the only cautious and responsible strategy at this point is to 'take one step back' with the intention of then going 'two steps forward'. The supply of food and other basic consumer goods has to be made to recover, they argue, before one can proceed with market reforms.

*Réculer pour mieux sauter?* A foreign visitor is hardly in a position to pronounce on the chances that 'discipline' can be restored in the command economy without also returning to other aspects of the Stalinist system that glasnost and perestroika have left behind. What is obvious, however, is that retreat now will undermine public confidence in the very possibility of reform, just as the continuation of the current situation is undermining the faith of many ordinary people in the desirability of moving toward a market economy. They do not much like what they see – shops with empty shelves, farmers who do not harvest for lack of goods to buy, miners on strike for lack of affordable food, and black market dealers making tons of rubles the easy way – and they tend to associate it all with the new economic policy of moving toward a market economy.

In fact, of course, all these phenomena are the result of not permitting market mechanisms to work. Prices must be allowed to respond to supply and demand if markets are to regulate economic activities. But they are not allowed to move and so the market mechanisms do not function. Prices fixed at a level below the free market level will keep the shelves empty indefinitely. And it is the discrepancies between controlled prices and market prices that create the black market profits. In an operating market economy, competition eliminates the easy profits of black markets. The black marketeers that so preoccupy Soviet thinking are the product, not of free markets, but of government-imposed price controls. Price and wage controls are maintained for the purpose of *suppressing inflation.* The failure to contain inflationary pressures and the decision, instead, to keep the lid on legal prices have put a stop to the creation of a private sector.

So inflation is the key to the major policy dilemmas at present. Economists and policy-makers in the USSR express great alarm over the danger of inflation, yet they underestimate it. The error is rife in Soviet circles of focusing on the measured rate of inflation rather than on the underlying determinants of inflation. The official price index has only the most tenuous links to economic realities. This is most obvious in so far as it includes the legal prices of goods that are simply unavailable at those prices. But, even apart from this point, it is a serious mistake to think that a slowdown in the rise of controlled prices is a policy success and an acceleration necessarily a failure. If policy-making were to be guided by such feedback, it would end up out of touch with realities.

Soviet economists express alarm that the inflation rate this year might be 'in double digits'. But the inflation rate that people should think about is not that at which the controlled prices rise, but the rate at which prices would rise if they were liberalized and hence were market-determined. Policy should focus, therefore, on the *determinants* of inflation, not on the measured inflation. The main determinant of inflation in the Soviet Union today is simply the combined government sector deficit which, in the absence of a market for Soviet public debt, has to be monetized. The figures for this deficit are unreliable – no two Soviet economists will give you the same number – but few dispute that it is running at a rate at least equal to 10–12 per cent of annual GNP. A deficit of that magnitude, we know from experience in other countries, will generate an inflation, not in double digits per year, but in *double digits per month*!

The market economy cannot function under suppressed inflation. Nor can it function well under open inflation. And an open inflation on the order, say, of 30 per cent per month is a tremendous disorganizing force that will destroy the financial structures that a private enterprise economy requires in order to function efficiently and in order to mobilize the capital for growth. The USSR has yet to develop these financial institutions. It cannot hope to create them under the kind of inflationary conditions that have destroyed them elsewhere in the world.

The government has concluded that to liberalize prices and let inflation rip is out of the question. It is realized that the current deficit is highly inflationary and, more terrifying yet, that the so-called 'monetary overhang' might trigger immediate price rises of such magnitude as to send the economy into a hyperinflationary spiral that could be nearly impossible to bring under control later. Recent policy, therefore, has sought on the one hand to reduce the monetary overhang by measures that, it was hoped, would succeed in expropriating the profits of black market operators and, on the other hand, to suppress price rises as far as possible but to allow the controlled prices to be adjusted from time to time when the inflationary pressures become impossible to contain.

There is no hope in such a policy. It does not try to cope with the causes of inflation but only to delay its consequences. Although the controlled prices are revised upward periodically, they remain far below the time path that market prices would follow if they were freed. Unless the underlying inflationary pressures are dealt with, such fitful price adjustments will *never* catch up with the level of free market prices that the monetary situation would dictate. The use of the market mechanism to call forth supplies will then be postponed indefinitely. The very fact that the consumer price increases that will take effect in early April were announced many weeks in advance proves how far out of touch with market determinants current prices were. To announce 'we will not raise prices now, but we are going to do so in a few weeks' is an elementary mistake that would normally cause chaos in markets anywhere in the world. That the Soviet authorities can do so without 'life' teaching them never to do so again shows how fantastically large excess demands in these markets already are.

What kind of policy ought then to be pursued in this situation? The basic strategy should be to *bring the free market price level down* to the general neighbourhood of the current price level, to get the *determinants of inflation under control*, and to *liberalize prices* – in order then to start on the tasks of *privatization*.

The first step in this strategy requires dealing with the so-called 'monetary overhang'. The second requires the elimination of the current Union budget deficit. The first task is far easier than the second, but it would be a serious mistake to do the easy one and not undertake the difficult one.

*The budget deficit problem is far more important than the monetary overhang.* It is important to understand why this is so. In a system of free prices, the fundamental determinant of the price level is the money supply, but the determinant of inflation is the rate at which the money supply is growing. In an economy lacking a well-developed financial market in which the government can borrow, the government budget deficit determines the rate at which money is being created. Reducing the size of the money supply at a particular point in time may provide a *pause* in the inflation, but, if the deficit is not cured, the money supply will soon grow back to its former size and then grow beyond that. At best, all that has then been achieved is that inflation has been postponed a bit. At worst, this kind of policy can produce a sharp contraction of activity without significant anti-inflationary impact. The experience of Brazil in 1990 is an example.

By the monetary overhang, one means the difference between the money stock actually in existence and the money stock that would just suffice to transact the nation's business at the present, controlled prices. Since the latter is a hypothetical magnitude, the monetary overhang is not easily measured. Past data give little guidance in trying to estimate a money demand function for the Soviet Union. So the size of the overhang is to some extent a matter of guesswork. It may amount to 50 per cent of the present money supply. In any case, an overestimate is safer than an underestimate, since the policies designed to eliminate the overhang are easily relaxed, but cannot be costlessly tightened, in a second round.

The objective of eliminating the overhang should be to make possible the liberalization of all consumer goods prices without causing a large immediate rise in the consumer price level. It can be done in the following manner.

1.  *Forced conversion of large bank deposits.* Bank deposits above certain values (to be determined) are converted into *privatization bonds*. These bonds should be of fairly long maturity, perhaps 10 years, but carry an interest rate somewhat higher than that currently paid on bank deposits. Privatization bonds can be used in payment for state assets being privatized and will be accepted at face value for that purpose. Owners will have the alternative of holding the bonds to maturity or of selling them to other parties for cash at whatever price the market provides.

2.  *Currency reform.* All old ruble notes are to be withdrawn from circulation and no longer be legal tender beyond some specified date. Individuals can exchange a certain amount (to be determined) of old notes for the same amount in newly issued notes. It is much to be preferred that there be no further attempt to expropriate money balances from private parties in connection with this currency conversion. People should be allowed, therefore, to exchange any amount of currency exceeding that which can be converted into new money for privatization bonds, and to do so with no questions asked.

It is important to note that dealing with the overhang in this manner will *not be worth doing unless the Union budget deficit is also corrected.* If the deficit cannot be tackled now, these currency reform measures should be postponed until it can be done.

The most common error in attempts to stabilize is to design a program with no tolerance for miscalculation or unanticipated disturbance. An unanticipated rise in consumer prices will force the government to compensate low and fixed-income groups; this would put a just-balanced budget back into deficit, renew the printing of money, and thus start a fresh inflationary spiral. Ideally, therefore, one should – if at all possible – *aim for a slight budget surplus* so as to provide a margin of error.

Whether the Union government will be able to master the deficit is now in doubt. The purely economic and technical difficulties would be formidable, even were there no challenges to the central government's authority.

Cutting subsidies while raising taxes is not a program designed to court popularity. The suggestion that the deficit must be brought under control meets with immediate warnings in Soviet circles: eliminating subsidies will cause the productive sector to collapse and raising taxes would cause most of the household sector to fall below the poverty level. Yet, look behind the 'veil of money' for a moment: it cannot be true that *all* of the productive activities in an economy are unprofitable; nor can it be true that total income is insufficient to buy the national product. At the bottom of the fiscal problem, therefore, lies a structural one, that is, one of relative prices and income shares. And such a problem is not to be solved, or in any degree ameliorated, by printing more rubles.

One of the legacies of socialist planning is its almost completely arbitrary system of prices. When some industries are taxed in order to subsidize others, we cannot conclude that the former should be allowed to expand and the others made to contract, for the profits of the first category and the losses of the second are calculated at prices that provide little in the way of reliable guidance to the allocation of resources. That planning on the basis of too low (or even a zero) rate of interest causes much waste of capital has been pointed out innumerable times. But wages that are too low is an equally pervasive problem.

Labor is not paid the value of its product under socialism. Instead, most of it enters into the command economy to be physically allocated to various uses; some of it is eventually returned to labor in the form of goods and services (health care, education, housing) provided by the government more or less 'for free'.

Labor is paid its product under (competitive) capitalism – and then much of it is taxed away. Some of the things that the worker received free of charge under socialism, the capitalist worker pays for with his taxes; others he pays for privately out of a larger after-tax income.

In moving from a command economy toward a market economy, the public sector has to change from commanding the uses of physical products to the taxing and spending of money. This will require, among many other

things, a *substantial rise in the level of real pre-tax personal income* throughout the economy. It is now far too low. Fear of wage-push inflation makes the
government keep a lid on wages – and then refrain from raising income taxes
because wages are so low. If the government were to double all wages (and
pensions) paid by the state and then tax half of them away, neither the
finances of the citizens nor those of the state would improve *at first*. But it
would make the public finances look a good deal more like those of a market
economy with a sizeable public sector and it would make state enterprises
calculate with a higher, and more realistic, cost of labor. This would make
profits and losses better indicators of what activities should be expanded and
which curtailed. *Over time*, moreover, any transfer of productive activities
and labor from the public to the private sector would improve the fiscal
position of the state.

This suggests the general direction in which the finances of the public
sector should be moving. But there is also the matter of the relationships
between the different levels of government.

On this political front, the threat of mounting inflation should be to the
advantage of President Gorbachev in dealing with the republics – or, rather, it
is to his advantage to the extent that the main actors understand the economics of the situation (and they might not). Unless the common currency for the
Union is to be abandoned, it will not be in the interest of the constituent
republics *as a group* to deny the Union the revenues necessary for defense
and other Union functions. Individually, the republics will be tempted to do
their utmost to keep all revenues raised on their territories, but such free-
riding would force the Union to rely on inflationary financing. And inflation,
whether open or suppressed, will thwart all ambitions for economic development in the republics.

Perhaps the new policies announced in the first week of April will be found
effectively to address some of the problems outlined above. It remains to be
seen whether a Union–Republics treaty will be reached that makes non-
inflationary policies by the central government feasible.

# NOTE

* Written in March 1991.

# 16. Problems of socialist transformation: Kazakhstan 1991*

The undoing of a totalitarian state does not make a functioning democracy. The undoing of central planning does not make a working market system. Simple truths sometimes make bitter lessons. After the initial euphoria over the undoing of the communist regimes, these lessons have by now sunk in.

The literature on the problems of the socialist transformation is already large and it is growing faster than a reader's eye can follow. Case studies may be more useful than further disquisitions on general principles at this point. The actual reform work has to be carried out under political conditions that vary widely between the various countries and that in almost all instances have been changing very rapidly. In this paper, I will discuss recent reform efforts in the Kazakh Republic and try to put them in their political context. The reader should be warned that Soviet studies has never been my field and that, even though I spent much time on some of the economic reform problems of Kazakhstan last year, I spent only a few weeks in the country and do not, by any means, consider myself an expert. Much of what follows is personal impressions and opinions based on fragmentary and not always reliable information.

## ECONOMIC GEOGRAPHY AND DEMOGRAPHY

Kazakhstan stretches some 1,800 miles from the Caspian Sea to the Chinese border. It is more than four times the size of France and six times the size of California. Yet, while the republic is rich in mineral resources, including oil, most of this vast area is poor steppe lands and the total population is only about 17 million.

There are as many ethnic Russians as Kazakhs in the republic, about 7 million of each. The remaining 3 million are composed of many ethnic groups, with Volga Germans and Koreans the most numerous. The Germans and the Koreans are in Kazakhstan as a result of two of Stalin's pre-World War II mass deportations.

Such simple facts of geography and demography do much to dictate the policies of the present government. Kazakhstan's main trade routes to the rest of the world will go north and west, to and through Russia. Long-term economic interests will tie it to a greater Russian trade area. Ethnic tensions are not severe at present, but if the Kazakhs, who are politically in control, were either to overdo their emerging nationalism or to orient themselves altogether toward the Muslim-dominated Central Asian neighbours, a Russian separatist movement would surely result that could split the republic.

## PRESIDENT NAZARBAEV

So far, the policies of the government have very largely meant the policies of President Nazarbaev. For the last two years or more, Nursultan Nazarbaev has played a role in the politics of the Soviet Union and now the Community of Independent States (CIS) politics out of all proportion to the importance of his republic in the scheme of things. In late 1990 and through 1991, he managed far better than either Gorbachev or Yeltsin to project himself as standing both for political stability and for economic reform. Gorbachev sought above all to ensure constitutional continuity and political stability. For years, he maneuvered with great skill to prevent the political center from melting away toward the extremes. But his successive maneuvers to keep the support, now of the moderate conservatives, now of the moderate liberals, set an unsteady, zig-zag course in economic matters that in the end led nowhere. Yeltsin, on the other hand, was impatient for economic reforms to move forward and had come to care little, if at all, for political continuity. Large segments both of the party and the public were fed up with the one and afraid of the other. The Kazakh President gained popularity and influence, also in Russia, as a consequence.

During this period, Nazarbaev devoted all his political skills and much of his time and energy to achieving a Union Treaty. His main objective was for Kazakhstan to escape the stifling economic control of the Moscow ministries and, above all, to gain ownership of its own natural resources. The Gosplan-imposed terms of trade, whereby Kazakhstan exported raw materials at prices far below world market prices and had to import consumer goods at Russian retail prices, had short-changed the republic for decades in the President's view. His campaign to extricate the republic from this situation began with a series of bilateral agreements with other republics, notably Yeltsin's Russia, the Ukraine and Kazakhstan's four Central Asian neighbours. These agreements were to be a prelude to a Union Treaty. They were directed against the center and at this stage therefore against Gorbachev. Nazarbaev at one point went so far as to suggest that a treaty might be reached among the republics that could exclude the central government.

The objective, however, was for Kazakhstan to gain a measure of control over its own economic fate, not to dissolve the USSR. From the perspective of Alma-Ata, whether the distant Baltic republics or Moldavia were to secede or not was hardly worth bothering about. But it was not in Kazakhstan's interest to have the core republics break apart. When, after the August 1991 coup, Nazarbaev continued to strive for his 9 + 1 Union concept, this distanced him from Yeltsin and Kravchuk. Having conceived this policy in opposition to Gorbachev, he ended up Gorbachev's last ally of significance. When Russia, Bielorus and the Ukraine met in Minsk to torpedo the Union and form the improvised Commonwealth, Nazarbaev was left out. But his hand had been forced and he had no alternative but to join the CIS.

## ECONOMIC REFORM

Back in mid-1990, it appeared that Gorbachev, after five years of irresolute economic policies, was finally going to back genuine market reform. Shatalin's protegé, Grigor Yavlinsky, who became the main architect of the '500-day Plan', spent half of his time in Gorbachev's Kremlin and half in Yeltsin's White House and expected the joint support of them both. But at the crucial juncture, Gorbachev again compromised with the conservatives, withdrew his support from the Shatalin plan, and backed the alternative proposed by his Prime Minister, Ryskov. Ryskov's plan was itself a non-starter. Aganbegyan was called in to craft yet another compromise, more palatable to reformers, but to little avail. By year's end, it was obvious that the stalemate in Moscow on the economic front would not soon be resolved.

President Nazarbaev had a keen sense of the dangers of marking time in a situation where the command economy no longer worked and a market economy did not yet work. Following the defeat of the Shatalin plan, he decided that Kazakhstan would have to move ahead on its own. It should be made clear that his goal is not a socioeconomic system on a West European or North American pattern. Nazarbaev is not looking West for his models, but to the East, to South Korea, Taiwan and Singapore, that is to countries that have combined fairly autocratic regimes with rapid economic growth.

In January 1991, he created a new High Economic Council consisting of top-level representatives from various sectors of the economy and also an Economic Expert Committee with himself as chairman and with two vice-chairmen: Dauton Sembayev, subsequently Vice-Premier for Economic Affairs, and Chan Young Bang, a Korean-American economist, who had already been an informal advisor to the President for some time. I became a member of this committee and so, for a time, did Yavlinsky.

The Economic Expert Committee of the President (informally often referred to as the Economic Reform Committee) was an ad hoc creation. It fitted nowhere in the organization chart of either government or Party. Initially, this seemed to be an advantage. The President used the committee to make the coming of reform seem credible both to the citizenry and to foreign media and diplomats, leaving the impression that the committee's proposals were very likely to become policy. The various staged appearances of the committee or its members attracted a great deal of attention, therefore, particularly from the government and Party bureaucracies. But this was not a sustainable situation. The committee did not sort under the Prime Minister, and when it started to produce proposals 'out of the blue', the Council of Ministers and the higher-level bureaucracy (still red at that time) must, I imagine, have found it a loose cannon on the deck. Apart from the President's personal backing, it had no legitimacy whatsoever. As, toward mid-year, Nazarbaev's energies became increasingly absorbed by the power politics of the disintegrating Union, he had correspondingly less time to push the implementation of reforms. By late Fall, the government 'couldn't find' the hard currency for the committee's travel expenses. By year's end, although not officially abolished, it had for all practical purposes ceased working. The structural problem was regularized by moving Mr Sembayev into the cabinet with the rank of Vice-Premier.[1]

## FEBRUARY 1991

I first visited Kazakhstan in February. The main question put to the Committee at that time was straightforward: 'What in the way of economic reform could be undertaken in Kazakhstan as long as there was stalemate in Moscow?' A great many desirable things were indeed not possible at that time (without a break with the Union). The main reasons were two: (a) the strong inflationary pressures, and (b) the uncertainties surrounding the rights of the republics to control the economic resources on their territories.

### Inflation Issues

At this time, the republics were of course in no position to have macroeconomic policies of their own. The high and mounting inflationary pressures created a number of problems that the Kazakh government could do nothing about. But they also posed policy issues, such as what stand to take on revenue-sharing with the Union.

The Union government was still suppressing inflation by means of comprehensive price controls and did not dare to lift them in the face of the monetary overhang. With price mechanisms thus disabled, not only was the scope for market reforms limited, but it was even difficult to design small-scale measures that had some promise of demonstrating to the public the advantages of market-regulated resource allocation. The suppression of inflation produced thriving black markets and almost universally 'empty shelves' in the legal retail sector. Normally, retailing would be the most natural place to begin privatization.

The growth of black markets was of course the result of six years of dithering and inaction over market reform. They nonetheless became a threat to the legitimacy of market reform. At the inconsistent planned prices, huge profits could be made with the greatest of ease by those able to command supplies. Organized 'mafias', using strong-arm tactics, were increasingly controlling the black markets, and the consumption of their members was blatantly conspicuous whereas the bosses of the communist era had done theirs in the discreet isolation of guarded government compounds. Many Soviet citizens took these black market phenomena as a foretaste of what a system of free markets would be like: capitalism pretty much as portrayed by 70 years of traditional communist propaganda! It is an open question whether market reform would really be backed by a democratic majority today.

The dangers of inflation were little understood in the Soviet Union. In part, policy-makers and their economists simply underestimated the inflationary pressures being created (and also overestimated the chances of keeping them contained by traditional methods of suppression). It was a commonly expressed apprehension at the beginning of the year that inflation might be in the double digits, and perhaps over 20 per cent, for the year. But the deficit of the central government was running at a rate that made *double digits per month* the more realistic fear.

Very few people in the entire USSR had any idea of what a double-digit monthly inflation would entail either for the (hopefully) emerging private sector or for the government itself. Experience elsewhere has shown that such high inflations tend to eliminate the contract forms and destroy the intertemporal markets that the Soviets were hoping soon to establish. Even with decades of experience in coping with inflations, Latin American populations have not been able to 'neutralize' the disorganizing forces of high inflations. The Soviet citizenry had had no such experience.

The government in a market economy appropriates resources by *paying* for them, preferably out of tax proceeds. This is a simple point, but not on that account an intuitive idea to officials whose whole careers have been in the command economy. Consequently, they did not (and do not) really understand how very powerless the government will be, once its ability to 'command' is gone, if it renders money worthless through hyperinflation. To avoid hyperinflation, however, the republics would have had to share sufficient revenues with the central government to enable it to finance remaining Union functions. A stable and enforceable agreement to do so would have been difficult to reach under the best of circumstances. In this instance, as became evident later in the year, Yeltsin's Russia and Kravchuk's Ukraine in particular were bent on starving Gorbachev's Union of taxes – even at the cost of hyperinflation.[2]

## Who Owned the Command Economy?

About three-fourths of the economy of Kazakhstan had been controlled by the central planning apparatus in Moscow. Yet Soviet law did not make clear whether the central government or the government of the Kazakh Republic 'owned' the natural resources and industrial capital stock located in Kazakhstan, and there appeared to be almost complete uncertainty concerning which property rights would be accorded the republics and which retained by the Union. It was the main objective of Nazarbaev's Union Treaty policy to achieve a settlement of these issues. But, in the meantime, it was for the most part not yet possible to move toward privatization of the manufacturing and extractive industries. It was not within the power of the Kazakh Republic to create secure private property rights to the *kombinate* that are the industrial legacy of 70 years of central planning.

## Privatization Proposals

President Nazarbaev wanted a significant move toward privatization that would signal the intention of the Kazakh SSR to move decisively on market reform. The main proposal of the committee became to *privatize housing* throughout the republic. Under the conditions of the moment, this was the biggest chunk of wealth that could be moved from the state into private hands. We also saw it as a big step toward improved labor mobility and, to the extent that it would ease the state out of subsidizing housing, as a small step toward budget balance. As the proposal was worked out, it came to involve also the introduction of *mortgages*, and various measures designed to make it possible for private firms to operate in *residential construction*. Other proposals concerned limited privatization of retail and service establishments and doubling the size of private plots in agriculture.

## Criteria for the Distribution of State Property

Kazakhstan was pretty close to the communist ideal of the state owning everything and the people nothing. Privatization by sale, therefore, was basically out of the question. Auctions, stock markets or mutual funds managed by European investment bankers are not likely to come to Central Asia very soon. Clearly, state property had to be distributed directly, and the problem was finding a practical means of doing so that would be accepted as legitimate and fair by a substantial majority of the population.

Dr Bang had already been arguing for privatization by *vouchers* before the Committee was formed.[3] We sought to provide a suitable ideological basis for the voucher scheme by pointing out that 'under socialism, the worker is not paid his product' (sic!) but that the state takes a substantial portion of it as a tax in kind. The means of production in the possession of the state have been accumulated from past taxes of this sort. If they were now to be privatized, therefore, the distribution should bear some relation to the efforts that present citizens have expended in the past to achieve this accumulation of capital. The size of individual vouchers, it was proposed, should be based on two factors: (a) age or number of years in the labor force, and (b) average salary over a number of past years. The weights were of course left for the relevant political bodies to determine.

## Privatization of Housing

In the case of housing, we recommended a variant of the voucher scheme *based solely on age*. In brief outline, the following was proposed:

1.  *All* residential housing presently belonging to the state, with the exception of state residences for officials, were to be transferred to current residents. The terms of this transfer would, however, vary with the age of the head of household.
2.  Heads of household above a certain age, to include in particular all persons already on pensions, were to receive full title to the apartment or house without payment being required or financial obligation incurred.[4] Full title was to entail the right to bequeath the apartment to heirs or to sell it for whatever price the free market might pay.
3.  Younger residents with fewer years in the labor force would have to assume a financial obligation in the form of a mortgage in exchange for the property right. The size of the mortgage as a proportion of the property's value should decline with the age of the prospective owner. Thus the equity share of the citizen would increase with age, becoming 100 per cent at or near retirement age.
4.  Ownership of houses or apartments should be encumbered by property taxes payable to the municipality. These should be set at a level sufficient to maintain streets, waterlines and sewers provided (where provided) by the municipality. In addition, apartment owners would have to contribute to their respective apartment house cooperatives for the maintenance and repair of collective facilities.

Both the state and the public in Kazakhstan face what theorists are pleased to call 'imperfect capital markets'. It was the Committee's intention not only to transfer a large block of wealth into private hands, but at the same time to improve (however marginally) the budget position of the republic, by letting maintenance expenses fall on private owners and by levying a modest amount of property taxes. Rents were, however, often set at such a low level as not to cover minimal maintenance. The staff of the High Economic Council feared, therefore, that housing privatization might be unpopular with many people. In the early stage, it was made voluntary, which became one of the factors slowing the process down.[5]

## Introduction of Mortgage Financing

The Committee wanted the government of the republic to get out of subsidizing housing. Newly constructed housing, therefore, would have to be sold at prices covering the cost of construction. Few people, other than black market dealers, would be able to pay cash for housing. Thus the State Savings Bank should get into the entirely novel business of providing mortgages for buyers of new residential housing.

To create and put into operation this system of housing financing would be a start on a more modern financial sector. It would give bank officers experience in appraisals of real estate and in evaluating loan applications. The banks would have to create computerized systems of accounting, bill collecting and so on. With perhaps a few exceptions, banking officials in Alma Ata had practically no experience with any other banking function than the transmittal of money to and from Moscow. In this sector, as in most, there was much talk of needed training programs.[6] Such programs certainly were needed, but some of us came to regard the demand for training as a tactic for postponing change of any kind. The mortgages created as a result of the distribution of apartments and houses to not yet retired citizens would add large sums of assets to the state banking system. The learning-by-doing that this would force on the banks would, we hoped, accomplish much of the required training of the personnel of the new financial system.

Two sets of problems were foreseen to complicate the modernization of the financial sector.

1.  The inflation then underway – and, more particularly, the much higher inflation that was waiting to happen – was bound to reduce the real value of simple ruble-denominated mortgages quite rapidly. More of the housing stock would end up being simply given away than the privatization plan intended.

    Since Kazakhstan could do nothing about the inflation rate, these mortgages ought to be indexed. For obvious reasons, we proposed indexing to the taxable money income of the individual household, rather than to the consumer price index.

2. Many families lacked sufficient money income to be able to shoulder the payments on a substantial mortgage. To the extent that Kazakhstan might succeed in creating a large private sector, however, wage and salary incomes would rise so that the ability to service debt would rise in the future. This problem could be dealt with by initially setting mortgage payments quite low and letting them rise more than in proportion to the real income of the household until a reasonable rate of interest and amortization was reached.

At this time, I do not have any information on how these problems were eventually handled.

## Residential Construction

There had been previous episodes of liberalizing private construction. But these had been rescinded as soon as it became clear (a) that private builders made money, and (b) that in one way or another they succeeded in siphoning off building supplies from the state sector. The Committee wanted to open up this sector to private activity, not only because this would 'fit' with the privatization of housing, but also because this was one sector where it should be possible to see a substantial expansion of employment even as employment in a number of other sectors inevitably started to decline.

The proposals made here are not of much general interest except for one point: economists usually preach reliance on the division of labor and are not used to finding themselves recommending self-sufficiency. But in the economy that Gosplan has bequeathed to the people, it is likely that all faucets come from Novosibirsk, say, and all electrical wall outlets from Odessa – and that each is controlled by some horrendous ministry in Moscow. In that setting, local diversification and smaller production units have much to recommend them.

## Agriculture

The Committee did not have an agricultural economist. But we were well aware that a good many ambitious land reforms in various parts of the world have been fiascos. A good many people were calling for the breaking up of collective farms in Eastern Europe and the USSR. The incentive structure of family farms, the high productivity of private plots in Russia and the success of Chinese agricultural reforms were constantly cited as conclusive arguments or evidence for dismantling Soviet *kolchozes*.

But these commonplace observations do not give much guidance in practice. The new Chinese 'private' farms require neither tractors nor other purchased inputs for their economical operation. It is not obvious, therefore, what lessons they provide for the reform of agriculture in the former Soviet Union. In much of Kazakhstan, economies of scale may preclude family farms. Historically, the steppe had supported not family farms but nomadic herders. The comparative advantage of most of Kazakhstan in agriculture should lie in large-scale sheep and cattle (and perhaps camel!) ranches.[7] Admittedly, today's large Kazakh *kolchozes* are not grazing large herds over extensive areas. Instead, they have pursued an ideal of 'industrialized' production, whereby the feed is trucked in to animals crowded into feedlots. With this pattern of production, the argument for maintaining large units (in terms of acreage) is not strong, but it is probably the wrong technology for Kazakhstan.[8] The present *kolchozes* are also horrendously overmanned by Western standards, but that is true of the republic's industries as well, and it is in any case not obvious that parceling out the land to all those now living on it is the proper solution.

In sum, we were (as you can see) too ignorant in this field to make sweeping recommendations. Just as well, as we quickly learned, because one recommendation was made. Already in early 1991, concern was widespread over the provisioning of the cities next winter. With that concern in mind, we recommended quite simply that the size of private plots on the *kolchozes* should be doubled. (The private plots are a vanishingly small proportion of the land.) This recommendation, I learned later, was simply 'politically impossible'. This little incident was a lesson in the political realities of Kazakhstan to which I will return below.

## JUNE–JULY 1991

By mid-June, there were some reasons for optimism. A very comprehensive 'Privatization and Destatization Bill' had just been enacted. The morale of the High Economic Council staff was very high at this time. They had done an enormous amount of work in a short span of time inventorying the housing stock and implementing the voucher system.[9] The privatization of housing was to begin in mid-September. In addition, some privatization of retail establishments and small and medium-size manufacturing plants through employee buy-outs was beginning.

The political assumptions for the reform work had changed a great deal since February. The main question put to the Committee now was how to proceed with the privatization of the big manufacturing enterprises. Their legal status was still not clear but it was assumed that a Union Treaty would be achieved and that it would put most of the manufacturing and extractive industries under the control of the republic. Moscow had previously insisted on Union control of transportation and energy, but at this time the Union Oil Ministry withdrew from the Tenghiz field negotiations, leaving Kazakhstan to deal with Chevron on its own.

## LARGE MANUFACTURING ENTERPRISES

On this issue, there was not a consensus within the Committee. What follows should be understood, therefore, as giving my own position.[10]

### Obstacles to Immediate Privatization

The manufacturing sector built up under central planning relied to a dysfunctional extent on very large plants. Individually, these plants tend to be technologically inflexible and so is the entire system consisting of such plants. The 'gigantomania' of the planners has left a very vulnerable legacy: many large plants depend on a single or at least dominant supplier for raw materials or intermediate goods and, similarly, have one dominant customer. If one of these gigantic plants ceases operations, others are left without customers or without supplies. Failure in one part of the system, therefore, can cascade through a large part of it.

Failures in this system constitute the most intractable part of the current crisis in the Soviet economy, and the aspect of it, moreover, that is not at all amenable to macroeconomic stabilization measures of the type traditional in capitalist systems. The collapse of trade with the former 'satellite' (CMEA) had already shown how vulnerable the system was. During 1991, the Soviet economy became increasingly susceptible to such failures caused by the new tensions among the republics; cessation of deliveries from one republic would interrupt production in others.[11] These problems were already multiplying half a year before the break-up of the USSR and the creation of CIS.

In this sector, privatization and economic reform in the East European countries were not going well. The East European countries have advantages that Kazakhstan lacks: proximity to alternative markets for both inputs and outputs, and somewhat better access (so far) to foreign capital and foreign technical expertise. The cascading collapse of the East German manufacturing sector, considered by many to have been the technologically most advanced among the command economies, was particularly alarming. Kazakhstan had no West Kazakh big brother. Privatization was proving not to be an easy panacea. It is not only state ownership that ails the command economies, but also the way in which their manufacturing sectors have been built up.

The centrally planned manufacturing sector may be likened to the assembly lines of a single plant.[12] For a single line, we have the following propositions.

1.  If any one work station breaks down or fails to receive necessary intermediate inputs, the whole assembly line comes to a halt – output becomes zero. This is the extreme case of the vulnerability discussed above.
2.  The assembly line is the simplest example of *vertically integrated production*. The work stations on an assembly line cannot be made into individual firms, each one selling its output to the next, because no determinate set of equilibrium prices can be found for such a chain of bilateral monopolies.
3.  The physical assets that together make up the assembly line have little market value separately. The *liquidation value* of the machinery is only some small fraction of the value of the going concern. The whole is worth more than the sum of the parts.

Obviously, the analogy is hard-drawn, and the applicability of the propositions derived from it is easily exaggerated. Nevertheless, the inherited manufacturing structure could hardly be more vulnerable to supply interruptions if it had been designed by the US Strategic Bomber Command in the worst days of the Cold War. Privatizing the large Soviet manufacturing plants would in many cases surely have the same consequences as would the breaking up of a vertically integrated multi-plant conglomerate. In many instances, bilateral monopoly situations would be created with two firms facing each other, one without alternative suppliers for one of its inputs, the other without alternative customers for most of its output. In some of these cases, moreover, the bargaining situation is inflamed from the start when the relationship between the two plants spans the boundary between two republics, one of which (and sometimes both of which!) feels historically exploited by the other.

My own conclusions from the above were as follows.

1.  The so-called *valuation problem* is not just due to having operated at arbitrary plan prices in the past. Simply deregulating prices will not reveal the 'true' value of plants that are elements in a vertically integrated production chain.
2.  For plants of this description, net current revenues (or losses, mostly) will *not* provide a reliable indicator of their social value, even if all prices have been liberalized. Note, in particular, that forcing such a plant into bankruptcy may, by the 'cascading effects', cause social losses that vastly exceed the losses recorded at the plant.

3.  If the plants in a vertically integrated chain were to be privatized individually, the productive assets may fetch no more than *liquidation sale values*.

## Large Manufacturing Enterprises: Approach to Market Reform

It is true enough that the arbitrary price systems of centrally planned economies do not give us much of a clue to what enterprises are socially efficient or inefficient. The already conventional wisdom on this subject is that rationalization of these economies can only be achieved by (a) privatizing all enterprises, and (b) letting the market weed out the inefficient ones through bankruptcy. And it is also conventional wisdom that it is best to get this all over with quickly – the quicker the better – so that the emerging market economy can take off from as clean a slate as possible.

The points made above are meant to throw doubt on this conventional wisdom. They do not mean, however, that one should be satisfied to make permanent either the inherited manufacturing structure or the state ownership of the manufacturing sector. They must not become the excuse to keep truly inefficient plants in operation indefinitely with the help of state subsidies that drain the budget of the republic. They do mean that one should look for more gradual, less destructive strategies to accomplish the transition to a market economy – but not so gradual as to postpone the transition indefinitely. In my opinion, the immediate steps to be taken were the following.

1.  To convert all large enterprises to corporations partially owned by their employees but with the state retaining a large majority interest. The state should exercise control through boards with the power to hire and fire management, and composed of representatives of the State Committee on Management of State Property and of the State Banks. The objective of control should be the enforcement of 'hard' budget constraints on these enterprises. Legislation changing the conditions under which workers could be laid off or fired was also needed if overmanning was not to become a permanent condition. This in turn required some overhaul of social legislation dealing with unemployment.
2.  To pursue a consistent policy of reducing the vulnerability of the inherited manufacturing structure to supply disruptions. A number of concrete measures could easily be taken, such as having the big metal working *kombinate* spin off their machine and repair shops and allow these to diversify. The objective of this should, of course, not be self-sufficiency but a degree of diversification normal to an economy of Kazakhstan's size.

# AFTER AUGUST

The August coup and the process of political disintegration that followed became a considerable set-back to the reform process. Nonetheless, in September, President Nazarbaev signed the High Economic Council's three-stage plan and timetable for privatization. It envisaged the privatization of 50 per cent of small and medium-size industrial and agro-business enterprises, of the great majority of small retail and service establishments, and of all housing by the end of 1992(!). By the year 2000, the entire privatization process should be completed.

Implementation got underway only slowly, however. With the President otherwise occupied, the Alma-Ata bureaucracy was not pushing the reforms effectively and local authorities in many areas were clearly dragging their heels. In late Fall, Nazarbaev dismissed the Prime Minister and reshaped the Council of Ministers and, in December, replaced all *oblast* leaders with his own appointees. The pace of privatization is now picking up. In early 1992, the *New York Times* reported that 16 per cent of housing had been privatized and that the proportion was 40 per cent in Alma-Ata.[13] A recent IMF report notes that 400 small to medium industrial establishments have been privatized. This number is now growing rapidly.

As previously mentioned, a third working trip to Alma-Ata was cancelled. The intention had been to bring a small team out that would concentrate on fiscal and financial issues. But Kazakhstan has in fact done pretty well – ending the first quarter of 1992 with a small budget surplus(!)[14] – and now has the assistance of IMF and World Bank teams.

The Tenghiz field negotiations have finally produced a signed contract and the Chevron Overseas Corporation will begin the multi-billion dollar investment project that will bring Kazakh oil to world markets. Meanwhile, there are reports of a new strike in a different region of the republic that may be of a size similar to Tenghiz (est. at 25 bn barrels).

Obviously, I have left a number of important policy issues out of this narrative. In addition to those having to do with the utilization of Kazakhstan's oil riches, there is, for example, the question of an independent currency. But I will confine myself to one more point.

## The Old Economy and the New: The Legal Framework

Up to this point, I have written in 'transformation' terms of how to change the socialist economy into a free market system. But it is sometimes useful to think of the problem differently, in two parts. One set of questions concerns what to do with the *old economy*, what can and cannot be salvaged, and so on. The other set of questions has to do with how to make the *new economy* grow. There is a tendency, I think, to get so preoccupied with the many difficult and technical problems of how to convert the old economy that we do not give enough attention to the relatively simple matter of establishing the right conditions under which private sector activity will thrive.[15]

Kazakhstan passed a rather revolutionary 'Privatization and Destatization Act' in June 1991. 'Privatization' carries the connotation of putting assets in private hands and (implicitly) under the protection of property and contract law. 'Destatization' is, of course, a curious term that probably has no legitimate existence in English. What it suggests is the removal of assets from state control. It is much the better word for describing what is actually going on. 'Destatizised' assets are not taken out of the command economy to be put into the legal and institutional context of a free market economy. Rather, they end up in a legally indeterminate or less than determinate status.

There has been a spate of important acts of this sort. One does not need to be a lawyer to realize that, as a body of law, all this recent legislation has many holes, much ambiguity and not a few contradictions. The new laws assert rights of private property – but it is not clear that the agents of the state are giving up the corresponding powers to intervene, to permit or prohibit, or to take control. The omissions and ambiguities of the new laws (and the lack of independent judicial power backing them) provide the ecological niches where officialdom can and will continue to thrive.

It is too much to ask that a legislature consisting almost entirely of former communist apparatchiks, with no experience and little understanding of free economic systems, should be able in a few sessions to develop a civil code as consistent and comprehensive as the bodies of law that have evolved over centuries in the West. It is obviously not just unlikely, but simply impossible. Nothing remotely like it is going to be accomplished.

It would be far better if Kazakhstan were to import the entire body of property and contract law from a Western country and let its legislature work on modifying and adapting it to local conditions and traditions. I am told, for example, that the old German *Handelsrecht* forms the core of the commercial law of some 80 countries. It would be a good idea[16] for Kazakhstan to join the 80 and to start training the judges and lawyers it will need in that well-developed body of law.

Nothing is more important for the new economy to grow and prosper than well-defined and secure economic rights, enforced by 'impartial arbiters' and protected also against the agents of the state.

## PROSPECTS

If political stability can be maintained and conflicts with neighboring republics be avoided, the medium-term economic prospects for Kazakhstan look
rather good to me. The republic's natural resource endowments are really
very impressive. But even as they constitute the republic's best hope for the
near future, they also constitute a clear threat to Nazarbaev's dream of emulating the socioeconomic systems of resource-starved South Korea, Hong
Kong, Taiwan or Singapore. The danger is that the erstwhile *nomenklatura*
will transform itself into an oligarchy commanding much of the oil revenues
and other resource rents for its own purposes and that, rather than the alert,
innovative and always hardworking businessmen of the 'Tigers', the future
elite of Kazakhstan might bear a closer resemblance to Latin-American rent-
seekers or the sheiks of Kuwait.

Nazarbaev will try to avoid this, but it will not be easy. His present
widespread popularity does not translate into the effective support of a broad-
based, organized political movement. There has been very little turnover
among the ruling strata of the republic. The Communist party is gone but all
the same people are in much the same powerful positions. Without the party's
authority over them, moreover, many may now have a degree of independent
power that they did not have before. Consider, for example, the chairmen and
party secretaries of the *kolchozes*. A friend once characterized them as 'feu-
dal rulers lording it with almost absolute power in the countryside'. These
people, running the collective farms that were established with such a terrible
toll among the Kazakhs, now find support in their opposition to any kind of
land reform from Kazakh traditionalists who abhor private property in land as
alien to the culture of the nomads that once ruled the steppe. Will Nazarbaev
be able to govern without the support of these people?

## NOTES

\*   Written in March 1992.
1.  Dr Bang's official position is now that of Director of the newly created Kazakhstan
    Institute of Management and Economics (KIME); unofficially, he continues as a personal
    economic advisor to the President. KIME, which has inherited the physical facilities of
    the Institute of the Central Committee of the Kazakh Communist Party, will use teachers
    from the West to teach management, business law and economics courses to Kazakh
    officials and students. The plans for the Institute were drawn up by the Expert Committee
    and it is partly funded by the European Community.
2.  In the last months of the USSR, Ukraine was persistently complaining that Moscow was
    not printing rubles fast enough for the needs of Ukraine. The response from the center was
    that the mints were running around the clock.
3.  One of the problems we encountered was that some well-known Soviet economists had
    argued that the issue of privatization vouchers would be inflationary!

4.  Actually, no other obligation than property taxes and possible condominium fees. See below.
5.  At this time, however, it is the declared policy of the government that the privatization of 'all' housing will be completed before the end of 1992.
6.  The Kazakhstan Institute of Management and Economics is being created to conduct such programs on a fairly large scale.
7.  It is worth noting that Western investors are interested in East German state farms today because agricultural units of that size can hardly be assembled in the West any longer.
8.  The collectivization of agriculture in Kazakhstan in the 1930s had been one of this century's more horrible tragedies, with a loss of life in the millions. It seems that, even fifty years later, the communist regime is not willing to let these erstwhile nomads loose to herd their animals on the steppe where the Party might not be able to keep an eye on them!
9.  In the meantime, the voucher system had gotten a bit more complicated than I would have liked. The usufruct rights to the existing stock of housing were of course not equitably distributed at all. The voucher scheme was modified in an attempt to make the property rights distribution resulting from privatization more equitable than the pre-existing usufruct distribution. At this time I do not know the actual outcome.
10. In Frydman and Rapaczynski (1991a), I have found some support. This was particularly welcome since I had found the previous papers by Frydman and Rapaczynski for my purposes the most insightful contributions to this literature that I have come across. See Frydman and Rapaczynski (1991b, 1991c).
11. A large furniture manufacturing plant in Kazakhstan was not producing at this time because all the furniture glue originated in Azerbaijan, and the Azeris were not delivering. A year later, lumber from Russia was not forthcoming, although the Kazakhs kept up their own deliveries.
12. For further discussion of production systems of this type, see Leijonhufvud (1986b, Chapter 13 in this volume) and Leijonhufvud (1989, Chapter 14 in this volume).
13. I have not been able to confirm these numbers. I am told that, by Spring 1992, housing privatization is proceeding considerably faster *outside* Alma-Ata than in the capital. This may reflect the fairly unchecked executive powers of Nazarbaev's new *oblast* 'prefects'.
14. Under current conditions in the CIS, this is quite an achievement. It is hardly possible that it will last, however. Russia will determine the rate of inflation for the ruble area and it will be high. Kazakhstan is bound to see the real value of tax revenues seriously reduced by the Oliveira-Tanzi lag effect.
15. To take the example most to the point: China has done remarkably well in making the 'new economy' grow but has not even attempted to tackle the 'old economy'. China is growing rapidly *despite* the drag put on the economy by the completely unreformed system of state enterprises.
16. It is of course an 'academic' idea. The signs are unmistakeable that it will share the fate of most other recommendations from the ivory tower.

# 17. The nature of the depression in the former Soviet Union*

Several years ago, the Soviet economy reached a point where: (a) the command economy system had been fatally damaged, while (b) the minimal institutions required for a private-sector market economy to function had not been put in place, and where (c) the state had made almost no progress toward creating for itself the public finance system of a mixed economy. Many things have changed in the interim but these three broad statements remain basically descriptive of the state of affairs. From a macroeconomic standpoint, this had all the marks of an unsustainable situation – and, of course, it has not been sustained. Russian industrial production has declined by more than 30 per cent at the same time as the economy is now entering hyperinflation.

To belabor the obvious: the depression in the former Soviet Union (FSU) fits neither Keynesian nor Monetarist theory and certainly not real business cycle theory. The ruble inflation also has features that make it *sui generis*. Western macroeconomics, whether traditional or modern, does not provide a ready-made guide to how the present FSU dilemmas should be dealt with. It appears that every economist and newspaper columnist around feels able to offer the Russians advice purported to be more valuable than the price charged for it. The truth is that we need to understand the situation better. I have had some first-hand exposure to the problems while a member of the Economic Expert Committee of the President of Kazakhstan,[1] but my professional background is not that of a Soviet expert.

I will sketch three themes: the first concerns the structure of industry, the second money and finance, and the third some of the legal and political aspects.

## THE GOSPLAN INHERITANCE

The manufacturing sector built up under central planning is characterized by a high degree of vertical industry integration and reliance on very large plants. Individually, these plants tend to be technologically inflexible and so is the entire system consisting of such plants. The planners had exaggerated notions

of the economies of plant scale and little understanding of the systemic economies of scale external to the plant. Their 'gigantomania' left a very vulnerable
legacy: many large plants depend on a single or at least dominant supplier for
some of their raw materials or intermediate inputs and, similarly, have one
dominant customer. If one such gigantic plant ceases to operate, others are left
without supplies or without customers. Failure in one part of the system,
therefore, can cascade through a large part of it. Such failures are now occurring on a large scale and, in my judgment, constitute the most intractable part
of the current crisis in the FSU economy and the aspect of it, moreover, that is
not at all amenable to traditional macroeconomic prescriptions.

A large proportion of the final goods output of this industrial structure has
been what we call 'defense production' when referring to the United States or
'armaments' when talking about foreign countries. Military production on
anything like the old scale will no longer be sustained, but conversion to
civilian production is far more difficult in the FSU than in the United States.
In the United States, land, labor and capital trickle away from military into
civilian uses via thousands of market channels. These markets have yet to
develop in the FSU. Besides, the mania for gigantic plants, combined with a
mania for secrecy, created a number of towns totally dependent on military
production and utterly lacking alternative employment opportunities. The
Russians, therefore, are more or less forced to convert existing plants to
entirely different uses. Western defense firms have not been successful at this
kind of conversion, although they have no difficulty changing the mix of
inputs that they buy. The Gosplan input–output table is far more inflexible,
making the difficulties of switching a particular plant from tanks to refrigera-
tors all but insurmountable.

The Gosplan system was not only larger than Russia, it lapped over the
borders of the Soviet Union into the 'satellite' Eastern European nations. The
plan prices underlying the terms of trade between political units bore little
relation to potential market prices. Trade was based not on mutually recognized gain but on Moscow's political hegemony. The loss of it, therefore, has
a lot to do with the breakdown of the system. The collapse of CMEA trade
already showed how vulnerable the system was. From early 1991 onwards,
new tensions among the republics of the Soviet Union began to disrupt trade
between them, also. The threat to withhold deliveries became part of the
political game between republics even before the break-up of the USSR and
the creation of the CIS. The Gosplan legacy of vertically integrated industries
of gigantic plants made such threats highly effective: cessation of deliveries
from one republic could seriously disrupt production in others. When Yeltsin
and Kravchuk torpedoed the Union, the result was a 'commonwealth' within
which the relationship between republics came to be negotiated very largely
through threat games of this sort.

The Gosplan legacy would have made rapid progress on market reform exceedingly difficult in any case. The basic problem is not political, although it is greatly exacerbated by political disintegration. Consider the classroom example many of us use to explain the vertical-integration theory of the firm: if production is organized as an assembly line, why is not every work station on that line a separate firm, buying its intermediate good input from the preceding station and selling to the succeeding one? Because (we tell our students) such firms would be without alternative suppliers for their inputs and without alternative customers for their outputs, and this creates a game with an empty core. The analogy likening the Gosplan system to a set of such assembly lines is easily overdrawn, of course. But one is more nearly right thinking of the Soviet manufacturing sector in these terms than in terms of the usual Cobb–Douglas production function. For instance:

1.  If one workstation on an assembly line breaks down or fails to receive required intermediate inputs, the whole line comes to a halt.
2.  The workstations on an assembly line cannot be made into individual firms, each one selling its output to the next, because no determinate set of equilibrium prices can be found for such a chain of bilateral monopolies.
3.  The physical assets that together make up the assembly line have little market value separately. The whole is worth more than the sum of the parts.

Privatization is no panacea when dealing with a productive structure of this kind and liberalizing prices will not automatically replace the arbitrary plan prices with market prices truly reflecting relative resource scarcities. The price explosion following the elimination of price controls was no doubt in large measure due to the government's inexplicable failure first to convert the pre-existing monetary overhang into illiquid securities. But it also demonstrated the monopoly powers of the *kombinate*, giving a first taste of the problems that privatization of these enterprises might bring.

It is obviously true that the inherited, utterly arbitrary system of prices offers hardly a clue to what enterprises are socially efficient or inefficient. It is a widespread opinion that rationalization of the FSU economies can only be achieved by: (a) privatizing all enterprises, and (b) letting the market weed out the inefficient ones. It is also argued that it is best to achieve this as rapidly as at all possible, before pressure groups can form to block the 'weeding-out' process. But the 'sink or swim' test of what enterprises deserve to survive can very easily go horribly wrong. It will go wrong not only because some plants will fail that would survive if prices were competitive, but because forcing individual loss-makers into bankruptcy may force a cascade of failures up and down the vertical chain of plants. The gain from eliminating the losses recorded at one plant can easily be completely swamped by the social loss resulting from a vertical cascade of failures.

Privatizing Gosplan, Inc. is a rather more complicated task than breaking up AT&T or deregulating the airlines. When dispensing advice to the former socialist countries, we should be quite careful not to oversimplify. More is involved than deciding how ownership is to be distributed and by which means ownership control may be exercised.

## MONEY AND CREDIT

Inflation in 1992 has been at least 1200 per cent. Some Russian economists would put it at 2000 per cent. Yet, Prime Minister Gaidar fell prey to an opposition in a fury over his policy of 'monetary restraint' and supposed subservience to the dictates of the IMF. The Civic Union people, who are gaining increasing influence in the government, seem to have little idea about how to handle the present situation – except to print money faster. So the ruble zone is headed for hyperinflation.

High inflation has overtaken the Russian public finances before a modern tax system and administration could be put in place. We must suppose that real tax revenues are now significantly diminished by the Oliveira–Tanzi lag effect. To govern without the printing press has become nearly impossible; the near impossibility of governing by means of the printing press remains to be demonstrated. Already, the 'mafias' find it easier than the government to pay the police a living wage. Most of the Soviet leaders have been terribly slow to grasp the dangers of inflation. Accustomed to the command economy, they are trying to get used to a system where the government rules not by the power to command but by the power of the purse. Day by day, the power to control events is slipping through their fingers, but many of them still fail to see that the ability to govern will be gone when the money in the purse is worth no more than the paper it is printed on.

High inflations have destroyed the financial systems of countries with long and unbroken experience with the market system. Russia cannot hope to create functioning intermediaries and securities markets under conditions of high inflation. The conditions are far off, therefore, under which capital formation in significant volume can resume. The efficiency with which exist-ing resources are utilized (never very high) will also suffer. Standard accounting practices are little known in Russia and inflation accounting is, I believe, totally unknown. Under high inflation, many Russian enterprises will have little or no idea of whether they are running at profit or loss.

Of course, they may not care. State enterprises have never operated under *hard budget constraints* in the communist past and have proved quite effectively resistant to such constraints in the non-communist present. With the help of the ministries that once controlled them, many of the vertically integrated industries try to keep going with the same plant-to-plant delivery patterns as before – transacting at arbitrary prices, but without settling accounts out of their own revenues. Instead, they turn to the government for subsidies to keep production going and unemployment from skyrocketing. If subsidies are denied, 'enterprise arrears' are allowed to pile up so that some money creation is postponed. If they are granted, the money presses roll at once. The subsidies that keep the manufacturing sector from total collapse have become the central crux of the inflation problem.

Why does not the government impose hard budget constraints on these enterprises? The answer, I believe, comes in three parts. First, Soviet enterprises never had to maintain a sound financial working capital position to operate. The present FSU enterprises are largely without financial working capital. Were the stream of subsidies (and/or permitted arrears) to suddenly dry up, many firms would simply lack the wherewithal to continue production. Second, the financial institutions or securities markets that might be able to provide the required working capital on business-like terms do not exist. Third, the government cannot credibly threaten large *kombinate* with bankruptcy, particularly not if it concerns the dominant enterprise in a particular location or if the failure would 'cascade'.

## THE OLD ECONOMY AND THE NEW: ESTABLISHING THE PREREQUISITES OF A MARKET ORDER

The discussion of the socialist transformation problem in the West seems to be stuck on the theme that one is to 'create the New economy by privatizing the Old'. Two things tend to go wrong when the discussion proceeds from this simplistic slogan. First, it is only too easy to become cavalier about the preservation of the productive capital – both human and physical – inherited from the communist system. Not all destruction is 'creative'. Second, the insistent focus on privatization easily diverts attention from what needs to be done to put the minimal prerequisites for a functioning market order in place.

Instead of starting directly with the intricate and difficult problems of how to privatize so as to create corporations with a workable governance structure, I think it is useful to begin by considering two sets of questions. One concerns what to do with the various elements of the old economy, what can and cannot be salvaged, and how that may be done. The other concerns how to make the new economy grow. Privatization of state assets will be *part* – but only part – of the answer to both questions.

## Salvaging the Old

It is only too easy for Western visitors to declare all Soviet plant and equipment hopelessly outmoded and uncompetitive. But it is the only industrial capital they have, and most of the former Soviet republics cannot look forward to capital inflow from abroad on the scale that East Germany or even Poland or Hungary are receiving. A 'big bang' privatization of the various enterprises in a vertically integrated Gosplan industry risks causing a cascade of failures. The unemployment and capital destruction that would ensue will be of a kind, moreover, that cannot be remedied through macroeconomic stimulus.

I am not of the 'privatize everything as fast as possible' school, therefore. I do believe that enterprises that produce final consumer goods should be privatized as soon as possible. But most of FSU heavy industry should, I think, first be converted to state-owned corporations with their privatization postponed, in some cases indefinitely. It will be difficult enough, without privatization, to keep these industries going in all those instances where the vertical chain of enterprises crosses the new inter-republican borders.

## The Prerequisites of the New

The proper functioning of a market economy depends on well-defined property rights, on a comprehensive commercial code and on the impartial and dependable enforcement of these laws. Well, the FSU republics are passing economic legislation at a tremendous rate, but the bodies of law that result are full of lacunae, ambiguities and contradictions. The new laws assert all sorts of rights to private property. But for these private rights to be meaningful and dependable, the agents of the state must also relinquish sundry powers to intervene, to prohibit or to control. It is far from clear that they are doing so. The omissions and ambiguities of the new laws and the lack of an independent judicial power give officialdom plenty of room where it can continue to thrive. Private economic rights have seen little dependable enforcement since perestroika, and law enforcement is now deteriorating in a very serious fashion. In the big cities, private rights cannot be dependably defended against the 'mafias'.

The term 'privatization' carries the misleading suggestion that the assets removed from state control are put into the legal and institutional context of a free market economy. But 'destatized' wealth is more likely to end up in some sort of insecure legal limbo. The framework within which a private enterprise economy can grow is still largely missing.

The Chinese have hardly allowed market reform to touch the 'old' state enterprises that are their Gosplan legacy. They have kept them producing, however inefficiently. Meanwhile, they have concentrated on providing the conditions under which their 'new' market sectors are able to grow at extremely impressive rates. Soviet conditions were not right for emulating the initial Chinese successes in agriculture. But they might emulate the Chinese in not tearing the 'old' economy apart before the 'new' has gotten under way.

## A POLITICAL REFLECTION

Finally, I have come to doubt the common wisdom also on a political issue. Let me emphasize that I am expressing doubts, not claiming to know a different truth.

The 'industrial managers' of Russia are routinely portrayed as the enemies of economic reform in the Western press. On economic matters, they have been the most effective opponents of Gaidar as they were of Gorbachev. Economists writing on the transformation problem routinely assume, it seems to me, that the industrial managers criticize policies of privatization and monetary restraint purely out of personal self-interest, and that because a free market would threaten their present powers, they will not support economic reform.

This view of the managers as party hacks who would not be able to compete in a free market (and know it) is no doubt true of a fair number of them. But making it into a cliché makes us forget that it is also in this group – and for present purposes virtually nowhere else, I would say – that we find 'the best and the brightest' in the FSU. Brezhnev-era corruption was so widespread that it has made us all but forget the meritocratic aspects of Soviet society. But it is worth recalling that men like Yeltsin, Gorbachev and Nazerbaev rose to the top from very poor backgrounds and did so by merit. They proved their merit, moreover, in economic management. Some of the present managers are simply first-rate people – and many of them clearly want the transformation to a market economy to succeed.

When they express opposition to the policies by which the transformation is being attempted, therefore, we should not be too quick to dismiss their criticisms. They do understand the system in which they have been operating. Consequently, it may well be that they sometimes understand the immediate economic consequences of certain policies better than we newcomers do. A Russian manager with an engineering degree and some schooling in Marxist economics, let us say, will not express himself in the terms we use. But he may still understand perfectly well that pell-mell privatization may wreak havoc with vertically integrated industries and that the sudden imposition of 'hard budget constraints' will simply shut down enterprises that have no working capital and cannot raise it in any credit market.

On this political matter, the coming months will test our differing perceptions of the Russian managers. The increasing influence of Volsky's Civic
Union in the government has been seen by an almost unanimous Western
press as presaging defeat for the entire reform effort. I am very much afraid
that it spells the end, for now, of any serious effort to contain inflationary
pressures – and hyperinflation is likely to prove disastrous. But I do not
expect to see a general retreat from pro-market reforms.

## NOTES

\*   Written in December 1992.
1.   See Leijonhufvud (1993a – Chapter 16 above).

# PART V

# Reflections

# 18. Ideology and analysis in macroeconomics

Economists converse and quarrel with one another as if it were obvious where the line between normative and positive propositions runs. In macroeconomic controversy, specifically, each side will dismiss some set of statements by the opposing side as 'ideological' in the sense of 'normative'. In my view, this dismissal often means that one fails to address and appraise important positive beliefs. The example of such a belief that we will consider is 'the market system will coordinate individual economic activities'. But there are others, such as beliefs about 'basic' human nature.

The formalization of economics and increasing specialization among economists aggravates the problem. These 'cosmological' beliefs are on the whole not appropriately addressed when controversy proceeds in obedience to the overt standards of mathematical and statistical precision. Thus, it seems to me, there are crucially important areas of substantive belief that are not at present subject to any orderly (well, more or less orderly) 'conjecture and refutation' process. At the same time economists have become much more narrowly educated and specialized. This 'division of knowledge' tendency we allow to run its course in the belief that mathematics can by itself maintain the intellectual coherence of the social sciences. But I do not believe we have reached the state yet where it can.

## THEORY AND ADVOCACY

### Macroeconomic Battlelines

The major controversies in macroeconomics since the publication of Keynes's *General Theory* have left behind a legacy of shorthand labels for the respective contending groups. Disturbingly, these paired labels are often perceived as indicating not just a 'scientific' but also something of an ideological battleline. Consider: Keynes versus classics; new economics versus Chicago school; income expenditure versus quantity theory; fiscalists versus Monetarists. And at times, not too distant, some economists have tended to tar with the same brush the distinction (however defined) of macro versus micro theory.

Each one of these dichotomies we usually strive to present in purely analytical terms. And it is important to do so, of course. Yet, from the above list it may seem a small step to add, say, interventionists versus automatists – at which point someone is apt to mumble 'liberals versus conservatives' or 'Democrats versus Republicans' ... and some seemingly feline creature is out of the bag.

The terms on the left side (or on the right) above are definitely not synonymous. Clearly, then, analytical issues are being fudged by lumping them together. This suggests that ideological contention over the scientific issues is going to be unhelpful. But one cannot retire from the field with that pious observation. It is a behavioral fact that many people perceive the categories above as having common 'left' and 'right' denominators. Modern macroeconomics emerged in the ideological hothouse of the 1930s and, ever since, has been less than successful in repelling injections of ideological matter. Less so, probably, than most other fields of economics. If scientific progress in the field has been less than encouraging, lack of clarity on this score is partly to blame.

Students do not like to be snowed. At some point in their training, most economics students feel compelled to worry over whether, in the often fairly frantic race to ingest a heavy diet of diagrams and algebra, they are not also being made to swallow a dose of potentially toxic ideology. It is a question the student should ask and is obliged to try to make up his mind about. But he will not find it an easy one, and it is not at all unlikely that he will find his instructors consistently avoiding it in favor of stressing the purely logical properties of the economic models taught in the courses. This avoidance behavior is to be expected, for professionals are trained to regard ideologies as 'unclean' and know that one requirement for respectability is to keep above suspicion.

If it is true, however, that ideology has been and is an obstacle to progress, then we should try to bring the problem out in the open and not avoid or try to suppress it. By avoiding it we fail to understand what our disagreements are about and why we seem condemned to relive the same old quarrels over and over again.

It might help, to begin with, if economists could resign themselves to the fact that, whatever they do, they will live 'below suspicion' of ideological bias for some time to come. The road between economic theory and policy recommendation is a two-way street, but the direction of traffic on it is hard if not impossible for outsiders to judge. The proper scholar derives his policy pronouncements from that theory which he believes has the most empirical support. The ideologue starts from the policies he favors and shops around for the theory that provides the most ample supply of rationalizations. The public observes in each case only the suspiciously neat dovetailing of theory and advocacy.

Naturally, the difficulty would not exist if there were not several theories in contention for the ideologically motivated to choose from. If by empirical investigations all theories but one were eliminated from serious scientific consideration, whoever backed up his policy recommendations with arguments not consistent with accepted doctrine would be discredited. This point would seem to lay the troubles and tribulations of the discipline at the door of the empiricists. That, however, is too simple a view of the matter. There certainly are issues in economics which remain outstanding because no one has come up with the empirical tools sharp enough to discriminate convincingly between contending hypotheses. But with the great ideological issues, it would be unwise to do nothing but wait for a breakthrough in econometric technique to bring the resolution. A large part of the problem lies in the failure of proponents of different 'theories' (a word used loosely in economics) to state some of their most basic beliefs about what the world is like in forms that could be subjected to any kind of quantitative test. As a short-hand label for such non-testable beliefs, let us refer to them as 'cosmological'. To work them into statements amenable to direct confrontation with specified bodies of data would require (where it can be done at all) a major analytical effort. The economist, who is (with reason) anxious not to be tagged as a carrier of ideological contamination, is likely to avoid putting out that effort, however.

In so doing, he is following a recipe honored by tradition for keeping social science 'value free'. The prescription builds on a distinction between 'means' and 'ends'. Let 'ends' be understood as alternative states of the economic system achievable as the outcomes of different sets of policies, these being the 'means'. The task of the economist, as a social scientist, is to explain the linkage between means and ends – a task that requires thoroughly objective understanding of the workings of the system on which policy actions impinge. Subjective, 'political' values are said to pertain only to 'outcomes'. If the economist wants to keep his nose entirely clean – as this tradition insists he ought – he should, strictly speaking, make no policy recommendations at all but confine himself to the role of separating unachievable from achievable outcomes, the latter to be presented to the appropriate 'political' decision-maker. In this scheme, values have a place only in arguing about the choice to be made among feasible outcomes; the functional relationships of the economic system that link means and ends as cause and effect are value neutral – objects of understanding, not of valuation. To avoid confounding the two, the economic scientist should watch his terminology: value-laden words (consider 'free enterprise' or 'exploitation') have their place in arguing the desirability of actual or feasible outcomes; scrupulous care should be taken to keep them out of the description of the actual workings of an economy – of how these outcomes are brought about.

While articulate critics have argued that all of this vastly oversimplifies the problem of the role of value in social science,[1] this traditional view is still the standard one. When today's textbooks and instructors concentrate on the properties of geometric or algebraic models of systems, these prescriptions for the ethical scholar are scrupulously adhered to – where, after all, do you hide your personal biases in a bordered Hessian? Yet, decades of this have not sufficed for macroeconomic science to emerge from under the ideological penumbra that clouded its birth. Our antiseptic-looking model machinery persists in generating political heat along with scientific light. Adhering to the traditional recipe for a value-free science has not sufficed to expunge ideology from macrotheory to everyone's satisfaction. It remains a fact that the traditional prescription worked pretty much to the 'satisfaction of most people' – before Keynes, when the great majority of English-speaking economists could be described as Marshallians. Why not since?

Basically, I believe, the prescription worked (or was perceived as working) because 'everyone' was a Marshallian – because economists shared a common framework of analysis, a common methodology and a set of basic assumptions about the nature of the economic system. Broad agreement on all this will create the confidence that 'objective' scientific propositions can be recognized by their form and content, and that, correspondingly, 'subjective' ideological statements can fairly easily be sorted out. This broad agreement was shattered by the Keynesian revolution. In its turbulent wake a pervasive uncertainty surfaced, for classics and Keynesians could not recognize each other's analytical propositions as purely objective. In the social sciences, easy identification of the line separating objective from subjective statements requires established ground rules of analysis. The very perception of objective and subjective statements as mutually exclusive, non-overlapping classes of propositions must be based on a shared 'cosmology'.

Note what my argument implies with regard to the interpretation of the term 'ideology'. It is clear that in the view that became well entrenched before Keynes, the problem of ideology and analysis was perceived as – very simply – that of keeping the personal political valuations of professionals out of economic theory. But disciplining the members of the profession in this regard has not sufficed. Thus, equating 'ideology' with 'personal bias' has proved too simplistic a view of the problem. Ideologies have two components: one stating preferences among attainable states of the system, the other stating beliefs about what the system is in fact like in what we may call its 'global properties' and, therefore, what states are attainable and which ones are not. The first component is obviously scientifically illegitimate; the proper role of the second – of economic cosmologies – is a much more difficult matter to decide, but it clearly cannot be relegated to the same low status as personal political biases. The common, simplistic identification of ideology with personal bias has been unfortunate in several respects. It has made honest and unbiased investigators the target of unfair – and worse, pointless – vituperation. And it has directed attention away from the source of the problem that has seriously impeded progress in macroeconomics.

It has also made the economist neglect a most important task, namely that of communicating with yon mythological creature, 'the intelligent layman'. By and large, what economists think they have learned about the economic system has to be imparted to the general public on the level of cosmological beliefs. It matters little how many hundreds of thousands of college students are each year taught the elements of an array of simple economic models. Those who do not continue to graduate study and beyond – obviously the great majority – are not in later years going to dust off their old lecture notes as an aid to making judgments on the economic issues of the day. Their thinking on such matters will be formed in terms of grand generalities on a level of discourse akin to that of serious economics in that distant epoch when the science was still struggling to emerge from social philosophy in general – at which time 'the intelligent layman' did inform himself (and could ill afford not to) about what economists had to say. The audience is still there – as Galbraith knows – but few professional economists choose to address it. Some, perhaps, have nothing intelligible to say to outsiders. But many are no doubt inhibited by the notion that discourse on the level of grand generalities is professionally illegitimate, because 'ideological'.

## COSMOLOGIES, THEORIES AND MODELS

There is, then, more to 'ideology' as I use the term than the exercise of pernicious personal bias. As usual, however, clarifying our usage of one term propels us into the fog surrounding another – there never can be an end to the game of 'define what you mean'. The (somewhat) more respectable component of ideologies I described as a set of 'beliefs about what the world is in fact like'. Such beliefs, obviously, in some sense or other form 'theories'. 'In some sense or other', however, is not good enough. 'Theory' is a term used loosely by economists, as is another which is frequently treated simply as interchangeable with 'theory', namely 'model'. We need to come to some tolerable degree of agreement about how these terms are to be employed.

Consider the following two statements as examples of what economists tend to say.

1.  If all commodities are gross substitutes, then equilibrium is unique and globally stable.

2.   In the current era of capitalism, wage and price controls are the only
     means whereby inflation can be halted.

These two, it would seem, are animals of different species. Yet, in general
usage, the word 'theory' may refer to a collection of statements of either sort.
What do we make of this kind of thing?

Let me – provisionally and without claim to epistemological profundity or
rigor – distinguish three 'levels' on which statements of beliefs about economic phenomena may be made. Begging the reader's indulgence, I will refer
to the three as 'cosmologies', 'theories' and 'models'. In referring to 'levels
of beliefs' I do not intend to convey a strictly discrete compartmentalization;
the three categories shade into one another along a continuum. In the most
general terms, this continuum may be thought of as running – from the
cosmology end to the model end, respectively – from the 'general' to the
'specific', from the 'ambiguous' to the 'precise' or (and here is where the
trouble comes in) from a strong and mostly non-cerebral commitment to
basic beliefs to a conditional, and hence more tentative, and 'reasonable'
adherence to certain hypotheses.

At all three levels, I am dealing with structures of interrelated statements.
In trying to evaluate such structures, one poses two types of questions. One
concerns the association of variables appearing in certain of these statements
with observable (and hopefully measurable) entities in the external world.
The other concerns the relationships between the statements themselves. The
ultimate criterion one endeavors to apply to the system of beliefs is, in the
one instance, empirical truth and, in the other, logical consistency. On either
ground, cosmologies appear ambiguous: terms referring to the real world
tend to be of a kind such that specific measurement procedures for the
corresponding phenomena are not just hard to devise but hard to conceive of;
terms used to assert relationships tend to have boundaries that are too ill-
defined for demonstrations of either logical consistency *or* inconsistency to
be possible.

At the other extreme good models are, relatively speaking, very precise at
least in one or the other of these two respects, much more seldom in both.
The very striving for precision, it appears, brings out a tension between the
dual desiderata of empirical applicability and logical consistency which is far
less bothersome in theories and never apparent in cosmologies. Thus, some
modern 'pure' models are wonders of logical–mathematical precision, but the
pursuit – necessary for that objective – of exact definition of the logical
boundaries of the terms employed tends to drain them of assured association
with the 'messy' empirical data that is all the economist has to work with.
Axiomatic models are capable of conclusive *proof* that, *if* a world such as that
postulated were to exist, it must have such and such properties – but they

leave us uncertain about how one would go about establishing the isomorphism of the model with, say, the US economy in recent decades. A single-equation regression may be considered as the opposite case. It will specify quite precisely what measurements will yield the data for the values of its variables, but in this pursuit of empirical operationality, liberties often have to be taken with the logic of economic analysis. In some cases, the question about the end product may be whether it can be derived from any logical model; in others, the equally troubling question is, from how many?

So, we can have precision of logic or of empirical reference but, in the current state of macroeconomics, it is hard to point out examples that will satisfy the discriminating taste in both these respects.[2]

So cosmologies are ambiguous and models precise. You will not be surprised if I mention that I want 'theory' to refer to a set of beliefs more precise than a cosmology, less precise than a model. You might wonder, however, why I do not dispense with the cosmologies (since they are so obviously 'unscientific'), and why I want to employ 'theory' as a separate concept (since it seems to have no independent status once the extremes of ambiguity and precision have been indicated). To take the second question first, I conceive of theories as more complex than either cosmologies or models. The theory level is the professional economist's working habitat; it is where he does his thinking, where new hypotheses are formed. An economist's theory, in this sense, comprises a very large set of beliefs about 'facts' – beliefs about individual markets and their mode of operating, about the behavior of households, different types of firms and various government agencies, about what happened and why in sundry economic historical episodes and so forth. Such a theory will also comprise beliefs about what kind of logical arguments are capable of making the interrelationships between the believed 'facts' intelligible. Most of the beliefs about 'facts' will be products of casual empiricism rather than of controlled measurement procedures. Similarly, the faith that the entire structure of beliefs forms a logically consistent system must be less than absolute – the structure is too large and complex, and some of its terms insufficiently precise, for a demonstration of consistency to be feasible.

'Cosmologies' are less complex than theories since they consist of a limited number of grand generalities. Models are less complex because that is part of their *raison d'être*. The motive for their construction is to clarify the logical or empirical status of *some aspect* of a theory. Models, then, are in a sense 'special cases' of theories, and the simplifications introduced in their construction mean that the strength of the beliefs attached to them is less than that associated with the more 'general' theories.

# COMMUNICATION AMONG ECONOMISTS

The point of all this (if any) has to do with the way in which beliefs about economic matters are confirmed or revised and with the manner in which economists communicate with each other.

The quest of the entire enterprise is to have the belief systems of individuals converge with each other and, more importantly, toward an increasingly accurate image of the real world. The theories held by individuals are, to varying degree but often in important respects, shaped by 'what he thinks before he starts thinking',[3] that is, by his pre-analytic 'cosmological' beliefs. His choice of models to work with (or at) are in turn motivated by his theory. As the discussion in any given subject area progresses, however, the requirements of precision in scientific communication are increasingly felt and dictate that communication be in terms of the properties of explicit models. Serious professional discussion in the learned journals concerns mostly models; theories will admit of informal but still fairly systematic discourse, preferably among friends; communication about cosmological beliefs is more or less taboo in professional contexts. Statements of this sort sometimes do surface but (when not made by people who are simply unaware of breaching the proprieties) tend then to be addressed, not to a professional audience, but to fellow believers.

The trouble with this is that communication at levels of belief 'deeper' than that of models is so faulty that the mechanism for the orderly revision of beliefs, which every science must have, operates only very weakly: 'in a subject where there is no agreed procedure for knocking out errors, doctrines have a long life'.[4] When an economist addresses you in terms of an explicitly presented model, it is usually perfectly clear what he is *saying*. But what is he *talking about*? That this question bothers economists more or less all the time is a fact revealed in their behavior. You cannot be around economists very long without hearing someone complain that he cannot understand why the distinguished Professor X persists in 'playing around' with a particular class of 'obviously unrealistic' axiomatic models, or why Professor Y attaches such importance to certain regression results that 'do not mean anything'. This is because, explicit as are their models, the theories held by X and Y remain in large measure private, so that the role of the hard-earned results in clarifying or strengthening aspects of their theories is not fully perceived by outsiders.

Any seminal theory is potentially capable of fathering a large number of offspring. This accounts for another type of complaint that economists make of each other, namely that although Professor Z's model has failed in the public arena, 'he won't change his theory'. This is because, in introducing a number of simplifications (that he hopes will work out), Z's belief in the resulting model will be of a lower order than that vested in his theory. If his model succumbs in professional crossfire, therefore, he will merely conclude that some simplifying assumption or choice of empirical proxy-variable was at fault – and return another day with a new brainchild of the same brood.

The above observations pertain to the difficulties we have in settling differences of opinion. Another problem of some consequence has to do with the spurious appearance of agreement. If it is the case that several models may correspond to one theory, it is also true on occasion that a single model may be a special case of more than one theory and, indeed, of theories which in turn relate to sharply divergent cosmologies. The potential consequences of this for the progress of the quest are obvious. I will return to a case of this sort later.

The communication process in economics is pretty good at 'knocking out errors' in models, and economists are – they have to be – pretty decent about renouncing their beliefs in models that have been shown faulty. On this level, out in the open, the process would appear to work with the efficacy attributed to the 'exact sciences'. On the theory level, matters are in a less healthy state. It does indeed happen that economists do revise their theoretical views, but this may occur for reasons almost entirely unrelated to the professional communication process, and it may indeed be questioned whether that process, taken by itself, is the most important of the causes of such occurrences. At one more remove, finally, mathematical argument and empirical work have entirely negligible impact on cosmological beliefs. If the psychological cost of giving up a theory, on which much thought and effort has been spent, is high, giving up one's cosmology is positively traumatic. For revision of a widely prevalent economic world view, one will have to look to great traumatic events – the Great Depression of the 1930s, say – or else put one's hope in generational change. So the trouble is not that cosmologies are frozen and unchanging, but that there is hardly any reason at all to believe that the laws governing their change operate so as to make them steadily converge toward an accurate image of the economic system.

I previously raised the question of why we bother with beliefs as woolly and unscientific as these and do not cast cosmologies out into that outer darkness beyond the friendly confines of the economics profession – there to be fought over, perhaps, by political scientists, sociologists and such like. Maybe 'theories' should go the same way and reputable men confine themselves to models – and talk only about topics where we know what we are saying? The mountain climber's classic rationale – 'because they are there' – is in essence the answer. Strongly held beliefs cannot be treated as nonexistent just because they are ill-defined. One should insist on bringing them out in the open (which is why I am averse to sweeping 'ideologies' under the rug) and on striving for their better definition. Operational definition should be the ultimate goal. But meanwhile it is simply naive to believe that cosmologies are dispensable in economics – or in any other science. It is possible to be unaware – happily unaware, maybe – of their existence and the role they play, but that bespeaks only one's limited perspective, not one's scientific attitude. You cannot start out on the intellectual journey to a scientific theory with a map that is 'a perfect and absolute blank' as did Lewis Carroll's Snark-hunters. Some pre-analytic cognitive elements must be present at the genesis of a theory to guide the choice of its first building blocks, to pose the questions and determine the perception of what things are relevant 'facts'.[5]

The trouble with macroeconomics, then, is not that beneath the sunlit surface, whereon its various models sail fishing for the truth, there lurks a cosmology in the murky depths. Every lake should have its Loch Ness monster. Our problem is having more than one – God knows how many – and that the suspicion of unseen, furious battles in the deep makes existence on the surface so uncomfortable.

## FOUR COSMOLOGIES

It is now time to proceed to a description of the cosmological beliefs of concern in this area. (A ticklish task, it must be realized, for if cosmologies are ill-defined, by definition it follows that it is impossible to provide universally acceptable characterizations of them. What follows must be understood as an account of the monsters of Loch Econ by, as the phrase goes in these contexts, an otherwise reliable observer.)

My concern is with the coordination of economic activities. To allow us the simplicities of two-dimensional illustration, let deviations from the equilibrium level of employment serve as a measure of the extent to which such coordination is achieved. In the following diagrams (18.1–18.4) the schedule $EE^*$ is in each case taken to represent the time path that total employment would follow were the system to maintain itself in general equilibrium over time.[6] I will sketch four cosmologies but do not intend to suggest that they make an exhaustive list.

### Cosmology I

The 'gross properties' of this system are, first, that if undisturbed, it will tend to follow the $EE^*$ path over time, and second, that if exposed to a shock that propels it off the path (to a point such as A), it will automatically and 'fairly rapidly' return itself to the track (Figure 18.1). Thus, the economy is portrayed as a *self-regulating* system. In tending to return to the $EE^*$ path, it exhibits what is usually referred to as 'equilibrating behavior', but since this term has come to be used in economics also with reference to systems that lack this tendency towards equilibrium employment, we will occasionally find it convenient to import a term from other fields dealing with self-regulating systems, namely 'homeostatic behavior'. The biological mechanisms that maintain body temperature, the glucose and cholesterol content of blood and so on are examples of homeostats. In Cosmology I, of course, the mechanisms that account for the system's homeostatic properties are the markets. In this cosmology, moreover, the system is believed to exhibit these homeostatic tendencies at all points off $EE^*$ in the field and they will in general be stronger the farther off the track the system happens to be (that is, the greater is the gap between supply and demand in the various markets).

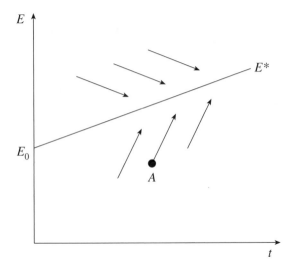

*Figure 18.1    Cosmology I*

This, then, may be taken as a crude sketch of a 'classical' cosmology. Note, however, that it is not by itself a full-blown laissez faire ideology, for it may well be desirable to use government policy instruments to speed up the system's return to the equilibrium path thus to lessen the social costs of being off it. Stabilization policy in this view, however, would be confined to the role of speeding up the system's adjustment; it is not necessary to use it in order to ensure the system's return to the path or in order to keep it there once the path has been reached.

### Cosmology II

This world view (see Figure 18.2) is most easily described simply by denying the beliefs about the economic system that characterize Cosmology I. Thus the economy is *not* a self-regulating system, exhibiting automatic tendencies toward coordinating all activities. Consequently, its motion in a space such as that given by Figure 18.2 proceeds without reference to the *EE\** path, which is viewed as strictly hypothetical – the product of some academic exercise without the slightest relevance to the behavior of the real world. Suppose, for example, that the economy were at point B – a situation of vast unemployment. The supply of labor would not be among the determinants of the rate of change of employment. This time path of total employment might then be as indicated by the arrow.

   If our first cosmology was 'classical' (or even super-classical), this is intended to sketch one world view of early, 'revolutionary' Keynesianism. Consider, as an example, Lekachman's characterization:[7]

> In the Keynesian universe, equilibrium could be reached at any level of employment and income between zero and full employment. Moreover, no theoretical reason existed for saying that one level of employment was more likely to occur than any other level of employment.

   In a Cosmology I world, in contrast, the probability distribution over alternative states of the economy would show higher densities near rather

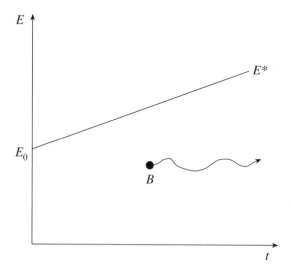

*Figure 18.2   Cosmology II*

than far from the equilibrium level of employment. The economy envisaged in Cosmology II is still presented as a system whose behavior over time may be mathematically described. But it is a system of a qualitatively different kind from that envisaged in Cosmology I, lacking the self-organizing properties of the latter. This qualitative difference is at this stage best explained by resorting to analogies. The market mechanisms central to our first world view have a plethora of analogies in other fields, such as biology or engineering, where self-regulating mechanisms tending to maintain 'desired' values for certain variables are studied (for example, desired body temperature, or desired course in the case of an automatic pilot).[8] The second world view, in contrast, tends to be portrayed as a plumbing system – as a system of interconnected pipes, with 'leakages' and 'injections' of purchasing power at various points, from the end of which gushes aggregate demand. (To its sworn enemies, it is all an intellectual sewer.) This system determines the flow of aggregate demand – but not with reference to some 'appropriate' or 'desired' level. It determines a level of activity for the system as a whole but does not coordinate activities in it.

A world of this type will exhibit either 'chronic' inflation or 'chronic' unemployment, if not 'interfered' with – it is extremely improbable that it would tend to maintain an equilibrium level of employment for any prolonged period. Chronic large-scale unemployment was the relevant concern during the revolutionary phase of this 'Keynesian' doctrine. The appropriate medicine: to step up the 'injection' of government expenditures (and/or decrease the 'leakage' that taxes constitute) sufficiently so as to bring the system to full employment. This policy is viewed not just as a way of speeding up the movement of the system to full employment; it is necessary to bring it there. Furthermore, the policy program cannot be phased out once the system has reached the desired level; it is necessary to maintain it in order to keep it there. If government spending is reduced, for example, when full employment is reached, the system will promptly backslide into depression. Advocacy of a permanently enlarged government sector is not a necessary consequence of this cosmology; in practice, however, those who believe that the private sector of the system lacks homeostatic controls of the activity level have regarded a large government sector as the proper long-run cure.

## Cosmology III

Cosmology III characterizes the system's behavior over time as exhibiting 'bounded instability'. There are many variations on this theme, so that Figure 18.3 gives only a rather arbitrarily chosen example, introduced here, in fact, mostly as a convenient counterpart to Cosmology IV below. In our version of Cosmology III, the system is incapable of settling down in the neighborhood

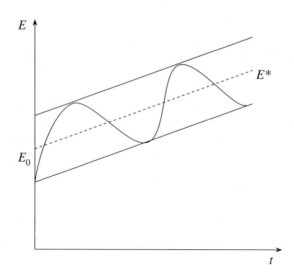

*Figure 18.3    Cosmology III*

of equilibrium employment; instead, it oscillates around it in a perpetual 'business cycle' pattern. Whether in expansion or contraction, the motion of the system generally tends to accelerate rather than slow down when approaching equilibrium, as in Cosmology I. This system is each time speeding up as it passes through the equilibrium level. But there are limits[9] to how far these inherently explosive motions may go, so that the system never actually explodes. Bouncing between the two limits set around the $EE^*$ path in Figure 18.3, it will tend to produce a 'cycle' of constant period. Stabilization policy in this system is the art of reducing the amplitude of these fluctuations and is, in this context, appropriately described as 'countercyclical' – fiscal and monetary policy instruments will be employed in a cyclical pattern of the same periodicity to counteract the inherently oscillatory behavior of the private sector.

## Cosmology IV

Cosmology IV comes with the forewarning that my own theory belongs under this heading. In Figure 18.4, we have again (as in Figure 18.3) marked a corridor around the $EE^*$ path, depicting what we will refer to as the 'equilibrium neighborhood'. The diagram is intended to show that the system is viewed as exhibiting 'nicely' homeostatic behavior in the equilibrium neighborhood – much as Cosmology I claims for the system over the entire field. Its capacity for self-regulatory behavior is here limited, however. Thus,

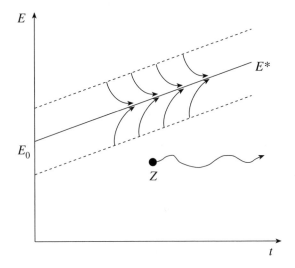

*Figure 18.4 Cosmology IV*

if the system is exposed to disturbances of a magnitude great enough to shock it to a position, such as Z, *outside* the equilibrium neighborhood, it is found that its homeostatic controls are severely impaired in their functioning so that it behaves, in effect, much more as a Cosmology II than a Cosmology I economy.

Something of this sort, it turns out, is true in general of self-regulatory systems. The human body contains, as an illustration, mechanisms designed automatically to maintain body temperature at, or restore it to, 98.6° F. But the range of effective control is limited to something of the order of ±6 degrees (at an uneducated guess). Outside this range, the dynamic behavior of the system proves – in a most distressing way – to be qualitatively different. Similarly, we are able, without conscious effort, to maintain our balance erect while buffeted by disturbances of some limited force, but the range does not include the force of a charging bull, for instance. Again, there are situations when the flight captain had better take over from the automatic pilot, or else.

As will become evident, all this is a very rough sketch indeed. The theory does not indicate a sharply defined 'classical corridor' through an otherwise 'Keynesian' field, but rather that the equilibrating tendencies of the system beyond some point get gradually weaker, not stronger, with distance from the $EE^*$ path.

On policy, two cursory observations will suffice. In contrast to the Cosmology I view, in which policy speeds up the equilibrating adjustment but is never necessary to ensure that it takes place, this system can get into disequilibrium states from which it will not extricate itself unaided by policy intervention. In contrast to Cosmology II, on the other hand, this system does not require the indefinite continuation of these policies in order to maintain itself in the equilibrium neighborhood once it has been reached.

These, then, are my four cosmologies in outline. The four do not, to repeat, exhaust the possibilities – one can easily imagine worlds the 'global properties' of which would be differently described – but four is enough. A somewhat distasteful metaphor may help in fixing their respective salient features in mind for future reference. Let us imagine some cosmic police station into which four suspected drunk drivers are brought. They are to be tested by being required to walk a chalk stripe down the middle of a corridor in the precinct house. Driver I is able to walk the line quite precisely with ease and confidence. If pushed off it, he immediately gets back on. (Actually, he is capable of this stellar performance whether drunk or sober.) Driver II is in a sorry state – completely uncoordinated – and has to be held up at the beginning of the line by the sergeant. As soon as he is let go, he will collapse on the floor and show no further signs of purposeful activity. Driver III is in only modestly better shape, lurching zigzag-wise from one wall to the other down the corridor. Driver IV, finally, is like most people – well-behaved when sober, but ...

## MARKETS AND THE COORDINATION OF ACTIVITIES

Of these deep-dwellers in Loch Econ, it is monsters I and II that have been responsible for the most ideological contention and confusion. Letting the others rest, therefore, the remainder of this paper will collect some notes on these two.

The two basic beliefs juxtaposed are 'the market system works' versus 'the market system does not work'.[10] This is putting it in the ill-defined terms characteristic of cosmological contention, of course. In the history of economics up to the 1930s, Cosmology I reigns – it is the world view of professional economists. The growing edifice of academic economics from Adam Smith to Keynes is primarily a growing, gradually more rigorous, analysis of how markets work, for which the implicit belief that they do work is the foundation. Dissenting writers elaborating a disbelief in the proposition that 'the market system works' – and note that Marx and Engels, as examples very much in point, are not to be counted among them – are by professional consensus at best interesting laymen dabbling in economics, but more often simply irritating cranks. When John Maynard Keynes, toward the end of his great theoretical investigation into the malfunctions of a market system, felt the impulse to dig up a few intellectual progenitors, his search could produce only names like Malthus, Hobson, Mandeville, Gesell and Douglas. None of them icons of academic economists, now or then.

The trauma of the Great Depression changes all this. That 'the market system does not work' is visible to the naked eye and whoever doesn't see it would think the Emperor has clothes. Millions upon millions are unemployed and remain unemployed for years on end. Tempted eyes are cast on the economic organization of totalitarian regimes – communist or fascist as one's leanings may dictate. Cosmology II is in the ascendance and becomes, for a time, predominant. In the most general terms, the doctrine – that left to itself the economic system degenerates into chaos – is not new, but simply pre-Smithian, which is to say, antedating the emergence of economics as a distinct academic field of study. Modern Cosmology II economics is 'neo-mercantilist'. The undisputed predominance of this world view does not last, but when economics settles down again there are two monsters in the lake.

## COSMOLOGIES AND THEORETICAL PROPOSITIONS

For the last 35 years or so, economists have had to accommodate themselves to this situation and have, on the whole, learned to live with it rather well.[11] We know – with some regret – that once upon a time here ruled an era of a single, unified (all but holy in fact!) economic theory, but we also know that, some time around 1940, the Reformation occurred, since when there have been microeconomics and macroeconomics. The beginning of this paper gave brief consideration to the phrases economists use in explaining to students why economic theory is split in this way and, hence, why the diagrams they learn in micro courses happen to be of no help in macro-courses, and vice versa. One should not be misled by these ceremonial rationalizations! The basic reason why micro is taught in one classroom and macro in another is that, historically, the former theory has a Cosmology I and the latter a Cosmology II origin.[12] Since, referring to the same real world, both cosmologies cannot be entertained at once, cultural shock is minimized by scheduling micro classes on Mondays, Wednesday and Fridays and macro classes on Tuesdays and Thursdays.

Naturally, the schizophrenia cannot be confined to 'pure' theory but has spread to applied fields, such as public finance and international economics, where some problems are analysed with the help of micro models and others with macro models. Unfortunately, some problems (for example, balance of payments adjustments) positively invite the use of both models. The resulting conclusions will not agree. This by itself would not be so confusing, if only one model was 'true' and the other 'false'. However, as things stand, the economist is only able to swear that either one tells 'part of the truth and something else than the truth'.

A historian colleague has saved an old Peanuts cartoon wherein Peppermint Patty takes a history examination: 'Explain World War I' – (!?) – 'Use both sides of paper if necessary'. One might imagine Patty sitting down to her final exam in economics and reading: 'Does the market system work? Time: 20 minutes. Weight: 50 per cent'. She may have learned quite a few things, we may suppose, about how economists usually go about producing answers to questions. But what does she do with this one? It may not be a 'good question', but the economics student who does not make a major effort to form a broad judgment of his own on this issue will have gained little from his studies of the subject. There are not that many worthwhile questions in economics that have the same answer whether or not markets do function to coordinate activities. Although the question is a central one in macroeconomics, the student who 'hasn't thought about it' is not safe even if he manages to stay away from the standard macro issues for the rest of his life. One example will suffice to illustrate.

Consider being put in the situation of having to evaluate a proposed large-scale government investment project in an underdeveloped country. The project will introduce a new technology that will substantially reduce the required input of labor. If the setting is that of a system that will absorb the released labor into other employment, then the present value of the labor costs saved should be credited to the project. If the released labor is going to be a permanent addition to the pool of unemployed, the reduced labor costs are not part of the social benefits of the project. The two alternative calculations of the project's value will be far apart and, we assume, make the difference between going ahead and not going ahead. Not knowing which assumption is appropriate means that one is incapable of making an informed decision.

Within macroeconomics, conflicting answers to questions that are at one and the same time the most elemental and the most fundamental have also to be sorted out according to their respective cosmological origin. Consider the following:

1. 'The higher the level of private investment, the higher the levels of consumption, aggregate income and employment.' – 'The higher the level of private investment, the lower the level of consumption.'
2. 'The larger the public sector, the higher (and more stable) the level of income and employment.' – 'The larger the government sector, the smaller the private sector.'
3. 'A rise in private saving will lower income and increase unemployment.' – 'A rise in private saving will increase the wealth of the Nation.'

The task of guiding the economic development of a low-income country, for example, is not made easier by conflicting advice on these issues.[13]

## COSMOLOGIES AND THE 'FACTS'

We have mentioned that it was the horrifying depression decade of the 1930s that broke the faith in the old cosmology. Some observations on developments since then are in order.

At the depth of the Great Depression in 1933 there were about 13 million people unemployed in the United States, an unemployment rate of very nearly 25 per cent. By the end of the decade, in 1939, unemployment was still between 9 and 10 million (17 per cent). Neither the automatic workings of the market system nor government policies brought the depression to an end. The war finally did it – the enormous war demands upon the nation's resources coupled with the equally enormous expansion of the Armed Forces made an end to large-scale unemployment. Up to the end of the war, nothing happened that would challenge the new neomercantilist faith.

As the end of hostilities approached, two developments were clearly in the cards: the return of servicemen to swell the supply of labor, and the end of the thoroughly abnormal government expenditures associated with the war. The elimination of the latter component of aggregate demand implied, from a Cosmology II point of view, an even larger reduction in total demand and, therefore, in the demand for labor. This being the prevalent world view, a return to the disastrous employment picture of the previous decade was generally forecast. What was held in prospect was not just an exceedingly severe 'business-cycle' downturn (with an upturn, even if distant, to look forward to) but permanent deep depression with large-scale unemployment. The theory predicting secular depression was known as the 'stagnation thesis' and was by that time already well entrenched.

By this time, some eight years after the appearance of Keynes's *General Theory*, much work had already been done on constructing explicit models incorporating the world view of our Cosmology II. These models were, in addition, structured so as to conform in a rough way with the schema of the National Income Accounts recently developed by Kuznets. These were, in effect, our first macromodels – the term 'macroeconomics' and the micro–macro distinction enters economics at this time, and it is the twin Kuznets/ Keynes parentage that historically defines macroeconomics as a field. Explicit numerical estimates of the levels of aggregate demand and unemployment in prospect were made utilizing these models.

What followed has come to be generally referred to as the 'postwar forecasting debacle'. The quantitative forecasts indicated depression and large-scale unemployment. In fact, the economy's readjustment to peace-time conditions was unexpectedly rapid, unemployment levels were much lower than in the preceding decade, and inflation turned out to be the predominant problem that policy-makers had to face. Actual events thus generated a most decisive falsification of scientific prediction. The aftermath is quite interesting.

A student's first lesson in scientific methodology tells him that a theory is discarded when falsified. (The second lesson is that, no matter how decisive the falsification, it is not discarded until those in the field have something better to put in its place. Meanwhile, the old theory sails on 'jury-rigged'.) Following this procedure, however, is not as easy as it sounds. When the falsified prediction has been generated by a fairly complex model, what exactly is it that this methodological prescription obliges us to discard? Some part of the model (but which)? The entire model (but what exactly would it mean to discard an 'entire model'?)? The underlying theory? The cosmological perspective? From the vantage point of 35 years of cultivated hindsight, it appears that the prediction of a postwar return to the conditions of the 1930s was so dramatically at variance with 'the facts' that an agonizing reappraisal of Cosmology II might already then have been in order. In fact, however, the agonizing reappraisal of Cosmology I was not even half over yet. Economists were still too busy sifting through the intellectual rubble left over from the old edifice for workable parts that might be worth keeping to even consider turning the wrecker's ball on the structure that was even then a-building. The revision of beliefs made necessary by the forecasting debacle therefore took place almost altogether *within* the New Faith – all the basic outlines of the (income–expenditure) model were retained. The failure of the model to predict with reasonable accuracy was in the event ascribed for the most part to the form of its consumption function. It is an important part of the story that this diagnosis of what ailed the model led, over the next ten years or so, to much valuable work culminating in the 'new theories of the consumption function'.

What really happened during the decade of the Great Depression?[14] There is no more important historical question in macroeconomics than this one. The interpretations of the events of this period continue to this day to shape the entire approach that economists take to the field of macroeconomics – the research methodology that they favor, with respect to both the brand of theory or type of model to be used and the type of statistical tools deemed required for empirical confirmation, and also the 'meaning' they find in the recorded 'facts' about historical episodes subsequent or prior to the 1930s.

In the 35 years since the postwar forecasting debacle, unemployment levels have never again approached those experienced all through the depression decade, either in the United States or in the United Kingdom. The specter of secular stagnation has receded, year by year, from a horrifying immediate prospect into the shadowy realm of the 'merely academic' possibility (or, even, improbability). Was it ever an actual prospect, from the realization of which the system was saved either by action based on foreknowledge or by a lucky concatenation of unforeseen developments? Or was the stagnation hypothesis simply a prophecy generated by a seriously defective economic theory? Most economists have simply been content to let the hypothesis slowly sink from view in the accumulated sediments of their neglect, and it would be risky to infer a professional consensus from their silence. But here is one voice:[15]

> In essence my stagnation thesis contends that the US propensity to save outruns the inducement to invest. Vast governmental outlays, induced partly by three wars, have indeed in large part filled the gap. Still, despite the greatly enlarged role of government, we averaged 4.7 per cent unemployment in 1947–1968 inclusive. No one can claim that the 'self-sustaining economy' has proved its capacity to produce full employment.[15]

A modest dose of historical background may help to lend perspective to Hansen's view. Computing the (unweighted) average unemployment rates in the United States for three other 20th-century periods, and listing also the figure cited by Hansen, we have the following picture:

| | |
|---|---|
| 1900–1913 | 4.2% |
| 1920–1929 | 5.0% |
| 1930–1940 | 17.9% |
| 1947–1968 | 4.7% |

To Hansen, the economic system revealed its true nature in the 1930–40 period. Although the post-World War II unemployment average lies in the same range as the pre-1930 averages, this is not taken as indicating a reversal to the pattern of behavior of the earlier periods (a pattern which, since it antedated the 'vast governmental outlays', is recognized as produced by a once 'self-sustaining economy'). Instead, the growth of the government sector is interpreted as explaining the fact that post-1947 unemployment rates have averaged less than one-third of those observed during the depression decade.

Now, contrast this with the judgment arrived at by Matthews[16] (in 1968) after having addressed the same question to the British 20th-century unemployment experience. He cited these approximate unemployment averages:

| | |
|---|---|
| Before 1914 | 4.5% |
| Between the World Wars | 10.5% |
| Since World War II | 1.8% |

Matthews' discussion of this record leads him to two conclusions: (a) that, at best, only a quite small part of the improvement in the system's employment performance from the interwar to the post-World War II period can be attributed to government fiscal policies; and (b) that there are good demographic and industry-structural reasons to adduce in explanation for the pre-World War I unemployment rates having been more than double the post-World War II rates.

The tentative conclusion of this 1968 study, therefore, was that the improved employment performance of the British economy from World War II to the mid-1960s was due, not to better-informed policies applied to a depression-prone system, but rather to a reversal of the system to its pre-World War I 'form'. Needless to say, the British debate on this issue has flared up again with new intensity in the 1980s.

The contrast between the two views is very sharp. One lesson is also clear – the meaning of 'facts' depends upon the cosmological perspective in which they are perceived. Which cosmology – I or II – do we find puts the most strain on our credulity? Nearly three decades of experience very different from that of the Great Depression has loosened the grip of conviction once exercised over economics by Cosmology II. Should we revert to Cosmology I? The collective memory may grow dim as generations change, but the Great Depression is, once and for all, in the historical record and the macro-economist has to come to terms with it. There are many reasonably respectable schools of thought on matters of scientific method, but one thing none of them will allow – namely 'the exception that proves the rule'.

Actually, of course, if the reader feels any tendency to make up his mind at this point, he simply must resist it (and if it was made up before he began reading this paper, he must unmake it). A certain paucity of empirical information (seven figures, for two different countries, on average annual unemployment rates over periods that may have been arbitrarily chosen) should discourage quick conclusions. Even if it doesn't, consider that even these numbers will mean something very different to someone who believes 9.5 per cent to be a reasonable figure for 'equilibrium unemployment' and to someone who believes that figure should be nearer 5 per cent.

Consider, finally, one more attempt to obtain evidence pertaining directly to the 'global properties' of the economic system. Cosmology I involves the belief that the economy is a self-regulating system. Suppose we add to this the separate further belief that the hypothetical equilibrium activity levels of the system are to be found distinctly nearer to the peaks than to the troughs of historically recorded 'business cycles'. The two beliefs together yield the compound hypothesis that contractions in activity, being departures from the equilibrium neighborhood, ought to be followed by expansions that (when corrected for the secular growth trend) are of approximately the same magnitude. The amplitude of a past recovery, on the other hand, is not expected to bear any systematic relation to the next contraction, the magnitude of which will depend upon the force of the next disturbance that shocks the system away from the equilibrium path. Milton Friedman and Anna Schwartz have tested this hypothesis, using what is known as the 'Moore index of business activity' together with the calendar of past peaks and troughs of the National Bureau of Economic Research (NBER). Their findings:[17]

> [W]hen the amplitude of an expansion is correlated with the amplitude of the succeeding contraction, the resulting correlation is negligible ... [On the other hand, a] large contraction in output tends to be followed on the average by a large business expansion: a mild contraction, by a mild expansion.

## CONCLUSION

We have juxtaposed the mutually opposed beliefs that markets will and markets won't work to coordinate activities in economic systems. Each has been made the basis for elaborate attempts to organize the data of economic experience into an 'understandable' pattern that would be an effective guide to legislation and government policy. Neither doctrine, in my opinion, is safe – either one is capable of betraying the believer in a most costly manner. There is then little point in debating which of the two will most regularly send you on costly excursions down the garden path. We have to get away from blanket assertions or denials of faith in the efficacy of market mechanisms as alternative foundations for macrotheory. The only way to remove the matter from this level of 'unreasoned beliefs' – and thus to escape what has become an ideological battle – is to buckle down to the business of studying what the market system (unaided) will do and will fail to do for you.

## NOTES

1. Among the critics, Gunnar Myrdal (1958) has been the most influential. His *Value in Social Theory* restates the case first made by Myrdal in Swedish some 25 years earlier.
2. The fairly concerted drive for greater precision – for 'quantification' as the term went – might be dated back to the founding of the Econometric Society, forty years ago. The thrust went in two directions in the ensuing development of mathematical economics and econometrics. If 'quantification' so far has not paid off quite as handsomely as its pioneers hoped, our uncertainty principle is part and parcel of the controversies in macroeconomics.
3. In an earlier paper, I used the term 'presuppositions' for these beliefs. See Leijonhufvud (1976), especially section I: 3.
4. Robinson (1963), p. 79.
5. Examples from economics of the problem stated here will follow later. Meanwhile, consider the illustration used by Hansen (1958, Chapter 1). Hansen has us imagining Kepler and Tycho Brahe on a hill at dawn. Kepler entertains a heliocentric cosmology,

Brahe still a geocentric. Their sense impressions are the same – but what 'facts' do they observe? Brahe sees the sun rise (as the English language insists to this day) on its way around the stationary earth; Kepler sees the horizon dip down and away from the fixed star as the earth spins.

6. An economy is said to be in general equilibrium when quantities demanded and quantities supplied are equal for each and every good in the system. Note that the equilibrium level of employment, not 'full employment', is used as the reference point. If some percentage of unemployed, say 4 per cent, is arbitrarily specified as representing 'full' employment, equilibrium employment may alternately exceed and fall short of 'full' employment over time.

7. Lekachman (1966), p. 90. The frame for this quote as well as the other statements in the text may be taken to be the simple '45-degree' aggregate demand diagram familiar from introductory economics courses.

8. Cybernetics is the name given by Norbert Wiener to the theoretical study of the general properties of such systems, independent of the field in which they appear. For an introduction see, for example, Wiener (1954). For the more ambitious: Ashby (1956).

9. There are 'ceilings' and 'floors' to the fluctuations, in the terminology of Sir John Hicks (1950).

10. Whether it works *to coordinate economic activities* is, of course the issue. Whether the market system brings about *efficient* states, or whether it produces *fair* and *just* states, is not at issue here. With people who can only perceive these statements in ideological terms, it is hopeless even to attempt to keep efficiency and justice out of the discussion. But, although ideologies were the starting point, at this point we are concerned with the above propositions interpreted, not as normative, but as positive, beliefs.

   A note in passing to those with an avid interest in the wider issues: in reading the literature which argues the pros and cons of market solutions to a variety of social problems, there is some advantage in sorting out the arguments in terms of their immediate pertinence to: (a) efficient allocation, (b) management of conflict, or (c) coordination. Pro-market writers tend to stress arguments pertaining to (c) and (b), arguing, on the one hand, that market coordination functions better than coordination by planning, and on the other, that intragroup strife will be less if resources are allocated through markets than if scarce resources have to be rationed according to 'political' criteria. Anti-market writers tend to stress arguments pertaining to (a), arguing the several ways in which the real world fails to conform to the assumptions of the 'perfectly' general equilibrium model of modern welfare economics and the consequent departures from Pareto-optimal resource allocation. Naturally, there is no hope whatsoever of progressing toward a resolution of this decades-long debate as long as people insist on talking about different issues. But then, can we be sure that people really want to have ideological questions settled?

11. For a largely parallel discussion, see Leijonhufvud (1976).

12. From this perspective, any attempt to construct systematic 'microfoundations of macrotheory' must be seen as a simply ridiculous quest. (The reader will understand that this refers to the situation before New Classical Economics put macroeconomics back in a Cosmology I context.)

13. See Johnson (1971) for a discussion critical of the economics training given to the students from low-income countries in the post-World War II period.

14. The debate has recently flared up again. See especially Brunner (1981).

15. Hansen (1971), p. 276. Alvin H. Hansen is an important figure in the history of American economic thought for at least two reasons: first, as the main advocate of the stagnation thesis – no other writer could possibly refer to it as 'my thesis'; and second, as a major contributor to, and probably the main popularizer of, the brand of American Keynesianism that gradually became standard textbook doctrine in macroeconomics (a doctrine involving substantive modifications of Keynes's own theory).

   I maintained previously that students who see no professional use for macroeconomic analysis in their future also need to make up their minds on what I have called the 'cosmological' issues about the nature of the economic system. Hansen's quoted statement brings up another illustration. Note his reference to war-time expenditures and his inference that, in their absence, the system's performance would have been considerably worse than that indicated by the 4.7 per cent average unemployment figure. Some readers may recall the argument, frequently seen and heard in the early days of opposition to the Vietnam war (before the inflation of the late 1960s became serious), that the United States derived an economic benefit from the war in decreased unemployment at home. To someone with Cosmology II beliefs, this strand of 'economic imperialism' doctrine is plausible enough to merit consideration. To someone with Cosmology I beliefs, wars are unambiguously resource consuming rather than employment creating.

During the decade following Hansen's postscript, the US propensity to save fell so low that domestic savings could no longer finance both investment and governmental deficits – but unemployment rose to a decade average of over 6 per cent.

16. Matthews (1968). It is worth noting that Matthews is best known in the United States for his book *The Business Cycle* (1959) – a work largely devoted to the exposition of models of the Cosmology III variety.

17. Friedman (1964), pp. 14 ff.

# 19. Time in theory and history, or why I am not a historian

Addressing an audience of historians is for me a daunting task. I would have become a historian myself, had I dared. Instead, I chose the simplest of the social sciences from whence I can from time to time take a look at the activities of historians from a relatively short, yet safe, distance. I do so always with both admiration and envy. Envy, because history often seems so much more fun than economics; admiration, because it seems so forbiddingly difficult.

Time, I take it, is an essential element in History. This simple observation is quite enough to give the economic theorist pause – he knows there is trouble ahead if he ventures into such territory.

All economists have heard Joan Robinson quoted to the effect that 'time is a device to prevent everything from happening at once'. (To which adage someone else has added the observation that 'space is a device to prevent everything from happening in Cambridge' … and if it did, one can only imagine what that would do to the lawns at the Backs!) But economic theorists have terrible trouble trying to prevent everything from happening at once in their models. They have found no easy way to make use of Joan Robinson's device.

Economists tend to believe that in order to make sensible and informative statements you have to have a model. Most of them are also quite attached to the belief that models should be built on optimizing behavioral foundations. Now, it is not at all easy to model a world that is, as Sir John Hicks likes to say, 'in time', but if you insist on describing all behavior as optimizing, the task becomes just about impossible.

For a theory to be 'in time' in the Hicksian sense, its future has to become the present and the present turn into the past. For agents immersed in the flow of time, the unknowable becomes the conceivable and then the possible; the possible, drawing nearer, becomes the probable and then experienced and known; the experienced becomes a matter of record … and eventually, at least if historians are in short supply, most of it becomes a matter of lost records.

Now, optimizing models will deal easily with the probable and the known, but will not accommodate the merely possible or conceivable, much less the inconceivable that is nonetheless going to happen. But in model-worlds where everything is known either for certain or as a certain probability, agents will make all their allocation and trading decisions at the outset. Nothing prevents 'everything from happening at once'. Time has escaped. And history, then, has no place.

I would like to bring to your attention a brave but neglected attack on this formidable problem. The author is Raymond Guarnieri (1973). Guarnieri actually began by considering the problem of predicting the future, and thus backed into the problem of the historical past rather inadvertently – which is probably the safest way to approach it.

Guarnieri's point of departure was the somewhat trite observation that, for some centuries now, economists have done rather badly at prediction. He conjectured, as I'm sure we all would, that the trouble must be that divination of the future had not been put on a completely rigorous foundation. It was not immediately obvious, however, how the requisite rigor was to be supplied and Guarnieri was apparently stuck at this point for some time. Then, in his own words:

> The light dawned on me some days later when I was calling my broker to place an order to buy short. Of course, thought I, the exact counterpart of the futures market with perfect certainty is the pasts market. Accordingly, if we could rigorously prove existence, uniqueness, and stability of pasts, we should obviously have come a long way toward prediction – albeit in the wrong direction. But this could be corrected – or so I was assured by an excellent second-rate mathematical economist – by appropriate changes in sign.

The *existence* of the past posed no problems for Guarnieri. Given a number of quite conventional assumptions, he found that he could prove existence by a straightforward application of 'Krakatoa's pointless theorem', for which he credits the French colonial mathematician Pacifique Krakatoa, whose dates are given as 1947–1883. There remain some doubts in my mind, however, how robust this result is.

The existence of the past is, in fact, a difficult problem and one that historians, in particular, do not seem to have taken seriously enough. We find the fundamental problem, perhaps in its original form, in the medieval scholastic dispute over Adam's navel. The issue, as you will recall, was whether Adam should be depicted with or without a navel. One theological faction maintained that one should not attribute meaningless or superfluous actions to the Lord; a navel would be superfluous on Adam; ergo, Adam had no navel. The opposed faction argued that Man is made in God's image; men have navels; ergo, the Lord and Adam have navels.

Now, clearly, the second faction had the stronger argument. In any case, it had the winning argument – as a check of a few churches and museums will quickly prove. So, it is agreed that Adam had a navel. The problem with that conclusion, however, is that it admits into the world strong and convincing *evidence of a past that never was* – in this case, evidence that would seem to indicate that Adam had a mother.

It may be that few modern historians have taken the problem of Adam's navel seriously, since the contemporary theory of evolution has no place for Adam himself. But to dismiss it in this way is to miss the more general version of the argument which is credited to Phillip Gosse. Gosse defended the creationist position against the use by evolutionists of geological evidence that seemed to show that the Earth was older than indicated in the Bible. He argued that when the Earth was created it was created with the geological strata laid down as we see them today – and containing, from the outset, the bones from extinct species and so on. It is an incontrovertible argument and you will appreciate at once how it puts the *existence* of the past in doubt. It is, after all, quite conceivable – isn't it? – that we were all created an instant ago, complete with memories of a nonexistent past, including the memory of the first half of this talk![1]

Guarnieri's use of the Krakatoa Pointless Theorem, therefore, will hardly put all doubts to rest on the existence issue. When it came to uniqueness, he also took a much different tack, seeking to ascertain the uniqueness of the past inductively by comparing commodity-market quotations in old newspapers. He satisfied himself in this manner that the past market was indeed unique up to the occasional misprint. The Guarnieri approach to the future is seen, somewhat surprisingly, to be philosophically grounded in the Rankean approach to the past – *mutatis mutandis*.

The stability of the past and what it may – or may not – imply about the stability of the future turns out to be the perhaps most difficult problem in this general area and it gave rise to some discussion already before the publication of Guarnieri's paper. (I think that, after the lapse now of more than ten years, I may reveal that I was the anonymous reviewer who recommended publication of the paper to the then editor of the then *Western Economic Journal*, Robert Clower. And I still think that Guarnieri's contribution certainly deserves being neglected in *Economic Inquiry*, as it is called today, rather than in some less prominent journal.)

In the original version of Guarnieri's manuscript, he claimed to have demonstrated the stability of pasts. He concluded that the future, therefore, would be stable too. This, I thought, was an error:[2] if the past could be shown to be stable as time goes to minus infinity, then one must conclude that the future is *unstable*. Our disagreement on this point gave rise to a voluminous correspondence back and forth between us. Unfortunately, time will not allow me to go into all the technical details.

Consider an Einsteinian universe. Next, abstract from the three Newtonian dimensions. (This kind of elegant analytical simplification may give pause to physicists, but economics training, which accustoms you to turning *n* goods into one GNP, imparts an intellectual daring sometimes lacking in other fields.) Einstein minus Newton leaves us with one dimension, a time line. Now, imagine a scientific observer in this universe. We position him at $t = 0$, facing the past and with his back to the future. His task is to draw inferences about what is going on behind his back from what he can observe in front of him.

Such an observer has to choose in which sequence to make his observations. He may deal with time retroactively, starting with states of the world farthest away from himself and arriving eventually to what is right under his nose. Or he may adopt a retrospective procedure, taking near observations first and proceeding toward minus infinity. The retroactive treatment of time is that commonly used by historians. Economists may, therefore, suspect it to be suboptimal. And, indeed, if one assumes a quadratic utility function attaching greater value to information about 'near' than about 'distant' states – as seems only sensible – one will reject the retroactive in favor of the retrospective approach.

The question of stability is a question about whether such sequences of observations show convergence or not. (The notion of convergence may at first seem an intuitively difficult one in the single-dimensional universe of our conceptual experiment. The best way to think about it is to suppose that past states of the world are color-coded and that we know, for instance, the sequence green–blue–red to be convergent whereas red–blue–green is divergent.) My position, in brief, was and remains that rational observers must be assumed to adopt the retrospective mode; if retrospective sequences are seen to converge, the rational inference to be drawn is that *the future is surely exploding behind our backs!*

At this point Guarnieri tentatively advanced the notion that, perhaps, one should think of the observer as facing forward after all and as observing the past through a rearview mirror. I forbear on this occasion to analyse this theory in detail. Suffice it to say that, while the use of mirrors may seem convenient in the single-dimensional case, it produces horrendous problems as soon as we start to restore dimensions by disaggregation. The use of mirrors necessitates a clear definition of the relevant axis of symmetry. Passing over the complications of general equilibrium, consider just the simplest case of an isolated market. Which of the two mirror models on p. 336 is the relevant one?

This, on the whole, is where the matter still stands today. It should be clear to everybody that we have much work to do before history can be put on a sound theoretical foundation. We ought then to heed the poet's admonition: *Dum loquimur fugerit invida eatas* – 'Who knows, alas!, whether it is coming or going?'

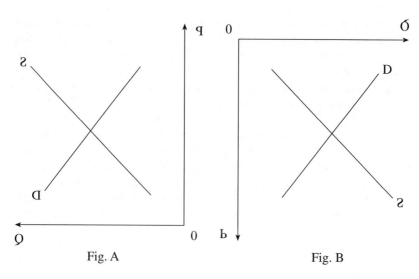

Fig. A                          Fig. B

*Figure 19.1*

## NOTES

1. The Gosse impossibility theorem, according to which there can be no empirical proof of the existence of pasts, and its antecedents are lucidly discussed in Gardner (1957), pp. 124–6.
2. In correspondence, I went so far as to call it the sort of error that could do 'irrevocable damage' to one's reputation. That, of course, was my error. It simply showed that I had not yet grasped the power of Guarnieri's sign-reversal technique.

# Bibliography

Adrogue, M. (1985), *La reforma monetaria: el Austral*, Buenos Aires: Plus Ultra.

Alchian, Armen and Harold Demsetz (1972), 'Production, Information Costs, and Economic Organization', *American Economic Review*, **62**(5), pp. 777–95.

Alterini, A. (1985), 'Los honorarios de abogados y el regimen del Austral', *La Ley*, Buenos Aires.

Arida, Persio and Lara Resende (1985), 'Inertial Inflation and Monetary Reform: Brazil', in J. Williamson (ed.), *Inflation and Indexation: Argentina, Brazil and Israel*, Washington, D.C., Cambridge, Massachusetts, London: MIT Press.

Arrow, Kenneth (1979), 'The Division of Labor in the Economy, the Polity, and Society', in Gerald P. O'Driscoll, Jr. (ed.), *Adam Smith and Modern Political Economy*, Ames, Iowa: Iowa State University Press, pp. 153–64.

Ashby, W.R. (1956), *An Introduction to Cybernetics*, London: Chapman & Hall.

Babbage, Charles (1833), *On the Economy of Machinery and Manufactures*, London: Charles Knight (3rd edition).

Bailey, M.J. (1956), 'The Welfare Cost of Inflationary Finance', *Journal of Political Economy*, **64**(2), pp. 93–110.

Bamford, J. (1987), 'The Family, Agriculture, and the Community', in R. Goffee and R. Scase (eds), *Entrepreneurship in Europe: The Social Processes*, London: Croom Helm, pp. 37–45.

Barro, Robert J. (1974), 'Are Government Bonds Net Wealth?', *Journal of Political Economy*, **82**(6), pp. 1095–117.

Barro, Robert J. (1976), 'Rational Expectations and the Role of Monetary Policy', *Journal of Monetary Economics,* **2**(1), pp. 1–32.

Barro, Robert J. (1980), 'A Capital Market in an Equilibrium Business Cycle Model', *Econometrica*, **48**(6), pp. 1393–417.

Barro, Robert J. (1986), 'Rules versus Discretion', in C.D. Campbell and W.R. Douglas (eds), *Alternative Monetary Regimes*, Baltimore, M.D.: John Hopkins University Press, pp. 16–30.

Barro, Robert J. and S. Fisher (1976), 'Recent Developments in Monetary Theory', *Journal of Monetary Economics*, **2**, pp. 133–67.

Barro, Robert J. and David B. Gordon (1983a), 'Rules, Discretion and Reputation in a Model of Monetary Policy', *Journal of Monetary Economics*,
**12**(1), pp. 101–21.

Barro, Robert J. and David B. Gordon (1983b), 'A Positive Theory of Monetary Policy in a Natural Rate Model', *Journal of Political Economy*, **91**(4),
pp. 589–610.

Barro, Robert J. and Hershel I. Grossman (1971), 'A General Disequilibrium
Model of Income and Employment', *American Economic Review*, **56**(1),
pp. 82–93.

Benassy, Jean-Pascal (1975), 'Neo-Keynesian Disequilibrium Theory in a
Monetary Economy', *Review of Economic Studies*, **57**(4), pp. 503–24.

Bewley, Truman (1989), 'Market Innovations and Enterpreneurship: A
Knightian View', *Cowles Foundation Discussion Paper No. 905*, New
Haven, Conn.: Yale University.

Black, Fisher (1970), 'Banking and Interest Rates in a World without Money:
The Effects of Uncontrolled Banking', *Journal of Bank Research,* 2 January, 20 August.

Blejer, M. and L. Leiderman (1980), 'On the Real Effects of Inflation and
Relative Price Variability: Some Empirical Evidence', *Review of Economics and Statistics*, **69,** pp. 539–44.

Bresciani-Turroni, C. (1937), *The Economics of Inflation*, London: Barnes
and Noble.

Brunner, Karl (1970), 'The "Monetarist Revolution" in Monetary Theory',
*Weltwirtschaftliches Archiv*, **105**(1), pp. 1–31.

Brunner, Karl (1971), 'A Survey of Selected Issues in Monetary Theory',
*Schweizerische Zeitschrift für Volkswirtschaft und Statistik*, **107**(1), pp. 1–
146.

Brunner, Karl (ed.) (1981), *The Great Depression Revisited*, Boston: Kluwer-
Nijhoff.

Buttrick, John (1952), 'The Inside Contracting System', *Journal of Economic
History,* **12**(3), pp. 205–21.

Cagan, Philip (1956), 'The Monetary Dynamics of Hyperinflation', in M.
Friedman (ed.), *Studies in the Quantity Theory of Money*, University of
Chicago Press, pp. 25–117.

Cagan, Philip (1982), 'A Review of the Report of the Gold Commission and
Some Thoughts on Convertible Monetary Systems', Columbia University,
mimeo.

Cardoso, E. and Rudiger Dornbusch (1987), 'Brazil's Tropical Plan', *American Economic Review,* **77,** May.

Chipman, J.S. (1965), 'A Survey of the Theory of International Trade: Part 2,
The Neoclassical Theory', *Econometrica,* **33**(4), pp. 685–760.

Chipman, J.S. (1970), 'External Economies of Scale and Competitive Equilibrium', *Quarterly Journal of Economics,* August, **84**, pp. 347–85.

Clower, Robert W. (1954), 'An Investigation into the Dynamics of Investment', *American Economic Review,* **44**, pp. 64–81.

Clower, Robert W. (1965), 'The Keynesian Counter-Revolution: A Theoretical Appraisal', in F.H. Hahn and F.P.R. Brechling (eds), *The Theory of Interest Rates*, London: Macmillan.

Clower, Robert W. (1967), 'A Reconsideration of the Microfoundations of Monetary Theory', *Western Economic Journal*, **6**, pp. 1–8.

Clower, Robert W. (1975), 'Reflections on the Keynesian Perplex', *Zeitschrift für Nationalökonomie,* **35**, pp. 1–24.

Clower, Robert W. and Axel Leijonhufvud (1973), 'Say's Principle: What It Means and Doesn't Mean', *Intermountain Economic Review*, **4**(2), pp. 1–16 (reprinted in Leijonhufvud 1981a).

Clower, Robert W. and Axel Leijonhuvud (1975), 'The Coordination of Economic Activities: A Keynesian Perspective', *American Economic Review,* **65**(2), pp. 182–8.

Coddington, Alan (1976), 'Keynesian Economics: The Search for First Principles', *Journal of Economic Literature*, **14**(2), pp. 1258–73, reprinted in idem., *Keynesian Economics: The Search for First Principles*, London: Allen & Unwin, 1983.

Coddington, Alan (1983), *Keynesian Economics: The Search for First Principles*, London: Allen & Unwin.

Crabbe, Leland (1988), 'Monetary Regimes, Unit Roots and Variance Bounds on Long-term Bonds', in Leland Crabbe, *Three Empirical Essays on Interest Rates and Inflation under Alternative Monetary Regimes*, UCLA doctoral dissertation.

Cukierman, A. (1979), 'The Relationship Between Relative Prices and the General Price Level: A Suggested Interpretation', *American Economic Review*, **69**, pp. 444–7.

Cukierman, A. and P. Wachtel (1979), 'Differential Inflationary Expectations and the Variability of the Rate of Inflation: Some Theory and Empirical Evidence,' *American Economic Review,* **69**, pp. 595–609.

Dahlman, Carl J. (1980), *The Open Field System and Beyond*, New York: Cambridge University Press.

Dahmen, Erik (1971), *Entrepreneurial Activity and the Development of Swedish Industry, 1919–1939*, Homewood, Ill.: Richard D. Irwin.

Darby, Michael (1976), *Macroeconomics*, New York: McGraw-Hill.

Darby, Michael and J.R. Lothian *et al.* (1983), *The International Transmission of Inflation*, Chicago: Chicago University Press for NBER.

Eden, B. (1979), 'The Nominal System: Linkage to the Quantity of Money or to Nominal Income', *Revue Economique*, **30**(1), pp. 121–43.

Eilbaum, R. (1985), 'Reforma monetaria y oblicaciones de afar sumas de dinero', *La Ley,* **148**, Buenos Aires.

Fama, Eugene G. (1980), 'Banking in the Theory of Finance', *Journal of Monetary Economics*, **6**(1), pp. 39–57.

Farmer, Roger E.A. and Michael Woodford (1984), 'Self-fulfilling Prophecies and the Business Cycle', *CARESS Working* Paper, Philadelphia: University of Pennsylvania, April.

Fellner, William (1979), 'American Household Wealth in an Inflationary Period', *Contemporary Economic Problems 1979*, Washington, D.C.: American Enterprise Institute.

Fischer, Stanley (1985), 'Inflation and Indexation: Israel', in J. Williamson (ed.), *Inflation and Indexation: Argentina, Brazil and Israel*, Washington, D.C., Cambridge, Mass., London: MIT Press.

Fitoussi, Jean Paul (ed.) (1983), *Modern Macroeconomic Theory*, Oxford: Blackwell.

Fremling, G.M. (1982), 'A Stock Equilibrium Model of the Gold Standard', UCLA, mimeo.

Frenkel, Roberto (1984), 'Salarios industriales e inflacion: el periodo 1976–82', *Desarrollo Economico*, **24**(95), pp. 387–414.

Friedman, Milton (1956), 'The Quantity Theory of Money: A Restatement', in M. Friedman (ed.), *Studies in the Quantity Theory of Money*, Chicago: University of Chicago Press.

Friedman, Milton (1964), 'The Monetary Studies of the National Bureau', *NBER 44th Annual Report*, New York: NBER.

Friedman, Milton (1968), 'The Role of Monetary Policy', *American Economic Review*, **58**, pp. 1–17.

Friedman, Milton (1976) 'Comment', in Jerome L. Stein (ed.), *Monetarism*, Amsterdam: North Holland.

Friedman, Milton (1977), 'Inflation and Unemployment', *Journal of Political Economy*, **85**, pp. 451–72.

Friedman, Milton and Anna J. Schwartz (1963a), *A Monetary History of the United States, 1867–1960*, Princeton: Princeton University Press..

Friedman, Milton and Anna J. Schwartz (1963b) 'Money and Business Cycles', *Review of Economics and Statistics*, **45** (supplement), pp. 32–64.

Frydman, Roman and Edmund S. Phelps (eds) (1983), *Individual Forecasting and Aggregate Outcomes: 'Rational Expectations' Examined*, New York: Cambridge University Press.

Frydman, Roman and Andrzej Rapaczynski (1991a), 'Evolution and Design in the East European Transition', *Rivista di economia politica*, **81**, pp. 63–103.

Frydman, Roman and Andrzej Rapaczynski (1991b), 'Markets and Institutions in Large-scale Privatization: An Approach to Economic and Social

Transformation in Eastern Europe', in Vittorio Corbo et al. (eds), *Reforming Central and East European Economies*, Washington D.C.: World Bank, pp. 253–74.

Frydman, Roman and Andrzej Rapaczynski (1991c), 'Privatisation and Corporate Governance: Can a Market Economy Be Designed?', in G. Winckler (ed.), *Central and Eastern Europe: Roads to Growth*, Washington D.C.: International Monetary Fund and Vienna: Austrian National Bank, pp. 255–85.

Gardner, Martin (1957), *Fads and Fallacies in the Name of Science*, New York: Dover Publications.

Georgescu-Roegen, Nicholas (1972), 'Process Analysis and the Neoclassical Theory of Production', *American Journal of Agricultural Economics,* **54**(2), pp. 279–94.

Georgescu-Roegen, Nicholas (1976), *Energy and Economic Myths*, New York: Pergamon Press.

Gerchunoff, P. and M. Bozalla (1987), 'Posibilidades y limites de un programa de estabilizacion heterodoxo: el caso argentino', Buenos Aires: Instituto Torcuato Di Tella, mimeo.

Gibson, William E. (1970a), 'Interest Rates and Monetary Policy', *Journal of Political Economy*, **78**(3), pp. 431–55.

Gibson, William E. (1970b), 'The Lag in Effect of Monetary Policy on Income and Interest Rates', *Quarterly Journal of Economics*, **84**(2), pp. 288–300.

Gioja, Melchiorre (1815), *Nuovo prospetto delle scienze economiche*, Milan: G. Pirotta.

Glasner, David (1985), 'A Reinterpretation of Classical Monetary Theory', *Southern Economic Journal,* **52**(1), pp. 46–67.

Goldin, Claudia and Kenneth Sokoloff (1984), 'Women, Children and Industrialization in the Early Republic: Evidence from the Manufacturing Censuses', *Journal of Economic History*, **42**(4), pp. 741–74.

Goodwin, Richard M. (1951), 'Iteration, Automatic Computers, and Economic Dynamics', *Metroeconomica*, **3**(1), pp. 1–7.

Gordon, Robert J. (ed.) (1974), *Milton Friedman's Monetary Framework: A Debate with His Critics*, Chicago: Chicago University Press.

Gordon, Robert J. (1981), 'Output Fluctuations and Gradual Price Adjustment', *Journal of Economic Literature*, **19**(2), pp. 493–530.

Gramley, Lyle E. and Samuel B. Chase (1965), 'Time Deposits in Monetary Analysis', *Federal Reserve Bulletin*, **51**, pp. 1380–406.

Grandmont, Jean Michael (1977), 'Temporary General Equilibrium Theory', *Econometrica*, **45**(3), pp. 535–72.

Grossman, Herschel I. (1972), 'Was Keynes a "Keynesian"? A Review Article', *Journal of Economic Literature,* **10**(1), pp. 26–30, reprinted in J.C.

Wood (ed.) (1983), *John Maynard Keynes: Critical Assessments, Volume III*, London: Croom Helm, 1983.

Guarnieri, Raymond L. (1973), 'A Suggestion for Rigorizing the Theory of Prediction', *Western Economic Journal*, **11**(2), pp. 147–9.

Haberler, Gottfried (1977), 'Stagflation: An Analysis of the Causes and Cures', in B. Balassa and R. Nelson (eds), *Economic Progress, Private Values and Public Policy: Essays in Honor of William Fellner*, Amsterdam: North Holland.

Hahn, Frank H. (1973), *On the Notion of Equilibrium in Economics*, Cambridge: Cambridge University Press.

Hahn, Frank H. (1983), *Money and Inflation*, Cambridge, Mass.: MIT Press.

Haltiwanger, John and Michael Waldman (1985), 'Rational Expectations and the Limits of Rationality: An Analysis of Heterogeneity', *American Economic Review*, **75**, pp. 326–40.

Haltiwanger, John and Michael Waldman (1989), 'Limited Rationality Synergism: The Implications for Macroeconomics', *Quarterly Journal of Economics*, **104**, pp. 463–83.

Hansen, Alvin H. (1971), 'Economic Progress and Declining Population Growth', M.G. Mueller (ed.), *Readings in Macroeconomics*, 2nd edition, New York: Holt, Rinehart & Winston (first published in 1939).

Hansen, Gary D. (1985), 'Indivisible Labor and the Business Cycle', *Journal of Monetary Economics*, **16**(3), pp. 309–27.

Hansen, N.R. (1958), *Patterns of Discovery*, Cambridge: Cambridge University Press.

Hart , A.G. (1942), 'Risk, Uncertainty and the Unprofitability of Compounding Probabilities', in Oscar Lange (ed.), *Studies in Mathematical Economics and Econometrics*, Chicago: Chicago University Press, reprinted in W. Fellner and B.F. Haley (eds) (1951), *Readings in the Theory of Income Distribution*, Philadelphia: Blakistone.

Hart, Oliver (1987), 'Incomplete Contracts', in John Eatwell, Murry Milford and Peter Newman (eds), *The New Palgrave,* London: Macmillan.

Hayek, F.A. von (1928), 'Das intertemporale Gleichgewichtssystem der Preise und die Bewegungen des "Geldwerts"', *Weltwirtschaftliches Archiv*, **64**, pp. 33–76.

Hayek, F.A. von (ed.) (1933), *Beiträge zur Geldtheorie*, Wien: Springer Verlag.

Heiner, Ronald A. (1983), 'The Origin of Predictable Behavior', *American Economic Review,* **73**, pp. 560–95.

Heiner, Ronald A. (1986), 'Uncertainty, Signal-Detection Experiments and Modeling Behavior', in Richard N. Langlois (ed.), *Economics as a Process: Essays in the New Institutional Economics*, New York: Cambridge University Press, pp. 59–115.

Helpman, Elhanan (1984), 'Increasing Returns, Imperfect Markets, and Trade Theory', in R.W. Jones and P.B. Kenen (eds), *Handbook of International Economics,* Amsterdam: North Holland.

Helpman, E. and P.R. Krugman (1985), *Market Structure and Foreign Trade,* Cambridge: MIT Press.

Heymann, Daniel (1986), *Tres ensayos sobre inflacion y politicas de establizacion,* Santiago de Chile: CEPAL.

Heymann, Daniel (1987), 'The Austral Plan', *American Economic Review,* **77**(2), pp. 284–7.

Heymann, Daniel and Axel Leijonhufvud (1995), *High Inflation,* Oxford: Oxford University Press.

Hicks, John R. (1933), 'Gleichgewicht und Konjunktur', *Zeitschrift für Nationalökonomie,* reprinted as 'Equilibrium and the Cycle' in J.R. Hicks (1982).

Hicks, John R. (1935), 'A Suggestion for Simplifying the Theory of Money', *Economica,* **2**, pp. 1–19.

Hicks, John R. (1936), 'Mr Keynes's Theory of Employment', *Economic Journal,* **46**, pp. 238–53.

Hicks, John R. (1937), 'Mr Keynes and the Classics: A Suggested Interpretation', *Econometrica,* **5**, pp. 147–59, reprinted in Hicks (1982).

Hicks, John R. (1939), *Value and Capital,* Oxford: Oxford University Press.

Hicks, John R. (1950), *A Contribution to the Theory of the Trade Cycle,* Oxford: Clarendon Press.

Hicks, John R. (1956), 'Methods of Dynamic Analysis', in Economisk Tidskrift (ed.), *25 Economic Essays in Honour of Erik Lindahl,* Stockholm: Svenska Tryckeri AB.

Hicks, John R. (1957), 'A Rehabilitation of "Classical" Economics?', *Economic Journal,* **67**, pp. 278–89.

Hicks, John R. (1963), *Theory of Wages,* 2nd edition, London: Macmillan.

Hicks, John R. (1965), *Capital and Growth,* Oxford: Oxford University Press.

Hicks, John R. (1967a), *Critical Essays in Monetary Theory,* Oxford: Oxford University Press.

Hicks, John R. (1967b), 'Monetary Theory and History – An Attempt at Perspective', in John R. Hicks, *Critical Essays in Monetary Theory,* Oxford: Oxford University Press.

Hicks, John R. (1973), *Capital and Time: A Neo-Austrian Theory,* Oxford: Clarendon Press.

Hicks, John R. (1974), *The Crisis in Keynesian Economics,* Oxford: Blackwell.

Hicks, John R. (1977), *Economic Perspectives: Further Essays on Money and Growth,* Oxford: Oxford University Press.

Hicks, John R. (1979a), *Causality in Economics,* Oxford: Blackwell.

Hicks, John R. (1979b) 'The Formation of an Economist', *Banca Nazionale del Lavoro Quarterly Review*, September, pp. 195–204.

Hicks, John R. (1979c), 'On Coddington's Interpretation: A Reply', *Journal of Economic Literature*, **17**, pp. 989–95.

Hicks, John R. (1981), *Wealth and Welfare: Collected Essays on Economic Theory I*, Oxford: Blackwell.

Hicks, John R. (1982), *Money, Interest and Wages: Collected Essays on Economic Theory II*, Oxford: Blackwell.

Hicks, John R. (1983a), *Classics and Moderns: Collected Essays on Economic Theory III*, Oxford: Blackwell.

Hicks, John. R. (1983b), 'IS–LM: An Explanation', in Jean Paul Fitoussi (ed.), *Modern Macroeconomic Theory*, Oxford: Blackwell, pp. 49–63.

Hicks, John R. and R.G.D. Allen (1934), 'A Reconsideration of the Theory of Value: Parts I and II', *Economica N.S.*, **1**, pp. 52–76, 196–219.

Ippolito, Richard S. (1977), 'The Division of Labor in the Firm', *Economic Inquiry*, **15**(4), pp. 462–92.

Jaffee, Dwight and E. Kleiman (1977), 'The Welfare Implications of Uneven Inflation', in E. Lundberg (ed.), *Inflation Theory and Anti-inflation Policy*, London: Macmillan.

Johnson, H.G. (1971), 'A Word to the Third World', *Encounter*, **37**(4), pp. 3–10.

Joint Economic Committee (1981), *Expectations and the Economy*, Washington, D.C.: U.S. Government Printing Office.

Jonung, Lars (1981), 'Perceived and Expected Rates of Inflation in Sweden', *American Economic Review*, **71**(5), pp. 961–8.

Kaldor, Nicholas (1982), *The Scourge of Monetarism*, Oxford: Oxford University Press.

Keynes, J. Maynard (1936), *The General Theory of Employment, Interest and Money*, London: Macmillan.

Keynes, J. Maynard (1971a), *Collected Writings IV: A Tract on Monetary Reform*, Cambridge: Macmillan.

Keynes, J. Maynard (1971b), *Collected Writings V–VI: A Treatise on Money*, Cambridge: Macmillan.

Keynes, J. Maynard (1972), *Collected Writings IX: Essays in Persuasion*, Cambridge: Macmillan

Keynes, J. Maynard (1979), *Collected Writings XXIX: The General Theory and After, A Supplement*, Cambridge: Macmillan.

Klein, Benjamin (1975), 'Our New Monetary Standard: The New Measurement and Effects of Price Uncertainty 1880–1973', *Economic Inquiry*, **13**(4), pp. 461–84.

Klein, Benjamin (1976), 'The Social Costs of the Recent Inflation: The

Mirage of Steady "Anticipated" Inflation', *Carnegie–Rochester Conference Series, Volume III*, Amsterdam: North Holland.

Klein, Benjamin (1977), 'The Demand for Quality-Adjusted Cash Balances: Price Uncertainty in the U.S. Demand for Money Function', *Journal of Political Economy*, **85**, pp. 691–716.

Klein, Benjamin (1978), 'Competing Monies, European Monetary Union and the Dollar', in Michele Fratianni and Theo Peeters (eds), *One Money for Europe*, London: Macmillan.

Klein, Benjamin and Keith B. Leffler (1981), 'The Role of Market Forces in Assuring Contractual Performance', *Journal of Political Economy,* **89**(4), pp. 615–41.

Klein, Benjamin, Robert G. Crawford and Armen Alchian (1978), 'Vertical Integration, Appropriable Rents, and the Competitive Contracting Process', *Journal of Law and Economics,* **21**(2), pp. 297–326.

Kornai, Janós (1980), *Economics of Shortage*, Amsterdam: North-Holland.

Kornai, Janós (1986), 'The Soft Budget Constraint', *Kyklos*, **39**, pp. 3–30 (first published in 1980).

Koyck, L.M. (1954), *Distributed Lags and Investment Analysis*, Amsterdam: North Holland.

Kydland, Finn and Edward C. Prescott (1982), 'Time to Build and Aggregate Fluctuations', *Econometrica*, **50**(6), pp. 1345–70.

Laidler, David (1981), 'Monetarism: An Interpretation and an Assessment', *Economic Journal,* **91**(361), pp. 1–28.

Laidler, David (1983), 'Did Macroeconomics Need the Rational Expectations Revolution?', in G. Mason (ed.), *Macroeconomics: Theory, Policy and Evidence,* Winnipeg: Institute for Economic Research, University of Manitoba, reprinted in David Laidler (1997), *Money and Macroeconomics, The Selected Essays of David Laidler*, Cheltenham, UK: Edward Elgar, pp. 215–32.

Lane, Frederic C. (1973), *Venice, A Maritime Republic*, Baltimore: Johns Hopkins University.

Lange, O. (1942),'Say's Law: A Restatement and Criticism', in O. Lange et al. (eds), *Studies in Mathematical Economics and Econometrics*, Chicago: University of Chicago Press.

Lange, O. (1944), *Price Flexibility and Full Employment*, Chicago: Cowles Commission.

Laslett, Peter (1973), *The World We Have Lost: England Before the Industrial Age*, New York: Scribner's (2nd edition).

Latsis, Spiro (ed.) (1976), *Method and Appraisal in Economics*, Cambridge: Cambridge University Press.

Leijonhufvud, Axel (1968a), 'Comment: Is There a Meaningful Trade-off

Between Inflation and Unemployment?', *Journal of Political Economy*, **76**, pp. 738–43.

Leijonhufvud, Axel (1968b), 'Keynes and the Effectiveness of Monetary Policy', *Western Economic Journal*, reprinted in Axel Leijonhufvud (1981a).

Leijonhufvud, Axel (1968c), *On Keynesian Economics and the Economics of Keynes: A Study in Monetary Theory*, New York: Oxford University Press.

Leijonhufvud, Axel (1969), *Keynes and the Classics: Two Lectures*, London: Institute of Economic Affairs, reprinted in Axel Leijonhufvud (1981a).

Leijonhufvud, Axel (1973), 'Effective Demand Failures', *Swedish Economic Journal*, **75**(1), pp. 27–48, reprinted in Axel Leijonhufvud (1981a).

Leijonhufvud, Axel (1976), 'Schools, Revolutions and Research Programmes in Economic Theory', in S. Latsis (ed.), *Method and Appraisal in Economics*, Cambridge: Cambridge University Press, reprinted in Axel Leijonhufvud (1981a).

Leijonhufvud, Axel (1977), 'Costs and Consequences of Inflation', in G.C. Harcourt (ed.), *The Microeconomic Foundations of Macroeconomics* , London: Macmillan, reprinted in Axel Leijonhufvud (1981a).

Leijonhufvud, Axel (1979), 'Review of Economic Perspectives by Sir John Hicks', *Journal of Economic Literature,* **17**, pp. 525–7.

Leijonhufvud, Axel (1980), 'Theories of Stagflation', *Revue de l'Association Francaise de Finance*, **1**(2), pp. 188–201.

Leijonhufvud, Axel (1981a), *Information and Coordination: Essays in Macroeconomic Theory*, New York: Oxford University Press.

Leijonhufvud, Axel (1981b), 'The Wicksell Connection: Variations on a Theme', in Axel Leijonhufvud, *Information and Coordination: Essays in Macroeconomic Theory*, New York: Oxford University Press.

Leijonhufvud, Axel (1981c), 'Monetary Theory in Hicksian Perspective', in Axel Leijonhufvud (ed.), *Information and Coordination: Essays in Macroeconomic Theory*, New York: Oxford University Press.

Leijonhufvud, Axel (1982), 'Rational Expectations and Monetary Institutions', in Marcello de Cecco and Jean-Paul Fitoussi (eds), *Monetary Theory and Economic Institutions*, London: Macmillan, 1987.

Leijonhufvud, Axel (1983a), 'Review of Studies in Business Cycle Theory by Robert E Lucas Jr', *Journal of Economic Literature*, **21**, pp. 107–10.

Leijonhufvud, Axel (1983b), 'What was the Matter with IS–LM?', in Jean-Paul Fitoussi (ed.), *Modern Macroeconomic Theory*, Oxford: Blackwell, pp. 64–90.

Leijonhufvud, Axel (1983c), 'What Would Keynes Have Thought of Rational Expectations?', in David Worswick and James Trevithick (eds), *Keynes and the Modern World,* Cambridge: Cambridge University Press.

Leijonhufvud, Axel (1983d), 'Keynesianism, Monetarism, and Rational Expectations: Some Reflections and Conjectures', in Roman Frydman and

E.S. Phelps (eds), *Individual Forecasting and Aggregate Outcomes: Rational Expectations Examined*, New York: Cambridge University Press.

Leijonhufvud, Axel (1984a), 'Inflation and Economic Performance', in Barry N. Siegel (ed.), *Money in Crisis: Government, Stagflation, and Monetary Reform,* San Francisco: Pacific Institute for Public Policy Research, and Cambridge, Mass.: Harper & Row.

Leijonhufvud, Axel (1984b), 'Constitutional Constraints on the Monetary Powers of Government', in Richard B. McKenzie (ed.), *Constitutional Economics: Containing the Economic Powers of Government*, Lexington, Mass.: D.C. Heath Co., pp. 107–205, reprinted in James A. Dorn and Anna Schwarz (eds) (1987), *The Search for Stable Money*, Chicago: Chicago University Press, pp. 129–43.

Leijonhufvud, Axel (1984c), 'Hicks on Time and Money', in D.A. Collard et al. (eds), *Economic Theory and Hicksian Themes,* New York: Oxford University Press, pp. 26–46.

Leijonhufvud (1984d), 'Stability of Monetary Policy, Federal Reserve Accountability, and Alternative Institutional Arrangements', in *Monetary Reform and Economic Stability*, Joint Economic Committee, Washington, D.C.: US Government Printing Office.

Leijonhufvud, Axel (1986a), 'Real and Monetary Factors in Business Fluctuations: Comment on Yeager', *Cato Journal*, **6**, pp. 409–20.

Leijonhufvud, Axel (1986b), 'Capitalism and the Factory System', in Richard Langlois (ed.), *Economics as a Process: Essays in the New Institutional Economics*, New York: Cambridge University Press, pp. 203–23.

Leijonhufvud, Axel (1986c), 'Rules with Some Discretion: Comment on Barro', in C.D. Campbell and W.R. Douglas (eds), *Alternative Monetary Regimes*, Baltimore: Johns Hopkins University Press, pp. 38–43.

Leijonhufvud, Axel (1987), 'Whatever Happened to Keynesian Economics?', in David A. Reese (ed.), *The Legacy of Keynes*, New York: Harper & Row, pp. 57–73.

Leijonhufvud, Axel (1988), 'Did Keynes Mean Anything? Rejoinder to Yeager', *Cato Journal*, **8**, pp. 209–17.

Leijonhufvud, Axel (1989), 'Information Costs and the Division of Labour', *International Social Science Journal*, **41**(2), 165–76.

Leijonhufvud, Axel (1993), 'The Nature of the Depression in the Former Soviet Union', *New Left Review*, **119**, May–June, pp. 120–26.

Lekachman, R. (1966), *The Age of Keynes*, New York: Random House.

Leland, Jonathan W. (1988), 'A Theory of Approximate Expected Utility Maximization', Carnegie-Mellon University Working Paper.

Levine, David K. (1989a), 'Efficiency and the Value of Money', *Review of Economic Studies*, **56**(1), pp. 77–88.

Levine, David K. (1991), 'Asset Trading Mechanisms and Expansionary Policy', *Journal of Economic Theory*, **54**(1), pp. 148–64.

Logue, Dennis E. and Richard J. Sweeney (1981), 'Inflation and Real Growth: Some Empirical Results,' *Journal of Money, Credit, and Banking*, **13**, pp. 497–501.

Lucas, Robert E. Jr. (1972), 'Expectations and the Neutrality of Money', *Journal of Economic Theory*, **4**(2), pp. 103–24 .

Lucas, Robert E. Jr. (1975), 'An Equilibrium Model of the Business Cycle', *Journal of Political Economy* , **83**(6), pp. 1113–44.

Lucas, Robert E. Jr. (1978), 'Unemployment Policy', *American Economic Review*, **68**(2), pp. 353–7.

Lucas, Robert E. Jr. (1980), 'Methods and Problems in Business Cycle Theory', *Journal of Money, Credit and Banking*, **12**(4), Part 2, pp. 696–715.

Lucas, Robert E. Jr. (1981), *Studies in Business Cycle Theory*, Cambridge: MIT Press.

Lucas, Robert E. Jr. (1986), 'Adaptive Behaviour and Economic Theory', *Journal of Business*, **59**(4), Part 2, pp. S401–26.

Lucas, Robert E. Jr. and Thomas J. Sargent (1978), 'After Keynesian Macroeconomics', in *After the Phillips Curve: Persistence of High Inflation and High Unemployment*, Conference Series No. 19, Boston, Massachusetts: Federal Reserve Bank of Boston.

Lundberg, Erik (1959), 'The Profitability of Investment', *Economic Journal*, **69,** pp. 655–77.

Machinea, José Luis and José Maria Fanelli (1988), 'Stopping Hyperinflation: The Case of the Austral Plan in Argentina, 1985–87', in M. Bruno, G. Di Tella, R. Dornbusch and S. Fischer (eds), *Inflation Stabilization: The Experience of Israel, Argentina, Brazil, Bolivia and Mexico*, Cambridge, Mass.: MIT Press, pp. 111–52.

Machinea, J. and J. Fanelli (1991), 'Inflation Stabilization in Argentina', in Michael Bruno, S. Fischer, E. Helpman, N. Liviatan and L. Meridor (eds), *Lessons of Economic Stabilization and Its Aftermath*, Cambridge, Mass.: MIT Press.

Malinvaud, Edmond (1977), *The Theory of Unemployment Reconsidered*, Oxford: Blackwell.

Mantoux, Paul (1962), *The Industrial Revolution in the Eighteenth Century*, New York: Harper and Row (revised edition).

Marglin, Stephen A. (1974), 'What Do Bosses Do? The Origins and Functions of Hierarchy in Capitalist Production', *Review of Radical Political Economics* , **6**(2), pp. 60–112.

Marshall, Alfred (1928), *Principles of Economics*, London: Macmillan (8th edition).

Marx, Karl (1906), *Capital*, New York: Modern Library.

Matthews, R.C.O. (1959), *The Business Cycle*, Chicago: University of Chicago Press, p. 383.

Matthews, R.C.O. (1968), 'Why Has Britain Had Full Employment Since the War?', *Economic Journal*, **78**, pp. 555–69.

Mill, John Stuart (1964), *Principles of Political Economy*, New York: Ashley Edition (first published in 1848).

Modiano, E. (1991),'The Cruzado First Attempt', in M. Bruno, S. Fisher, E. Helpman, N. Liviatan and L. Meridor (eds), *Lessons of Economic Stabilization and Its Aftermath*, Cambridge, Mass.: MIT Press.

Modigliani, Franco (1944), 'Liquidity Preference and the Theory of Interest and Money', *Econometrica*, **12**, pp. 45–88, rev. reprinted in Andrew Abel (ed.) (1980), *The Collected Papers of Franco Modigliani, I*, Cambridge Mass.: MIT Press.

Moisset De Espanes, L.J. et al. (1985), *El Desagio*, Santa Fe, Argentina: Rubinzal-Culsoni.

Mossetti, Giovanna (1986), 'Inside Money, Output and Inventories in a Real Business Cycle', UCLA, mimeo.

Myrdal, Gunnar (1933), 'Der Gleichgewichtbegriff als Instrument der Geldtheoretischen Analyse', in F.A. von Hayek (ed.), *Beiträge zur Geldtheorie*, Wien: Verlag von Julius Springer.

Myrdal, Gunnar (1958), *Value in Social Theory*, New York: Harper.

Nef, J.U. (1934), 'The Progress of Technology and Growth of Large-scale Industry in Great Britain, 1540–1640', *Economic History Review*, **5**(1), pp. 3–24.

Niehans, J. (1978), *The Theory of Money*, Baltimore–London: Johns Hopkins Press.

O'Driscoll, Gerald (1986), 'Deregulation and Monetary Reform', *Federal Reserve Bank of Dallas Economic Review*, July, pp. 19–31.

Okun, Arthur M. (1981), *Prices and Quantities: A Macroeconomic Analysis*, Washington, D.C.: Brookings.

Palerm, Angel Viquiera (1990), 'Price Formation and Relative Price Variability in an Inflationary Enviroment: Mexico 1940–1984', *UCLA Doctoral Dissertation*.

Parks, R. (1978), 'Inflation and Relative Price Variability,' *Journal of Political Economy*, **86**, pp. 79–96.

Patinkin, D. (1948), 'Price Flexibility and Full Employment', *American Economic Review*, **38**, pp. 543–64.

Patinkin, D. (1956), *Money, Interest, and Prices*, Evanston, Ill.: Row, Peterson & Co.

Patinkin, D. (1959) 'Keynesian Economics Rehabilitated: A Rejoinder to Professor Hicks', *Economic Journal,* September, **69,** pp. 582–7.

Pelaez, C. (1986), *O Cruzado e o Austral: analise das reformas monetarias do Brasil e de Argentina*, Sao Paulo: Editora Atlas.

Phelps, Edmund S. (1968), 'Money Wage Dynamics and Labor Market Equilibrium', *Journal of Political Economy*, **76**, pp. 678–711, reprinted in Phelps et al. (eds), *Microeconomic Foundations of Unemployment and Inflation Theory*, New York: Norton.

Phelps, Edmund S. and Roman Frydman (1983a), 'Introduction', in Roman Frydman and Edmund S. Phelps (eds), *Individual Forecasting and Aggregate Outcomes*, New York: Cambridge University Press, pp. 1–30.

Phelps, Edmund S. (1983b), 'The Trouble with Rational Expectations and the Problem of Inflation Stabilization', in Roman Frydman and Edmund S. Phelps (eds), *Individual Forecasting and Aggregate Outcomes*, New York: Cambridge University Press, pp. 31–41.

Power, E. (1963), *Medieval People*, New York: Barnes & Noble (10th edition).

Pratten, Clifford F. (1980), 'The Manufacture of Pins', *Journal of Economic Literature,* **18**(1), pp. 93–6.

Rae, John (1964), *Statement of Some New Principles on the Subject of Political Economy*, New York: Augustus M. Kelley (first published in 1834).

Robbins, Lionel (1932), *An Essay on the Nature and Significance of Economic Science*, London: Macmillan.

Roberts, John (1987), 'An Equilibrium Model with Involuntary Unemployment at Flexible Competitive Prices and Wages', *American Economic Review,* **77**(5), pp. 856–74.

Robertson, Dennis (1954), 'Thoughts on Meeting Some Important Persons', *Quarterly Journal of Economics,* **68**, pp. 181–90.

Robinson, Joan (1963), *Economic Philosophy*, Chicago: Aldine Publishing Co.

Romer, Paul M. (1986), 'Increasing Returns, Specialization, and External Economies: Growth as Described by Allyn Young', Working Paper No. 64, Rochester Center for Economic Research, December.

Romer, Paul M. (1987), 'Growth Based on Increasing Returns due to Specialization', *American Economic Review,* **77**(2), pp. 56–62.

Rosenberg, Nathan (1965), 'Adam Smith on the Division of Labour: Two Views or One?', *Economica*, **32,** pp. 127–39.

Samuelson, Paul A. (1947), *Foundations of Economic Analysis*, Cambridge, Mass.: Harvard University Press.

Samuelson, Paul A. (1983), 'Sympathy from the Other Cambridge', *Economist*, 25 June–1 July, pp. 21–7.

Sargent, Thomas J. (1973), 'Rational Expectations, the Real Rate of Interest, and the Natural Rate of Unemployment', *Brookings Papers on Economic Activity*, **2**, pp. 429–72.

Sargent, Thomas J. (1981), 'Stopping Moderate Inflations: The Methods of Poincaré, and Thatcher', in *Economic Policy in the United Kingdom*, Proceedings of a conference sponsored by the General Mills Foundation, University of Minnesota.

Sargent, Thomas J. (1987), *Dynamic Macroeconomic Theory*, Cambridge: Harvard University Press.

Sargent, Thomas J. and Neil Wallace (1976), 'Rational Expectations and the Theory of Economic Policy', *Journal of Monetary Economics*, **2**(2), pp. 169–83.

Sargent, Thomas J. and Neil Wallace (1981), 'Some Unpleasant Monetarist Arithmetic', *Federal Reserve Bank of Minneapolis Quarterly Review*, **9**(1), pp. 15–31.

Schacht, H. (1927), *The Stabilization of the Mark*, London: Allen and Unwin.

Schotter, Andrew (1981), *The Economic Theory of Social Institutions*, Cambridge: Cambridge University Press.

Shackle, G.L.S. (1967), *The Years of High Theory: Invention and Tradition in Economic Thought, 1926–1939*, Cambridge: Cambridge University Press.

Shackle, G.L.S. (1972), *Epistemics and Economics: A Critique of Economic Doctrines*, Cambridge: Cambridge University Press.

Simonsen, Mario (1983), 'Indexation: Current Theory and the Brazilian Experience', in R. Dornbusch and M. Simonsen (eds), *Inflation, Debt and Indexation*, Cambridge, Mass.: MIT Press, pp. 99–132.

Sims, Christopher A. (1980), 'Comparison of Interwar and Postwar Business Cycles: Monetarism Reconsidered', *American Economic Review*, **70**(2), pp. 250–57.

Sims, Christopher A. (1983), 'Is There a Monetary Business Cycle?', *American Economic Review*, **73**(2), pp. 228–33.

Smith, Adam ([1776], 1937), *An Inquiry into the Nature and Causes of the Wealth of Nations*, New York: Modern Library edition.

Sokoloff, Kenneth L. (1984a), 'Investment in Fixed and Working Capital during Early Industrialization: Evidence from US Manufacturing Firms', *Journal of Economic History*, **44**(2), pp. 545–56.

Sokoloff, Kenneth L. (1984b), 'Was the Transition from the Artisanal Shop to the Non-mechanized Factory Associated with Gains in Efficiency?: Evidence from the US Manufacturing Censuses of 1820 and 1850', *Explorations in Economic History*, **21**(4), pp. 351–82.

Solow, Robert M. (1980), 'On Theories of Unemployment', *American Economic Review*, **70**(1), pp. 1–11.

Sowell, Thomas (1980), *Knowledge and Decisions*, New York: Basic Books.

Stigler, George (1951), 'The Division of Labor is Limited by the Extent of the Market', *Journal of Political Economy*, **59**(3), pp. 185–93.

Thompson, Earl A. (1974), 'The Theory of Money and Income Consistent with Orthodox Value Theory', in George Horwich and Paul A. Samuelson (eds), *Trade, Stability, and Macroeconomics*, New York: Academic Press.

Thompson, E.P. (1967), 'Time, Work-Discipline, and Industrial Revolution', *Past & Present,* **38**, pp. 56–97.

Tobin, James (1963), 'Commercial Banks as Creators of Money', in Deane Carson (ed.), *Banking and Monetary Studies,* Homewood, Ill.: Richard D. Irwin.

Tobin, James (1972), 'Inflation and Unemployment', *American Economic Review*, **62**, pp. 1–18.

Tobin, James (1981), 'The Monetarist Counter-revolution Today – An Appraisal', *Economic Journal,* **91**(361), pp. 29–42.

Trigo Represas, F. (1985), *El Austral y el Desagio*, Buenos Aires: Depalama.

Tumlir, Jan (1983), 'J M Keynes and the Emergence of the Post-World War II International Economic Order', Paper presented at a conference on 'Tactics of Liberalization', Madrid, Spain, March.

Velupillai, Kumaraswamy (1999), 'Undecideability, Computation Universality, and Minimality in Economic Dynamics', *Journal of Economic Surveys*, **13**(5), pp. 653–73.

Vining, D.R. and T.C. Elwertowski (1976), 'The Relationship between Relative Prices and the General Price Level', *American Economic Review*, **66**, pp. 699–708.

Wallace, Neil (1981), 'A Modigliani–Miller Theorem for Open Market Operations', *American Economic Review* , **71**(3), pp. 267–74.

Wallace, Neil (1983), 'A Legal Restrictions Theory of the Demand for "Money" and the Role of Monetary Policy', *Federal Reserve Bank of Minneapolis Quarterly Review,* **7**, pp. 1–7.

Weintraub, E. Roy (1979), *Microfoundations: The Compatibility of Microeconomics and Macroeconomics*, New York: Cambridge University Press.

Weitzman, Martin L. (1982), 'Increasing Returns and the Foundation of Unemployment Theory', *Economic Journal,* **92**(368), pp. 787–804.

West, E.G. (1964), 'Adam Smith's Two Views on the Division of Labour', *Economica*, **31**, pp. 23–32.

White, Lawrence H. (1984), 'Competitive Payments Systems and the Unit of Account', *American Economic* Review, **74**(4), pp. 699–712.

Wiener, Norbert (1954), *The Human Use of Human Beings*, Garden City, N.J.: Doubleday & Co.

Williamson, Oliver E. (1975), *Markets and Hierarchies*, New York: The Free Press.

Williamson, Oliver E. (1980), 'The Organization of Work: A Comparative Institutional Assessment', *Journal of Economic Behavior and Organization*, **1**(1), pp. 5–38.

Williamson, Oliver E. (1986), 'The Economics of Governance: Framework and Implications', in R. Langlois (ed.) *Economics as a Process*, Cambridge: Cambridge University Press, pp. 171–202.

Witte, James R. (1963), 'The Microfoundations of the Social Investment Function', *Journal of Political Economy,* **71**, pp. 441–56.

Woodford, Michael (1988), 'Expectations, Finance and Aggregate Instability', in Meir Kohn and S.C. Tsiang (eds), *Finance Constraints, Expectations, and Macroeconomics*, Oxford: Clarendon Press, pp. 230–61.

Yeager, Leland B. (1973), 'The Keynesian Diversion', *Western Economic Journal*, **11**(2), pp. 150–63, reprinted in C. Wood (ed.), *John Maynard Keynes: Critical Assessments, Volume IV*, London: Croom Helm, pp. 7–20.

Yeager, Leland B. (1986), 'The Significance of Monetary Disequilibrium', *Cato Journal,* **6**(2), pp. 369–99.

Yeager, Leland B. (1988), 'On Interpreting Keynes: Reply to Leijonhufvud', *Cato Journal,* **8**(1), pp. 205–8.

Young, Allyn (1928), 'Increasing Returns and Economic Progress', *Economic Journal,* **38**, pp. 527–42.

# Index

# Economists of the Twentieth Century

The History of Economics
The Collected Essays of Takashi Negishi
Volume II
*Takashi Negishi*

Studies in Econometric Theory
The Collected Essays of Takeshi Amemiya
*Takeshi Amemiya*

Exchange Rates and the Monetary
System
Selected Essays of Peter B. Kenen
*Peter B. Kenen*

Econometric Methods and Applications
(2 volumes)
*G.S. Maddala*

National Accounting and Economic
Theory
The Collected Papers of Dan Usher, Volume I
*Dan Usher*

Welfare Economics and Public Finance
The Collected Papers of Dan Usher, Volume
II
*Dan Usher*

Economic Theory and Capitalist Society
The Selected Essays of Shigeto Tsuru,
Volume I
*Shigeto Tsuru*

Methodology, Money and the Firm
The Collected Essays of D.P. O'Brien
(2 volumes)
*D.P. O'Brien*

Economic Theory and Financial Policy
The Selected Essays of Jacques J. Polak
(2 volumes)
*Jacques J. Polak*

Sturdy Econometrics
*Edward E. Leamer*

The Emergence of Economic Ideas
Essays in the History of Economics
*Nathan Rosenberg*

Productivity Change, Public Goods and
Transaction Costs
Essays at the Boundaries of Microeconomics
*Yoram Barzel*

Reflections on Economic Development
The Selected Essays of Michael P. Todaro
*Michael P. Todaro*

The Economic Development of Modern
Japan
The Selected Essays of Shigeto Tsuru
Volume II
*Shigeto Tsuru*

Money, Credit and Policy
*Allan H. Meltzer*

Macroeconomics and Monetary Theory
The Selected Essays of Meghnad Desai
Volume I
*Meghnad Desai*

Poverty, Famine and Economic
Development
The Selected Essays of Meghnad Desai
Volume II
*Meghnad Desai*

Explaining the Economic Performance
of Nations
Essays in Time and Space
*Angus Maddison*

Economic Doctrine and Method
Selected Papers of R.W. Clower
*Robert W. Clower*

Economic Theory and Reality
Selected Essays on their Disparities and
Reconciliation
*Tibor Scitovsky*

Doing Economic Research
Essays on the Applied Methodology of
Economics
*Thomas Mayer*

Institutions and Development Strategies
The Selected Essays of Irma Adelman
Volume I
*Irma Adelman*

Dynamics and Income Distribution
The Selected Essays of Irma Adelman
Volume II
*Irma Adelman*

The Economics of Growth and
Development
Selected Essays of A.P. Thirlwall
*A.P. Thirlwall*

Theoretical and Applied Econometrics
The Selected Papers of Phoebus J. Dhrymes
*Phoebus J. Dhrymes*

Innovation, Technology and the
Economy
The Selected Essays of Edwin Mansfield
(2 volumes)
*Edwin Mansfield*

Economic Theory and Policy in Context
The Selected Essays of R.D. Collison Black
*R.D. Collison Black*

Location Economics
Theoretical Underpinnings and Applications
*Melvin L. Greenhut*

Spatial Microeconomics
Theoretical Underpinnings and Applications
*Melvin L. Greenhut*

Capitalism, Socialism and Post-
Keynesianism
Selected Essays of G.C. Harcourt
*G.C. Harcourt*

Time Series Analysis and
Macroeconometric Modelling
The Collected Papers of Kenneth F. Wallis
*Kenneth F. Wallis*

Foundations of Modern Econometrics
The Selected Essays of Ragnar Frisch
(2 volumes)
*Edited by Olav Bjerkholt*

Growth, the Environment and the
Distribution of Incomes
Essays by a Sceptical Optimist
*Wilfred Beckerman*

The Economics of Environmental
Regulation
*Wallace E. Oates*

Econometrics, Macroeconomics and
Economic Policy
Selected Papers of Carl F. Christ
*Carl F. Christ*

Strategic Approaches to the
International Economy
Selected Essays of Koichi Hamada
*Koichi Hamada*

Economic Analysis and Political
Ideology
The Selected Essays of Karl Brunner
Volume One
*Edited by Thomas Lys*

Growth Theory and Technical Change
The Selected Essays of Ryuzo Sato
Volume One
*Ryuzo Sato*

Industrialization, Inequality and
Economic Growth
*Jeffrey G. Williamson*

Economic Theory and Public Decisions
Selected Essays of Robert Dorfman
*Robert Dorfman*

The Logic of Action One
Method, Money, and the Austrian School
*Murray N. Rothbard*

The Logic of Action Two
Applications and Criticism from the Austrian
School
*Murray N. Rothbard*

Bayesian Analysis in Econometrics and
Statistics
The Zellner View and Papers
*Arnold Zellner*

On the Foundations of Monopolistic
Competition and Economic Geography
The Selected Essays of B. Curtis Eaton and
Richard G. Lipsey
*B. Curtis Eaton and Richard G. Lipsey*

Microeconomics, Growth and Political
Economy
The Selected Essays of Richard G. Lipsey
Volume One
*Richard G. Lipsey*

Macroeconomic Theory and Policy
The Selected Essays of Richard G. Lipsey
Volume Two
*Richard G. Lipsey*

Employment, Labor Unions and Wages
The Collected Essays of Orley Ashenfelter
Volume One
*Edited by Kevin F. Hallock*

Education, Training and Discrimination
The Collected Essays of Orley Ashenfelter
Volume Two
*Edited by Kevin F. Hallock*

Economic Institutions and the Demand
and Supply of Labour
The Collected Essays of Orley Ashenfelter
Volume Three
*Edited by Kevin F. Hallock*

The Economic Structure of the Law
The Collected Economic Essays of Richard
A. Posner
Volume One
*Richard A. Posner*
*Edited by Francesco Parisi*

Measurement and Meaning in
Economics
The Essential Deirdre McCloskey
*Deirdre McCloskey*
*Edited and introduced by*
*Stephen Thomas Ziliak*

Growth Theory, Nonlinear Dynamics
and Economic Modelling
Scientific Essays of William Allen Brock
William Allen Brock
*Edited by W. Davis Dechert*